D0270696

Aberdeenshire Library and Information Service
www.aberdeenshire.gov.uk/libraries
Renewals Hotline 01224 661511

HEADQUARTERS

3 0 MAY 2007

1 7 JAN 2012

2 6 NOV 2008   - 3 JUN 2014

2 7 JUN 2009   1 0 AUG 2015

2 3 JUL 2009
1 8 AUG 2009

2 1 SEP 2009

WITHDRAWN
FROM LIBRARY

- 3 AUG 2016

- 8 MAR 2010

2 2 MAR 2011

SPURR, Barry

Studying poetry

A L I S

2553608

To Leonie Kramer

Studying Poetry

Poetry

Second Edition

BARRY SPURR

© Barry Spurr 1997, 2006

All rights reserved. No reproduction, copy or transmission of
this publication may be made without written permission.

No paragraph of this publication may be reproduced, copied or
transmitted save with written permission or in accordance with
the provisions of the Copyright, Designs and Patents Act 1988,
or under the terms of any licence permitting limited copying
issued by the Copyright Licensing Agency, 90 Tottenham Court Road,
London W1T 4LP.

Any person who does any unauthorised act in relation to this
publication may be liable to criminal prosecution and civil
claims for damages.

The author has asserted his right to be identified as the author
of this work in accordance with the Copyright, Designs and
Patents Act 1988.

First edition published 1997
Second edition published 2006 by
PALGRAVE MACMILLAN
Houndmills, Basingstoke, Hampshire RG21 6XS and
175 Fifth Avenue, New York, N.Y. 10010
Companies and representatives throughout the world

PALGRAVE MACMILLAN is the global academic imprint of the Palgrave
Macmillan division of St. Martin's Press, LLC and of Palgrave Macmillan Ltd.
Macmillan® is a registered trademark in the United States, United
Kingdom and other countries. Palgrave is a registered trademark in the
European Union and other countries.

ISBN-13: 978–1–4039–4561–7
ISBN-10: 1–4039–4561–6   hardback
ISBN-13: 978–1–4039–4562–4
ISBN-10: 1–4039–4562–4   paperback

This book is printed on paper suitable for recycling and made
from fully managed and sustained forest sources.

A catalogue record for this book is available from the British Library.

10   9   8   7   6   5   4   3   2   1
15 14 13 12 11 10 09 08 07 06

Printed and bound in China

ABERDEENSHIRE LIBRARY AND	
INFORMATION SERVICES	
2553608	
HJ	490320
821.009	£15.99
AD	PORP

Contents

Preface

The purpose of this book is to provide a comprehensive guide to the study of poetry in English for senior secondary pupils and undergraduates and their teachers. Poetry is often regarded by students of literature as the least approachable of the literary genres. The complexities and compression of its language, the elusiveness of its meaning and the artificiality of its forms combine, for many readers, to prevent both the understanding and enjoyment of a poem. This is profoundly regrettable, for poetry represents not only an extraordinary testament to human creativity, but an incomparable treasury of insights into and interpretations of the human condition, in all its variety of experience. 'Poetry is the honey of all flowers', wrote Thomas Nashe in the sixteenth century, 'the quintessence of all sciences, the marrow of wit, and the very phrase of angels.' Poets confront us and delight us, as another of them – Alexander Pope – has testified, with 'what oft was thought, but ne'er so well expressed'.

This book is addressed to a specific audience of those completing English studies at school or pursuing the study of poetry further at college and university. More specifically, it is a response to perceptions of difficulties that students of mine and of colleagues are encountering when required to discuss literary texts, whether in class or in their essays. The most significant of these are problems associated with the 'close reading' of a poem – the explication of the text, thematically and stylistically – and with appreciating the importance of setting literary texts, such as poems, in various contexts: historical, biographical, aesthetic and so forth.

There are various explanations for these difficulties. Certainly, a lack of instruction in the technical aspects of language inhibits both textual analysis and its lucid explanation and expression: if we are to describe and evaluate a poet's use of language, it is easier if we have familiar terms and concepts to hand, which the formal study of grammar provides. This book cannot fill this need, but I hope that in the use of elementary grammatical and other technical terms, I can demonstrate both their simplicity and the need to apply them to the discussion of poetry.

Then there is insufficient knowledge, today, of the broad outline of British and European history and cultural evolution. This restricts the reading of texts that have arisen from (and have often been influential upon) those circumstances and developments. *Studying Poetry* aims to introduce the periods of history which are relevant to the understanding and appreciation of the cultural heritage to which English literature belongs.

There are the more practical problems, too, arising from the vanishing discipline of the sustained reading and scrutiny of literary texts. The 'instant gratification' provided by other media – most notably, television – does not accustom the mind to the concentration which poetry (in particular) requires in order to yield its profound rewards. In reading numerous poetic texts in close detail, I emphasise the need for this process and the stimulation which it provides.

In later twentieth-century philosophical and socio-political theory, which continues to have significant impact on English studies today, there has been formidable opposition to the appreciation of texts as literary works of art, rather than as cultural and social commentary, even polemical tracts. The study of poetry, in particular, as the most highly wrought of literary forms, the most 'artistic', has suffered from this revulsion from the aesthetic component of literature. John Keats's equation of beauty with truth is rejected. Poetry (like literature at large) is read for what it has to teach us about a philosophical or sociological issue and, preferably, in order that its teaching will lend support to this or that 'correct' cultural or political theory, in ignorance of how it says it and the appreciation and evaluation of that mode of saying. Thomas De Quincey asked, 'What do you learn from *Paradise Lost?*' in his essay on Alexander Pope in 1848. 'Nothing at all.' What we learn, in fact, is that the ways in which poets express their ideas provide readers with unique kinds of enjoyment, emotionally and intellectually. Studying poetry begins (and, in a sense, ends) with the recognition of this truth: that a poem is a poem, as T. S. Eliot argued, and 'not another thing'.

To focus on a poet's skilful and beautiful use of language has come to be regarded as the quintessence of decadence and social irresponsibility. Yet prior to the enlightenment of Postmodernism, these aspects of poetry were esteemed. It could be argued that it is another species of intellectual and aesthetic decadence to demand that only certain poets and poems be studied, and appreciated aright, because they endorse currently fashionable social theories.

In *Studying Poetry*, I have chosen poets and poems which have been long regarded as the most significant in themselves and/or representative of the evolution of poetry in English, through the centuries. Only in the last chapter, 'Contemporary poetry', do we enter (inevitably) the area of speculation about literary value and reputation. So, the majority of the poets to whom I refer or discuss in detail are English-born and male. They have been significant in our evolving literary culture. Wishing, for racial and sexual reasons for example, that this were not so does not alter their significance and it would be to rewrite literary history to present the situation otherwise. We need not automatically agree with Samuel Johnson's statements that Shakespeare is 'above all writers . . . the poet who holds up to his readers a faithful mirror of manners and of life' and that Milton's *Paradise Lost* 'with respect to design, may claim the first place, and with respect to performance, the second, among the productions of the human mind', or with Harold Bloom's (and other commentators') assessment of Dr Johnson himself as the greatest of critics. But it could be argued that the need to study these writers and their works is urgent today precisely because they fail to endorse contemporary ideas about human existence. Matthew Arnold believed that poetry was a 'criticism of life' and Milton, in his own time as in our own, presents a challenging assessment of it. He was, as Percy Bysshe Shelley affirmed, 'a bold inquirer into morals and religion'. However this is different from asserting that Milton's poetry is merely didactic: 'nothing can be equally well expressed in prose', Shelley continues, 'that is not tedious and supererogatory in verse'. 'We hate poetry', Keats wrote in a letter, 'that has a palpable design upon us.'

Yet, we should not censor the unique ways in which poetry can question and disturb our presuppositions, particularly when it is the creation of writers from societies and with philosophies of life far removed from our own. We should certainly resist the temptation to remake and rewrite such poems in our image. Dr Johnson loathed Milton's politics and religion and had little regard for his character, but this did not prevent him from recognising the genius of his poetry which included Milton's convictions and personality. One of the greatest rewards of the study of poetry is the insight it gives into the human experience in lives and ages so different from ours.

Whether to begin (as I have) with the section on 'Reading poetry' or on the historical periods of literature is arbitrary. Readers may choose to reverse this order according to their requirements. To prioritise 'Reading poetry', however, has this justification: the skills referred to there are universally applicable.

I speak deliberately of 'skills', for the study of poetry is a discipline and it is wise to understand its basic techniques before pursuing it further. It is pertinent to compare it with the study of music as the two have much in common: the identification of a theme, the mastery of a rarefied notation, of matters of rhythm and tone, and so on. While a musical piece may be enjoyed immediately, at a certain level, and by those without any technical knowledge in the art, that appreciation is widened, deepened and made available to others once the technical terminology and its application have become familiar. In stressing the need to acquire literary-critical skills and techniques in the reading of poetry, I would argue against the notion that appreciating a poem is merely a matter of a subjective response and of 'taste'. It is not a science (pace I. A. Richards), but nor should it be restricted to the excitement of an individual sensibility. Ultimately, the study of poetry is, as T. S. Eliot suggested, 'the common pursuit of true judgment'.

More mundanely, examinations and essay-writing need to be addressed. Accordingly, I have punctuated the text with examples of the kinds of questions that are asked and assignments that are set in these circumstances. I am often puzzled by the revulsion – for example, of poets themselves – from this aspect of reading poetry, as if it were disreputable. The formal study of harmony and counterpoint and the examining of music students in those procedures enriches their appreciation of Bach, Mozart and Beethoven. Similarly, an assignment on the use of metaphor in George Herbert or a question on Christina Rossetti's lyricism, arising out of a study of those matters in the broad reading of their poetry, should refine rather than dampen our enthusiasm for those writers. Of course, poetry is not written so that examinations can be taken in its discussion or essays written about it. It is meant to be enjoyed:

> All art [wrote Friedrich Schiller] is dedicated to joy, and there is no higher and no more serious problem, than how to make men happy. The right art is that alone, which creates the highest enjoyment.

But the enjoyment of a complex art such as poetry comes from knowledge about it and it is a fact of educational life that the testing of knowledge concentrates the mind in the acquisition of that knowledge.

In any case, if it were not for the compulsory study of poetry in secondary schools, very few people today would ever encounter it. Some, no doubt, are put off poetry for life by that experience. Many more are at least acquainted with the possibility of its pleasure. The seed is sown and has the chance of growing into informed appreciation. Poetry is such an important expression of our humanity that it needs to be made as widely available as possible.

At the end of the book are a glossary of literary terms and historical tables for reference.

The opportunity to prepare a second edition of *Studying Poetry* has enabled me to add a chapter on medieval poetry, to increase the number of Special Studies of poets, to expand several of the original Special Studies and provide additional questions and assignments. Most significantly, I have divided the final chapter in the original book, 'Postmodernism and the future', into two chapters – 'After Modernism' and 'Contemporary poetry' – which has enabled me to bring the book up to date.

I am most grateful to the staff of Palgrave Macmillan, especially to my commissioning editor Kate Wallis, as well as Sonya Barker and Felicity Noble for their professional assistance and enthusiasm during the preparation of the book. Its purpose will have been achieved if students and teachers find it helpful in enriching their reading of poems and if they experience even a portion of the pleasure I have derived, in writing it, from revisiting and discovering these poets. It is dedicated, with respect and affection, to a former Chancellor of the University of Sydney, Dame Leonie Kramer, who, in a series of lectures on William Blake a third of a century ago, was the first of several university teachers to reveal to me the challenges and the rewards of the study of poetry.

Barry Spurr
Sydney

Acknowledgements

The author and publisher wish to thank the following for permission to use copyright material:

ETT Imprint, for 'Woman to Man', from *Selected Poems*, by Judith Wright.

Faber and Faber Ltd, for extracts from: 'Requiem for Croppies', from *Door in the Dark*, by Seamus Heaney; 'Mr Bleaney', 'Talking in Bed', 'The Large Cool Store' and 'The Whitsun Weddings', from *The Whitsun Weddings*, and 'Annus Mirabilis' from *High Windows*, by Philip Larkin; 'Lady Lazarus', from *Collected Poems*, by Sylvia Plath; 'Twelve Songs IX', from *Collected Poems*, by W. H. Auden; *Medieval English Lyrics*, by R. T. Davies; 'Preludes', 'Rhapsody on a Windy Night', 'The Love Song of J. Alfred Prufrock', 'Portrait of a Lady' and *Four Quartets*, from *Collected Poems 1909–1962*, by T. S. Eliot; 'Fulbright Scholars', 'The Minotaur', 'Sam' and 'Red' from *Birthday Letters*, by Ted Hughes.

HarperCollins Publishers Australia, for 'Sleep', from *Selected Poems*, by Kenneth Slessor.

Les Murray, for 'The Widower in the Country' and 'The Mitchells', by Les Murray.

Penguin Group (Australia), for extracts from 'In the Park', from *Selected Poems*, by Gwen Harwood.

Penguin Group (UK), for extracts from 'Howl', from *Howl and Other Poems*, by Allen Ginsberg.

University of Queensland Press, for extracts from *on a clear day*, by Joanne Burns.

A. P. Watts Ltd on behalf of Michael B. Yeats, for extracts from 'Byzantium', 'Ben Bulben', 'Easter 1916'. 'The Second Coming', 'Sailing to Byzantium' and 'Among School Children', from *The Poems*, by W. B. Yeats.

Every effort has been made to trace the copyright holders but, if any have been inadvertently overlooked, the author and publisher will be pleased to make the necessary arrangements at the first opportunity.

PART ONE

Reading poetry

Reading aloud

1

Our first encounter with a poem should involve reading it aloud, after a preliminary silent reading. The silent reading prepares us for any complicated or surprising features within it. These might include obscure words, a striking change in rhythm (the 'metre' of the poem: see the Glossary for definitions of this and other technical terms), the insistence or otherwise of its rhyming pattern, the presence of more than one speaker, and so on. If it is a long poem, then we will read and consider it, section by manageable section.

The essential point about these first readings, both silent and aloud, is that as any good poem is inexhaustible, we should treat our initial meeting with it as an introduction. If we can absorb something of the poem's meaning and tone, that is a sufficient beginning. A poem that revealed all of itself on the first reading would be a very shallow work.

Reading aloud recognises that poets want their works to be heard. A slower process than reading silently, it encourages us to savour the words – their sounds as much as their sense. These qualities, in fact, are usually intimately related. Poetry began as an oral art where rhythm and rhyme assisted memory in the preservation of poets' works. Today, we most often encounter poetry in printed form, yet even contemporary poets who know that their poems will be presented in that medium, write with their ears attuned to the sounds of their speech and the voice of their poetry. This is evident if we look closely at their use of language.

The aural appeal of words is not cultivated by poets for its own sake. The characteristics of the sounds of language reveal its meanings, just as groupings of words, phrases and stanzas contribute to the subtleties of thought and emotion that even an apparently straightforward lyric may convey.

Consider this poem by William Shakespeare from his play *As You Like It*:

> Blow, blow, thou winter wind,   ['wind' is pronounced to rhyme with 'rind']
> Thou art not so unkind

As man's ingratitude;
Thy tooth is not so keen,
Because thou art not seen,
Although thy breath be rude.
Heigh-ho! sing, heigh-ho! unto the green holly:
Most friendship is feigning, most loving mere folly:
Then, heigh-ho, the holly!
This life is most jolly.

Freeze, freeze, thou bitter sky,
That dost not bite so nigh
    As benefits forgot:
Though thou the waters warp,   [warp = to roughen by freezing]
Thy sting is not so sharp
    As friend remembered not.
Heigh-ho! sing, heigh-ho! unto the green holly:
Most friendship is feigning, most loving mere folly:
Then, heigh-ho, the holly!
This life is most jolly.

Our preliminary silent reading alerts us to the regularity of the poem's metrical and rhyming scheme, and to its strikingly boisterous refrain at the end of both stanzas. More significantly, however, our first reading should reveal that the poem treats two different ideas held in a tension: while nature's cruelties are recognised by the speaker, humanity's behaviour is judged to be far worse and so, in a backhanded way, nature emerges praised, in spite of its harshness, and is even encouraged in its brutality.

Much of the impact of the meaning of the poem is communicated through the sounds of its words, which can only be fully appreciated if we read it out loud, with careful attention to those sounds. The opening line alone is replete with aural appeal:

Blow, blow, thou winter wind.

First there is the repetition of the verb, giving further insistence to its imperative form. The speaker is wilfully encouraging nature in its assault as if to prove his point that it is less painful than humanity's cruelties, and he imitates the sound of wind in the device of onomatopoeia (see Glossary). This opening to the work is surprising and arresting, for we could not imagine that anyone would be so receptive to the wintry tempest. Thus we are encouraged to read on for an explanation. In a poem in which the perversity of human nature is the principal subject, Shakespeare has aptly appropriated a perverse attitude for his speaker. A recognisable truth of human experience is being approached in an oblique and, therefore, captivating way.

In 'blow', we hear the wind even as it is being addressed. The repetition is introduced by a strong alliteration on 'b' which is paralleled by that on 'w' in 'winter wind'. We sense the impact of the blustery wind as we speak those initial words. The old pronunciation of 'wind' contains within it also the echo of the word 'whined' — onomatopoeic again, and associated with a cry of complaint. We can hear how all these elements of sound are being orchestrated. Then, the personification of wind in the address to it as 'thou' (in the formal second person) brings it disturbingly close to human life: it appears that it has motivations like ours — unkindness, for example. And, again, the sound of the word, particularly the vowel combination 'ou', reminds us of wind's howling. In just five words, Shakespeare combines a series of sounds to evoke the experience to which he is referring. By focusing on them in this way, we can explain in detail how the effect is achieved and appreciate it more fully.

The clever subtlety of the poem's argument — its 'wit' — is revealed most strikingly in its aural qualities. There is, for example, its longest word — 'ingratitude' — with its four syllables. Reading aloud, we must dwell on that abstract noun, and because it is at the end of a line which ends with a semi-colon, we pause further to absorb the fullness of its unpleasantness. The speaker's point is that this is worse than wind's assault. This point is aided by our extended enunciation of 'ingratitude', particularly as it contains that grating, accented second syllable after the negative prefix. Reading this poem and concentrating on this word, we are also introduced to the wider world of Shakespeare's thought. Ingratitude was an evil that especially agitated him. He isolates it for denunciation later in his great tragedy *King Lear*, again emphasising how humanity's display of this vice puts us at a disadvantage with respect to nature:

> Ingratitude! thou marble-hearted fiend,
> More hideous, when thou show'st thee in a child,
> Than the sea-monster!

There, as in this poem, the dramatic sound of the word is essential to its impact.

We return to the contrast of monosyllables, just as we return to nature and wind in particular. The negativity (although qualified) of nature's processes is again captured in the reference to its 'rude' breath. The adjective sounds as coarse as the attribute itself. Reading the poem silently, we note the attribution. Reading it aloud, we hear it and the reference is more forceful.

Then there is the violent contrast in tone:

> Heigh-ho! sing, heigh-ho! unto the green holly:
> Most friendship is feigning, most loving mere folly:
> Then, heigh-ho, the holly!

This different tone (see Glossary) of over-pitched merriment — in the laughing language of the repeated 'heigh-ho!' — balances the bitter allusions to nature's and humanity's unkindness. The glib alliteration on 'f' – 'friendship is feigning' (pretence) – serves almost to dismiss this most serious indictment, especially as it is framed by 'Heigh-ho!' The overall effect is a recognition of the fallibility of human behaviour combined with a determination not to be oppressed by it. *As You Like It*, where the poem appears, is a comedy, not a tragedy. The jocular sounds of the words, to which even such neutral elements as 'holly' contribute, achieve the comedic resolution: 'This life is most jolly'.

This forced merriment leaves a bitter after-taste (or, more accurately, after-sound) of something imperfectly resolved, perhaps like life itself. The aural impression of the earlier negative concepts has not been entirely dispelled by this too-aggressive jocularity. A refrain usually confirms the subject of a poem. Shakespeare, in the abundant variety of his genius, uses the device here, but subversively, imaginatively, provocatively.

No one would suggest that all of the above features would be noted, or should be, on the initial reading aloud of 'Blow, blow, thou winter wind'. But that experience opens our ears as well as our eyes to the poem's several dimensions of meaning.

> **Question**
> To what other qualities of the language of this poem would you draw attention?

To hear some different sounds, we now look at 'A Birthday', in which the Victorian poet, Christina Rossetti, enunciates an emotion rarely encountered in her writings. She was described by her brother as 'replete with the spirit of self-postponement'. That is to say that Christina Rossetti is usually a poet of unhappiness, especially of the lack of fulfilment in love. But this is not so here, and we should note, in reading the poem aloud, the way the sounds of her words and the cadences of her phrases convey the unusual experience, in her poetry, of the celebration of joy:

> My heart is like a singing bird
>   Whose nest is in a watered shoot;
> My heart is like an apple tree
>   Whose boughs are bent with thickset fruit;
> My heart is like a rainbow shell
>   That paddles in a halcyon sea;   [halcyon = tranquil]
> My heart is gladder than all these
>   Because my love is come to me.
>
> Raise me a dais of silk and down;
>   Hang it with vair and purple dyes;   [vair = squirrel fur]
> Carve it in doves and pomegranates,

> And peacocks with a hundred eyes;
> Work it in gold and silver grapes,
>> In leaves and silver fleurs-de-lys; [fleur-de-lys = iris flower, heraldic lily]
> Because the birthday of my life
>> Is come, my love is come to me.

The essence of the artistry of this poem is in the repetition accumulating to exultation in the use of the present tense. In the first stanza there is the series of similes, introduced in the usual way by 'like'. This is how the speaker defines her mood of joy. But splendid as they are in their beauty, fecundity and peacefulness, they do not do justice to her sublime happiness:

> My heart is gladder than all these
>> Because my love is come to me.

The meaning is clear. How do the sounds of the poetry assist it? Why must it be read aloud to be fully appreciated?

In reading it aloud, the repetitions, with their rhythmical pulse, are more insistent; the phrase 'like a singing bird' actually sings as we say it; there is an aural exhilaration in 'a watered shoot', and those boughs heavily hung with abundant fruit are more immediately envisaged, bearing their glad burden in the sound of 'thickset fruit'. We hear the rainbow shell (as well as picture its beauty) paddling in a tranquil sea, in that onomatopoeic verb with its implied personification.

The second stanza has a ceremonious tone in the use of the imperative verb which opens it: 'Raise'; in the series of these (a grammatical repetition) which follow – 'Hang', 'Carve', 'Work' – and in the depiction of the dais on which she will indeed be raised as she has been exalted by her lover. These strong verbs are declarative in sound, indicating an emotion that is definite in its happiness and secure in its triumph. But even more significant is the decoration of the platform and its strange details: 'carve it in doves and pomegranates'. It is exotic because such happiness is rare. But we do not merely see it or picture it in our mind's eye. The sound of a word like the deliciously polysyllabic 'pomegranates' – a word which we would probably never utter in our lifetimes were it not for reading it aloud in a poem such as this – emphasises the distinctiveness of the emotion and the occasion. The same is less ostentatiously true of 'fleurs-de-lys'. In savouring those words and phrases we are linked to the special experience they communicate. Again, repetition is important; the adjective 'silver', for example, abets the exquisite luxury of the occasion.

The culmination of Rossetti's accomplished technique of repetition and of our understanding of the need to read the poem aloud is in the closing lines:

> Because the birthday of my life
>> Is come, my love is come to me.

The caesura, or brief pause, after 'come' (signalled by the comma) introduces the final repetition of the declaration of the arrival of love and her birth as a human being as a consequence of it. In reading aloud, our pause there might seem to be a preparation for a new revelation about the experience. The surprise, of course, is that there is no surprise, nor can there be. She has attained the summit of human happiness and no amount of repetition can exhaust it. Our reading aloud of that last clause is both especially emphatic and conclusive: it reveals that the knowledge of love is the ultimate truth and the consummation of life. This is enacted by the accumulating repetitions and the air of finality at the close. The device of enjambement in those last two lines assists this, as the penultimate line runs on into the last. It is another technique of accumulation. Such devices are not used by poets merely for decoration. They assist the communication of meaning and, in recognising them, we can explain and communicate our enjoyment of the work.

> **Question**
> What is the significance of the natural imagery, used throughout the poem?

Finally, we should read aloud the following poem, 'Sleep', by the twentieth-century Australian poet, Kenneth Slessor. In writing about his choice of language here, Slessor referred to the 'narcotic effect of the repetition of certain consonant-structures and vowel sounds'. This is proof, if it were needed, that poets want us to hear their poems:

> Do you give yourself to me utterly,
>   Body and no-body, flesh and no-flesh,
> Not as a fugitive, blindly or bitterly,
>   But as a child might, with no other wish?
> *Yes, utterly.*
>
> Then I shall bear you down my estuary,
> Carry you and ferry you to burial mysteriously,
> Take you and receive you,
> Consume you, engulf you,
> In the huge cave, my belly, lave you   [lave = wash]
> With huger waves continually.
>
> And you shall cling and clamber there
> And slumber there, in that dumb chamber,
> Beat with my blood's beat, hear my heart move
> Blindly in bones that ride above you,
> Delve in my flesh, dissolved and bedded,
> Through viewless valves embodied so –

> Till daylight, the expulsion and awakening,
>   The riving and the driving forth,
> Life with remorseless forceps beckoning –
>   Pangs and betrayal of harsh birth.

'Sleep' seeks to induce the pleasurable sensation of being lulled into the experience it describes, through such rhythmical rhymes as 'utterly' / 'bitterly', the
cadence of 'Take you and receive you', with long 'u' sounds which are continued
in 'Consume you, engulf you'. The effect is of a lullaby in a poem that would take
us back to our pre-existent state, before birth, in the womb. Those 'u' sounds are
reminiscent of a mother's cooing to a baby.

   Slessor draws upon a variety of sounds to achieve his 'narcotic' effect – sounds
which we can only appreciate if we read the poem aloud. The gentleness of the
verb 'slumber', echoed in the neighbouring adjective 'dumb' and sustained in the
'amb' of 'chamber', modulates to the more assertive development of the
implicit alliteration on 'b' in those words, in the following line:

> Beat with my blood's beat . . .

Slessor's point (articulated through the technique of his diction) is that sleep has
its own activity, for all its peacefulness and womb-like security. This is asserted
further in the next line, with its stronger alliteration on 'd' which is consummated in the conjunction with the earlier 'b' alliteration in the last word:

> Delve in my flesh, dissolved and bedded . . .

The sequence of narcotic effects concludes with a final, gentler alliteration on
'v' in a lulling rhythm:

> Through viewless valves embodied so.

To close the poem, in contrast, Slessor brings us back to our waking existence.
Daily awakening is akin to being born anew and both are judged negatively by
the poet. Their criticism is articulated through the sounds of the words in his last
stanza. 'Expulsion' is not only a negative concept, but its sound is brusque,
almost violent. We notice how carefully Slessor has placed it before the otherwise neutral (even positive) 'awakening', thereby investing that concept with
negativity too. The violence of the verbs in the next line:

> The riving and the driving forth . . .

with their relentless emphasis and harsh assonance on 'i' makes a clear judgement of the daily process which is intensified as the comparison with birth
focuses specifically on a difficult, reluctant birthing. Life is seen as an insistent
doctor or midwife, dragging us protestingly into this world:

> with remorseless forceps beckoning –

Pangs and betrayal of harsh birth.

The consonant dominating these grim lines is 's', to the point of a hiss in 'remorseless'. It contrasts harshly with such gentle sounds (most notably 'b' sounds and the gentle 'lave' with its echo of 'love', at the poem's centre) earlier in the poem as Slessor explores the antithesis between sleep and waking, our pre-existent womb-life and life itself.

Question
How and why does the reading aloud of this poem help us to memorise it?

Whenever possible, we should take the opportunity to listen to poets reading their works – whether on recordings or live at poetry readings. There are accounts of at least two enjoyable occasions when Alexander Pope, in the early eighteenth century, read his *Rape of the Lock* aloud to appreciative audiences. At the end of that century, the essayist William Hazlitt recorded that when he heard the Romantic poet Samuel Taylor Coleridge reading aloud, 'the sense of a new style and a new spirit in poetry came over me'. Tennyson's resonant voice, 'mouthing out his hollow o's and a's / Deep-chested music', thrilled his audiences in the nineteenth century. Recordings by W. B. Yeats and T. S. Eliot in the twentieth century give surprising insights into the meaning of their poems as we listen to how they hear them. P. J. Kavanagh remarks that

> I made nothing of John Berryman's Dream Songs until
> I heard him recite them. He ranted, raved, he went
> falsetto on occasion, individualising the different voices
> that intrude into the poem, 'Henry', 'Mr Bones', and so
> on. It was a crazed performance, but it made perfect
> sense of the poems. Afterwards I could read, because I
> could 'hear', the Songs.[1]

Our own reading aloud of poetry has the advantage, too, that the process will help us to remember those lines of poetry, especially if we repeat the poem or passage a few times. We will come to know them 'by heart'. Abiding in our subconscious, phrases and cadences will be recalled and their meanings pondered anew. A poem remembered reveals the riches of its meaning throughout our lives.

Sample question with guidelines
How do the sounds of this poem by Seamus Heaney augment its meaning?

---

1. 'Ranting and anting', *The Spectator*, 2 December 1995, p. 52.

REQUIEM FOR THE CROPPIES
The pockets of our greatcoats full of barley –
No kitchen on the run; no striking camp –
We moved quick and sudden in our own country.
The priest lay behind ditches with the tramp.
A people, hardly marching – on the hike –
We found new tactics happening each day:
We'd cut through reins and rider with the pike
And stampede cattle into infantry,
Then retreat through hedges where cavalry must be thrown.
Until, on Vinegar Hill, the fatal conclave.
Terraced thousands died, shaking scythes at cannon.
The hillside blushed, soaked in our broken wave.
They buried us without shroud or coffin
And in August the barley grew up out of the grave.

Notes:
* The 'croppies' were so called because of the short-cropped hair of these Irish rebels who sympathised with the French revolutionaries at the end of the eighteenth century.
* A requiem mass is offered in Roman Catholicism for the souls of the departed – 'requiem', meaning 'rest', being the initial Latin word of the mass. This poem is a rite of commemoration of these dead ones.

■ 'Requiem for the Croppies' is a sonnet, so it is in a form which is notable for the compression of meaning and intensity of utterance. This is suitable for conveying the excitement and danger of the croppies' story.

■ The brisk sounds of the opening phrases and lines – particularly the 'c' sounds – capture the 'quick and sudden' action of the rebels' progress through the countryside.

■ Alliteration on 'r', in the phrase 'reins and rider', adds to the aural immediacy of flight and pursuit, and the noise of a word such as 'stampede' is climactic in this context.

■ The second section of the poem is quieter as the slaughter of the croppies on Vinegar Hill in 1798 is remembered. The impetus of the earlier lines is now replaced by a series of closed units:

Until, on Vinegar Hill, the fatal conclave.

■ The emotive element in Heaney's presentation is conveyed aurally, as well as visually, in a word such as 'blushed', which alliterates with 'broken' and 'buried' to intensify the sense of grief appropriate to a requiem. These words are almost blurted out in the sadness of the memory of the occasion.

Question

How does your reading aloud of the following sonnet by Shakespeare assist
your appreciation of its subject matter?

When to the sessions of sweet silent thought
I summon up remembrance of things past,
I sigh the lack of many a thing I sought,
And with old woes new wail my dear time's waste:
Then can I drown an eye (unused to flow)
For precious friends hid in death's dateless night,
And weep afresh love's long cancelled woe,
And moan th' expense of many a vanished sight:
Then can I grieve at grievances foregone,
And heavily from woe to woe tell o'er
The sad account of fore-bemoaned moan,
Which I new pay as if not paid before.
But if the while I think on thee, dear friend,
All losses are restored and sorrows end.

Assignment

Consider the issue of reading aloud and memorising poetry, for recitation
and personal satisfaction and pleasure. Choose two or three poems (or
sections from longer poems) which you would learn by heart, explaining your
choice and the matters of technique, in the poetry, which assist the process
of memorising.

Describing a poem

Theme

In using the term 'theme' for the subject matter of a poem, we are reminded of a musical piece and particularly that a complex composition, in music (such as the classical sonata) as in poetry, may have sub-themes that complement, and even contradict, the principal subject. In our first encounter with a poem, we should endeavour to identify its principal theme.

TITLE

The best introduction to the theme of a poem is its title. Some poems have no title (such as Emily Dickinson's short lyric pieces) or may have been given a title by a later editor of the work. Sometimes the title is merely the opening word or phrase of the poem, as in George Herbert's poem 'Death' (beginning: 'Death, thou wast once an uncouth, hideous thing . . .') or his third poem on the subject of love, entitled 'Love' and beginning: 'Love bade me welcome: yet my soul drew back'. Nonetheless, those simple titles are the key to the subjects of the poems that follow.

In contrast, a title may be as significant (and sometimes nearly as long) as the poem itself. The most extraordinary titles in English poetry are those of Richard Crashaw, in the seventeenth century. His poem addressed to the Countess of Denbigh has a title twelve lines long and is itself prefaced by a heart-shaped emblem. The late Romantic Irish poet W. B. Yeats, entitled one of his poems thus:

> TO A WEALTHY MAN WHO PROMISED A SECOND
> SUBSCRIPTION TO THE DUBLIN MUNICIPAL GALLERY
> IF IT WERE PROVED THE PEOPLE WANTED PICTURES

– a title which is both a dedication and an introduction to the theme of the work.

More usually, titles are introductions to the substance of the poem and its tone. John Keats's sonnet, 'On First Looking into Chapman's Homer', introduces us to three beings: the speaker of the poem (who had looked into Chapman), George Chapman – the Elizabethan poet who had translated Homer – and, finally, the Greek epic poet himself. W. H. Auden's elegy entitled 'In Memory of W. B. Yeats' announces its subject and the tone of celebratory commemoration of a life in its title. But when John Dryden, in the seventeenth century, entitled a poem 'Absalom and Achitophel', the names of two figures from the Old Testament, he was being deliberately misleading. The satire adapts the biographies and circumstances of those figures to contemporary events and personages to expose and correct their faults. If we had expected a serious work on a biblical theme from that title, then we would be surprised and amused by the disparity between that expectation and the reality of the poem, even as we admire the parallels that Dryden sustains with the original scriptural material. Such surprise and amusement is a method of satirists. In retrospect, the title is essential to the meaning and purpose of the poem.

A title can be ironic, as is the case of 'Dulce et Decorum est', by the First World War poet Wilfred Owen. He borrowed this Latin title (meaning 'it is sweet and meet [that is, appropriate] to die for one's country') from the odes of the Roman poet Horace. In the poem that follows, however, Owen rejects this teaching, calling it 'the old Lie'. The title thus prepares us for the purpose of the poem in the sense that it lulls us into a false sense of what is to follow and this makes the shock of Owen's revelations more powerful.

Irony characterises the titles of many twentieth-century poems. Perhaps the best example is T. S. Eliot's 'The Love Song of J. Alfred Prufrock', which is not a song but a dramatic monologue and which has as its theme not the presence but the absence of love from Prufrock's life.

Assignment

Consider the titles of a range of poems by different poets, preferably from different centuries. Note the variety of ways in which titles are used – simply to introduce, to entice, to surprise, and (most often) to summarise: portentously, incisively, ironically.

SUBJECT

We have considered the possible implications of the title of a poem for its theme (and we should remember to return to it as part of the poem when we are describing its meaning and reviewing it as a whole). We then take the next step in the exploration of the subject by concentrating on what is said in the body of the poem. We leave stylistic matters aside for the moment because we need to define the subject first, before we examine a poet's animation of it through the use of devices and techniques of poetic language.

I

In 'Dover Beach', by the Victorian poet Matthew Arnold, we observe the skilful development of the theme in the context of a vividly presented natural setting. This grows into a seascape representing in metaphor the ideas of the speaker. The work closes in a highly charged emotional climax:

> The sea is calm tonight.
> The tide is full, the moon lies fair
> Upon the straits — on the French coast the light
> Gleams and is gone; the cliffs of England stand,
> Glimmering and vast, out in the tranquil bay.
> Come to the window, sweet is the night air!
> Only, from the long line of spray
> Where the sea meets the moon-blanched land,
> Listen! you hear the grating roar
> Of pebbles which the waves draw back, and fling,
> At their return, up the high strand,
> Begin, and cease, and then again begin,
> With tremulous cadence slow, and bring
> The eternal note of sadness in.
>
> Sophocles long ago
> Heard it on the Aegean, and it brought
> Into his mind the turbid ebb and flow
> Of human misery; we
> Find also in the sound a thought,
> Hearing it by this distant northern sea.
>
> The Sea of Faith
> Was once, too, at the full, and round earth's shore
> Lay like the folds of a bright girdle furled.
> But now I only hear
> Its melancholy, long, withdrawing roar,
> Retreating, to the breath
> Of the night wind, down the vast edges drear
> And naked shingles of the world.
>
> Ah, love, let us be true
> To one another! for the world, which seems
> To lie before us like a land of dreams,
> So various, so beautiful, so new,
> Hath really neither joy, nor love, nor light,
> Nor certitude, nor peace, nor help for pain;
> And we are here as on a darkling plain

> Swept with confused alarms of struggle and flight,
> Where ignorant armies clash by night.

The title of 'Dover Beach' establishes the setting of the poem on the southern coast of England. To Arnold's readers it was a familiar location, with a reassuring resonance of Englishness. It also has a contrasting sense of apprehension as it is the island's closest point to continental Europe, whence so many enemies had come through the ages. In Shakespeare, it is the setting ('The Country near Dover') of the cliff over which the blind Gloucester in *King Lear* would jump; in Elizabeth Barrett Browning's *Aurora Leigh* (1853–6), its 'frosty cliffs/Looked cold upon me', while in the Second World War, the song 'The White Cliffs of Dover' inspired an Empire with its vision of the cliffs in the future, undarkened by war clouds.

Matthew Arnold spent some days there after his marriage in June 1851 when he probably wrote this poem. Dover is an ambiguous location. So a work with the title 'Dover Beach' prompts a complex response at the outset.

Our first impression of the poem is of its four verse-paragraphs – longer units than stanzas and with looser rhythmical and rhyming structures. Such divisions signal stages in the speaker's thought, in the 'argument' of the poem, but it is better to leave these subdivisions for the moment as we grasp its overall idea.

The first perception that we gain of 'Dover Beach' is a criticism of life, which is what Matthew Arnold believed that poetry should be. Various key words and phrases establish this central idea: 'the eternal note of sadness', 'human misery', 'melancholy', 'neither joy, nor love, nor light,/Nor certitude, nor peace, nor help for pain'. We notice that each verse-paragraph contains a word or phrase of this kind. And we note also, at this stage of interpretation, how the poem closes. This is at least as important as its title and opening:

> Where ignorant armies clash by night.

That is a triply negative conclusion, with its references to ignorance, violent warfare and night (in the sense of a time without illumination).

Having established that the poem is a criticism of life, we need to specify those aspects of life about which it is critical and the reasons that are given for the critique. At this point we are detailing the theme in its sub-themes and may also watch for a contrasting theme that might suggest a solution to these grave problems. Describing the process of reading the poem in this theoretical way inevitably sounds mechanical. But, in practice, we find that this is in fact the way we do read a poem, if we attend to its meaning closely.

It is at this point that we begin to look at the work systematically, line by line. We notice that the first five lines are descriptive, in a seascape. When we consider the style of 'Dover Beach' in the next section, we will note these lines' importance to the introduction of the subject. For the moment it is sufficient to recognise that the scene is set. In the sixth line, we notice that the speaker is not alone; he addresses a beloved (as she turns out to be, later, when he calls her 'love'). That the speaker is male and his sweetheart female is arbitrary. But as the poem was written by a man (and, so it is believed, shortly after his marriage), we may refer to the speaker here as 'he' for convenience.

Much more importantly, we should regard him as the speaker and not necessarily Matthew Arnold. In their poems, poets assume the identities of their speakers, who may express ideas identical to their own or explore different views or embrace larger ideas than the poet's individual convictions. They may even enter into experiences entirely outside the poet's autobiography. With these possibilities in mind (and there are many examples of what T. S. Eliot described as the 'escape from personality' in poetry) it is better to refer to the poem's 'speaker' rather than to the poet's name. Of course, we can draw conclusions about a poet's thoughts and feelings even when the speakers used are fanciful or far removed from the writer's biography. The desire to create such beings – as in Robert Browning's dramatic monologues – reveals traits of the author's personality in the desire to escape from it.

In 'Dover Beach', the speaker establishes a connection between what he sees before him physically, and his metaphysical sense of a timeless grief. The behaviour of the sea, with its relentless activity, is like a 'tremulous cadence' of persistent sorrow.

It is not until the second verse-paragraph that the speaker particularises the 'eternal note of sadness'. From the first, we might have supposed that it was the created world in general that he was lamenting. But now he speaks of 'human misery'.

The expectation of the reader, aroused by the initial reference to an apparently universal tragedy, is intensified as the speaker has specified that it is a 'human' phenomenon to which he is referring. We are therefore implicated in what has moved him. The third verse-paragraph explains that it is the loss of 'Faith', of religious belief and spiritual certitude, that has brought us to this sad condition. At this point, if we are familiar with the character of Victorian thought (treated in detail in the section on Victorianism in Part 2), we would recognise the mid-nineteenth-century 'crisis of faith' in this observation.

In the final verse-paragraph, we encounter a dilemma of meaning which is familiar in great poetry. There seems to be a solution to the despair caused by the loss of 'Faith' and the recognition of the futility of human suffering. The speaker appeals to his beloved:

> Ah, love, let us be true
> To one another!

The Romantic exclamation seems to modify, and even cancel, the Victorian melancholy. Human love will absolve all metaphysical sorrow. But the closing stanza is not as straightforward as this, for at least two reasons. Firstly, after this brief passion the speaker returns to contemplate the world bereft of all hope (and it is in his vision of despair and chaos that the work closes). Secondly, we note that his address to his lover is not a celebration of fulfilled desire but merely a plea that this might come about: 'let us be true. . .'. Nonetheless, that element is in the poem as a possible, if desperate, solution.

The ambiguous close of 'Dover Beach' shows us that we will reach limits in our quest for the meanings of poems. As William Empson has shown, there are numerous types of ambiguity in poetry. These subtleties encourage us to look more closely at works such as 'Dover Beach' and to explore their meanings more deeply. It is at this point that a close analysis of linguistic style, which is considered in the section on style (where we return to 'Dover Beach'), is so important.

Question
What is the thematic point and significance of Arnold's reference to Sophocles in 'Dover Beach'?

II

With reference to the identification and description of theme, we should now consider a modern poem by Les Murray, 'The Widower in the Country', from his collection *The Ilex Tree,* of 1965:

I'll get up soon, and leave my bed unmade.
I'll go outside and split off kindling wood
from the yellow-box log that lies beside the gate,
and the sun will be high, for I get up late now.

I'll drive my axe in the log and come back in
with my armful of wood, and pause to look across
the Christmas paddocks aching in the heat,
the windless trees, the nettles in the yard...
and then I'll go in, boil water and make tea.

This afternoon, I'll stand out on the hill
and watch my house away below, and how
the roof reflects the sun and makes my eyes
water and close on bright webbed visions smeared
on the dark of my thoughts to dance and fade away.
Then the sun will move on, and I will simply watch,
or work, or sleep. And evening will come on.

Getting near dark, I'll go home, light the lamp

and eat my corned-beef supper, sitting there
at the head of the table. Then I'll go to bed.
Last night I thought I dreamed – but when I woke
the screaming was only a possum ski-ing down
the iron roof on little moonlit claws.

'The Widower in the Country' is addressed to the reader by the first-person speaker who is the subject of the poem. The repeated use of 'I' focuses the work on this individual. It also emphasises his aloneness – not only as a widower, but as a man isolated in the Australian bush.

The poem anticipates his day. That he can be so sure of its trivial events, in advance, indicates that his is a life in which there are no surprises. This is Murray's way of suggesting that since the widower's wife's death, vitality has gone from the man's existence. The theme of the poem, in other words, includes a judgement of what is being described.

There is a striking change of tense at the end, in the last verse-sentence, when the speaker recalls his experience 'last night':

I thought I dreamed – but when I woke
the screaming was only a possum ski-ing down
the iron roof on little moonlit claws.

Even that startling event turned out to be mundane. Again, there is the sense that this is a life from which excitement has absented itself. The widower cannot even dream himself into a world removed from his ordinary circumstances. The theme of the poem is negative in its controlled pathos.

The domain of the widower is simply but effectively captured in the image of the unmade bed in the opening line. In retrospect, reviewing the subject of the poem as a whole, we can understand the poignancy of this sight. The bed would not have been left unmade by his wife. The widower is not domesticated, but quickly escapes the indoors for 'outside', where he will engage in primeval agri-cultural activities. The man's work is not judged, yet there is the underlying impression of an individual reluctantly performing his accustomed tasks:

and the sun will be high, for I get up late now.

Before, presumably, he had risen with the sun – not simply because he was younger and had more energy, but because there was a purpose in his life. As in 'Dover Beach', nature here reflects the emotions of the speaker:

the Christmas paddocks aching in the heat.

We are surprised to find that it is Christmas. This adds to the sense of poignancy in the poem, for the absence of joy is more acutely felt when we realise that we are listening to the widower's listless lament during the supposedly festive season.

The stanzas of the poem are growing in line lengths. It is not that the speaker is warming to his day's activities. Rather, the increasing length of the stanzas relates to the long drawn-out day, as the hot afternoon wearily declines into evening. The style is expressive of the themes of the poem.

The widower is seen in a detached position, looking down on his house from the hill. This is realistic in the picture it presents of the spaciousness of such a property in the bush, but it is also an image of his detachment from his earlier life. Again, realistically, his eyes water because of the reflection of the sun from that iron roof. But his explanation is not entirely convincing. He is crying, but he will not confess it, nor define precisely the cause of his grief:

> bright webbed visions smeared
> on the dark of my thoughts to dance and fade away.

It is the one point in the poem of reflection (not only from the sun, but of introspection by the widower): then 'the sun will move on'.

Pathetically, he is seen at his solitary dinner. He sits pointlessly 'at the head of the table', in the position he had taken when his wife and family were about him. His memory of the previous night's screaming possum scarcely makes the prospect of bedtime alluring. Once again the loveless, companionless present is set against the shared bedtime of the past. The poem's main theme is constantly offset by that contrary theme of what his life had been like before. The term 'widower' in the title implicitly introduces that other life as well as the idea of its absence.

Question

How does the technique of the poet restrain the poem from becoming grief-stricken and, therefore, more powerful in the presentation of the grief?

Sample question with guidelines

How would you describe the theme(s) of this poem by Judith Wright?

WOMAN TO MAN

The eyeless labourer in the night,
the selfless, shapeless seed I hold,
builds for its resurrection day –
silent and swift and deep from sight
foresees the unimagined light.

This is no child with a child's face;
this has no name to name it by;
yet you and I have known it well.

This is our hunter and our chase,
the third who lay in our embrace.

This is the strength that your arm knows,
the arc of flesh that is my breast,
the precise crystals of our eyes.
This is the blood's wild tree that grows
the intricate and folded rose.

This is the maker and the made;
this is the question and reply;
the blind head butting at the dark,
the blaze of light along the blade.
Oh hold me, for I am afraid.

■ The poem explores the relationship between a particular man and
woman, from the woman's perspective. She is the speaker of the poem,
addressing him — as the title indicates.

■ The opening stanza introduces negative ideas. Is the relationship going to
be assessed critically, or unromantically? Is the poem going to be a
complaint? Yet the language, in words like 'resurrection', suggests a religious, supernatural quality in the relationship.

■ The second stanza indicates that the aspect of the bond the speaker is
describing is their sexual encounter, personified as 'the third who lay in
our embrace'. The negativity and the spirituality of the first stanza are
now resolved in the mystery of that relationship which is, at this point,
'no child', but may lead to conception.

■ The fourth stanza focuses on the sub-theme of the difference and reciprocity between women and men, in a series of images (see Glossary). A
poem of very personal address, 'Woman to Man' has a more general
dimension too. Notice the absence of names to achieve this. Sometimes
what is left out of a poem is as significant as what is there.

■ The climax of the poem in the last stanza accompanies the climax of
their love-making. The speaker would convey the uniqueness of the act,
which is not without violence, but which is also complete in itself, and in
the contemplation and experience of which she is 'afraid'. Those definitions and that response sound contradictory and ambiguous, but taken
together they also reveal the complexity of an act that may symbolise
human life. In particular, we should note the final appeal of the woman to
the man: 'Oh hold me, for I am afraid' for its thematic significance and
linguistic impact.

Style

The style in which a poem is written is as important as its theme. Poets communicate their ideas and emotions through their use of language. While this is also true of prose and dramatic literature, in poetry the complexity, concentration and compression of language forge a unique bond with the subject to the point where the manner of the poem is indistinguishable from its matter. The style determines our understanding of the thought or feeling which the poet would convey or describe. In other words, style is the expression of poetry.

While first we seek the theme of a poem we are reading, its appreciation truly begins once we understand how the language of the poem is not only the means by which the theme is stated, but essential to its substance. We can paraphrase or summarise a poem's subject. But valuable as that exercise can be for our understanding, what we produce can never be anything other than a substitute for the poem itself – that unique linguistic combination of ideas and their expression.

Because of the importance of style in poetry, we should never ignore stylistic matters, or even consider them as less significant than theme and subject. We should combine thematic and stylistic commentary and interpretation in our appreciation of the unity of matter and form in poetry.

I

In the previous section we looked at Matthew Arnold's 'Dover Beach' in thematic terms. We should now complete that study by showing how the poet's style of utterance is not only intrinsic to the ideas and emotions of his speaker, but brings them to life. The style excites the readers' attention and draws them into the subtleties of the poem's thoughts and feelings. This enables the readers to evaluate the writer's artistry.

Stylistic analysis requires the closest possible attention to the details of vocabulary (word-usage), syntax (or grammatical structure), punctuation, rhythm and rhyme and all the host of components and devices of poetic diction. Readers cannot be expected to notice all of these in their early encounters with a poem such as 'Dover Beach'. But various features are both obvious and vital to the communication of the work's meaning. We notice, for example, that in the opening lines, the first of these is a simple sentence:

> The sea is calm tonight.

Setting his scene, the poet, through his speaker, gently introduces the reader to his subject. 'Dover Beach', as we have seen, is a grim analysis of the tragedy of the human condition. But Arnold has chosen to begin serenely – particularly in the monosyllable 'calm', which sounds as benign as the sea itself. The reader is drawn alluringly into the poem to ponder the beautiful sight of a tranquil evening seascape. And the impression is sustained in the style of the following lines, especially in the device of alliteration – on 'l': 'full', 'lies', 'light', 'Gleams', 'cliffs', 'England', 'Glimmering'. This concludes, appropriately, at the end of the second verse-sentence, with the adjective which summarises this scene and its initial effect on the observer: 'tranquil'.

The matter, however, is not as simple as this – it seldom is, in poetry. As we know from our previous readings of the work, both aloud and silent, a darkening vision is to unfold. And these lines would be irrelevant to 'Dover Beach' were they merely tranquil. Rather, we notice that Arnold has included elements in these opening lines which anticipate the disturbance of tranquillity and even something of the urgency of the poem's development. The 'French coast' and 'cliffs of England' are juxtaposed, for example – a juxtaposition emphasised by the crisper alliteration on 'c' (contrasting with that on 'l') in 'coast' and 'cliffs'. That opposition in geography stirs up a sense of contrarieties in life, as for all the intimacy of this opening, its unthreatening quality, the sublimity of the cliffs and the sound of 'vast' combine to suggest that more may be at stake than a pleasant Victorian sea-picture. A larger truth may be being communicated.

Just as the attentive reader is beginning to discern these implications, a different tone is introduced in the speaker's address to his beloved, as the poem's complexity grows:

Come to the window, sweet is the night-air!

This is a command, with the imperative use of the verb emphasised by the exclamation mark. Arnold is not merely being correct in his use of punctuation. The sight of that mark on the page is a sign of the urgency that attends this arresting call, initiated by the strong consonant and the direct monosyllabic word at the beginning of the line.

As at the opening of the poem, the sensual experience of the sea, at this point, is positive: 'sweet is the night-air!' The adjective is deliciously aural in its impact even as the scent of the night-air is being evoked. And the presence of the speaker's beloved adds to the positive impression. These attractive techniques draw us further into the vision, but even as this occurs – as much through the sounds of the words as their sense – we see (or rather, hear) that, in the next verse-sentence, the sounds change strikingly. In particular, we notice its opening word – 'Only' – and the poem's first example of onomatopoeia: 'grating roar'. The visual darkness of night (an ambiguous phenomenon) is now being accompanied by aural features that are disturbing rather than 'sweet'. 'Only' has a moan in it, like the sea, and the harshness of 'grating roar' insistently turns our minds to other aspects of the sea's behaviour and what they might suggest, as metaphors.

These negative impressions accumulate around the second imperative, 'Listen!', which in turn intensifies the motion of the poetry to destabilise completely the initial calm of 'Dover Beach'. This climaxes in the repetitive writing which closes the first verse-paragraph, as the rhythms of the words enact the restless turbulence of the sea:

> Of pebbles which the waves draw back, and fling,
> At their return, up the high strand,
> Begin, and cease, and then again begin.

This endless motion is tormenting, to read and to imagine. And the paragraph closes with a 'tremulous cadence' and the 'eternal note of sadness' in a musical metaphor, as we recognise how far we have travelled, thematically and stylistically, from the serene opening of the work.

In the four lines introducing the second verse-paragraph, a similar progression is achieved, but in a much more compact space. There is nothing especially striking about the language of the initial lines: the reference to Sophocles is in itself sufficiently arresting – such an allusion to ancient wisdom is vital to the process of validating the speaker's perception. But then we are again confronted with poetry which, in its sound and its rhythm, takes up the negative aspect of the first verse-paragraph and advances it by defining the 'sadness' generally referred to there:

> the turbid ebb and flow
> Of human misery.

The sea's movement has now become metaphorical of our condition: 'turbid' sounds turgid, while 'misery' sounds like the state it describes and the accent falls heavily on it after the 'm' of 'human'.

In the metaphorical vein, Arnold begins the third verse-paragraph with 'The Sea of Faith'. We notice the capitalisation. This is ironic, for the device usually signals something of significance, even of Godlikeness. But this 'Sea' has, for the speaker and his times, receded. He remembers its former grandeur in a resplendent painterly simile: once it lay, around the world, 'like the folds of a bright girdle furled'. Notice again the 'l' alliteration, adding to the sumptuousness of that now past glory.

In aural contrast is the alarming onomatopoeia of 'roar' which accompanies the withdrawal of the 'Sea of Faith'. The adjective 'drear' also contributes to this negative perception – in its sound as much as its sense.

The third exclamation of the poem opens its final paragraph. That this is a heartfelt plea for reciprocated love, in the presence of human despair, is animated by the cry of passion which introduces it: 'Ah, love. . .'. And to bring his poem to a climax, Arnold uses a technique of urgent, pulsing rhythm in a catalogue of the ills of contemporary life. This is registered in staccato monosyllables:

> neither joy, nor love, nor light…,

and is then intensified in a polysyllabic word which animates another collection of single-syllabled negatives to give the sense that there is no end to these pangs, metaphysical and physical: 'Nor certitude, nor peace, nor help for pain'. We notice in particular that Arnold has not directly named the negatives themselves: unhappiness, hatred, darkness, uncertainty, war, helplessness. Instead, we have a rhythm of negation in those sequences of 'neither' and 'nor' to emphasise their negativity. The naming of what is absent is stronger in its cumulative effect than the cataloguing of the negative presences would be. Multiple absences intensify the negativity.

The rhyming scheme of the poem also contributes to this plaintive atmosphere in the closing lines as 'pain' and 'plain', 'flight' and 'night' end 'Dover Beach' crisply and decisively, but also darkly. It is a tone-poem of several contrasting thoughts and emotions, articulated as much through the manner as the matter of its diction.

Assignment

Review these thematic and stylistic analyses of 'Dover Beach'. Do you agree with the readings? Would you refer to other features of the poem as important to its theme and style? Do you enjoy the poem, or not? Give reasons for your response.

II

The skilful combination of subject and style, matter and manner, is a mark of good poetry. In a twentieth century poem with a nautical setting, Stevie Smith's 'Not Waving but Drowning', we appreciate, again, the matching of theme and technique:

> Nobody heard him, the dead man,
> But still he lay moaning:
> I was much further out than you thought
> And not waving but drowning.
>
> Poor chap, he always loved larking
> And now he's dead
> It must have been too cold for him his heart gave way,
> They said.
>
> Oh, no no no, it was too cold always
> (Still the dead one lay moaning)
> I was much too far out all my life
> And not waving but drowning.

Reading the poem aloud, three of its elements strike us initially: the repetition of the title in the course of the poem and in its last line, the repetition of the onomatopoeic 'moaning' and the insistent 'no no no' in the third stanza.

Stevie Smith accompanied many of her poems with simple line drawings, recalling something of the 'emblem poems' of the seventeenth century. In this case it is an image of a swimmer emerging from the water with tear-like strands of hair over his or her face (the figure is androgynous, although referred to as 'he' in the poem). In the text, the principal image, obviously, is of the swimmer's gesture which might be construed as a wave to friends on shore, but which in reality was a signal for help as he drowns. Because it is the central image of the poem, Smith emphasises it by repetition. Then the moan of 'moaning' and the insistent negativity of 'no' make it clear – as 'drowning' in the title and elsewhere would suggest – that the poem is concerned not only with a death by water but with that event in a single life as emblematic of the tragedy of the human condition. Accordingly, *Not Waving but Drowning* is also the title of Stevie Smith's collection of poems of 1957 and the illustration accompanying the poem is also on the cover of her *Selected Poems* of 1983. In her worldview, the image has universal application.

The accumulation of negativity in the poem begins with its first word: 'Nobody'. Smith is concentrating (as she does in much of her work) on the isolation of individuals in society. This is one of the principal themes of twentieth- and twenty-first-century literature. We notice, too, in the time-scheme of the poem that the man, although dead, is still moaning. The poet is dislocating her work from the realism of its immediate setting and events. The suggestion is that we may know death in life, spiritually speaking; it is as if we cannot distinguish the dead man from his live self. Yet that immediate setting of seaside bathing perfectly embraces both joy and sadness in its connotations of the delights and dangers of the sea:

I was much further out than you thought.

The point is that human life is as deceptive as a group of bathers seen from the shore. They are apparently together, but there are those on the extremities of the community, whose calls for help are misconstrued: their apparently happy gestures are signals of desperation.

Even in the face of the corpse, washed up on the beach, the anonymous 'they', representative of society's opinion, misunderstand the significance of the tragedy of his life, condescending to him:

Poor chap, he always loved larking
And now he's dead.

But he was always 'dead', in his alienation, his failure (in E. M. Forster's phrase) to 'connect'. To absolve themselves from any responsibility and the terror of contemplating this reality in their own lives, 'they' content themselves with a medical explanation:

It must have been too cold for him his heart gave way.

We notice the absence of punctuation midway in the line which suggests that the convenient diagnosis is rapidly mouthed. What they recognise physically emphasises what they have ignored emotionally, in his dead existence: life was always too cold for him.

Insistently, but with the sense that the world will always be deaf to such cries, the dead man continues his complaint in the last stanza. This is the point of Stevie Smith's technique of repeating the title phrase which also closes the poem and which is, in effect, a text for her poetry and all poetry: that the function of a poem is to confront us, time and again, with the truths of life while leaving us to draw our own conclusions. That confrontation is achieved through striking words and images, such as the central image of the poem and the work's accumulating negativity, which is communicated as much through its style as its theme. Once again, indeed, we see that the style is the theme.

Question

What is the effect, thematically and stylistically, of Stevie Smith's use of repetition in this poem?

Sample question with guidelines

How does the combination of ideas and style convey the meaning of the following poem by Philip Larkin?

TALKING IN BED

Talking in bed ought to be easiest,
Lying together there goes back so far,
An emblem of two people being honest.

Yet more and more time passes silently.
Outside, the wind's incomplete unrest
Builds and disperses clouds about the sky,

And dark towns heap up on the horizon.
None of this cares for us. Nothing shows why
At this unique distance from isolation

It becomes still more difficult to find
Words at once true and kind,
Or not untrue and not unkind.

- The poem is about language, as its title indicates and its first phrase – the title repeated – emphasises language as representative of human behaviour, thoughts and emotions. Reading it initially, we identify the theme and the speaker's attitude towards it: talking in bed (in a relationship, especially in marriage) begins easily and honestly, truly and kindly, but in time becomes difficult, dishonest and unkind. It is implied that what is true of bed, furthermore, is representative of human relationships in general.

- The division of the poem into stanzas traces the stages of this decline in speech and love. Particularly, we notice the second stanza's first word: 'Yet'. This disjunction marks the dawning recognition of the failure of the conversation of lovers. We might see it anticipated, indeed, in the first line of the poem, in 'ought'. What should be the case is often not so, as here.

- The repetition of 'more and more' indicates the onset of the silent situation and the double negative of 'incomplete unrest', relative both to the wind and the couple in bed, emphasises their unsatisfactory condition. The effect of the wind is registered in the verbs: 'Builds and disperses'. This emblematises the developing destructiveness and the contradiction of unity, which is caused by silence in a relationship. In poetry, clouds are typically associated with the onset of gloom.

- As the stanzas accumulate, so too do the negative images as Larkin, with an ironic style, talks fluently about silence:

  dark towns heap up on the horizon.

  Even as he has established a connection with these disturbing images, the doomed speaker then derives a further negative meaning from them by observing that 'None of this cares for us'. In other words, nature and human life proceed with their unattractive processes, indifferent to individual deprivation. The only solution is for individuals to establish bonds with each other, in love and in language: 'at this unique distance from isolation'. But these connections, as he shows, do not last. It is a despairing worldview – of life in general and individual lives in particular. Such was Larkin's philosophy.

- The style of the poem comes to a decisive conclusion as the speaker, in a poem about language, toys with words:

      at once true and kind
  Or not untrue and not unkind.

  In seeking and finding the precise words to describe the situation (always the poet's quest), he simultaneously shows how this is the linguistic nightmare of a failing relationship. The irony of the style of the poem is that its fluency and honesty expose the halting and dishonest discourse of the couple trapped in their bed.

Question

Apart from the obvious stylistic device of the catalogue of her love, how, in other ways, does the speaker in this sonnet by Elizabeth Barrett Browning stylistically animate her theme of passion?

> How do I love thee? Let me count the ways.
> I love thee to the depth and breadth and height
> My soul can reach, when feeling out of sight
> For the ends of Being and ideal Grace.
> I love thee to the level of everyday's
> Most quiet need, by sun and candlelight.
> I love thee freely, as men strive for Right;
> I love thee purely, as they turn from Praise.
> I love thee with the passion put to use
> In my old griefs, and with my childhood's faith.
> I love thee with a love I seemed to lose
> With my lost saints – I love thee with the breath,
> Smile, tears, of all my life! – and, if God choose,
> I shall but love thee better after death.

Assignment

Read Thomas Gray's 'Elegy Written in a Country Churchyard'. Describe its principal theme and sub-themes, giving an account of its style: the lyrical stanza, the vocabulary and imagery, the combination of thought and emotion (as appropriate for an elegy).

Varieties of poetic style

In considering the style of poetry in English, we find, as we read widely in the different 'schools' of literary composition (which are treated in detail in Part 2), that various characteristics of style are apparent at different times in its history and in the works of individual poets.

Most striking is the contrast between conventions of poetic language in the past and the comparative plainness of much contemporary writing. Analogies may be drawn with the visual arts and music: with the richly detailed paintings and the musical polyphony of the High Renaissance, for example, in comparison with the spare qualities of modern art and contemporary 'serious' music.

It is important not to exaggerate what sometimes appears to be a rejection of artifice in modern writing. However, where stylistic features have been pared down in a minimalist utterance, it is difficult to argue that the style is as important as the subject and to identify that component for discussion. To observe that the absence of style is itself a stylistic strategy may be true, but it does not take us very far in the aesthetic interpretation and appreciation of such works. Yet, as in abstract art and contemporary musical composition, the search for meaning in modern poetry through style is often as challenging as our reading of works from the past which are firmly based in established and well-recognised conventions.

To show some of the rich variety of characteristics of poetic style through the centuries, and to consider the particular problem of stylistic interpretation of modern poetry, we should now look at some representative works over the centuries. This will lead us into Part 2 of the book where the various periods are treated in detail.

(1)   Let us begin in the Renaissance with this stanza from the fourth canto of the first book of *The Faerie Queene*, an incomplete epic poem, by Edmund Spenser:

> Now whenas darkesome night had all displayd
>   Her coleblacke curtein over brightest skye,

> The warlike youthes on dayntie couches layd,
> Did chace away sweet sleepe from sluggish eye,
> To muse on meanes of hopèd victory.
> But whenas Morpheus had with leaden mace   [Morpheus = god of
> Arrested all that courtly company,   sleep]
> Up-rose Duessa from her resting place,
> And to the Paynims lodging comes with silent pace.   [Paynims = Pagan's]

Stylistically, we are struck first of all by the rhyming and rhythmical regularity of the stanzaic design. In particular, there is a sense both of closure and anticipation in the last long line. Spenser maintains this pattern throughout the six books of the twelve he intended. It gives each stanza the sense of a completed unity and of being an integral component of the entire poem (although, ironically, unfinished) as an authoritative statement. The 'finish' of the style is representative of how the insights are presented with assurance. This is appropriate and conventional. The epic poet, in the Renaissance, was meant to have this kind of total vision and accomplishment.

The vocabulary of this stanza, like its rhyme and rhythm, is so artificial that it draws attention to itself. Today, in an informal age, we may be suspicious of such qualities, or find them contrived. But it was that very contrivance which delighted the Renaissance mind. In Spenser's *Amoretti*, or little love poems, for example, the themes and ideas are conventional in terms of Renaissance expectations of a sonnet sequence. What is remarkable is the skill with which he uses a complex rhyming scheme throughout. This facility would have delighted his contemporary readers at least as much as what his speaker had to say.

In this stanza from *The Faerie Queene*, night is personified; there are many epithets (adjectives) which are juxtaposed, and there is some alliteration for good measure: 'darkesome', 'coleblacke', 'brightest', 'warlike', 'dayntie', 'sweet', 'sluggish'. This is decorative writing, although not simply for the sake of decoration. It is detailed to convey the variety of life. This variety testified to the abundance of the created order and so to the munificence of the Creator. This may seem far-fetched to us. But to a Christian Humanist, like Spenser, it was at the heart of his epic undertaking.

The Faerie Queene is also an allegory, operating on several levels of meaning simultaneously. Realistically, this stanza is part of the narrative, the progression of the story or plot. But more is being conveyed than a sequence of events. It is being assessed as it unfolds. Symbolically, 'darkesome night' is a time of evil deeds; spiritually, it is synonymous with blindness to truth. That the youths, in quasi-Homeric epithet, are 'warlike' but on 'dayntie couches' suggests that they may be corrupted, for all their bravery. When we encounter a 'daintie couch' later in *The Faerie Queene* (Book 3, Canto 2, 28) it is the resting place of the beautiful damsel Britomart. Here, it has the disturbing implication of effeminacy;

that the young men 'muse' is similarly, although less gravely, juxtaposed with their normal vigorous activity. The large debate in the Renaissance between the lives of action and contemplation is glanced at in small here, as musing changes to Morpheus, the god of sleep, through alliteration, and his 'mace' – the heaviness of which is conveyed as much by the sound of 'leaden' as by its sense.

Both the story and the style prepare us for the evil Duessa's bad influence. That her moment has come is captured in the vigorous verb 'Up-rose' and in the decisive action of 'pace' which closes the stanza. This is animated by the last long Spenserian line. His metre is well-paced, like her walking.

A highly ornamented style such as this can be enjoyed for its own abundance of connotation and precise diction. Its enjoyment depends on our careful consideration of all the details which contribute to the meaning. The way in which the circumstances are presented, stylistically, is crucial to our evaluation of them.

(2)   A century later, in the late Metaphysical poetry of Andrew Marvell, we find a style that is less concentrated than Spenser's – there are not (at least to the same extent) compressed allusions or copious references – but which is finely polished and lyrically graceful. There is, however, as T. S. Eliot observed, a 'tough reasonableness', an argumentative strenuousness, beneath the deceptively straightforward vocabulary and cadence:

> THE MOWER TO THE GLOW-WORMS
> Ye living lamps, by whose dear light
> The nightingale does sit so late,
> And studying all the summer night
> Her matchless songs does meditate,
>
> Ye country comets, that portend
> No war nor prince's funeral,
> Shining unto no higher end
> Than to presage the grass's fall;
>
> Ye glow-worms, whose officious flame
> To wand'ring mowers shows the way,
> That in the night have lost their aim,
> And after foolish fires do stray;
>
> Your courteous fires in vain you waste,
> Since Juliana here is come,
> For she my mind hath so displaced
> That I shall never find my home.

The title introduces the poem as a pastoral work and an address by the conventional figure of Damon the mower (the subject of four poems by Marvell) to creatures which, since antiquity, have been praised in poetry for their light-bringing powers.

Stylistically, we notice that the poem is one sentence, impelled by three 'apostrophes' or addresses to the creatures: 'Ye living lamps', 'Ye country comets', 'Ye glow-worms'. The repetition accumulates to a compliment to the glow-worms for their generosity, harmlessness and care in providing their light to 'wand'ring mowers'. This makes the conclusion of the poetic sentence all the more striking, as the speaker announces, in the final stanza, that these lights are wasted, for a stronger power, exercised by Juliana, has displaced his mind and 'I shall never find my home'.

Beneath the restrained delicacy of the writing, Marvell's serious point concerns the power of passion. The simple word 'home' and the concept of never finding it are charged with significant moral and spiritual meanings which, paradoxically, are more powerful for the simplicity of the style.

Further, in terms of the vocabulary, we notice the archaic second-person plural address, 'Ye', which we cannot ignore because it insistently introduces three of the four stanzas. This style was used most often in religious and liturgical contexts by Marvell's time, and it invests the glow-worms with supernatural significance, which makes the surprise of the mower's rejection of them even more striking and reckless. Notice too that in speaking of the glow-worms' benefit to the nightingale, the melodious bird of poetry, Marvell writes:

> And studying all the summer long
> Her matchless songs does meditate.

The simple alliteration of 's' and 'm' heightens the language at precisely the point where poetic artistry is being described. There is the juxtaposition, too, of two kinds of 'fires' in the third and fourth stanzas, in succeeding lines. When poets repeat themselves in such proximity, there is a particular reason. The effect here is to contrast false fires which lead men astray with kindly lights that lead to virtue. The closeness of these on the page, in the course of the 'argument' of the poem, shows how life's pilgrimage (a favourite image in seventeenth-century poetry) is conducted in the midst of opposing forces of vice and virtue.

The most important stylistic component of the poem, however, is its simplest and most conventional: the contrast between 'light' and 'night', illumination and darkness, with their metaphorical implications. This symbolism is as old as poetry, but Marvell brings it to life again in the unique context of this poem.

(3)   In the eighteenth century, the stylistic gestures could be broad and resonant to match a generalising interpretation of human existence. In his description of the poet's craft, in the philosophical fable *Rasselas*, Samuel Johnson has Imlac remark that

> The business of a poet is to examine, not the individual,
> but the species; to remark general properties and large
> appearances; he does not number the streaks of the tulip.

Johnson's own poetry follows these principles, as in the opening paragraph of 'The Vanity of Human Wishes':

> Let Observation, with extensive view,
> Survey mankind, from China to Peru;
> Remark each anxious toil, each eager strife,
> And watch the busy scenes of crowded life;
> Then say how hope and fear, desire and hate
> O'erspread with snares the clouded maze of fate,
> Where wavering man, betrayed by venturous pride
> To tread the dreary paths without a guide,
> As treacherous phantoms in the mist delude,
> Shuns fancied ills, or chases airy good;
> How rarely Reason guides the stubborn choice,
> Rules the bold hand, or prompts the suppliant voice;
> How nations sink, by darling schemes oppressed,
> When Vengeance listens to the fool's request.
> Fate wings with every wish the afflictive dart,
> Each gift of nature, and each grace of art;
> With fatal heat impetuous courage glows,
> With fatal sweetness elocution flows,
> Impeachment stops the speaker's powerful breath,
> And restless fire precipitates on death.

The title announces both the general subject – human aspirations – and, in 'Vanity', Johnson's critique of them. As he is proposing an analysis in poetry of the human condition, the style, at the outset at least, is philosophical:

> Let Observation . . .

The opening imperative verb is the same linguistic gesture which a philosopher would use to introduce his major premise in a scholarly argument. The capitalisation of 'Observation' gives it an all-seeing power which, in a sense, validates the conclusion of the argument before the evidence has been presented. Observation, thus dignified, could scarcely be fallible.

The ordered quality of Johnson's poetic language – its sense of balance and completeness (as in 'hope and fear', 'desire and hate') – proposes the notion that these are the last words on the matter. The regular rhythm and the rhyming couplets also contribute strongly to the idea of finalised truth.

The style is not only rational or philosophical, however. As the lines proceed, aural qualities give an emotive force to the negative panorama which Observation is revealing. A word like 'wavering' has a quavering quality, and 'dreary paths' sound as depressing as they are. The 'treacherous phantoms' communicate their treachery in the aggressive sound of that adjective. The capitalisation of Reason and Vengeance draws attention to the conflict between those elevated and baser aspects of human nature; and the triumph of oppressive Fate is seen to be pervasive by the repetition of the associated adjective: 'fatal heat', 'fatal sweetness' – the second being an oxymoron. This makes us pause to consider how something sweet may be pernicious and to note how Fate may queer all things.

Johnson is the champion of Reason – which is at the centre of this verse-paragraph. His style, accordingly, although rotund, exhales reasonableness even though his assumption that his judgements are correct could be interpreted as a most unreasonable presupposition.

(4)   In the succeeding Romantic movement of the early nineteenth century, the style of the poets articulates their rejection of the Age of Reason and its principles. Romanticism was the most momentous revolution in sensibility since the Renaissance. It replaced the impersonal neo-classical style with an emphasis on individuality and imagination. The result, which continues to influence artistry to this day, is a wide variety of styles.

This is not to say that variety and experimentation did not exist before (Milton's bold stroke of the use of blank verse for his epic, *Paradise Lost*, in the seventeenth century, was a striking innovation, particularly in the wake of Spenser, the earlier epic model for English poetry) or that there has not been much derivative poetry since Romanticism – in theme as in style. But Romanticism freed poets from conventions of poetic diction, emphasising and celebrating the individuality – even idiosyncrasy and eccentricity – of the poet's voice as the expression of his or her unique visionary inspiration.

The variety of voices of the Romantic poet may be seen in the works of Samuel Taylor Coleridge who was one of the earliest exponents and theorists of the movement. He can be conversational, as in the casual opening to 'This Lime-Tree Bower My Prison':

> Well, they are gone, and here must I remain,
> This lime-tree bower my prison! I have lost
> Beauties and feelings . . .

This is very different from the formal beginning of 'The Vanity of Human Wishes'. Then there is his lyrical narrative style in 'The Rime of the Ancient Mariner' which is certainly formal, but quaintly archaic in its simplicity, recalling the troubadour poetry of the original Romance period in the Middle Ages:

It is an ancient Mariner
And he stoppeth one of three.

In 'Kubla Khan', Coleridge's style is ecstatic in expressing an exotic vision of oriental mystery and sensuousness:

But oh! that deep romantic chasm which slanted
Down the green hill athwart a cedarn cover!
A savage place! as holy and enchanted
As e'er beneath a waning moon was haunted
By woman wailing for her demon lover!
And from this chasm, with ceaseless turmoil seething,
As if this earth in fast thick pants were breathing,
A mighty fountain momently was forced.

This is a poetry, indeed, 'breathing' in 'fast thick pants'.

The variety of Coleridge's technique is just one example of the seemingly limitless stylistic possibilities of Romantic aesthetic theory, from the most primitive, even childlike lyricism of William Blake (in his *Songs of Innocence and of Experience*):

Little Fly
Thy Summer's play
My thoughtless hand
Has brush'd away.

to the complexities of Gerard Manley Hopkins:

Earnest, earthless, equal, attuneable, | vaulty, voluminous,
     ... stupendous
Evening strains to be time's vast, | womb-of-all, home-of-all,
     hearse-of-all night...

where intricacies of rhythm and a sinuous syntax seem at once to dislocate poetic language from the meaning while intensifying our contemplation of it. Yet Hopkins had his simplicities too, as in 'Spring and Fall' – a song of innocence and experience:

Margaret, are you grieving
Over Goldengrove unleaving?

Any mode of utterance was possible that spoke of the individual sensibility. This included, ironically, the reaction to Romanticism in Modernism, early in the twentieth century. Modernism rejected the decadence of much later Romantic and Victorian styles, yet it is a testament to the revolutionary individuality which inspired the movement.

(5)   Modernist and Post-Modernist poets were determined to confront and reveal the twentieth century to their readers and to reject what they regarded as the escapism of Romanticism. Thematically, their poetry is often much more direct, to the point of being brutal in its realism, than nineteenth-century verse. Stylistically, it can seem indistinguishable from prose in its conversational immediacy and the absence of all traditional kinds of decoration which are usually found in the lush lyricism of Romantic and Victorian poetry. A deliberately unlovely utterance was deemed appropriate to express the wasteland world and its life. Wyndham Lewis's literary magazine *Blast* (1914–15) and Allen Ginsberg's long poem of the mid-1950s *Howl* indicate in their titles the new voice of Modernism.

If we look more closely at *Howl*, however, while we certainly note the 'unpoetic' components of its subject matter – the moral despair of American urban youth culture – we also appreciate rhythmic patterns and the dynamic qualities of the poet's vocabulary:

> I saw the best minds of my generation destroyed by madness,
> > starving hysterical naked,
> dragging themselves through the negro streets at dawn looking
> > for an angry fix,
> angelheaded hipsters burning for the ancient heavenly
> > connection to the starry dynamo in the machinery of
> > > night,
> who poverty and tatters and hollow-eyed and high sat up
> > smoking in the supernatural darkness of cold-water
> > > flats
> > floating across the tops of cities contemplating jazz . . .

The elements of the poem may be prosaically familiar – perhaps more so today than they were when Ginsberg wrote *Howl* – but the language is far from prosaic. As the paragraphing indicates, the poetry has orderly divisions even as moral anarchy or madness is being described. As the divisions evolve – particularly, again, if we read the poetry out loud – we discern a chanting, incantatory pulse. The last quoted division beginning with 'who' is in fact the first of a sequence of numerous such beginnings in Part I of the poem. It is an accumulating catalogue of misery, stabbingly insistent. We notice, too, the activity of those described, in disturbing verbs such as 'dragging' and 'burning', and – in spite of all the degradation – the contrasting ethereal images of the 'starry dynamo' and 'supernatural darkness'. In this dimension, *Howl* is not far removed from Coleridge's pleasure dome in 'Kubla Khan'.

Of the same period and school of the 'Beat generation' is Jack Kerouac, who writes more sparingly than Ginsberg in his '113th Chorus' (note, nonetheless, the musical title) from his *Mexico City Blues*:

> Got up and dressed up
> > and went out & got laid
> Then died and got buried
> > in a coffin in the grave,
> Man –
> > Yet everything is perfect,
> Because it is empty
> Because it is perfect
> > with emptiness,
> Because it's not even happening.

The style here is highly concentrated even though the matter is by turns banal, cynical and deranged. The lilting rhythm of the opening line corresponds to the daily tedium of the automatic procedure it describes. It becomes syncopated – for this is a 'blues' poem – as the two heavily accented words, 'grave, / Man' jolt us out of the predictable lilt. 'Man' is at least as challenging as it is accommodating, in this context. It is colloquial but it is also universal – this is another version of Shakespeare's 'unaccommodated man': our essential animal being. The language then conveys the meaninglessness of life as emptiness and perfection resolve into each other. And the poem as a whole conforms to an artistic convention: that of the lament of the 'blues' lyric, even though it is radical in its vision.

Earlier in the twentieth century, the experimentation derived from Romanticism prompted Modernists to explore modes of abstraction, leading at times to seemingly impenetrable complexity. e e cummings (the decapitalisation of his name reflecting the most striking detail of punctuation, or its absence, in his writing) rejected the conventions of printing. This was a sign of a general assault on the Classical and Romantic traditions of poetry and even the requirement of meaning.

Another tradition of twentieth-century poetics preserved Romantic style in a modified form. This was under the influence of such later nineteenth-century poets as Thomas Hardy and A. E. Housman. Its principal exponent, Philip Larkin, was committed to lyrical regularity and to avoiding what he and others of this school (known as 'the Movement') regarded as the wilful obscurity of much Modernist writing.

(6)   The characteristic later twentieth-century style of poetry, however, was that of the 'confessional' school of writers such as Robert Lowell and Sylvia Plath. This remains the most pervasive tradition in poetry in English today, in the twenty-first century. It is, again, directly derived from Romanticism with its emphasis on individuality, which received its most extreme expression in the theory of the 'egotistical sublime' (see Chapter 9). Yet the self-centredness of confessional poetry is usually depressing in its revelations rather than exhilarat-

ing (see, for example, Robert Lowell's *Life Studies*, dealt with in detail in Special Study 14).

In Plath's poem 'The Hanging Man' (in the collection *Ariel*, published after her suicide in 1963), she recalls the bouts of electric-shock treatment she received for her mental illness in the 1950s. While we are struck by how directly the brutality is described here, it is important to appreciate how the experience, for all its terror, has been compressed and refined stylistically. This is not merely a direct transcription of this horrible experience, as we might expect of a 'confessional' poem. The title, in comparing the hospital official to an executioner, poeticises the event, dramatising it and exaggerating it, in a typically Plathian way. However, at the same time the analogy intellectualises the event, and thus makes it objective to a degree. By comparing the official to a 'god', Plath indicates her powerlessness in his presence – although we note that the 'god' is not 'God'. By having the attention of a divinity, like a desert prophet no less, her dominant emotion of self-pity is modified and replaced with a kind of martyrdom. Plath was often triumphant in her suffering. The onomatopoeia of 'sizzled' frighteningly conveys the sound and heat of the electric shock, as well as the sense of her mental powers being shrivelled up by it. The treatment is akin to death in the electric chair. She has been brought to this punishment by a 'vulturous boredom'. The adjective to describe the condition of being consumed sounds all-consuming as we enunciate it. And the closing line, deceptively simple in its sequence of monosyllables, insists that anyone else in her condition of boredom, including the executioner himself, would have behaved as she did. Plath is referring to her repeated suicide attempts.

This is modern poetry speaking directly of psychological suffering at its worst. However, in its various stylistic features – the use of two similes, for example, in the space of just six lines – it is traditionally concentrated in its artistry.

Question

How would you characterise the stylistic differences between Robert Browning's mid-nineteenth-century poem and Thomas Hardy's early twentieth-century poem, below? Remember to relate thematic concerns to stylistic features.

HOME-THOUGHTS, FROM THE SEA

Nobly, nobly Cape Saint Vincent to the northwest died away;
Sunset ran, one glorious blood-red, reeking into Cadiz Bay;
Bluish 'mid the burning water, full in face Trafalgar lay;
In the dimmest northeast distance dawned Gibraltar grand and gray;
'Here and here did England help me: how can I help England?' – say,

Whoso turns as I, this evening, turn to God to praise and pray,
While Jove's planet rises yonder, silent over Africa.

IN TIME OF 'THE BREAKING OF NATIONS'
Only a man harrowing clods
       In a slow silent walk
With an old horse that stumbles and nods
       Half asleep as they stalk.

Only thin smoke without flame
       From the heaps of couch-grass;
Yet this will go onward the same
       Though Dynasties pass.

Yonder a maid and her wight   [wight = man]
       Come whispering by:
War's annals will cloud into night
       Ere their story die.

Evaluation of poetry 4

The most difficult exercise in the study of poetry is the process of evaluating a poem. We can describe its theme and note how stylistic techniques are vital to the communication of the ideas and emotions which it embodies. But is it a great poem, good, bad, or indifferent? We may be asked whether or not we enjoy a particular poem and we can find it very difficult to justify our response.

One reason for the difficulty in evaluating poetry is that, through the centuries, contradictory expectations of poets and their art have been formulated, often with absolutist certainty. In practice, this has meant that while the works of writers of a particular age have been highly regarded, another age – usually the immediately succeeding one – rejects them, both for their subject matter and their style. The Modernists found the themes and mannerisms of Victorian poetry very risible: 'Lawn Tennyson, gentleman poet', muses Leopold Bloom, mischievously, in James Joyce's *Ulysses*, 'the rum tum tiddledy tum'. It is true that such variations in appreciation have produced the marvellous variety of poetry in English, but they are also confusing to those readers who seek standards by which to evaluate a poem.

That certain poets and their works have survived the violent waxings and wanings of canons of taste indicates that survival itself may be a measure of excellence. Ben Jonson, with commendable foresight, said of his contemporary, William Shakespeare, that he 'was not of an age, but for all time'. But different times have constructed different Shakespeares, to suit their preoccupations. In any case, when we are confronted with contemporary poetry, we cannot apply the test of endurance.

We should start with the individual reader's response to a poem. First (as we have seen) we read it aloud and silently, consider its theme and style and give a detailed analysis of both, showing their interdependence. Then we must ask ourselves if we like it and provide reasons for our approval or disapproval.

Before the Romantic movement of the nineteenth century, the judgement of poetry was easier because conventions and technical requirements needed to be fulfilled. What was required of an Elizabethan *aubade* (or morning song) to the beloved or in a sonnet sequence was generally understood, although individual poets made their own thematic and stylistic innovations within the broad conventions. In the courtly entertainment of the masque – a combination of poetry, music and theatricality which was popular in the early seventeenth century – Ben Jonson's 'Pleasure Reconciled to Virtue' (1618), for example, finds its thematic antithesis in Milton's 'Comus' of 1634, where the triumph of virtue over the 'god of cheer' is secured by Chastity. The stylistic contrast is also striking in Milton's use of blank verse. But other features of the masque are retained in 'Comus' – there are songs and the device of the antimasque. Milton subverts important components of the masque tradition even as he carefully submits to several of its thematic and stylistic conventions. So a contemporary reader may have been appalled or exhilarated by the innovations and evaluated the work accordingly.

The rhyming couplet dominated eighteenth-century poetry, although much innovative skill was brought to its use. What Dr Samuel Johnson required of a poem in the eighteenth century was very different from what Sir Philip Sidney had demanded in the sixteenth century. The similar aspect, however, was the objective tests that could be applied about subject matter and technique, and such critics as Sidney and Johnson set out their requirements in their literary-critical essays. So we are beginning to see that if we make clear the standards by which we are judging a poem, we are ready to argue our case for its worthiness.

The Romantics formulated their understanding of poetry and poetic artistry, too – but the emphasis in their writings moved from obedience to objective criteria to affirmations of the sovereignty of the individual artist's imagination and the spontaneous creativity which it generated. In spite of a vigorous reaction to this in twentieth-century criticism (most notably in T. S. Eliot's essays, where the anti-Romantic emphasis on impersonality attempted to recover some of the classical detachment of the pre-Romantic periods), readers of poetry today approach it with Romantic expectations: they seek the revelation of a personality, they expect sincerity from the writer about his or her convictions and want to be moved by the poem. The writer's artistic accomplishment, now, is probably of secondary importance. It is a significant rearrangement of the priorities of the pre-Romantic periods.

This is why so many readers today find that while they might be able to admire the poetry of the sixteenth, seventeenth and eighteenth centuries for its skill and learning, they do not find that it speaks to them personally by stirring their emotions. It is not merely because they are separated from the preoccupations of those beings from far-distant ages. We seek responses in ourselves which their poetry was not written to satisfy. If we read the love poems of Robert Herrick, the seventeenth-century 'Cavalier' poet, for example, as transcriptions of his emotional experiences and sexual adventures, we would be grossly misled. Herrick mentions a dozen mistresses by name in his verse, but all are imaginary, their names being used because they fit his metrical schemes. Where the bachelor-parson is sincere is where he tells us that 'jocund his muse was, but his life was chaste'. His love poems are not about love, let alone his own apparently non-existent love life. They are about love poetry and they are to be evaluated accordingly.

This is not, however, a counsel of despair. While always keeping our minds open to the possibilities of innovation and a new style of writing, it is possible to bring certain basic requirements to our evaluation of a poem from any century. The challenge of entering into the sensibilities of writers from different ages, and even, eventually, coming to a mastery of such an understanding of their contrasting worlds is one of the delights and rewards of studying poetry. How limited our worldview would be if it were confined to our own time and kind of experience!

1

Essentially, the poet should catch and retain our attention. Both in what is said and how it is said, the opening gestures of a poem – its title, the beginnings of its argument, its descriptive scene-setting, its mode of address – should be captivating, like the first few bars of an overture or a symphony. This certainly does not mean that the opening should be spectacular or noisy or shocking. A quiet introduction can cast its own spell. For example, the title to Philip Larkin's 'As Bad as a Mile' excites our interest as it urges us to remember the cliché: 'a miss is as good as a mile'. We are led to discover the reason for the poet's variation of that wisdom in the body of the poem, after it is so tantalisingly introduced in its title.

We find many examples of arresting openings in the works of the great poets - some because of the vocabulary that is used, others because of the attitude that is struck by the speaker:

> My mistress' eyes are nothing like the sun.
>
> SHAKESPEARE

> For God's sake hold your tongue, and let me love.
>
> DONNE

> This is the month, and this the happy morn.
>
> MILTON

> Shut, shut the door, good John! (fatigued, I said)
> Tie up the knocker, say I'm sick, I'm dead.
>
> POPE

> Milton! thou should'st be living at this hour.
>
> WORDSWORTH

No, no, go not to Lethe.

KEATS

Break, break, break,
On thy cold gray stones, O Sea!

TENNYSON

I will arise and go now, and go to Innisfree.

YEATS

April is the cruellest month.

ELIOT

I imagine this midnight moment's forest.

HUGHES

This last opening echoes and mimics Gerard Manley Hopkins's striking opening to 'The Windhover':

I caught this morning morning's minion.

Assignment

Consider some of these openings and the poems to which they belong. Give an account of the qualities of theme and style which make these beginnings apt and captivating.

II

Next, we require that what has been promised at the beginning, in matter and manner, should prevail throughout the work. Most poets can either begin well or end decisively. The later seventeenth-century poet Henry Vaughan is often cited (perhaps unfairly) as the example of the poet who begins arrestingly but who fails to sustain thematic and stylistic impetus. Few – Milton is one of them – can both start and finish memorably and maintain the original promise and design throughout, as he does repeatedly, even in the large scope of *Paradise Lost*.

That consistency of utterance entails the mastery of style. It is one of the marks of the great poets that they speak distinctively in their own voices, however conventional their subjects and techniques, and that each voice has a flexible range and variety.

Emily Dickinson, the American nineteenth-century poet, sounds like noone else, before or since. In discovering her own voice, she reveals its strange qualities of being ever-new while always recognisably the same. Superficially, her poems appear to be simplistic in their themes and lyrical technique. But through the combination of her unique vision of her subjects, perfectly mediated through her style, they present challenging interpretations of life:

> There's a certain slant of light,
> Winter afternoons,
> That oppresses like the heft
> Of cathedral tunes.
>
> Heavenly hurt it gives us.
> We can find no scar
> But internal difference
> Where the meanings are.
>
> None may teach it any –
> 'Tis the seal despair,
> An imperial affliction
> Sent us of the air.
>
> When it comes the landscape listens.
> Shadows hold their breath.
> When it goes 'tis like the distance
> On the look of death.

The familiar experience of melancholy is presented here in a poetry the style of which has a crisp, terse quality throughout. Dickinson does not diminish her knowledge of 'despair' by indulging in self-pity, or by writing in lugubrious language. There is, instead, objectivity and detachment in the impersonal speaker ('we' not 'I'), which also gives universality to the poem's meaning and in the use of extended imagery from nature. This reinforces the general application of the subject to the world and the idea that this affliction is at its heart.

The setting of the lyric, in the opening stanza, is most striking in the short second line, 'Winter afternoons', which establishes the ideas of death and decline. We need to remember the harshness of the winter in Massachusetts where Dickinson lived. However, on re-reading, the opening subtlety of description – 'a certain slant of light' – becomes more significant than the conventional winter imagery. The 'slant' suggests something awry – a perversion in creation – as well as the more obvious indication of light being seen from an oblique angle (and possibly even more accurately from that angle). It is also striking that it is 'light' which is disturbing, for light is usually associated with warmth, hope, even God's presence.

Light as it is seen here, however,

> oppresses like the heft
> Of cathedral tunes.

Again, Dickinson is contradicting expectation in this simile. For light as an adjective is understood as weightless, yet the heavy verb, 'oppresses', and the blunt 'heft' (or 'weight') show that this slant of light is entirely different in its effect. The burdensome quality of the light being like the resonant sound of cathedral music ascribes to it a religious portentousness that is not consoling, but oppressive. With a stylistic irony, Dickinson is writing of such heaviness in a poetry that is itself light and lyrical in manner. Within the discipline of the stanza convention the odd comparison almost seems normal, yet arresting implications are not dulled.

Dickinson indicates the theological significance of this 'certain' light in the second stanza. With her Calvinist Puritan background, she is referring both to the idea of Original Sin and the punishment of alienation from God ('Heavenly hurt') which was its consequence. We have but one 'scar', which is not like an external, physical wound, but the soul's affliction which has profoundly separated us from heaven – 'internal difference'. And this is the explanation of the human condition, the elucidation of its tragedy: 'where the meanings are'.

Despair is emphasised, in the third stanza, not only for its emotional impact of profound desolation, but for its precise theological meaning as the gravest of sins: the conviction that there can be no salvation from our mortality, no resurrection from death.

This concentration on a 'slant of light' reveals heaven's purposes as indifferent to the present condition of humanity:

> None may teach it any . . .

as being irreversible in their consequences:

> 'Tis the seal despair . . .

and imposed magisterially (with the implication of 'unjustifiably') from on high:

> An imperial affliction
> Sent us of the air.

For all its insubstantial character, Dickinson's speaker is not denying the light's overwhelming impact – not only on human lives, but on the creation at large:

> When it comes the landscape listens,
> Shadows hold their breath.

Nature is personified to establish its connection with humanity (and ours with it) in this affliction.

The closing lines

> When it goes 'tis like the distance
> On the look of death

release the tension that has been accumulating through the stanzas, but they do not relax the poem into consolation: there is consistency of theme and tone throughout.

The departure of the light is not absolute, as the poet's simile indicates. What this light represents is always present, though it may be removed and at a 'distance' from us. And what it signifies is the essential truth about all life - that it is touched by and will be consumed in death. Dickinson is suggesting that the 'slant of light' stands for a phenomenon that is at once at the heart of our being (our mortality, the scar within) and that yet seems so strange to us, as we pursue our ordinary existences. The 'look of death', so distant from us, is in essence what we are. Here, as elsewhere, the impression made by Dickinson's poetry is of the stylistic and thematic enactment of her unique and disturbing worldview. Her poetry combines two elements to achieve this: it is accessible through its apparent simplicity, and innovative images convey the strangeness of her vision.

III

Dickinson demonstrates a quality we require of good poetry at large: the exercise of restraint in thematic and stylistic presentation. All of life's experiences can be made poetic and the process of transforming an experience into a literary text (an experience in itself, on which poets often reflect) is bound to straiten that experience. Ben Jonson expounds the theory in his poem in praise of Shakespeare's 'well-turned and true-filed lines':

> For though the poet's matter Nature be,
> His Art doth give the fashion; and that he
> Who casts to write a living line must sweat
> (Such as thine are) and strike the second heat
> Upon the muses' anvil; turn the same,
> And himself with it, that he thinks to frame,
> Or for the laurel he may gain a scorn;
> For a good poet's made as well as born.

Even chaos and anarchy need to be controlled in order to be expressed, and, as Pope shows in *The Dunciad*, they may be most tellingly expressed when they are most rigorously controlled. In this case he satirises the triumph of dullness in poetry and other branches of learning:

> In vain, in vain, – the all-composing Hour
> Resistless falls: The Muse obeys the Power.
> She comes! she comes! the sable throne behold
> Of Night primeval, and of Chaos old!
> Before her, Fancy's gilded clouds decay,
> And all its varying rainbows die away.

Wit shoots in vain its momentary fires,
The meteor drops, and in a flash expires.
As one by one, at dread Medea's strain,
The sickening stars fade off the ethereal plain;
As Argus' eyes by Hermes' wand oppressed,
Closed one by one to everlasting rest;
Thus at her felt approach, and secret might,
Art after Art goes out, and all is Night.
See skulking Truth to her old cavern fled,
Mountains of casuistry heaped o'er her head!
Philosophy, that leaned on Heaven before,
Shrinks to her second cause, and is no more.
Physic of Metaphysic begs defense,
And Metaphysic calls for aid on Sense!
See Mystery to Mathematics fly!
In vain! they gaze, turn giddy, rave, and die.
Religion blushing veils her sacred fires,
And unawares Morality expires.
Nor public flame, nor private, dares to shine;
Nor human spark is left, nor glimpse divine!
Lo! thy dread Empire, CHAOS is restored;
Light dies before thy uncreating word:
Thy hand, great Anarch! lets the curtain fall;
And Universal Darkness buries All.

When the artistry of a poem is dull (unlike the example above) we find that the straitening has been insufficient, thematically and stylistically: grief over lost love may be mawkish, argumentativeness may be too abstruse or aggressive, patriotism may be jingoistic, a preoccupation with death maudlin, praise gushing, learning ostentatious, description unfocused and, perhaps most importantly, the style fails to constrain the subject matter even as it expresses it. Admittedly, in the cases of a handful of poets, the violation of restraint can become a form of artistry. Richard Crashaw, the only English 'baroque' poet, is one of very few examples of a successful excess. Christopher Smart of the eighteenth century and Gerard Manley Hopkins of the nineteenth are others. But in all their cases, the apparently undisciplined flamboyance has its justification and ultimate restraint in their poetry being faithful to recognisable varieties of orthodox Christian doctrine.

A modern example of the importance of this quality of restraint is W. H. Auden's 'Lullaby'. Its subject, the experience of passionate love, is difficult to treat with artistic rectitude. Ironically, the effect of straitening is that passion artistically controlled can make a more profound and lasting impression on the reader than writing which is intoxicated with emotion. It becomes (to borrow an image from W. B. Yeats) like a 'tightened bow'.

The quality of restraint in this poem is announced in its title: this will be a song-like poem sung to the beloved at bedtime – not as a prelude to love-making, but to sleep. As a lullaby, it must be rhythmically soothing throughout and aurally tender. The regular stanzaic arrangement also contributes to the ordering of the material, but the speaker's range is as wide as his passion is deep: life passes, the first stanza reminds us, so we must live it in love. This will take us beyond our concerns with mortality and our human imperfections, into a realm of enchantment.

The speaker, conveying this in the second stanza, nonetheless controls their ecstasy – located on a 'slope', out-of-doors – both by that literary allusion and the reference to them in 'their ordinary swoon'. The artistic discipline of the lullaby prevents an excessive outpouring here, even as absolute claims are made for Venus's vision and there are startling references to the 'hermit's carnal ecstasy' and the 'pedantic boring cry' of 'fashionable madmen'. If we look closely at those phrases, we notice how the vocabulary, too, is a technique of restraint. The classical etymology of 'carnal ecstasy' is almost clinical in its detachment even though the speaker refers to fleshly lust. The ironically elegant 'fashionable' carefully restrains the madmen's cry (already controlled by 'pedantic'). These phrases bring their subject matter to our attention, but then they are dismissed. Auden's technique is so secure that the lullaby is not destabilised by their inclusion.

The poem closes in a benediction as the speaker wishes his lover well in a hostile world. It has been said that the poem is an expression of homosexual love (for Auden was homosexual) and that this explains the closing reference to 'nights of insult' which his partner will endure. But 'Lullaby' is not explicit in this way, and this is another example of restraint. It is, as its closing phrase affirms, about 'human love' and that wider application is true to the absolute qualities of love referred to before yet agreeably contained, restrained and straitened in the work's aesthetic order.

Numerous other qualities of a good poem are revealed by wide reading, which is the best method for refining our appreciation of literature. It is important that the praise or criticism of a poem is justified as objectively as possible. This can only happen by firstly considering the poem as a poem and, as a consequence of this, focusing closely on the poet's use of language. To praise or criticise a poem because it seems to endorse (or fails to endorse, or contradicts) our personal opinions is to miss the point of poetry and of all art. Everything is susceptible to artistic treatment. What Virginia Woolf said of fiction is also true of poetry:

> 'The proper stuff of fiction' does not exist, everything is the
> proper stuff of fiction, every feeling, every thought; every
> quality of brain and spirit is drawn upon; no perception comes amiss.

As readers, we should strive to enter into the world of thought and imagination which the poet has created for us. If necessary - as Coleridge taught - we should suspend disbelief. The student of poetry should concentrate on determining whether or not a poem's treatment of its theme is artistic. We should clearly state the principles of aesthetic value which are being used to make the assessment. It is only by this method that we can explain our enjoyment of poetry to ourselves and to others.

Sample questions with guidelines

What is worthy of admiration in this poem by George Herbert?

LOVE III

Love bade me welcome: yet my soul drew back,
    Guilty of dust and sin.
But quick-eyed Love, observing me grow slack
    From my first entrance in,
Drew nearer to me, sweetly questioning
    If I lacked any thing.

A guest', I answered, 'worthy to be here':
    Love said, 'You shall be he'.
'I, the unkind, ungrateful? Ah, my dear,
    I cannot look on thee'.
Love took my hand, and smiling did reply,
    'Who made the eyes but I?'

'Truth, Lord; but I have marred them; let my shame
    Go where it doth deserve'.
'And know you not', says Love, 'who bore the blame?'
    'My dear, then I will serve'.
'You must sit down', says Love, 'and taste my meat'.
    So I did sit and eat.

- The title of the poem and its first word establish the theme, which is complicated by the ideas of secular and sacred love and the speaker's negative response to Love's invitation. The first two stanzas are ambiguous – they describe the worlds of courtly romance and the biblical 'love-feast' – while the third dramatically clarifies the ambiguity in an explicit address to God in the reference to 'Lord'. The poem presents a progression from worldliness to spirituality which is the essence of the Christian pilgrimage.

- Ordering the material further is Herbert's use of dialogue between the attentive courtly lady, 'quick-eyed Love' and the speaker, and then the Lord and the speaker. Statements and responses reveal his character –

sinful, unworthy and so on. Yet all is embraced by love, in the poem as in Christian doctrine. We notice also the change of tense between the first two stanzas and the third as the speaker draws nearer to the present revelation of Love in the Lord.

- While setting the poem in an accessible situation, like the parables in the New Testament, Herbert is using the lyric to indicate theological truths: the relationship between God and Love and the sacrificial death of Christ ('who bore the blame' for sin) which reveals it. Herbert celebrates the bounty of that heavenly love in the willingness of the Lord to serve the sinner and through the imagery of the banquet at the end.

- The simplicity of Herbert's style is commendable in a poem which deals with profound spiritual issues, as in the last line with its monosyllables: 'I did sit and eat'. It is his genius to express the Christian faith lucidly without descending to the banal or the simplistic.

- The lyrical quality of the poem is finally justified as its subject is resolved in harmony. Herbert (whose ear and imagery were attuned to music) anticipates this resolution in the work's title and opening word. All is ordered to bring the piece to a perfect cadence of style and theme at the end, but the drama of the dialogue provides a dissonant tension within the poem, requiring resolution and providing its 'human interest'.

Question

What would you commend in this poem by D. H. Lawrence? (You might focus on the poet's choice of vocabulary; the dramatic situation he describes; the changing tones and moods of the poem; its musical allusions.)

PIANO

Softly, in the dusk, a woman is singing to me;
Taking me back down the vista of years, till I see
A child sitting under the piano, in the boom of the tingling strings
And pressing the small, poised feet of a mother who smiles as she
    sings.

In spite of myself, the insidious mastery of song
Betrays me back, till the heart of me weeps to belong
To the old Sunday evenings at home, with winter outside
And hymns in the cozy parlour, the tinkling piano our guide.

So now it is vain for the singer to burst into clamour
With the great black piano appassionato. The glamour
Of childish days is upon me. My manhood is cast
Down in the flood of remembrance, I weep like a child for the past.

PART TWO

Poetry through the centuries

2

Introduction

Poems are not written in a vacuum: they are the products of individual men and women living in different societies at different times in history. Accordingly, we need to bring a measure of historical learning and biographical information to our reading of poetry if it is to be informed and persuasive. Our interpretation of a poem, both thematically and stylistically, depends on whether it was written in early nineteenth-century England by Lord Byron or later twentieth-century Australia by Gwen Harwood. It is futile to contend that the identity, biography and historical period of an author are irrelevant to the work he or she produced.

With knowledge of the 'life and times' from which a poem has derived, we can identify allusions and avoid making fundamental mistakes in our explanation of the references and the meanings of words and phrases. A dictionary based on historical principles, such as the Shorter Oxford, is an indispensable aid for the student of poetry. Words have changed their meanings and implications through the centuries and we can often solve what appears to be an incongruity in a text simply by finding the meaning of the word at the time the text was written.

In the seventeenth century, for example, 'prevent', which now means 'to hinder or stop', had the precisely opposite meaning (from its Latin origins) of 'to go before' or 'to guide'. So the prayer of that time which begins, 'Prevent us, O Lord, in all our doings...' is certainly not a request that God should hinder or stop our undertakings, but the very reverse. Similarly, if we are unaware that an angel was once a gold coin as well as a divine messenger, we would miss the point of many wry puns in Renaissance literature or the cynicism of John Donne's lines about marriage addressed to the 'Daughters of London' in his 'Epithalamion made at Lincolnes Inne':

> You which are Angels, yet still bring with you
> Thousands of Angels on your marriage daies.

Then, when John Milton wrote that Dalila was 'ornate, and gay' in *Samson Agonistes*, he did not mean to suggest that she was a lesbian, but splendidly bedecked in her finery. When your 'humour' was referred to, in the same period, it may have been to any one of four states of emotion – the 'cardinal humours' – including anger and melancholy; the word was not confined to jocularity as it tends to be today. When Lady Mary Wortley Montagu, in the eighteenth century, referred to 'madam's toilet', she was not describing a lavatory but a woman in the last stages of dressing.

The force of words changes, too, over the years. The adjective 'naughty', for instance – as in the seventeenth-century phrase 'this naughty world' – was once a serious indictment of wickedness. Now we usually apply it only to a mischievous child or, whimsically, to an adult. Our lame term of approval, 'nice', was once much stronger, meaning 'precise', even 'fastidious', as in Samuel Butler's phrase in *Hudibras* (1663): 'he could raise scruples dark and nice'. It is particularly important to be alert to such nuances in our reading of that most subtle of linguistic forms, the poem.

A fascinating aspect of studying poetry is the insight into different ways of thinking, along with the characteristics of individual human lives and aspects of social behaviour to which poems give concentrated artistic expression. Poetry liberates us from self-centredness and from the restrictions of our own societal preoccupations and prejudices, linking us imaginatively with men and women from different ages and cultures – as distant as the English Middle Ages or as recent as America in the 1960s. We return to our own world with a new and enlarged perspective, free from assumptions that our views of life are the only ones and necessarily superior to those of men and women in the past. We become aware, also, that the ideas and convictions even of our own time may change during the course of it: 'the genius of a nation', Jonathan Swift wrote, 'is liable to alter in half an age'.

Poems, of course, are not limited by the ages in which they were written or by their writers' experiences. In Robert Lowell's *Life Studies* of the 1950s, for example, the emphasis is on the particular – even peculiar – biographies of Lowell and his Bostonian family. The reader who knows about American east-coast society at that time (in the 'tranquillized *Fifties*', in Lowell's phrase) and the poet's troubled life-story will bring valuable information to the interpretation of many details in these works. But *Life Studies* (published in 1959) is also a statement about western civilisation in the later twentieth century and a probing psychological analysis of perennial problems in human relationships. One poem is entitled, for example, 'To Speak of the Woe That Is in Marriage'. *Life Studies* is about Lowell's life and life in general.

On the other hand, in John Dryden's Augustan poetry of the later seventeenth century, we search in vain for personal details in observations that are remarkable for their universality:

> All human things are subject to decay,
> And, when fate summons, monarchs must obey.
>
> *Mac Flecknoe*

Yet we need to understand the political and social attitudes of his age which his poetry so pointedly probes in order to appreciate his brilliant incisiveness. And Dryden's own views may be inferred from the disposition of his satire.

All poetry is, in varying degrees, autobiographical and a response to its times. Yet it is also striking to observe, especially in poetry written in societies and cultures far removed from our own, how insights into the human condition by a great poet such as Geoffrey Chaucer, writing in Middle English in the fourteenth century, are as immediate as today.

Assignment

Read the following poems and research the relationship of the texts to the historical circumstances in which they were written. Consider, too, whether the poems are constrained by those events or make larger statements about life.

'Avenge, O Lord, thy slaughtered saints . . .' (John Milton)

'The Charge of the Light Brigade' (Alfred, Lord Tennyson)

'September 1913' (William Butler Yeats)

'Still Falls the Rain' (Edith Sitwell)

Medieval poetry

Dating the beginning of the 'modern' period in literary history from the beginning of the sixteenth century is arbitrary, but not inexplicable, especially when we compare English literature of the sixteenth century with that which preceded it in the medieval period. The texts of the later Middle Ages – most notably Geoffrey Chaucer's (in poetry such as the *Canterbury Tales*, which was probably written from 1386 onwards) and even Sir Thomas Malory's *Morte Darthur* of the late fifteenth century – immediately confront us with the problem that a substantial portion of the language reads like a foreign tongue, resembling English, but requiring translation. Chaucer's 'language', wrote Matthew Arnold in the nineteenth century, 'is a cause of difficulty for us'. John Dryden, who was much closer historically and linguistically to Chaucer than ourselves (having lived in the seventeenth century), 'translated' several of the *Canterbury Tales*, although he also styled Chaucer the 'father' of English poetry. In the next century, Alexander Pope spoke of the failure to understand English from generation to generation and gloomily predicted:

> Our sons their fathers' failing language see,
> And such as Chaucer is shall Dryden be.

Yet sixteenth-century literature (as, indeed, sixteenth-century life) grew out of the medieval milieu. A poet of that century, Edmund Spenser, held Chaucer in veneration and modelled his *Shepheardes Calender* on Chaucer's style. Another, Sir Thomas Wyatt, in his didactic verse-letter to 'Mine Owne John Poins', cites Chaucer as an authority, while some Chaucerian verse-forms survive in Shakespeare's poetry. And even if we interpret the sixteenth- and seventeenth-century Renaissance as being a reaction against medievalism, it cannot be fully appreciated without an understanding of its genesis in the Middle Ages. Furthermore, certain traditions of poetic subject matter and style that have remained powerful presences in English poetry, through the centuries, have their origins in medieval poetry. The celebration of nature's regeneration in springtime is just one of these.

I

We need to be cautious in our use of the general phrase 'the Middle Ages', as it covers a period of some 800 years, from the seventh to the beginning of the sixteenth century, and two distinct periods in the history of English literature: the Old English (Anglo-Saxon) period and the Middle English period. These are decisively separated from each other by the Norman conquest of England by Duke William at the Battle of Hastings in 1066. This initiated a radical change in English culture, the English language and, therefore, in English literature.

From the conquest until about 1200, the English language was scarcely used in written literature, having been replaced by Latin (the language of the Church, whose influence was pervasive in that culture) or Anglo-Norman, the French dialect of the new rulers. English did not become the language of the court or of government until the later fourteenth century and there are few records of secular lyrical poetry in English until this time. Most of the surviving literature from the Middle English period is religious in character because literacy was almost entirely under the control of scribes who were monastic clerics. Most non-religious poetry in English was transmitted orally (in the traditional manner of the folk-song) and would, in any case, have been generally regarded as unsuitable for clerical transcription.

Here is one of the earliest surviving Middle English lyrics, of the thirteenth century, which has been preserved because it was transcribed in a religious house and set to music:

SUMER IS ICUMEN IN
    Sing! cuccu, nu. Sing! cuccu.
    Sing! cuccu. Sing! cuccu, nu.

Sumer is icumen in –
Lhude sing! cuccu.
Groweth sed and bloweth med
And springth the wude nu –
Sing! cuccu.

Awe bleteth after lomb,
Lhouth after calve cu,
Bulluc sterteth, bucke verteth,
Murie sing! cuccu.
Cuccu, cuccu,
Well singes thu, cuccu –
Ne swik thu naver nu!

[Sing! now, cuckoo. Spring has come in – sing loud! Cuckoo. The seed grows and the meadow flowers, and now the wood is in leaf. Sing! cuckoo. The ewe bleats for her lamb, the cow lows for her calf, the bullock leaps and the buck breaks wind (?). Sing, tunefully! cuckoo, cuckoo, you sing well – now don't ever stop![1]]

This poem's refrain (or chorus) – 'Sing! cuccu' – with its joyous monosyllabic imperative and the onomatopoeia of the bird's name (the cuckoo), echoing its song, punctuates a poem that we often find at the beginning of general anthologies of English verse. Here we encounter features of poetry which are perennial, such as the refrain and the technique of onomatopoeia. 'Sumer is icumen in' also demonstrates the origins of poetry in song and the oral tradition.

II

THE REVERDIE

The lyrical praise of new life in nature, in 'Sumer is icumen in', is known as the 'reverdie' – the literary celebration of the re-greening of the earth in spring. At the beginning of Chaucer's *Canterbury Tales*, in the 'General Prologue' to the stories, we find the reverdie again:

Whan that Aprill with his shoures soote
The droghts of March hath perced to the roote,
And bathed every veyne in swich licour
Of which vertu engendered is the flour;
Whan Zephirus eek with his sweete breeth
Inspired hath in every holt and heeth
The tendre croppes, and the yonge sonne
Hath in the Ram his halve cours yronne,
And smale foweles maken melodye,
That slepen al the nyght with open ye
(So priketh hem nature in hir corages);
Thanne longen folk to goon on pilgrimages.

[When April with its fresh showers has pierced the drought of March to the root and bathed every vein of the plants in such liquid, by the power of which flowers are born; when the west wind, also, with his sweet breath has breathed into every grove and field, the tender shoots and the young sun has in the Ram – the first sign of the zodiac in the solar year – run half of his course, and small birds make melody, who sleep all night with open eye (so does Nature prick them in their hearts), then do folk long to go on pilgrimages.[2]]

We notice here how wide-ranging, embracing the entirety of the created world, is this sense of new life – from the mighty sun to small birds to human beings. The whole of life is animated by this experience of seasonal rebirth.

---

1. Translation by R. T. Davies, *Medieval English Lyrics* (London: Faber, 1963), p. 52. All subsequent translations of medieval poems in this chapter are by Davies, unless indicated otherwise.

2. The text of the poem is from F. N. Robinson (ed.), *The Works of Geoffrey Chaucer* (London: Oxford University Press, 1957), p. 17. The translation is adapted from Margaret Ferguson, Mary Jo Salter, Jon Stallworthy (eds), *The Norton Anthology of Poetry*, 4th edn (New York: W. W. Norton, 1996), p. 17. All references to Chaucer in this chapter are from Robinson's edition.

Such tributes to seasonal change constantly recur in English poetry. Varying
the reverdie (having it in mind to vary it), John Keats, in the nineteenth century,
wrote an ode 'To Autumn':

Season of mists and mellow fruitfulness,
Close bosom-friend of the maturing sun . . .

Conscious of the tradition, he notes the absence of the reverdie – 'Where are
the songs of Spring? Aye, where are they?' – and praises Autumn for having
its own 'music'. Such 'Romantic' poets looked back to the original
'Romance' period of the Middle Ages, not only recovering medieval lyricism
and the love of nature, but the idea of the poet as a bard and singer, like the
troubadours (lyric poets originating in Provence in the eleventh century).
Especially, they renewed the concentration on love (both its joys and its
pains) as a subject for lyrical expression. This is a favourite topic of the original Romance poets too.

The recognition of the vitality of nature can stir up, contrastingly, a sense of
desolation in a person who feels bereft of the same life-force. In this lyric from
the later thirteenth century, the speaker notes his experience of love's sickness,
aggravated by the fecundity about him:

I LIVE IN GREAT SORROW
Foweles in the frith,
The fisses in the flod,
And I mon waxe wod:
Mulch sorw I walke with
For beste of bon and blod.

[Birds in the wood, the fish in the river, and I must go mad: I live in great sorrow because of the
best creature living.]

This psychological experience – of the exaggeration of emotional pain because
of the contrasting *joie de vivre* of burgeoning natural life, especially in spring – is
found seven centuries later in the famous opening lines of T. S. Eliot's Modernist
masterwork *The Waste Land*, a kind of mock-reverdie:

April is the cruellest month, breeding
Lilacs out of the dead land, mixing
Memory and desire, stirring
Dull roots with spring rain.

Eliot's poem draws extensively on medieval myth and legend – especially that of
the search for the Holy Grail – but specifically, here, in a poem which is also a
kind of compendium of English and European poetic traditions, Eliot begins by
ironically recalling Chaucer's opening to the *Canterbury Tales*, touching that buoyancy and optimism with the cynicism of disappointed passion. We might be

tempted to think that this was just a wry, modern response to the reverdie's
innocence, yet we find a similar emotion in 'I live in great sorrow'.

Variations of the reverdie account for many of the Middle English lyrics that
have survived. 'Fairest between Lincoln and Lindsey', for example, is a reduced
reverdie. The reverdie tradition is just glanced at, in the opening lines, and then
follows the main burden of the five-stanza lyric which is the singer's request for
his lady's love:

> When the nightegale singes,
> The wodes waxen grene:
> Lef and gras and blosme springes,
> In Averil, I wene.
> And love is to mine herte gon
> With one spere so kene:
> Night and day my blod it drinkes;
> Mine herte deth me tene.

[When the nightingale sings, the woods grow green; believe me, leaf and grass and blossom
springs in April. And love has gone to my heart with so sharp a spear: it drinks my blood night
and day; my heart is hurting me.]

> Ich have loved all this yer
> That I may love na more;
> Ich have siked mony sik,
> Lemmon, for thine ore.
> Me nis love never the ner,
> And that me reweth sore.
> Swete lemmon, thench on me:
> Ich have loved thee yore.

[I have loved all this year so that (? what) I can love no more; I have sighed many a sigh, sweetheart, for your favour. Love is not any the nearer me, which grieves me greatly. Dear sweetheart, think about me: I have loved you for so long.]

> Swete lemmon, I preye thee
> Of love one speche.
> Whil I live, in world so wide
> Other nulle I seche.
> With thy love, my swete lef,
> My blis thou mightes eche:
> A swete kos of thy mouth
> Mighte be my leche.

[Dear sweetheart, I pray for one word of love. As long as I live I will not seek another throughout the whole world. You could increase my happiness with your love, my dear: a sweet kiss from
your mouth might be my physician.]

Swete lemmon, I preye thee
Of a love-bene.
Yef thou me lovest, ase men says,
Lemmon, as I wene,
And, yef it thy wille be,
Thou loke that it be sene.
So muchel I thenke upon thee
That all I waxe grene.

[Dear sweetheart, I pray of you a lover's request. If you love me, as men say, sweetheart, as I think, and if it is your wish, please see that it is shown. I am falling ill with thinking so much about you.]

Between Lincolne and Lindeseye,
Northamptoun and Lounde,
Ne wot I non so fair a may
As I go fore ibounde.
Swete lemmon, I preye thee
Thou lovie me a stounde.
I wole mone my song
On wham that it is on ilong.

[Between Lincoln and Lindsey, Northampton and Lound, I know no maid so fair as I go in love-fetters for. Dear sweetheart, I pray you to love me a little while. I will sadly sing my song about the cause of my complaint.]

What we see here is a feature that we should be alert to, in general, in our study of poetry. It is the recognition of the observance of literary conventions and the application of them to the poet's specific situation and concerns, as well as the use of various strategies of discourse. Until comparatively recent times, in the history of poetry in English, traditions of approach to subject matter – often registered in a mere phrase – stirred up certain ideas in the readers' minds, leading to various expectations about the poem which was to follow and, often, producing surprise when the poet was found departing from, subverting or fulfilling the expectations in new or strange ways.

So, the unknown composer of 'Fairest between Lincoln and Lindsey' indicates to his listeners, initially, that his is to be a reverdie poem, by briefly introducing those conventional elements of birdsong, the greening of nature and the precise reference to April. But before the first stanza is over, he has moved from the general to the particular in contrasting this beauty with his extreme pain, because of his lover's refusal to reciprocate his passion.

We may argue that this, too, is conventional, but the naming of the towns in the fifth stanza adds geographical particularity to a general theme of the pains of unrequited love. It gives, in Shakespeare's phrase, a 'local habitation and a name' to a common idea.

Also, the process of directly addressing the beloved with regard to the pains she is causing him is a very familiar approach throughout love poetry, over the centuries. It is the usual manner of poems in the *carpe diem* ('seize the day') tradition, for example, where the beloved is directly addressed and urged to make love now. We notice, here, that the direct address is framed by the opening and closing stanzas where the speaker reflects on his situation. This combination of personal introspection and direct speech adds contrast and dramatic immediacy to the poetry, which a sustained complaint without personal address would lack. We need to be alert to such artistic intelligence in the often deceptively simple utterances of medieval lyrics.

III

THE BLAZON

One of the conventions of love poetry, very familiar in medieval lyrics and a rich subject for development later, was the representation of the physical beauties of the beloved which, in turn, represented her virtues. This was the rhetorical device known as *descriptio* in the context of the 'blazon' (deriving from the Old French *blason* and originally referring to the design on a shield, coat of arms or banner, describing various virtues). In medieval poetry it usually took the form of an ordered account of the lady's physical features, beginning with her hair, as in these lines from 'Love for a beautiful lady' (of the later thirteenth or earlier fourteenth century):

> Ichot a burde in bowre bright
> That sully semly is on sight . . .
> With lockes lefliche and longe,
> With frount and face fair to fonde,
> With murthes monye mote he monge,
> That brid so breme in boure.
> With lossom eye grete and gode,
> With browen blisful under hode . . .
> Hire lure lumes light
> Ase a launterne anight,
> Hire ble blikieth so bright
> So fair he is and fine,
> A swetly swire he hath to holde,
> With armes, shuldre ase mon wolde . . .

[I know a beautiful lady, radiant in her chamber, who is most comely to look on . . . With beautiful long hair, a forehead and a face fair to enjoy, with many pleasant things must she be compared, that damsel so excellent in her chamber. With lovely eye, large and good, with brows most happy under her hood . . . Her cheek shines alight like a lantern by night, her face gleams so bright, so fair is she and fine. She has a lovely neck to embrace, with arms, shoulder as you would wish . . .]

Particularly, we notice the mention of the qualities of her eye. This important organ was the window to the soul. That the lady's is large and good indicates that her soul, too, has these qualities. Two centuries later, in a sonnet, Shakespeare draws on this tradition to subvert it when he writes that 'My mistress' eyes are nothing like the sun . . . / If hairs be wires, black wires grow on her head', yet that poem turns out, too, to be a celebration of the beloved as her physical features are listed. He appreciates her for her ordinariness and, in that way, renews the tradition by applying it differently:

> My mistress, when she walks, treads on the ground.
> And yet, by heaven, I think my love as rare
> As any she belied with false compare.

Sample question with guidelines

Read this later thirteenth- or earlier fourteenth-century lyric. What ideas does it convey about medieval life, its literary traditions and the particular experience of this speaker/singer?

LENTEN IS COME WITH LOVE TO TOUNE

Lenten is come with love to toune,	Spring has come with love among us
With blosmen and with briddes roune,	With flowers and with the song of birds
That all this blisse bringeth.	
Dayseyes in this dales,	[this = these]
Notes swete of nightegales,	
Uch fowl song singeth.	Each bird sings its song
The threstelcok him threteth oo.	The song thrush wrangles all the time
Away is huere winter wo	[huere = their]
When woderofe springeth.	[woderofe = woodruff, white-flowered plant]
This fowles singeth ferly fele,	Vast numbers of birds are singing
And wliteth on huere wynne wele,	And warbling in their abounding joy
That all the wode ringeth.	
The rose raileth hire rode,	The rose puts on her rosy face
The leves on the lighte wode	The leaves in the bright wood
Waxen all with wille.	
The mone mandeth hire ble,	The moon sends out her radiance
The lilye is lossom to se,	[lossom = lovely]
The fennel and the fille.	[fille = wild thyme]
Wowes this wilde drakes,	These wild drakes make love
Miles murgeth huere makes,	Animals [?] cheer their mates

Ase strem that striketh stille.	Like a stream that flows softly
Mody meneth, so doth mo;	The passionate man complains, as do more
Ichot ich am on of tho	I know that I am one of those
For love that likes ille.	Who is unhappy for love
The mone mandeth hire light,	The moon sends out her radiance
So doth the semly sonne bright,	
When briddes singeth breme.	[breme = strongly]
Deawes donketh the dounes,	Dews wet the downs
Deores with huere derne rounes	Animals with their cries that we do not understand
Domes for to deme.	For telling their tales.
Wormes woweth under cloude,	Worms make love underground
Wimmen waxeth wounder proude,	Women grow exceedingly proud
So well it wol hem seme.	So well it will suit them
Yef me shall wonte wille of on,	If I don't have what I want of one
This wunne wele I wole forgon,	I will abandon all this happiness
And wiht in wode be fleme.	And quickly be a fugitive in the woods.

- First, we are struck by the opening line (indeed, word) of the poem: 'Lenten' (which is also used, by its modern editor, as a title for the poem, for such poems were usually not titled). This originally meant 'spring', whereas we might think it referred to the Church's penitential season of Lent, which occurs at that time of the year in the northern hemisphere, preceding the spiritual – and natural – new life of Easter. This would complicate the poem interestingly, but, etymologically, it is not an admissible reading. This shows, again, how important it is to read poems in historical and linguistic contexts.
- The device that dominates the opening lines of celebration of spring is alliteration, on 'l' and 'b'. This reminds us of the importance of alliteration in the oral tradition of poetry, as an aid to memory. We also notice how it is joined to rhythm, accentuating the buoyancy of the recognition of all that 'blisse bringeth'.
- There is the catalogue, too, of nature's delights. This is familiar in the reverdie, but also commonplace in poetry at large, where the writer substantiates what is being claimed with evidence, or exempla. Typically, flowers and birds are named.
- There is a significant key-change, however, in the middle of the poem when the singer announces that 'Ichot ich am on of tho / For love that likes ille'. While aspects of the reverdie continue to be listed, this negativity casts a pall over them. There seems to be a sinister element in those

worms making love underground, and certainly the proud women are sneered at. The speaker notes petulantly and lustfully that unless he gets what he wants from them, he will become a fugitive.

■   So the poem demonstrates something of the contrariety of medieval life, as of all life. There is happiness, but it is crossed with frustration and disappointment. There can be innocent joy in nature's processes, but this is mixed with a self-regarding physicality of a darker colouring. We see, again, the sense of the wholeness of the poet's view of the world, as he ranges from small details like 'dayeseyes' and 'nightegales', to the moon and the sun. He speaks of womankind in general, but of himself in partic-ular (while also belonging to a class of those who are disappointed in love). There is a balance between the conventional and the personal, registered in that specific petulance at the end (which may well be self-mocking).

Assignment

Read this poem, written in the west of England in the early fourteenth century, and identify aspects of theme and style which are characteristic of medieval lyrics.

ALISON

Bytwene Mersh and Averil	
When spray biginneth to springe	[spray = twigs; springe = leaf out]
The lutel foul hath hire wyl	[lutel = little; foul = bird; hire = its]
On hyre lud to synge.	[lud = birdsong]
Ich libbe in love-longinge	[Ich libbe = I live]
For semlokest of alle thinge -	[semlokest = seemliest]
He may me blisse bringe;	[he = she]
Ich am in hire baundon	[baundon = power]
An hendy hap ichabbe yhent -	[A happy chance I have received]
Ichot from hevene it is me sent	[Ichot = I know]
From alle wymmen mi love is lent	[lent = turned]
And lyht on Alysoun.	[lyht = fallen]
On heu hire her is fayr ynoh	[In colour her hair is fair enough]
Hire browe broune, hire eye blake –	
With lossum chere he on me lo -	[with lovely face she laughed at me]
With middel smal and wel ymake.	[middel = waist; ymake = made]
Bote he me wolle to hire take,	[bote = unless; he = she]
Forte buen hire owen make,	[for to be her own mate]
Longe to lyven ichulle forsake	[ichulle = I will]

And feye fallen adoun   [feye = dead, lifeless]
   An hendy hap ichabbe yhent – . . .

Nightes when I wende and wake -   [wende = turn]
Forthi myn wonges waxeth won -   [therefore my cheeks grow pale]
Levedi, al for thine sake   [levedi = lady]
Longinge is ylent me on.   [longing is come upon me]
In world nis non so wyter mon   [in the world there is no man so wise]
That al hire bounte telle con.   [bounte = excellence]
Hire swyre is whittore then the swon,   [swyre = neck; swon = swan]
And feyrest may in toune.   [may = maid]
   An hendy hap ichabbe yhent – . . .

Icham for wowyng al forwake,   [I am entirely worn out from wooing]
Wery so water in wore,   [weary as water in a troubled pool]
Lest eny reve me my make   [lest anyone deprive me of my mate]
Ichabbe y-yerned yore.   [whom I have desired a long time]
Betere is tholien whyle sore   [It is better to suffer sorely for a while]

Then mournen evermore.
Geynest under gore,   [kindest of ladies (under gown)]
Herkne to my roun.   [listen to my song]
   An hendy hap ichabbe yhent – . . .[3]

IV

RELIGIOUS LYRICS

The combination of religious material with the secular subject matter of the typical reverdie is another version of this common subject of medieval lyrical poems. A sophisticated example of this combination is in the negative reverdie of 'The penitent hopes in Mary' (later thirteenth/earlier fourteenth century), which has these opening stanzas:

> Now skrinketh rose and lilye-flour,
> That whilen ber that swete savour,
> In somer, that swete tide.
> Ne is no quene so stark ne stour,
> Ne no levedy so bright in bour,
> That Ded ne shall by glide.
> Whose wol flesh lust forgon

---

3 *Norton Anthology*, pp.15 16.

And Hevene blis abide,
On Jesu be his thoght anon,
That therled was his side.

From Petresbourgh in o morewening,
As I me wende o my pleying,
On my folye I thoghte.
Menen I gon my mourning
To hire that ber the Hevene King,
Of mercy hire besoghte:
'Ledy, preye thy sone for ous,
That so dere boghte:
And shild us from the lothe hous
That to the Fend is wroghte'.

[Now the rose and the lily wither that once bore that sweet smell in summer, that sweet time.
There is no queen so mighty and strong, nor lady so bright in her chamber, whom Death shall
not creep up on. Whoever will forgo bodily delight and wait for the bliss of Heaven, let his
thoughts be straightway on Jesus whose side was pierced. As I went out from Peterborough one
morning to enjoy myself, I thought about my folly (illicit love?). I began to express my grief to
her who bore the King of Heaven and begged her for mercy: 'Lady, pray for us to your son who
bought us dear, and defend us from the hateful house made for the Fiend'.]

Here, we see the sharp contrast, in the medieval mind, between the secular and
sacred domains of human experience. This is registered, poetically, in the withering of nature – and, so, the compromising of the reverdie's exultation – in the
recognition of the changeableness (or mutability) of natural, mortal life. The
theme of many medieval poems, *de contemptu mundi*, of contempt for the world,
was at least as strong as the desire to praise it, which should hardly surprise us
when we learn of the almost unimaginable pains of life for medieval people,
especially for example during the recurrent times of plague and famine. Human
existence was often violent and harsh. Of course, no one was immune to the
experience of death – here personified, to make his malevolent presence more
terrible (another enduring device: John Donne uses it, for example, in the
seventeenth century; Anne Finch, in the eighteenth). But the contemplation of
this common experience was intensified, in the Middle Ages, by the literal belief
in the afterlife, either of bliss in Heaven (after the intermediate state of
Purgatory) or terrible, eternal punishment in Hell, as a result of one's behaviour
on earth. The medieval mind, learned or simple, worldly and devout, was preoccupied with Christian teaching about the four 'Last Things': death, judgement,
Heaven and Hell.

In this poem, the singer, setting out to enjoy himself, contrasts the lady with
whom he may be planning some love-making with the Virgin Mary and, thereby,
juxtaposes a life that will lead to Hell ('the lothe hous' made for the Devil) and
that in Heaven, secured by the sacrifice of Christ for the sins of the world. He

closes by asking the Virgin to pray for him. So this negative reverdie is also a rejection of earthly loves for heavenly love.

Religious concerns dominated and permeated medieval life in a way virtually impossible for us to appreciate in the post-Enlightenment culture of the last 200 years, where religion has been progressively marginalised in the collective consciousness of most Western societies. In their theocentric (or God-centred) epoch, people of the Middle Ages experienced Christianity, principally, through the teachings, ministrations and liturgy of the Church and its clerical officials. It was a communal faith, mediated by the Church's ministers and her seven sacraments: the Eucharist, Baptism, Confirmation, Orders (for those being ordained to the ministry), Matrimony, Penance and Extreme Unction (the anointing of the sick).

No sacrament was more important than that of holy communion, where bread and wine were transubstantiated into the body and blood of Christ and received by the worshipper. Attendance at Mass on Sundays, when this miracle was performed, and on other holy days was at the heart of medieval religion. Worthy reception of communion depended upon being in a state of grace, which could be secured through sacramental confession to a priest, who would pronounce absolution and forgiveness, and prescribe a penance (such as the recitation of certain prayers) for the sins that had been confessed. Obviously, for these rites to be observed and regularised, places needed to be built and ceremonies followed for their decent and, indeed, beautiful administration. Hence the widespread construction of churches and cathedrals in medieval times and their adornment – for example, in the elaboration of the celebration of Mass, in Latin, with chant and intricately prescribed ceremonies.

As well as being the seats of bishops, cathedrals (from *cathedra*, Greek for a chair) often contained shrines and relics of holy people ('saints') who had been recognised by the Church for their piety and good works for the faith, often leading to their deaths (or martyrdoms). The pilgrims, in Chaucer's *Canterbury Tales*, are setting out on such a pilgrimage to the shrine of St Thomas Becket in Canterbury Cathedral, as the speaker of the Prologue to the *Tales* notes:

> And specially from every shires ende
> Of Engelond to Caunterbury they wende,
> The hooly blisful martir for to seke
> That hem hath holpen whan that they were seeke.   [holpen = helped; seeke = sick]

Becket had been murdered in 1170 and was canonised (formally declared a saint) by the Pope in 1173. His shrine in the cathedral became one of the principal pilgrimage centres not only of England, but of Christendom and was especially associated with healing.

As in the ordinary performance of their religious duties in their parish church, so on pilgrimage and on arrival at the shrine, medieval Christians would have regularly had the Mass celebrated for them. The following lyric from the middle or later fourteenth century indicates the centrality of the sacrament of the eucharist, a sacrifice offered repeatedly at the altar of every church, for the living and the dead. (Notice, now, as we move closer to the modern period in English history and literature, how the language is becoming more familiar and less translation is required.)

A PRAYER TO THE SACRAMENT OF THE ALTAR
Jesu, Lord, welcom thou be,
In forme of bred as I thee see.
Jesu, for thine Holy Name,
Shild me today from sinne and shame.
As thou were of a maide born,
Thou lat me never be forlorn.   [Don't ever let me be utterly lost]

Ne lat me never for noo sinne   [Nor let me ever for any sin]
Lese the joye that thou art inne.   [lese = lose]
Thou, rihtwise King of all thing,   [rihtwise = righteous]
Grant me Shrifte, Housil and good ending, [shrifte = absolution; housil = communion]

Riht beleve beforn my ded day,   [ded = death]
And blisse with thee that leste shall ay.

This simple-sounding prayer is, in fact, theologically replete with the details of medieval Catholic faith. It begins by acknowledging the 'real presence' of Christ in the sacrament, under the appearance or 'forme' of bread. In the second couplet, there is the straightforward recognition of the sin and shame of human existence, as a result of the Original Sin by Adam and Eve in Paradise. In the medieval mind, the spirit of evil was constantly roaming about, seeking to devour human beings. Next, the speaker refers to the Incarnation – the birth of Christ by the Virgin Mary. This balances the negativity of the previous couplet, with a recognition of the potential for blessedness in the created world which the choice of the humble maiden to bear God Himself indicates. The speaker would be like her and, so, partake of the joy of union with God. He closes sacramentally, as he opened, by requesting absolution (or forgiveness of his sins), worthy participation in holy communion, and that he will be acceptable to God on his deathbed and be granted eternal happiness in Heaven. The conclusion reflects the medieval preoccupation with the afterlife, even as the poem as a whole acknowledges the possibility of experiencing that union with God, on earth – or at least a foretaste of it – through the sacraments.

Question

In the following poem, how are doctrinal matters poeticised?

> **A NEW SONG OF MARY**
>   Of MARY
>   Sing I will a new song.
>
> Of thes four letters purpose I,
> Of M and A, R and Y.
> They betoken maid Mary –
> All our joy of her it sprong.
>
> Withouten wem of her body,   [wem = stain]
> M and A, R and Y,
> Of her was borne a King, truly,
> The Jewes dedin to deth with wrong.   [Whom the Jews wrongly put to death]
>
> Upon the mounte of Calvary,
> M and A, R and Y,
> Ther they beten his bar body
> With scorges that war sharp and long.
>
> Our der Lady she stod him by,
> M and A, R and Y,
> And wept water full bitterly,
> And teres of blod ever among.   [among = from time to time]

■ SPECIAL STUDY 1

Geoffrey Chaucer (?1345–1400)

ABOUT THE AUTHOR

The year of Chaucer's birth (?1345), in England, may only be deduced from later evidence, as in 1386 when he said of himself that he was 'forty years old and more'. His parents were John and Agnes and he had a sister Catherine. Geoffrey was to follow his family's career of public service, the earliest records of his life suggesting that he was a page in the households of the nobility.

Chaucer was in military service in France in 1359–60 and was taken prisoner. After his release, he appears to have returned to service and eventually to have been employed in the household of King Edward III.

Chaucer married Philippa Roet, possibly in 1366. They may have had both a son (Chaucer's treatise on the astronomical instrument, the astrolabe, is

■ addressed to 'little Lewis, my son') and a daughter. During the following decade, he travelled extensively in Europe and rose in public office, becoming Controller of Customs in the port of London in 1374, and this office continued under the new king, Richard II, who ascended the throne in 1377. This position, and his experiences on diplomatic missions abroad, brought Chaucer into contact with the most brilliant courtiers and men of affairs of his day.

By 1386, Chaucer had retired to Kent, but still his public service continued. In 1389 he was made Clerk of the King's Works, with responsibility for the maintenance of such buildings as the Tower of London and Westminster Palace.

Returning to London at the end of his life, occupying a house in the garden of Westminster Abbey, Chaucer died on 25 October 1400.

THE CANTERBURY TALES

The writing of *The Canterbury Tales* has been dated by scholars as occurring between the years 1387 and 1400, when Chaucer could draw on his rich experience of life. He never completed the sequence.

Thirty-one pilgrims are assembled at the Tabard Inn in Southwark (on the south side of the Thames, in London), preparing to leave for the shrine of St Thomas Becket in Canterbury Cathedral in Kent. In order to pass the time on the journey, the Host suggests that they tell tales. He will accompany them and make a judgement, at journey's end, about the tale that is most uplifting and diverting ('of best sentence and moost solaas' – 'General Prologue', 798). In addition to the General Prologue, each individual tale has its own prologue.

THE PARDONER'S TALE[4]

One of Chaucer's most accomplished texts, 'The Pardoner's Tale' is thought to belong to that stage in the evolution of *The Canterbury Tales* when Chaucer had fully developed the idea of the sequence of tales.

An understanding of the convention of a 'tale' and a recognition of 'The Pardoner's Tale' in the sequence are important if we are to set the work in its literary and sequential context. We need also to consider the tone of the piece, the arguments and ideas that it addresses and explores, and details of the language that is used: description, characterisation, dialogue, and so forth. And we may speculate about the author's intention in the work: for example, did Chaucer want us to learn from the narrative that the Pardoner unfolds, or to be entertained by it, or both?

---

4. You should refer to a complete text of the Introduction to 'The Pardoner's Tale', the Pardoner's Prologue and the Tale itself. Do not use a modern 'translation' of Chaucer.

■ The tale is told, by the Pardoner, to the pilgrims in the tavern, before they have set out for Canterbury: 'heere at this alestake [signpost of an inn]'. This setting is appropriate for the unmasking of the Pardoner's hypocrisy. For his tale is a sermon against the sins of gluttony and revelry, yet it is delivered in the very place where these vices flourish and, what is more, by a man who is scandalously addicted to them. In this sense, Chaucer's tale is a satire of its teller, who is before us as an individual and as a representative of a class of persons – pardoners – who were notorious in Chaucer's society for the abuses of their roles as licensed purveyors of papal pardons and indulgences.

For a price, the faithful could purchase relief (pardon) from the torment of the afterlife to which their sins would otherwise consign them. The corruptions of this system were of central importance in the Protestant Reformation of the Church, two centuries later, and Chaucer exposes not only the shortcomings of the 'bisynesse' but the hypocrisy of the individuals who managed it. His Pardoner's status in the Church is unclear. He may have belonged to a religious order of mendicant (begging) friars, but as he speaks (possibly only facetiously) of taking a wife, he may have been a layman.

In the Prologue to the Tale, the Pardoner expresses his determination to persist in his corrupt activities. He laughs to scorn the religious virtues of poverty and chastity:

> Nay, I wol drynke licour of the vyne,
> And have a joly wenche in every town.

Although he is a monster of immorality ('a ful vicious man'), he can tell a moral tale with exemplary skill. Chaucer is thus raising, in the prologue, one of the paradoxes of artistry – that great accomplishment in the arts (including that of story-telling) does not depend on the moral rectitude of the artist. The paradox is given an extra force in this context as the tale is explicitly designed to urge its hearers to righteousness.

His role as a pardoner maybe being satirised, but he is a man of rare wit and intelligence amongst the pilgrims, as his tale and its telling reveal. About his corruption there is no question, but he is a brilliant and skilful speaker. His tale has come to be regarded as the model of the perfect short story.

The Introduction

In the sequential organisation of *The Canterbury Tales*, the Host's reflections and introductions serve the important functions of both summarising the tales and linking the tellers. At the conclusion of 'The Physician's Tale' – 'a pitous tale for to heere' – the Host is keen to listen next to something unlike it, 'a myrie tale', in fact. So he turns to his good friend, the Pardoner, and exhorts him to

■   telle us som myrthe or japes right anon.

The Pardoner is keen to oblige, and exclaims:

It shal be doon, be Seint Ronyon.

Like the Host before him, he utters an oath (in swearing by St Ninian, of which 'Ronyon' is a corruption). This may be the first sign of Chaucer's characterisation of the Pardoner as a less than holy man. Certainly, his delay in beginning while he has a drink and some cake suggests his fleshliness. And the warning by those about him that they do not want to hear any 'ribaudye' suggests that this is precisely what they might have expected from the Pardoner:

Telle us som moral thyng, that we may leere
Som wit, and thanne wol we gladly heere.

Amusingly, the Pardoner accedes to their request for an edifying tale while he continues to delay its beginning in the enjoyment of his ale. Yet we should not over-emphasise the incongruity. The linking of the taking of a drink and the telling of a tale is conventional from antiquity.

The Tale

To introduce the story, in a preamble of some 200 lines, the Pardoner plunges his audience into a world of extreme decadence. The opening phrase, 'In Flaunders', immediately conveys licentiousness as Flanders was associated in the English mind with drinking – in the way, even to this day, that continental Europe is regarded, from the English perspective, as a place of loose morals. The Pardoner delights in providing copious examples of the debauchery of the 'yonge folk' of the place, through his catalogues of nouns: 'riot, hasard, stywes, and tavernes'; 'harpes, lutes, and gyternes'. He affects to be appalled by this diabolical excess in a splendidly polysyllabic phrase which is perfectly appropriate to the libertinism he is describing: 'superfluytee abhomynable'. We can imagine his audience thrilling to his account, while expressing their horror. As well as gluttony, there is 'lecherye', and all of the sinning has its source in 'wyn and dronkennesse'. We need to remember that all this is being described in the precincts of a tavern by a speaker who has delayed his story while he completes his ale.

As in a sermon, it is conventional for the Pardoner to give specific examples of the theme he is pursuing; preferably from the Bible. Such displays of learning establish his authority to comment on the matter. Accordingly, he refers to Lot in the Old Testament, who, drunk with wine, slept with his daughters 'unwityngly'. From the New Testament, Herod is cited. Then, the classical writer Seneca is alluded to, in the observation that no difference can be found

> Betwixt a man that is out of his mynde
> And a man which that is dronkelewe.

With this abundance of exempla, the Pardoner works himself up into a series of exclamations in denunciation of sin:

> O glotonye, ful of cursednesse!
> O cause first of oure confusioun!
> O original of oure dampnacioun.

As it suits his purpose to focus on gluttony, the Pardoner claims that the original sin of apple-eating, by Adam and Eve in the Garden of Eden, was the sin of gluttony and the root of our damnation. Theologically, of course, every sin was involved in that act – most notably, pride. But the Pardoner cleverly confines the apple-eating to its physical aspect, as fleshliness is his concern. He draws upon St Paul's denunciation of gluttony, which inspires him to further excessive exclamation against this excess:

> O wombe! O bely! O stynkyng cod,
> Fulfilled of dong and of corrupcioun!

The description following of the handiwork of cooks gives a delightful and alarming window into the medieval kitchen, and the subsequent portrait of a drunken man is one of those timeless moments in Chaucer's writing.

The Pardoner, a great lover of his drink, exhorts his listeners (in the tavern) to avoid its evils. The exhortation, however, in its detail, indicates that he is very knowledgeable and experienced in the effects of various wines.

Having defamed gluttony, with abundant biblical and other sources, the Pardoner turns next to gambling – 'hasardrye' – and pours his contempt upon it. Once again, we notice the process of the provision of exempla (such as Demetrius) from ancient sources to support his argument. We do not know whether the Pardoner was a gambler, but certainly he utters oaths. And his next subject for denunciation (hypocritically) is 'sweryng', as he urges his hearers to abandon this vice, in all its forms:

> Lete youre oathes, bothe grete and smale.

The tale itself follows this introductory material of moral discourse, learned and passionately delivered by one who has accurately introduced himself to us, in the Prologue, as a speaker skilled in winning the attention of his audience. We can imagine the pilgrims hanging on every word, but whether they are edified as well as entertained by this hypocritical moralising by the Pardoner is a moot point. And it is a question that we, as an audience, too, of the Pardoner, must ponder.

■   The setting of the Pardoner's story (like his telling of it) is a tavern, and the first event that we encounter is the chiming of the passing-bell that was rung, in the parish church, to alert the community that one of their number was about to be buried. The medieval obsession with death is emphasised by the priority given to this event in the story. To add to the 'gothic' quality of this incident, it appears that the dead one had been murdered 'to-nyght' (that is, the night before) while very drunk. His 'murderer', in fact, is 'Deeth' in the form of the plague, 'this pestilence' – reminding us that there were four serious plagues in the later fourteenth century. The 'boy' who is recounting this gruesome (but, no doubt, very commonplace) event closes by exhorting the reveller whom he is addressing to prepare himself for such an unannounced visitation. It is a warning, in other words, against drunkenness which would distract one's attention from the enemy 'Deeth'.

The innkeeper, in an oath – 'by seinte Marie' – acknowledges the truth of the boy's teaching, indicating the widespread deaths which the plague has wrought. This incites the reveller to encourage his friends to seek out 'this false traytour Deeth' and kill him before he kills others, and in nonsensical recklessness, aggravated by alcohol, they swear allegiance to each other, in a parody of a chivalric bond:

> To lyve and dyen ech of hem for oother,
> As though he were his owene ybore brother.

The Pardoner observes that their progress is accompanied by 'many a grisly ooth', recalling his teaching against swearing in the preamble to the Tale.

The revellers meet an aged man, who is vividly described in his decrepitude, and who is longing for death:

> Allas! whan shul my bones been at reste?

There is a warning here which the revellers in their inebriation fail to discern. The old man is an image of endless life, yearning for release, who cries out to death to take him. If the revellers could kill death, this would be their fate.

As he has referred to 'Deeth', the revellers imagine that the old man has spoken to him, and they demand to know where he is. The old man, under threat of punishment, directs them to a tree underneath which they will discover Deeth. Arriving there, they find 'floryns fyne of gold'. The Pardoner's text about the love of money is recalled as the revellers forget their quest after Deeth and 'down they sette hem by this precious hoord'.

The treachery of this threesome that had earlier sworn fidelity to each other, leads two to plan the murder of the third, and the third to plan the poisoning of the others. They murder him and then, unwittingly, drink from his poisoned bottles. All succumb to death, which they had set out to conquer, through their avaricious love of money and as a result of their drunkenness.

The Pardoner exclaims in denunciation of the revellers:

O cursed synne of alle cursednesse!
O traytours homycide, O wikkednesse!
O glotonye, luxurie, and hasardrye!

And he beseeches his congregation – for he is showing the pilgrims how he preaches to the people – not only to avoid such errors but to secure pardon from them by his offices, offering

nobles or sterlynges,
Or elles silver broches, spoones, rynges.

The abruptness with which he turns from his high moral indictment to the sordid practicalities of his avaricious trade is as startling as it is comical. After a moment of apparently genuine piety, he suddenly remembers that he has forgotten to include his discourse on relics and, concluding that, he mischie-vously turns on the Host, demanding that he heed his advice, 'for he is moost envoluped in synne'. But unlike his credulous congregations, the Host is equal to the Pardoner, and in a hilarious conclusion, he tells him exactly what he thinks of his pardons and relics. Instead of kissing the Pardoner's holy things, the Host would grab him by the testicles, cut them off and have them 'shryned in an hogges toord!'

The articulate Pardoner, for once, is at a loss for a word. But the suave Knight intervenes   calms the wrathful Pardoner amidst the hilarity of the pilgrims, and directs the rude Host to 'kisse the Pardoner' (if not his relics). All ends happily: 'Anon they kiste, and ryden forth hir weye'.

Plot(s)

The complete text of 'The Pardoner's Tale' in fact presents us with three plots. As a framework, there is the situation in the tavern, with the Host and the pilgrims, as part of the sequence of the *Tales*. Secondly, there is the plot or story of the Pardoner himself – the situation in which we find him, his revelations about himself, his tale-telling and the amusing close when he meets his match in the Host. Finally, there is the story which he tells itself, with its taut plot structure – succinct, suspenseful, and moving subtly to its conclusion. Chaucer is a master storyteller and he is at his most skilful in this section of *The Canterbury Tales*.

Question

How are the three 'plots' of the compete text of 'The Pardoner's Tale' related, and for what purposes?

■ *Characterisation*

In the Pardoner's story, the most striking character is the 'olde man'. It is argued that while the tale was a familiar legend, this personage is Chaucer's invention, and a richly conceived one. His portrayal of himself knocking on the earth to be interred is a striking image indeed. This immediacy makes him more real than a symbolic representative of Age. The revellers are not clearly distinguished one from the other, by character traits, but the presentation of them in their inebriated bravado, their seduction by the gold and their plotting against each other, has a universal familiarity.

Dialogue

Contrast is the life of dialogue, and we observe Chaucer's exemplary use of this device, in the Tale, in the interchange between the young boy, the tavern-keeper and the reveller. The different ways in which they speak reveal their very different characters. At the end, the suspense which resolves itself in happiness depends upon dialogue – in particular, the brief speech of the Knight which restores fellow-feeling to the company.

Tone and evaluation

To speak of the tone of the Tale is insufficient, as it has several tones, and the recognition of these complicates our description and assessment. Although the Host asks for a 'moral thyng', the self-revelation and the story which the Pardoner supplies, although intimately concerned with matters of morality, are certainly not sober in tone. There are outbursts of excessive denunciation, careful procedures for duping congregations, suavely described, and – in the story itself – suspense and drama; while at the conclusion of the Tale there is the obscenity of the Host's ridicule of the Pardoner and the onomatopoeia of 'kisse' and 'kiste' which conveys a tone of affectionate good humour.

The dominant tone, perhaps, is satirical; but it would be a mistake to imagine that Chaucer, for all his criticism of pardoners and their craft, does not find something humanly alluring in this particular Pardoner, with his cunning and his conscience, his lies and his consummate preaching and tale-telling, his hypocritical morality and – above all – his *joie de vivre*: 'a joly wenche in every toun'.

Questions

1. Why is the character of the Pardoner important to our understanding of the tale he is telling, its tone, meaning and purpose? (Think about the reasons why writers create characters as means of transmitting ideas and feelings and how a created character can either reflect or be distant from the author creating him or her.)

2. Is the effect of the Pardoner's posturing as a moralist undermined by our knowledge of his character? Is the posturing itself too excessive to be taken seriously? Or are moral truths more persuasive if their teacher is seen to be a person of flesh and blood who has experienced what he is denouncing?

3. To what extent – and how – does Chaucer define character by dialogue?

Assignment

View Samuel Raimi's film *A Simple Plan* (1998), which is based on 'The Pardoner's Tale'. Note significant similarities and changes. Does the abandonment of poetry in Raimi's text make important differences in our appreciation of the story? Can we make absolute distinctions between poetry and prose? Why might their effects be different on the audience?

The Renaissance

I

The Renaissance (from the French word meaning 'to be born again') refers to the rebirth of art and learning in Europe in the sixteenth century, under the influence of models from the classical civilisations of Greece and Rome. Francis Bacon writes in *The Advancement of Learning* (1605) that 'the ancient authors both in divinity and humanity, which had long slept in libraries began generally to be read . . . and thereof grew again a delight in their manner of style and phrase'. The poetic forms of the time drew their inspiration directly from classical examples. John Donne's elegies, for instance, written in the 1590s, derive from the *Amores* of the Roman poet Ovid, while Ben Jonson, immersed in the comedies of Terence and Plautus, used details from their plays in his own. Legends from classical literature, with all their details, were taken over into English poetry – such as that of Orpheus and Eurydice, used by John Milton in no less than four of his poems. The medieval Christian suspicion about 'pagan' culture was gradually replaced by the rise of humanistic values. Even Milton, with his Puritan reservations about the theatre, expressed his debt to 'Aeschylus, Sophocles, and Euripides, the three tragic poets unequalled yet by any, and the best rule to all who endeavour to write tragedy' in the preface to his 'closet-drama' (that is, one not intended for performance) *Samson Agonistes*.

In society, the communal, otherworldly Catholicism of the Middle Ages began to be superseded by a new humanistic emphasis on individualism and a concentration on the things of this world.

These momentous revolutions in thought and sensibility were not completed in the Renaissance, which includes the contemporary Protestant Reformation. Usually dated from 1517, when the German friar Martin Luther nailed his Ninety-five Theses in criticism of Catholicism to the church door in Wittenberg, the Reformation was a remarkable expression of the shift from communality to individuality. It repudiated medieval ecclesiastical authority, in particular the need for a mediating priesthood between God and the faithful, and it emphasised each Christian's personal access to God's grace. But the fact that such exaltation of individuality was expressed within the context of supernatural doctrine and the absolute authority of Scripture indicates that the Humanism of the Renaissance has to be firmly placed in the larger context of a God-centred world-picture. It was, even at its most liberal, a Christian Humanism.

The Renaissance was a period of complex tensions, in all aspects of its life, between the so-called Dark Ages and the apotheosis of Humanism in the eighteenth-century Enlightenment. A time of tension is propitious for artistic creativity, as several ages of this kind have shown. One of the most memorable expressions in English literature of the ambiguities of Renaissance thought is the famous soliloquy, in blank verse, of Shakespeare's Hamlet, a character who is individualistic to a tragic fault, yet keenly aware of the spiritual dimension in which his little world of experience must ultimately be placed:

> To be, or not to be, that is the question,
> Whether 'tis nobler in the mind to suffer
> The slings and arrows of outrageous fortune,
> Or to take arms against a sea of troubles,
> And by opposing, end them. To die, to sleep –
> No more, and by a sleep to say we end
> The heart-ache, and the thousand natural shocks
> That flesh is heir to; 'tis a consummation
> Devoutly to be wished to die to sleep!
> To sleep, perchance to dream, ay there's the rub,
> For in that sleep of death what dreams may come
> When we have shuffled off this mortal coil
> Must give us pause – there's the respect
> That makes calamity of so long life:
> For who would bear the whips and scorns of time,
> Th' oppressor's wrong, the proud man's contumely,
> The pangs of disprized love, the law's delay,
> The insolence of office, and the scorns
> That patient merit of th'unworthy takes,
> When he himself might his quietus make,   [quietus = release from life]
>
> With a bare bodkin; who would fardels bear,   [bodkin = dagger; fardels = burden]
>
> To grunt and sweat under a weary life,
> But that the dread of something after death,
> The undiscovered country, from whose bourn
> No traveller returns, puzzles the will,
> And makes us rather bear those ills we have,
> Than fly to others that we know not of?

Hamlet's juxtaposition here of the microcosm of his intensely experienced humanity and the macrocosm of the great world, including the 'undiscovered country' of eternity, was a favourite Renaissance idea or conceit. 'I am a little world made cunningly,' wrote John Donne, expressing delight in his individuality even as he assesses it in terms of its littleness.

Through Hamlet's speech, at the centre of his tragedy, Shakespeare typically queries the new conceptions of his age, such as uncertainty about the eternal nature of the individual's destiny, as he formulates a dilemma which not only reveals to the audience the psychological torment of the character, but a society torn between two worlds.

Hamlet is contemplating suicide, the ultimate act of self-will that perversely affirms individuality and which was a notable preoccupation of Renaissance minds at the turn of the sixteenth and seventeenth centuries. Donne wrote a treatise, *Biathanatos,* on the lawfulness of 'Self-homicide', unpublishable until 1646, after his death; while, on the other side of the debate, Hamlet had reminded himself (and his audience), in an earlier speech, that God had

> fixed
> His canon 'gainst self-slaughter.   [canon = edict; also a pun on 'cannon']

This explicit recollection of the canonical teaching here indicates, in an age when old certainties were being scrutinised, that such authorities were now in question.

There, as in the soliloquy before, we encounter a further tension of Renaissance thought – between the burgeoning confidence of the period manifested everywhere (for example, in the presentation of Elizabeth, its embodiment in England, as Gloriana) and a strikingly antithetical world-weariness:

> O God, God,
> How weary, stale, flat and unprofitable
> Seem to me all the uses of this world.

The medieval tradition *de contemptu mundi,* of disdain for earthly life, survived with ironic vigour into the Renaissance as a corrective to the over-reaching optimism of the new age. Such optimism had a certain justifiable basis and explanation in the momentous achievements (by England, for instance) in geographical exploration, scientific discovery and in the reborn literary and other arts themselves. National self-confidence was buoyant. Sir Thomas Wyatt could equate 'Kent and Christendom' (in 'Mine Owne John Poins'), while at the end of the Renaissance, Milton, in *Paradise Lost,* describes the Garden of Eden, before the Fall, as if it were an English country estate: 'a happy rural seat of various view'. But another who was in the midst of the achievements and agitations of his times, Sir Walter Raleigh, also recognised the mortal limitations of all humanity:

What is our life? a play of passion;
Our mirth the music of division;
Our mothers' wombs the tiring-houses be   [tiring-houses = dressing-rooms]
Where we are dressed for this short comedy.
Heaven the judicious sharp spectator is,
That sits and marks still who doth act amiss;
Our graves that hide us from the searching sun
Are like drawn curtains when the play is done.
Thus march we, playing, to our latest rest,
Only we die in earnest – that's no jest.

A generation later the theme persists, as in this grim expostulation by Bosola in John Webster's play *The Duchess of Malfi*:

Oh, this gloomy world,
In what a shadow or deep pit of darkness
Doth, womanish and fearful, mankind live!

In support of this idea and in tension with the progressive spirit of the Renaissance was the contemporary conviction that the world was drawing to its close, as encountered in Donne's 'First Anniversary', 'An Anatomy of the World', where he repeats Hamlet's observation that 'the time is out of joint':

so is the world's whole frame
Quite out of joint.

Donne similarly observes, in his third satire, that 'the world's all parts wither away and pass' in accordance with the common belief that the final stages had been reached of the progressive decline from a distant golden age, through silver and bronze, to the present decay of iron.

II

In religious terms, a critique of the expanding worldliness of the Renaissance mind can be found in the continued interest (also stemming from medieval times) in the so-called four 'Last Things' of life: death, judgement, Heaven and Hell. This was intensified in the widespread preaching on these topics and formal meditation about them. We need to remember that Heaven and Hell were not merely metaphors for Renaissance Christians (that is, for virtually everybody in the Renaissance world). As they had been for medieval people, they were physical locations and states of being for eternity, according to God's judgement of each man and woman. There is a palpable *joie de vivre* in so many Renaissance events, lives and literary texts which was, however, modified by the Christian idea of the imminent Second Coming of Christ, and secondly – and more immediately – the daily pain of existence. Hamlet refers to 'the thousand natural

shocks that flesh is heir to', and even the beginnings of modern medical science
(William Harvey published his discovery of the circulation of the blood in 1628)
had done nothing to alleviate them. Donne's 'Canonization' is one of these arrogantly life- and love-affirming celebrations, but it also includes his passing reference to the 'plaguy bill': the weekly reports from each parish of the deaths from
these repeated scourges. As Webster's Antonio realistically observes:

> Pleasure of life, what is't? Only the good hours
> Of an ague merely a preparative to rest,   [ague = fever]
> To endure vexation.

The popular theatrical metaphor of human existence was used to focus the
Renaissance tension between optimism and desperation. Ironically, while the
theatres were burgeoning in this period, the dramatic poets used the imagery of
the stage to convey their despair of life, as in numerous famous allusions in
Shakespeare and in the Duchess's complaint in Webster's play:

> I account this world a tedious theater,
> For I do play a part in 't 'gainst my will.

That one was forced to endure such a life was usually blamed on Fate, Chance
or 'Fortune's wheel'. This showed that as well as being, in Francis Bacon's
phrase, a time of the advancement of learning, of the pursuit of the empirical
principle and experimentation, and a time of almost universal Christian belief,
the Renaissance was also an age of gross superstition. Astrological predictions
were solemnly credited, by such as Bosola in *The Duchess of Malfi*:

> We are merely the stars' tennis balls, struck and bandied
> Which way please them.

The evil powers of witches and the possibility of possession by the devil were
taken for granted. For all its progressive learning, the contradictions of the
Ptolemaic and Copernican theories about the ordering of the universe remained
unresolved. Milton confessed, in the usually authoritative *Paradise Lost*, that it
was 'hard to tell' which was correct. And even Donne, with his innovative literary temperament, ridiculed the new science for calling 'all in doubt'. He interpreted it as a sign of the end of the world:

> 'Tis all in pieces, all coherence gone;
> All just supply, and all relation:
> Prince, subject; father, son, are things forgot,
> For every man alone thinks he hath got
> To be a phoenix, and that there can be
> None of that kind of which he is, but he.

Once again, Renaissance individuality is stressed, but here it is seen as a fearful
aberration.

Because of this individuality, authority and hierarchy were under threat: theologically and ecclesiastically, politically and socially. Doubt over the survival of authority is indicated in Renaissance literature by the impassioned defence of order and institutions on the one hand, and the satirical critique of their human representatives on the other.

Theologically, the concept of the 'great chain of being' – the hierarchy of the created world, descending from God to the humblest creatures – was evidence of the design of creation and, therefore, of the ultimate authority and benevolence of its Creator. But empirical science was beginning to erode both the God-centred view of the cosmos and the mystical approach of theology. In Francis Bacon's writings, while polite references are made to the Almighty, He is relegated to a pious afterthought. Bacon's pupil, Thomas Hobbes, preferred not to think of Him at all, as the tension with the inheritance of medieval Christianity began to be resolved. Not that Hobbes's lack of divine consolation was ameliorated by a faith in humanity, the life of which he summarised, in *Leviathan*, as 'solitary, poor, nasty, brutish, and short'.

Ecclesiastically, the Church was the temporal sign of spiritual certainty. But in the Reformation, conflicting Churches with contradictory theologies and liturgies led even those who were most earnest to believe in Christianity to be sceptical about all ecclesiastical authorities and hierarchies:

> To adore, or scorn an image, or protest,
> May all be bad; doubt wisely; in strange way
> To stand inquiring right, is not to stray;
> To sleep, or run wrong, is. On a huge hill,
> Cragged and steep, Truth stands, and he that will
> Reach her, about must, and about must go . . .

Donne's ecclesiastical agnosticism here – in his satire on religion – stands in striking contrast to the convictions of his immediate forbears who believed that no-one could be saved from damnation outside the (Roman) Catholic Church. The arduous search for Truth, in Donne's celebrated image of the mountain-climber, is that of a solitary aspirant divorced from a congregation of faith.

In tension with this, we have at the same time the confidence in Anglicanism of George Herbert, who praises its *via media* (or middle way) between the respective excess and meanness of continental Catholicism and Protestantism, in 'The British Church'. He placed this poem deliberately and appropriately at the centre of his long sequence *The Church*:

> I joy, deare Mother, when I view
> Thy perfect lineaments and hue
>   Both sweet and bright . . .

> A fine aspect in fit aray,
> Neither too mean, nor yet too gay,
>   Shows who is best.
> Outlandish looks may not compare:
> For all they either painted are,
>   Or else undrest . . .
>
> But, dearest Mother, what those misse,
> The mean, thy praise and glorie is,   [mean = moderation]
>   And long may be.
> Blessed be God, whose love it was
> To double-moat thee with his grace,
>   And none but thee.

Herbert's conceit of femininity is not only a poetic metaphor based on the traditional concept of the Church as Mother. He is thinking also of his mother,
Magdalen Herbert, one of the great Renaissance women who represented for
him and for many others (including Donne, who commemorated her in poetry
and preaching) an image of admirable Christian, Anglican faith and devotion.

III

The internal and external history of England in the fifteenth and early sixteenth
centuries was turbulent. In the wake of this, Tudor nationalism was triumphantly
affirmed as the guarantee of peace at home and the bulwark against threats from
abroad. The Pope might condemn Elizabeth (as he did in 1570), but her forces
defeated the Spanish Armada in 1588.

The goddess-like mystique of Elizabeth-Gloriana, celebrated in the greatest
poem of the earlier period of the English Renaissance, Spenser's *Faerie Queene*:

> Great Lady of the greatest Isle, whose light
> Like Phoebus lampe throughout the world doth shine . . .

depended substantially on the cult of her virginity. However, that very attribute
of Elizabeth, about which she herself was not always best pleased:

> the queen of Scots is this day leichter of a fair son, and I
> am but a barren stock . . .

meant that the matter of her successor, crucial to continued stability in the state,
could not be settled. In the closing years of Elizabeth's reign, confidence in the
throne was undermined.

A rising mercantile middle-class began to challenge the regal and aristocratic
monopoly of power, not only economically, but artistically. Early in the
Renaissance, poetry emanated from the courtly circle but by the turn of the

sixteenth and seventeenth centuries, the flowering of genius in literature came from the sons of the bourgeoisie: Milton's father was a self-made businessman and Ben Jonson's stepfather was a master bricklayer in Westminster. They were not necessarily iconoclasts (although Milton turned out to be) and, if they were, they were circumspect, for criticism of the state was tantamount to treason. The system of courtly patronage of writers, however, remained strong under Elizabeth's successors.

Shakespeare (whose father had been an alderman in Stratford) is usually portrayed as a defender of the 'divine right' of kingship (in his history plays, for example) and of the status quo in politics and society. Ulysses' great speech on degree in *Troilus and Cressida* seems to represent Shakespeare's own theory on order, authority and hierarchy:

> The heavens themselves, the planets, and this centre
> Observe degree, priority, and place,
> Insisture, course, proportion, season, form   [insisture = continuance]
> Office, and custom, in all line of order . . .
> O! when degree is shak'd,
> Which is the ladder to all high designs,
> The enterprise is sick. How could communities,
> Degrees in schools, and brotherhoods in cities,
> Peaceful commerce from dividable shores,
> The primogenitive and due of birth,
> Prerogative of age, crowns, sceptres, laurels,
> But by degree, stand in authentic place?
> Take but degree away, untune that string,
> And, hark! what discord follows; each thing meets
> In mere oppugnancy . . .   [oppugnancy = antagonism]
>
> Then everything includes itself in power,
> Power into will, will into appetite;
> And appetite, a universal wolf,
> So doubly seconded with will and power,
> Must make perforce a universal prey,
> And last eat up himself.

For this very reason, Shakespeare's criticisms of the court are more telling. In *King Lear*, the king himself, having attained wisdom after prolonged suffering, recognises (although too late) the corruption and futility of that domain in his moving speech to his daughter Cordelia, who had refused to submit to courtly duplicity at the beginning of the tragedy:

> Come, let's away to prison;
> We two alone will sing like birds i' the cage:

> When thou dost ask me blessing, I'll kneel down,
> And ask of thee forgiveness: so we'll live,
> And pray, and sing, and tell old tales, and laugh
> At gilded butterflies, and hear poor rogues
> Talk of court news; and we'll talk with them too,
> Who loses and who wins; who's in, who's out;
> And take upon's the mystery of things,
> As if we were God's spies: and we'll wear out,
> In a wall'd prison, packs and sets of great ones
> That ebb and flow by the moon.

Queen Elizabeth herself expressed the grief she had suffered because of the unnatural expectations of her regal position:

> I grieve and dare not show my discontent,
> I love and yet am forced to seem to hate,
> I do, yet dare not say I ever meant,
> I seem stark mute but inwardly do prate.
>> I am and not, I freeze and yet am burned,
>> Since from myself another self I turned . . .

She is referring to the failure of marriage negotiations between herself and the French duke of Anjou in 1582.

Within less than a century, English society, which was apparently so secure in the Elizabethan 'settlement' of Church and State, was turned upside down. In the Civil War, each of the orders, authorities and hierarchies of theology and politics were violently repudiated. This was symbolised by the execution of King Charles I in 1649. In the tensions of Renaissance life, as expressed in the literature of the period, we perceive the beginnings of that revolution.

IV

The 'rebirth' of classical civilisation and literature in the Renaissance is most evident in the poetry of the period. There was the imitation of formal modes, such as the elegy, the epithalamion (or marriage-song), the satire, the ode (as derived from the Greek poet Pindar, by such as Dryden) and so on. Many literary conventions were also appropriated; for example, the *carpe diem* ('seize the day') address in love poetry from the Roman poet Horace. Writers displayed both their knowledge and facility in the application of these classical models.

In the sixteenth century, English poetry was principally an amateur's and a courtier's art. The poets of the court, such as Sir Thomas Wyatt and Sir Philip Sidney, wrote poetry in the midst of their other activities in statecraft, diplomacy and warfare. It was one of several amateur skills, like horsemanship and musicianship, which presented the model of behaviour for Renaissance courtiers. There was no conception of the 'professional' poet.

Yet, in this era of change we can discern in the literary activities of Sidney, especially, the emergence of the 'man of letters'. For he was not only a prolific poet, but the author of the most important work of prose-fiction of the Elizabethan age, the *Arcadia*, and of its only significant essay in literary criticism, *The Defence of Poesy*.

Poems in this period were more often circulated in manuscript than published. Many were written to be sung to the accompaniment of the lute, such as Wyatt's 'My Lute, Awake!':

> My lute, awake! Perform the last
> Labour that thou and I shall waste,
> And end that I have now begun;
> For when this song is sung and past,
> My lute, be still, for I have done.

Very few of Wyatt's poems were published in his lifetime (he died in 1542). However, in the second half of the sixteenth century, as the transition began slowly to take place from the amateur to the professional role of the poet, several collections of poems appeared – most notably, in 1577, a 'miscellany' by several writers (including Wyatt) collected by the printer Richard Tottel.

As well as Wyatt's poems, the miscellany included forty by Henry Howard, Earl of Surrey. These two poets were responsible, through this collection, for introducing the sonnet into English. They imitated the principal Italian sonneteer Francesco Petrarch (1304–74), who, in his classical literary scholarship, was a precursor of the European Renaissance. The influence of Petrarch on English poetry remained powerful for a century, and is a sign of the pre-eminence of Italy as the source of Renaissance culture. The Italian journey (undertaken by Milton, for example) nurtured the appreciation of the flowering of artistry and learning in such centres as Florence. This coexisted with a view, particularly in English minds, of Italy as debauched and decadent. Ben Jonson's dramatic study of corruption, *Volpone*, is set in Venice.

The Italian sonnet provided the model for the formal, fourteen-line structure of the sonnet, with the division into octave (the first eight lines) and sestet (the remaining six). Its subject matter and various attitudes and references also came from the Italian sonnet: the address to the idealised woman (Laura, in Petrarch's case; Stella, in Sidney's) and the presentation of the extreme qualities of the speaker's passion. This passion was restrained by the formalities of the sonnet's strict literary arrangement and, eventually, the predictability of those very attitudes.

Petrarch's authority was not absolute, however. His Italian form of the sonnet was succeeded – in the sonnets of Shakespeare, for example – by the so-called

English form, which varied the octave/sestet structure with three quatrains (groups of four lines) and a concluding couplet, and which could satirically over-turn the idealisation of the typical Petrarchan speaker, most famously in Shakespeare's 'My mistress' eyes are nothing like the sun'. A generation later, in Milton's sonnet-writing career, we find both Petrarchan and other forms being used, including that of another Italian sonneteer, Giovanni Della Casa, who rejected Petrarch's metrical regularity.

While Wyatt and Surrey were both indebted to Petrarch, their versions of the Petrarchan models differed in character, as in these imitations of the same sonnet, '*Amor, che nel penser mio vive e regna*':

> The long love that in my thought doth harbour
> And in mine heart doth keep his residence,
> Into my face presseth with bold pretence,
> And therein campeth, spreading his banner.
> She that me learneth to love and suffer
> And will that my trust and lust's negligence
> Be reined by reason, shame and reverence,
> With his hardiness taketh displeasure.
> Wherewithal unto the heart's forest he fleeth,
> Leaving his enterprise with pain and cry,
> And there him hideth, and not appeareth.
> What may I do, when my master feareth,
> But in the field with him to live and die?
> For good is the life ending faithfully.
>
> WYATT

> Love, that doth reign and live within my thought,
> And built his seat within my captive breast,
> Clad in the arms wherein with me he fought,
> Oft in my face he doth his banner rest.
> But she that taught me love and suffer pain,
> My doubtful hope and eke my hot desire   [eke = also]
> With shamefast look to shadow and refrain,
> Her smiling grace converteth straight to ire.
> And coward Love, then, to the heart apace
> Taketh his flight, where he doth lurk and plain,
> His purpose lost, and dare not show his face.
> For my lord's guilt thus faultless bide I pain,
> Yet from my lord shall not my foot remove:
> Sweet is the death that taketh end by love.
>
> SURREY

The contrasts between these poems show both the fertility of the Italian model from which they derived and the different qualities of English poetry which they represent. Rhythmically, Surrey's is much more regular, to the point of a 'sing-song' metre. We also note, at the very beginning, his stricter fidelity to the Petrarchan original: 'Amor' is Petrarch's opening, 'Love' Surrey's. Wyatt, more interestingly, gives us 'The long love' with its alliteration and the sense (aurally), in that long heavy phrase, of *longueur* – protracted, even tedious presence. Wyatt's control of rhythm is less even, for which he was often criticised, but it is arguably more appropriate here to the subject of Cupid's unpredictable behaviour.

More striking, however, is the inventiveness of Wyatt's conception with regard to Surrey's – the vitality of his rendering of Petrarch's imagery. If we compare the first quatrain of each sonnet, we note the striking quality of Wyatt's verbs: 'harbour', 'presseth', 'spreading'. In contrast, Surrey is less dramatic: 'reign and live', 'built', 'clad', 'rest'. At the beginning of the sestet, Wyatt has Cupid, in a verb, fleeing into the forest; Surrey refers, in a noun, to the act of 'flight'. Wyatt's dramatic immediacy and lack of rhythmic polish present a rough-hewn quality, invigorating the material, and (whether stylised or not) they are indicative of the developing independence of the English voice in poetry. Within a generation, Donne's so-called 'Songs and Sonnets' (which are rarely lyrical and never, strictly speaking, sonnets) are stridently assertive, rudely rebuking all Petrarchans.

Question
Which do you prefer: Wyatt's or Surrey's poem? Why?

SPECIAL STUDY 2

Sir Philip Sidney (1554–86)

ABOUT THE AUTHOR

Sidney was born into an aristocratic family at Penshurst in the English county of Kent. He attended Shrewsbury School and Oxford and Cambridge. Three years spent travelling in Europe (1572–5) influenced Sidney's attraction to Protestantism which led to his criticism of a proposal that Queen Elizabeth should marry a French Catholic. This in turn brought about Sidney's banishment from the royal court. He spent the time composing poetry, literary criticism (the famous *Defense of Poesy*) and the pastoral romance *The Arcadia*. While fighting in the Low Countries in Europe for the Protestant cause, Sir Philip (who had been knighted in 1583) died from a leg wound. He is often regarded as the quintessential expression of the Renaissance man: brave, virtuous and cultivated.

■ ASTROPHIL AND STELLA

It is in Sidney's sequence of 108 sonnets and 11 songs, *Astrophil and Stella*, that we encounter the most sustained and brilliant appropriation of the Petrarchan subject and style in the Renaissance. In his literary-critical essay *The Defence of Poesy*, Sidney argues that poetry should both 'teach and delight'; through delighting, it should 'move men to take . . . goodness in hand', by presenting 'notable images of virtues, vices, or what else'. The theory had its source in Horace's *Art of Poetry*. In *Astrophil and Stella*, accordingly, virtuous counsel is provided about persistence in love and the idealisation of the beloved in the unfolding drama of the pair's relationship. Some of the poems and a number of references in them derive from Sidney's pursuit of Penelope Devereux for his wife. Representing Penelope, Stella, the star, is yearned for by Astrophil, the lover of the star, who is Sidney. However, in 1581, Penelope married Lord Robert Rich. This leads to some witty punning, such as the opening phrase of sonnet 24: 'Rich fools there be . . .'. But the poetry is not merely autobiographical. It has significance beyond these personal circumstances.

Nor is this first great sonnet sequence in English rigorously sequential: it ends inconclusively although it begins predictably and conventionally with a determination to speak from the heart. This is one of the witty poses of writers in the Petrarchan tradition:

> Loving in truth, and fain in verse my love to show,   [fain = eager]
> That the dear she might take some pleasure of my pain:
> Pleasure might cause her read, reading might make her know,
> Knowledge might pity win, and pity grace obtain,
> I sought fit words to paint the blackest face of woe,
> Studying inventions fine, her wits to entertain:
> Oft turning others' leaves, to see if thence would flow
> Some fresh and fruitful showers upon my sun-burn'd brain.
> But words came halting forth, wanting Invention's stay,   [stay = support]
> Invention Nature's child, fled step-dame Study's blows,
> And others feet still seem'd but strangers in my way.
> Thus great with child to speak, and helpless in my throes,
> Biting my truand pen, beating myself for spite,
> Fool, said my Muse to me, look in thy heart and write.

The wit of this opening sonnet is that it demonstrates what it would repudiate. As Sidney talks about the convolutions of the Petrarchan tradition, he writes in the manner of such ornateness. There is, for example, the rhetorical device of *gradatio* in the opening quatrain: his love (poetically expressed) might excite her pleasure; being pleased, she might read; reading would lead to knowledge of his devotion; knowledge might entail pity; pity could obtain grace. Cleverly, Sidney animates Astrophil's opening address, giving impetus to the poetry from the start.

He indicates his debt to the tradition – 'turning others' leaves'; the meteorological imagery is distinctively Petrarchan ('fresh and fruitful showers upon my sun-burn'd brain'); he talks about the 'halting' quality of his uninspired verse, and, sure enough, the poetry proceeds haltingly in the repetition:

> But words came halting forth, wanting Invention's stay,
> Invention Nature's child . . .

There is comedy in the personification of 'step-dame Study' and of himself 'great with child to speak' and in the representation of writer's block: 'biting my truand pen, beating myself for spite'. This is poetry as much concerned with poetry and the writing of it as it is with the subject itself – the desire to write tellingly about love.

The wit is extended to the second sonnet in the sequence, for, in spite of this submission to plain speaking, the next poem is firmly in the ancient tradition of Cupid as the agent of love and the extended metaphor of love as warfare and conquest:

> Not at first sight, nor with a dribbéd shot   [dribbéd = random]
> Love gave the wound, which while I breathe will bleed;
> But known worth did in mine of time proceed,   [mine = tunnelling under besieged walls]
> Till by degrees it had full conquest got.

Next, Sidney invokes (and complicates) the epic triplet from heroic writing, whereby momentous undertakings are elevated by the use of three verbs (such as Julius Caesar's '*veni, vidi, vici*' – 'I came, I saw, I conquered'). This is witty, too, as these personal problems in love are hardly of the same significance:

> I saw and liked, I liked but lovéd not,
> I loved, but straight did not what Love decreed:
> At length to Love's decrees, I forc'd, agreed,
> Yet with repining at so partial lot.

The sestet presents Astrophil in the woebegone state of the unrequited lover, paradoxically and wretchedly enslaved to one who is disdainful of him:

> Now even that footstep of lost liberty
> Is gone, and now like slave-born Muscovite,
> I call it praise to suffer tyranny;
> And now employ the remnant of my wit,
> To make myself believe, that all is well,

■   While with a feeling skill I paint my hell.

Notice how self-conscious the poetry is – not only of the lover's emotional state, but of the characteristics of his writing about it. We also notice the intrusion of a theological vocabulary – 'believe' and 'hell' – reminding us of the interaction of religious belief with all aspects of life in this period.

In the fifteenth sonnet Sidney's speaker affects to reject Petrarchan artificiality in the course of displaying his indebtedness to aspects of the Petrarchan tradition:

> You that do search for every purling spring
> Which from the ribs of old Parnassus flows,   [in Greece, sacred to the Muses]
>
> And every flower, not sweet perhaps, which grows   [flower = rhetorical figure]
>
> Near thereabout, into your poesy wring;   [poesy = poetry, bunch of flowers]
>
> You that do dictionary's method bring   [dictionary's method = esp. alliteration]
>
> Into your rhymes, running in rattling rows;
> You that poor Petrarch's long-deceaséd woes,
> With new-born sighs and denizen'd wit do sing;   [denizen'd = domesticated]
>
> You take wrong ways, those far-fet helps be such,
> As do bewray a want of inward touch,
> And sure at length stolen goods do come to light
> But if (both for your love and skill) your name
> You seek to nurse at fullest breasts of Fame,
> Stella behold, and then begin to indite.   [indite = write]

The sonnet embraces learning in the context of its rejection; the consummation of the strategy is the concluding, conventional determination to be natural and spontaneous. What brings the sonnet to life is not its subject matter but its style. The repeated use of 'You' has an accumulating, accusatory character; the extremity of verbs such as 'wring' (meaning 'insinuate', comically satirising the slavish imitators of classical poetry and rhetoric); the alliterated mimickry and mockery of the metrical rhymesters ('your rhymes, running in rattling rows'); the onomatopoeia of 'sighs'; and the physical immediacy of the concluding feminine imagery (appropriate in a sequence of addresses to Stella) of being nursed at Fame's breasts. This is a poetry as securely within its tradition as it is happily chafing against it. It is the expression of the tension between the indebtedness of English literary culture to the Italian and classical models and its determination to speak with its own voice.

We hear this impulse again in sonnet 74, with its speaker's affectation of amateurism in literary learning set within the context of its deft display. There is the subtext, too, of English suspicion about continental ways with a celebration of home-grown virtue:

> I never drank of Aganippe well,   [in Greece, sacred to poetry]
> Nor ever did in shade of Tempe sit;   [in Greece, sacred to poetry]
> And Muses scorn with vulgar brains to dwell;
> Poor layman I, for sacred rites unfit.
> Some do I hear of Poets' fury tell,   [‘fury’ of inspiration]
> But God wot, wot not what they mean by it;   [wot = knows]
> And this I swear by blackest brook of hell,
> I am no pick-purse of another's wit.
> How falls it then that with so smooth an ease
> My thoughts I speak, and what I speak doth flow
> In verse, and that my verse best wits doth please?
> Guess we the cause. 'What, is it thus?' Fie no.
> 'Or so?' Much less. 'How then?' Sure thus it is:
> My lips are sweet, inspired with Stella's kiss.

The construction of the speaker as a 'layman' is directly related to the cherished amateurism of Renaissance poetic composition. The Englishness of Astrophil's blustering – 'but God wot, wot not what they mean by it' – is amusingly and dramatically aural. It contrasts sharply with the preciosity of the ambience of Aganippe and Tempe which are decisively rejected at the beginning. Yet, in spite of his native vulgarity – expressed in the highly artificial form of the sonnet which Sidney sustains effortlessly – his poetry flows. He says it in this smooth gradation, assisted by enjambement:

> My thoughts I speak and what I speak doth flow
> In verse, and that my verse best wits doth please.

The bluster returns in the sharp dialogue, only to be resolved again – and finally – in the sweetness of reference and sound in the concluding 'kiss'.

There are many more poems in the sequence that are thoroughly Petrarchan in attitude and imagery, in spite of Sidney's ambivalence towards the tradition. However, Sidney imbues them with their own distinctive artistry and immediacy, as in this outpouring of exultation which, in its sounds, is as celebratory as its sense:

> O joy, too high for my low style to show,
> O bliss, fit for a nobler state then me!
> Envy, put out thine eyes, lest thou do see
> What oceans of delight in me do flow
> My friend, that oft saw through all masks my woe,

■ Come, come, and let me pour myself on thee:
Gone is the winter of my misery;
My spring appears; O see what here doth grow
For Stella hath, with words where faith doth shine,
Of her high heart given me the monarchy;
I, I, O I may say, that she is mine.
And though she give but this conditionly
This realm of bliss, while virtuous course I take,
No kings be crowned but they some covenants make.

The keynote of exultation is sounded in the opening combination of the ejaculation 'O' and the direct and delightful expression of happiness: 'joy'. Sidney
also introduces variations of 'i' sounds – as in 'high' – which, with the initial
outpouring of emotion, have their later consummation in the splendid exultation: 'I, I, O I may say...' as he announces that 'she is mine'. This is poetry
that enacts the mood of its speaker; it does not merely describe it. In addition to this inventiveness, however, Sidney includes conventional Petrarchan
references to the macrocosmic dimensions of the speaker's microcosmic
passion:

oceans of delight in me do flow.

The references to the 'winter of my misery' and the arrival of spring when
Stella acquiesces to him are also conventional. The speaker in the sonnet's
final conceit (in the sense both of metaphor and of over-reaching in the mood
of exultation) compares himself to a king. He has been enthroned in the
monarchy of love, the 'realm of bliss'. But, surprisingly, in the last stroke of
brilliance in the poem, there is a qualification at the end. Like a king, he must
enter into an undertaking when he receives the crown – to be a faithful
servant and pursue a 'virtuous course'. In other words, he must be true to
Stella. The poem is a wonderful expression of delight, but, in true Sidneian
fashion, it possesses the restraint of a certain didacticism.

Sample question with guidelines
What characteristics of theme and style would you identify for comment
in this sonnet, early in Sidney's sequence, *Astrophil and Stella*?

It is most true that eyes are formed to serve
The inward light, and that the heavenly part
Ought to be king, from whose rules who do swerve,
Rebels to nature, strive for their own smart.
It is most true, what we call Cupid's dart
An image is, which for ourselves we carve;
And, fools, adore in temple of our heart,

Till that good god make church and churchman starve.
True, that true beauty virtue is indeed,
Whereof this beauty can be but a shade,
Which elements with mortal mixture breed;
True, that on earth we are but pilgrims made,
And should in soul up to our country move;
True, and yet true that I must Stella love.

- Our first reading of the poem alerts us to a disjunction in its argument between reason linked to spirituality, on the one hand, and emotion on the other. In particular, we note that thirteen of the fourteen lines are devoted to the praise of thought and piety, and even the first word of the fourteenth confirms that praise. But the confession introduced by the disjunction 'yet' has the effect of demolishing all that has been established. This is emphasised not only by the expression of love but the personal naming of the beloved, 'Stella'.

- The speaker repeats the word 'true' numerous times, to emphasise the value of 'the inward light' of reason and the soul; the demerits of Cupid's religion as opposed to true religion; and the beauty of virtue in contrast to mere physical attractiveness. However, the repetition overstates the case and serves to dramatise his anxiety to persuade himself of these truths which should be self-evident.

- We notice the contingency of the argument at two points: in line 3 and line 13. He is contending that this is what we should do, rather than declaring a fact. In other words, he is articulating a tension between ideas and reality, between his spiritual and physical selves. This is a major debate in the Renaissance, represented in numerous dialogues between the body and the soul.

- The imagery of the poem is rich in its variety, bringing the elements of the argument before us. There is the popular monarchical image, in the first quatrain, and the reference to the temple of the heart where Cupid makes us worship. Further, the metaphor of this life as a pilgrimage is present. In contrast, the presentation in the disjunction of the last line is free of imagery (unless we count Stella herself as an image of elevated, shining perfection). The direct language emphasises the power of this alternative commitment.

- The wit of the poem is that its argument is unresolved. Early in the sequence this tension is dramatically appropriate as the relationship is introduced. And within the poem itself, there is the little world of the tension in each human being between reason and passion, spirituality and physical desire: 'the subtle knot', as Donne called it, 'that makes us man'. It is a major theme of *Astrophil and Stella*.

Questions

1. What does a close reading of the following sonnet tell us about Sidney's characterisation of Astrophil, Renaissance attitudes to love, and of the technical qualities of Sidney's poetry which might explain the enduring appeal it has had for readers over the centuries?

> I on my horse, and Love on me doth try
> Our horsemanships, while by strange work I prove
> A horseman to my horse, a horse to Love;
> And now man's wrongs in me poor beast descry.
> The reins wherewith my rider doth me tie,
> Are humbled thoughts, which bit of reverence move,
> Curb'd in with fear, but with gilt boss above   [boss = metal stud on the side of a bit]
>
> Of hope, which makes it seem fair to the eye.
> The wand is will, thou fancy saddle art,   [wand = riding crop]
> Girt fast by memory, and while I spur
> My horse, he spurs with sharp desire my heart:
> He sits me fast, how ever I do stir:
> And now hath made me to his hand so right,
> That in the manage myself takes delight.   [manage = art of training and handling horses]

2. In the *Defense of Poesy*, Sidney argues that poetry combines the functions of teaching and delighting. By looking closely at two or three of the sonnets in *Astrophil and Stella*, do you find that Sidney is true to his own claim about poetry?

3. Several songs are interspersed in the sonnet sequence. Look at two or three of them. How are they different from the sonnets, in their subject matter and the kind of poetic writing they present?

V

The element of delightful teaching, and of morality and spirituality pleasantly mediated, was an important component of Renaissance poetry in general and of the sonnet sequence in particular. While it may seem incongruous, in terms of the decorum of a collection of love poems, Edmund Spenser, in his *Amoretti*, proceeds from a sonnet in which he uses the conventional imagery of the hunt as a metaphor for the pursuit of the 'gentle deare' – 'Lyke as a huntsman after weary chace' – to this celebration of Easter Day in which 'deare' is repeated three times in a very different context:

Most glorious Lord of lyfe, that on this day,
Didst make thy triumph over death and sin:
And having harrowed hell, didst bring away
Captivity thence captive us to win:
This joyous day, deare Lord, with joy begin,
And grant that we for whom thou diddest dye
Being with thy deare blood clene washt from sin,
May live for ever in felicity.
And that thy love we weighing worthily,
May likewise love thee for the same again:
And for thy sake that all lyke deare didst buy,
With love may one another entertayne.
So let us love, deare love, lyke as we ought,
Love is the lesson which the Lord us taught.

This is not merely a reminder of the unrigorously sequential nature of the sonnet sequence, or the possibility of connecting earthly and heavenly loves, or of the Renaissance delight in variety of reference: *copia* (or copiousness). Most significantly, it reminds us again that in the Renaissance, unlike modern post-Christian civilisation, religious concerns were an integral part of life. The sensual and the spiritual were constantly interacting, and did so in Metaphysical poetry violently, as we shall see in the next chapter.

For this reason, the most important text for the student of English Renaissance poetry (and, indeed, for English poetry and literature at large) is the Holy Bible, for everyone at the time, learned and unlearned alike, was familiar with it. It had a mixture of literary modes, of prose and poetry, in its two testaments. The first complete Bible in English was by Miles Coverdale, published in 1535. The Great Bible appeared in 1540; it was the first English translation to be officially sanctioned. The Geneva Bible followed twenty years later, and the Bishops' Bible in 1568. King James's authorisation of the version of 1611 produced the translation that was not only a monument of scholarship but a masterpiece of language, and which remains today the single most important source in the study of English literary texts. The King James version was authorised to be read in churches, so, for centuries, it was the version heard in English in the liturgy. Everyone in the English-speaking world, literate and illiterate, pious and worldly, was once, to some degree, familiar with it. That it has now passed out of use and that people in Western societies, for a century, have ceased to be exposed to it, regularly, in church, or even irregularly in the wider culture – means that the numerous references to it and borrowings from it in English poetry until well into the twentieth century are now lost on most contemporary readers. It is the most significant instance of cultural forgetting in the history of the English language.

The poeticising of the already poetic psalms and other sections of the Bible was a favourite literary and pious exercise in the Renaissance. Poets such as Sidney and Donne undertook this, and even a libertine poet like Thomas Carew (pronounced 'Carey') translated nine of them. Donne, indeed, said of the translation of the psalms by Sidney and his sister Mary Herbert, Countess of Pembroke, that 'they tell us *why*, and teach us *how* to sing'.

There is no better way to enter the mind of the Renaissance and the seventeenth century, in England, than to read the King James version of the Bible. Milton, for example, knew it by heart and its presence is pervasive in his poetry. Bunyan's style is modelled on its prose. While there can be no substitute for reading it in its entirety, the compilation, *King James's Bible: A Selection*, edited by W. H. Stevenson (London: Longman, 1994) is an excellent introduction.

Further to the Bible of 1611, students of poetry in English should also acquaint themselves with the works of the great classical writers, such as Homer and Virgil, which were similarly well-known to Renaissance poets and which are accessible to the non-classicist in very readable translations.

Question

'In this sonnet from his *Amoretti*, Spenser uses a conventional Renaissance conceit. But his poetic style gives it new and unique vitality'. Do you agree? (Identify the conceit and think about why it was popular in this period. How does the poet relate to it, in terms of his personal life? What is he saying about his emotion and how does his use of language make that revelation vivid? What is the effect of the focus on the unnamed 'she' in the sestet, in terms of the arrangement of the poem and in explaining the more general emotions outlined in the octave?)

> Of this worlds theatre in which we stay,
> My love like the spectator ydly sits
> Beholding me that all the pageants play,   [pageants = roles]
> Disguysing diversly my troubled wits.
> Sometimes I joy when glad occasion fits,
> And mask in myrth lyke to a comedy:
> Soone after when my joy to sorrow flits,
> I waile and make my woes a tragedy.
> Yet she, beholding me with constant eye,
> Delights not in my merth nor rues my smart:
> But when I laugh she mocks, and when I cry
> She laughs and hardens evermore her heart.
> What then can move her? if nor merth nor mone,
> She is no woman, but a sencelesse stone.

■ **SPECIAL STUDY 3**

William Shakespeare (1564–1616)

ABOUT THE AUTHOR

William Shakespeare was born in Stratford-on-Avon in 1564, the son of a prominent citizen. He presumably attended the Stratford grammar school, but we know nothing certain about his young life, apart from his christening and then his marriage, eighteen years later, to Anne Hathaway. In 1583, they had a daughter and, in 1585, twins, a boy and a girl.

There is no more information until 1592, when Shakespeare is already well known in London both as an actor and a playwright. He belonged to the acting company, the Lord Chamberlain's Men, later (under James I) the King's Men. In 1599 this group built and became resident at the Globe, the leading Elizabethan theatre.

Shakespeare's writing, in his early years, included poetry as well as plays. *Venus and Adonis* was published in 1593 and *The Rape of Lucrece* in 1594. His contemporary, Francis Meres, records in 1598 that Shakespeare had circulated 'his sugared sonnets among his private friends'. But these were not published until 1609. Shakespeare's plays, moreover, contain a variety of songs, revealing his lyrical mastery.

In 1610, Shakespeare returned to Stratford, although he continued his dramatic writing. He died there in 1616. It was not until 1623, in the 'First Folio', that his plays were published in a collected edition.

THE SONNETS

The sonnet sequence, such as Sidney's *Astrophil and Stella*, was a popular literary form in the Renaissance. Shakespeare's sonnets, published by Thomas Thorpe in 1609, bear a dedication to 'Mr. W. H.'. There has been considerable speculation over the centuries as to the identity of the dedicatee, assuming that he must be the subject of at least some of the sonnets. A twentieth-century historian of the Elizabethan age, A. L. Rowse, argued that 'Mr. W. H.' was Sir William Harvey, who had married the mother of Shakespeare's patron, Southampton (the young lord of the poems), and who was therefore in a position of 'close proximity to Southampton' and able to get the manuscript for publication by Thorpe. The dedication, in other words, is Thorpe's, not Shakespeare's.[1] More recent scholarship tends to avoid this controversy (and other related arguments about the identities of the individuals in the sonnets, such as the 'fair youth' and the 'dark lady'). Helen Vendler's *The Art of Shakespeare's Sonnets* is representative of this emphasis in focusing – as its title suggests – on the poetic qualities of the poems.

---

1. See the introduction to A. L. Rowse, *Shakespeare's Sonnets* (3rd edition: London: Macmillan, 1984).

■   Whoever the 'fair youth' of the sonnets may have been, it is striking
indeed that he should be the subject of the male poet's love poems in the
earlier part of the sequence. This has led socio-psychological critics to speculate about Shakespeare's sexuality and, in general, about gender relations in
the Renaissance. Again, Professor Vendler provides a useful corrective to this
approach (while acknowledging its interest) by arguing that it is wrong to
read the sonnet sequence 'as if these lyrics were either a novel or a documentary of a lived life'. She points out that 'there is no social discourse which
[Shakespeare] does not interrogate and ironize', so his subversion of the
expected series of poems to a beautiful woman is of most interest as a literary strategy, in the context of the Petrarchan tradition.[2] This is true also of
the later poems' focus on the dark lady and of those that deal with a love
triangle, involving two men and a woman.

   This is not to argue, of course, that we cannot derive any autobiography
and biography from such works and that what the poems might say about
Elizabethan and Jacobean society is irrelevant to our consideration and
cannot assist our reading and appreciation. It is simply to note that we should
be wary of allowing these considerations to dominate, or even obliterate,
what is of most interest about the poems – their status and character as
poems, works of literary art.

SELECTED SONNETS

(i)   Shall I compare thee to a summer's day?
      Thou art more lovely and more temperate:
      Rough winds do shake the darling buds of May,
      And summer's lease hath all too short a date:
      Sometime too hot the eye of heaven shines
      And often is his gold complexion dimmed;
      And every fair from fair sometimes declines,
      By chance or nature's changing course untrimmed;
      But thy eternal summer shall not fade,
      Nor lose possession of that fair thou ow'st;   [ow'st = ownest]
      Nor shall death brag thou wander'st in his shade,
      When in eternal lines to time thou grow'st:
      So long as men can breathe, or eyes can see,
      So long lives this, and this gives life to thee.

This is a sonnet of sustained praise of the beloved. Although there appears to
be a disjunction at the beginning of the sestet – 'But thy eternal summer shall
not fade' – the compliment is a continuation of the praise in the opening lines

---

2. Helen Vendler, *The Art of Shakespeare's Sonnets* (Cambridge, MA: Harvard University Press, 1997), p. 2.

and has the same seasonal reference. The difference now is that the lover who is better than summer is now superlatively so, for he is not subject to the finiteness of a season, but an expression of the eternal.

The opening line of the poem is a proposition, in the manner of an intellectual exercise; thought and emotion are typically mixed in Renaissance poetry. But in the query there is already uncertainty about the validity of the comparison, which the second line emphasises with its two good reasons for this doubt by the repetition of 'more'. The subject of the poem is more lovely than summer and more temperate. The speaker, in this way, is showing that while he is interested in love, he is also preoccupied with time and its passing, as in the next line with its forceful impact in the first word:

Rough winds do shake the darling buds of May.

There is onomatopoeia here in both 'winds' and 'shake' as, even at its beginning, summer reveals its transitory 'lease'. The cherished buds symbolise its promise, but that can be – like the buds – short-lived. Shakespeare is thinking, of course, of an English summer which is always a dubious season. It can be scorching, or fitful, or even non-existent:

Sometime too hot the eye of heaven shines
And often is his gold complexion dimmed . . .

The speaker is referring both to the experience of a particular summer and of a succession of summers. In so doing, he is not only considering love by comparison, or time and its passing. He is reflecting most importantly on change and decay – 'mutability', as the Renaissance poets called it – as revealed by nature.

These negative ideas are complemented by the definition of the beloved's embodiment of their contradiction in an alternative sequence of negatives:

thy eternal summer shall *not* fade
Nor lose possession of that fair thou ow'st;
Nor shall death brag thou wander'st in his shade . . .

We can hear Death in that characterisation of his speech, even as Shakespeare is silencing him.

Apparently arrogantly, at the end, the guarantee of the beloved's eternal persistence as a beautiful being is the poet's celebration in this sonnet: 'this gives life to thee'. But it was conventional for the Renaissance poet to claim immortality for his lines. Shakespeare has arranged his appropriation of the convention so that the immortality ascribed to the lover is not diminished by this assertion, because it has already been established. Eternal beauty takes life from his lines, but they, in turn, have taken their life from the beloved.

■ (ii)   When, in disgrace with Fortune and men's eyes,
          I all alone beweep my outcast state,
          And trouble deaf heaven with my bootless cries,   [bootless = futile]
          And look upon myself and curse my fate,
          Wishing me like to one more rich in hope,
          Featured like him, like him with friends possessed,
          Desiring this man's art and that man's scope,
          With what I most enjoy contented least;
          Yet in these thoughts myself almost despising,
          Haply I think on thee, and then my state
          (Like to the lark at break of day arising
          From sullen earth) sings hymns at heaven's gate;
                   For thy sweet love remembered such wealth brings
                   That then I scorn to change my state with kings.

The focus of this sonnet is the speaker and his condition. It is an aggrieved reflection on his public, professional life and its problems. It is very different from a Petrarchan sonnet because it does not concentrate on the beloved or on love. Although at the end, of course, there is the exultant praise of both as liberating the speaker from his worldly cares.

We notice, in the opening line, the familiar Renaissance complaint about 'Fortune' capitalised for personification to make Fate's malignant processes more immediate. There is concentration, too, on his critics' 'eyes'. A very important organ for medieval, Renaissance and seventeenth-century writers, the eye was the window of the soul and expressed a person's true emotions.

The speaker's response to his divorce from favour is to lament it, in words – 'alone beweep' – that reflect the sounds of moaning and crying. Notice again the concentration on the eyes: weeping was a sign of genuine grief. There were even prayers for the 'grace' of tears to indicate a genuinely penitent soul.

More boisterously now, he pleads to heaven; but his pleas are futile. This agitation is captured stylistically in the forthright consonants and alliteration (on 'b') in the third line, which is perpetuated in the strong verb, 'curse', in the next. Having introduced Fortune at the beginning, the speaker now refers to 'my fate', emphasising (as Shakespeare often does in his plays) how he is subject to these capricious influences.

In such a situation, one envies others. And the speaker utters a heated catalogue of fortunate ones – the man with prospects, good looks, influential friends, talent and breadth of accomplishment. He would be a Renaissance man, a successful courtier. Emerging here is the familiar theme of the desire to rise in such circumstances, but it is held in a tension (particularly by outsiders like Shakespeare and Donne) with criticisms of the world of the court.

■   The speaker all but despairs – even his dearest pleasures have lost their appeal. But one consolation remains and it annihilates all his suffering and misfortune: it is the beloved. In contemplation of his love, the speaker undergoes a metamorphosis. His 'state' – his psychological and emotional condition – is transformed. Shakespeare is toying here with the political idea also of his speaker's position in society which is different from that of kings (as he says at the end), but not inferior, because he knows superlative happiness in love. It is too much to say that this is subversive of the court or the monarchy, but it certainly challenges absolute conceptions about kingship, and we note the strong verb, 'I scorn'. Further, we see that he speaks of kings in the plural which paradoxically minimises kingship: they are less remarkable for being numerous.

Most striking and memorable, however, is the splendid simile in the sestet, for his joyous soul:

>   my state
> (Like to the lark at break of day arising
> From sullen earth) sings hymns at heaven's gate.

Such poetry defies paraphrase in its perfection. But we might note the sounds of the words which contribute to this image (aural and visual) of sublime happiness. The language sings – in the 'k' alliteration, for example – as it enacts the birdsong it describes. And the enjambement – 'arising / From sullen earth' – describes the soaring impulse of that ecstasy.

(iii) Not marble, nor the gilded monuments
       Of princes, shall outlive this powerful rhyme;
       But you shall shine more bright in these contents
       Than unswept stone, besmeared with sluttish time.
       When wasteful war shall statues overturn,
       And broils root out the work of masonry,
       Nor Mars his sword nor war's quick fire shall burn
       The living record of your memory.
       'Gainst death and all-oblivious enmity   [enmity = the enmity of being forgotten]
       Shall you pace forth; your praise shall still find room
       Even in the eyes of all posterity
       That wear this world out to the ending doom.   [the ending doom = Judgement Day]
           So, till the judgement that yourself arise,
           You live in this, and dwell in lovers' eyes.

This sonnet takes up the theme we encountered in 'Shall I compare thee to a summer's day' – the immortality of the beloved's fame as a result of its

■ preservation in the poet's lines. Here, however, this idea is introduced at the beginning in the reference to 'this powerful rhyme'. To affirm the qualities of his literary commemoration, the speaker indicates that it will outlast even 'marble' and 'gilded monuments'. Both of these forms of memorial are initially attractive, but marble (often used for tombs) is cold and hard and the gilding of the monuments could suggest a memorial that was too ornate, or only superficially impressive. In any case, these are inanimate, funereal objects. The sonnet gives life to the beloved's memory. In particular, we notice – as in other poems in the sequence (as, indeed, in Shakespeare's plays) – that the world of the court is singled out ('of princes') for special repudiation. Shakespeare owed much to courtly patronage and was a defender of the monarchical system, but he was not uncritical of its realities.

The sounds of the words in the first quatrain clearly establish the antithesis between monumental and literary commemoration. The light and crisp consonants of 'you shall shine more bright in these contents' are juxtaposed with the sneering and guttural vowels of 'besmeared with sluttish time'.

The aural technique continues in the next quatrain, in the alliteration of 'wasteful war' which emphasises that calamity and the forceful 'broils' (conflicts) which 'root out' the stone-masons' commemorative handiwork. We can hear that tumult of destruction in the sounds of those words. Relentlessly, the god of war is enlisted in this catalogue of destruction and criticism of the way of the world, which is conquered, ultimately, by love and poetry. The antithesis, in essence, is between life and death, and the octave concludes with

The living record of your memory.

The image of the beloved in triumph is captured in the ceremonious verb 'pace'. This is appropriate as it idealises the presentation as well as the poetry which perpetuates it. The phrase paces forth too. This is emphasised, both thematically and stylistically, through the alliteration of 'pace' and 'praise', and is carried on into the next line, in 'all posterity'. The contrast with the terrible-sounding 'doom' of judgement, at the end of the third quatrain, makes the beloved's endurance until the end of time even more excellent.

There is also the familiar idea of Renaissance poets that the world was wearing out. Shakespeare may be projecting this event into the distant future – in order to stress the endurance of the beloved and his poetry. But the emphasis on that telling verb 'wear' reveals a contemporary anxiety about the end of things, which was in tension with the burgeoning optimism of Elizabethan England.

The sonnet concludes confidently in a compliment, with a vision of the resurrection of the beloved. The speaker has no doubt about God's verdict and may even be claiming knowledge of the divine intention. But the final

4

■ stroke is a compliment to himself for providing the living rhyme of the sonnet to preserve the beloved's being. It is not entirely self-centred, however: the poem and the image it reveals inspire all lovers who read it.

(iv) Let me not to the marriage of true minds
      Admit impediments; love is not love
      Which alters when it alteration finds,
      Or bends with the remover to remove:
      O, no, it is an ever-fixèd mark,
      That looks on tempests and is never shaken;
      It is the star to every wand'ring bark,
      Whose worth's unknown, although his highth be taken.
      Love's not Time's fool, though rosy lips and cheeks
      Within his bending sickle's compass come;
      Love alters not with his brief hours and weeks,
      But bears it out even to the edge of doom.
              If this be error and upon me proved,
              I never writ, nor no man ever loved.

The idealising vein of the Elizabethan love sonnet is apparent here, not only in its celebration of love's enduring quality but also in the initial reference to the marriage of 'true minds'. The speaker will not 'admit impediments' to this, echoing the marriage service in the Anglican prayer book. Unlike the prayer book, however, which speaks of the bodily as well as the spiritual aspects of wedlock, this sonnet concentrates on the marriage of minds. There is also a detachment on the speaker's part. He appears to be giving his bless-ing (another aspect recalling the liturgy) to a couple. It is an ideal partner-ship he is describing, but not one in which he is a participant.

The sonnet is no less passionate for these qualities, however. The dramatic, 'O, no, it is an ever-fixèd mark' is emphatic in its declaration of love's constancy.

Taking us into the contemporary world of sea-faring and navigation, Shakespeare develops the metaphor of ideal love as the true guide amid the tempests and other dangers of life. The image of the 'wand'ring' craft suggests the aimlessness of existence without love's inspiration. Once expe-rienced, love's worth (like the star's) is beyond calculation.

The preoccupation in the sonnets with time and its passing, and the related matter of mutability, is reintroduced in the sestet in a double person-ification of Love and Time. There is a reminiscence of the conventional *descriptio* or blazon of the beloved in the reference to 'rosy lips and cheeks'. But, differently, the speaker admits that these will be subject to Time's assaults. However, love outlasts bodily decay.

As in the previous sonnet we discussed, perfect love is projected 'to the

■ edge of doom', the Day of Judgement. Such repetitions are not, of course, the sign of failing creativity or lack of originality. They indicate the importance of such ideas to the poet and his age. The Last Judgement was of momentous significance to individuals within a Christian society. And as Shakespeare's quotation from the Book of Common Prayer at the beginning of this sonnet (and elsewhere in the sequence) indicates, we have good reason to suppose that he was not only informed about such Church teaching but subscribed to it. The reference to 'error' in the penultimate line sustains this idea. It signified not merely a mistake, but – frequently – theological error. Shakespeare is arguing that his idea of love and its survival to the end of time is as true as the existence of the poem he has just completed. On one level this is witty and tongue-in-cheek, but it cannot be entirely dismissed as flippant. The self-consciousness of the poet is conventional, as we have said, but it is given a force and purpose here, as elsewhere, as part of the larger convictions about life and love which the sonnet proposes.

Questions

1. 'Shakespeare's sonnets are not confined to matters of idealised love. They also provide telling reflections on life, in all its variety.' Do you agree? Use the following poem as a starting-point for your discussion of two or three sonnets.

> Th' expense of spirit in a waste of shame
> Is lust in action; and till action, lust
> Is perjured, murd'rous, bloody, full of blame,
> Savage, extreme, rude, cruel, not to trust;
> Enjoyed no sooner but despised straight:
> Past reason hunted; and no sooner had,
> Past reason hated, as a swallowed bait,
> On purpose laid to make the taker mad:
> Mad in pursuit, and in possession so;
> Had, having, and in quest to have, extreme;
> A bliss in proof and proved, a very woe;   [in proof = during the act]
> Before, a joy proposed; behind, a dream.
>   All this the world well knows; yet none knows well
>   To shun the heaven that leads men to this hell.

2. 'Shakespeare's manner, as a poet, is as important as his matter in communicating his ideas forcefully and memorably.' Do you agree? Refer in detail to two or three sonnets.

The early seventeenth century

THE PILGRIMAGE TO 'THE KINGDOM OF MAN'

The end of the Elizabethan age occurred on the peaceful accession, in 1603, of the Stuart king, James VI of Scotland, who became James I of England. The new Jacobean era, the subsequent Caroline age – under James's son, Charles I – and the Commonwealth and Protectorate, which were the result of the Civil War in the 1640s and 1650s under Oliver Cromwell, present complex political, theological, social and artistic responses to and reactions against the Renaissance and Reformation of the sixteenth century. But the continuing influence of those great historical and cultural movements is also remarkable. The poetry of Milton, who did not die until 1674, may be seen as the last word of Renaissance civilisation and literary culture, while his eccentric Puritanism had its origins in the individuality of Reformation theology more than a century before.

The story of the oscillating persistence and rejection of the poetic school of Petrarchanism, well into the seventeenth century, is a reflection of the debt to the cultural past and liberation from it. As early as *Volpone* (1606), Ben Jonson has the leading character express his torment of amorous suffering in tired Petrarchan terms. Jonson uses that affected language as a means of satirising the disreputable Volpone in his dated and debauched passion:

> angry Cupid, bolting from her eyes,
> Hath shot himself into me like a flame,
> Where now he flings about his burning heat
> As in a furnace.

And later in the play, Lady Politic, as if pondering a distant age, refers to 'your Petrarch . . . / In days of sonneting'. In the next generation, we find Carew sneering at 'Petrarch's learnèd arms' in 'A Rapture' (1640). However, in Marvell's poetry, written later still, in 'Damon the Mower', for example, the speaker conforms completely to Petrarchan attitudes. The seventeenth century is as much a part of the Renaissance as a departure from it.

A swelling theme in the seventeenth century (in prose as well as in poetry) is the Renaissance search for knowledge of the world and independence of thought (as revealed, for example, in Sir Thomas More's *Utopia* of 1516). But Donne's insistence, in his *Devotions Upon Emergent Occasions* (1623), that 'No Man is an Iland' might be read more as an urgent response to a sense of developing individualism than as confirmation of an accepted belief. The tensions between tradition and individuality in the Renaissance begin to be resolved in humanity's quest for self-realisation: 'the understanding thoroughly freed and cleansed', as Bacon envisaged it in his *Novum Organum* of 1620, would bring about 'the entrance into the kingdom of man, founded on the sciences'. The seventeenth century loosens the bonds with medievalism and anticipates the exaltation of Reason in the Augustan age of the eighteenth century as well as the antithetical celebration of Imagination in the Romantic movement of the early nineteenth century.

I

The first half of the seventeenth century was an age, metaphysically and physically, of increasingly vigorous and often individualistic pilgrimage and quest. Accordingly, that is one of the most prominent and persistent metaphors of its literature. The self-contained and apparently self-perpetuating domains of the Court and the Church were still at the centre of power and national life under James and Charles. However, they were no longer sufficiently sustaining or compelling, politically, theologically or socially for all of those within them or for many of those outside.

John Milton, whose academic training would normally have led to ordination in the Anglican Church, outspokenly rejected orders, preferring to become a poet-priest. The Pilgrim Fathers, unable to practise their rigorous Protestantism within the Anglicanism which they regarded as insufficiently reformed, had left for Amsterdam in 1608 and eventually, in 1620, settled in Plymouth, Massachusetts. Theirs was a geographically adventurous expression of the usually allegorical pilgrim's progress (as most famously described by John Bunyan later in the century). Richard Crashaw journeyed physically and metaphysically from Anglican Cambridge to Catholic Loreto. In 'Bermudas', Andrew Marvell combined geographical amplitude of reference with social commentary to take up the motif of journeying beyond the constrictions and constructions of society:

> Where the remote Bermudas ride,
> In th' ocean's bosom unespied,
> From a small boat that rowed along,
> The listening winds received this song:

> 'What should we do but sing his praise

That led us through the wat'ry maze
Unto an isle so long unknown,
And yet far kinder than our own?
Where he the huge sea monsters wracks,   [wracks = shipwrecks]
That lift the deep upon their backs;
He lands us on a grassy stage,
Safe from the storms, and prelate's rage'.

The buoyant rhythm expresses the exhilaration of being dissociated from repression. Yet in Marvell's public career (he was Milton's assistant as Latin Secretary for the Commonwealth) we witness a curious blend of radicalism and conservatism. This is brought into focus most memorably in the Horatian ode 'Upon Cromwell's Return from Ireland' — ostensibly in praise of the victory of Cromwell over the Irish, but in which the most celebrated lines are the description of the execution of Charles I by the Cromwellians. The king is presented as a tragic hero:

> thence the royal actor borne,
> The tragic scaffold might adorn;
> > While round the armèd bands
> > Did clap their bloody hands.
>
> *He* nothing common did or mean
> Upon that memorable scene,
> > But with his keener eye
> > The ax's edge did try;
>
> Nor called the gods with vulgar spite
> To vindicate his helpless right;
> > But bowed his comely head
> > Down, as upon a bed.

As the Civil War demonstrated, the pilgrimage to freedom could be arduous, its attainments fleeting and its consequences — as in the regicide — alarming. Journeying (intellectually, spiritually and materially) is usually seen as difficult in the literature of the seventeenth century: 'a cold coming they had of it', as Lancelot Andrewes, one of the great preachers of the day, put it with reference to the journey of the Magi to Bethlehem. This gives a heroic dimension to pilgrimage.

The speaker in George Herbert's poem 'The Pilgrimage' is not only undertaking a daunting role, but finds himself in the middle of his journey at the beginning of the poem. This indicates the combined persistence and urgency of the undertaking:

> I travelled on, seeing the hill where lay
> > My expectation.
> A long it was and weary way.
> The gloomy cave of desperation
> I left on th' one, and on the other side
> > The rock of pride.

As is so often the case with Herbert, the poetry is superficially simple, but it is both allegorical and theological. The progress of life is plotted as a pilgrimage between the deadly but opposite sins of despair and spiritual pride. It is another example of Herbert's search for the *via media*, but in this poem it is placed not in the domain of Anglican ecclesiology (as in his poem 'The British Church') but in the larger context of moral choice.

The following stanzas trace the stages of the pilgrim's journey. There are surprises – as in the fourth stanza, where it seems that the speaker has reached his destination:

> At length I got unto the gladsome hill
> > Where lay my hope,
> Where lay my heart; and, climbing still,
> When I had gained the brow and top,
> A lake of brackish waters on the ground
> > Was all I found.

The search for truth, an individual quest fraught with disappointment, is described here with a determination not to be thwarted in its pursuit. The verb is startling in Herbert's usually temperate discourse:

> My hill was further; so I flung away . . .

and the poem closes darkly with the surmise that all such journeying on earth may be futile – the only journey that matters begins with death.

In the most beautiful of laments by a husband for his wife, Henry King's 'Exequy' of 1624, we find the motif of the journey expressed in different terms:

> I am already on the way,
> And follow thee with all the speed
> Desire can make, or sorrows breed . . .
> But hark! my pulse like a soft drum
> Beats my approach, tells thee I come;
> And slow howe'er my marches be,
> I shall at last sit down by thee.

There, the very act of walking ('my marches') is heard like a heartbeat – its pulse is the speaker's impulse (onomatopoeically registered in 'drum' and 'beats' and rhythmically paced, like his pacing) as the slowing of age's steps is juxtaposed with the determination to finish the quest to reach his beloved. King's reflections on his condition are, not surprisingly, very close to melancholy (see John Bunyan's 'slough of despond' in his *Pilgrim's Progress*), that formidable obstacle to seventeenth-century hyperactivity in life's journey.

Robert Burton was true to his ruling passion of 'melancholy' both in his life and writing (in the famous *Anatomy*). He never travelled anywhere, geographically or emotionally, remaining unmarried in Oxford, amongst decaying books, all his adulthood. His dusty despair contrasts strikingly with the more characteristic attitude of the age as expressed in Milton's vision, a generation later, of strenuous, purposeful, revolutionary Englishness setting out on the venture of political and religious reform:

> methinks I see in my mind a noble and puissant nation
> rousing herself like a strong man after sleep, and shaking
> her invincible locks: methinks I see her as an eagle mewing[1]
> her mighty youth, and kindling her undazzled eyes
> at the full midday beam.
>
> *Areopagitica*

But the period's greatest poet of pilgrimage is Henry Vaughan. Vaughan was indebted to Herbert for the titles, some subjects and occasional mannerisms in his poems, but brings a unique interpretation to this contemporary preoccupation. Straightforwardly, in a work such as 'Regeneration', the individual freed from oppression,

> A ward, and still in bonds, one day
>   I stole abroad . . .

finds himself, vividly here, in imagery and alliteration, amidst the difficulties of the journey from bondage:

> My walk a monstrous, mountained thing.

Typically, the pilgrim's progress is frustrated by pains and disappointments, as nature reflects his 'humour':

>   as a pilgrim's eye,
> Far from relief,
> Measures the melancholy sky,
> Then drops and rains for grief.

In other poems, Vaughan strikingly varies the usual form of the quest motif in his description of journeying backwards in time and sensibility to the imagined pre-

---

1. Shaking off or possibly 'newing' from renewing.

existent world before birth. Touching his orthodox Christianity with Platonic teaching, Vaughan unwittingly anticipates Romanticism: Wordsworth drew upon the same theory of pre-existence in his Immortality Ode (see Special Study 8), and in the general desire to recover a lost innocence. Vaughan repeatedly expresses his quest to return 'unto that hour' when God was last revealed to him – most memorably in 'The Retreat' itself:

> Happy those early days! when I
> Shined in my angel infancy . . .
> When yet I had not walked above
> A mile or two from my first love,
> And looking back, at that short space,
> Could see a glimpse of His bright face . . .
> Some men a forward motion love;
> But I by backward steps would move,
> And when this dust falls to the urn,
> In that state I came, return.

It is a reactionary text in a time of progress. Vaughan, who was politically and religiously conservative, diminishes the very animating spirit of the age to the enthusiasm of 'some men' for a 'forward motion'. He vividly dramatises the complexities of his progress by developing his metaphor of walking, with an anxiety akin to Herbert's in 'The Pilgrimage':

> But, ah! my soul with too much stay   [stay = delay]
> Is drunk, and staggers in the way.

One's way and life, the *via* and *vita*, were synonymous and could lead to the truth. In 'The World', Vaughan seeks his 'way', repeating the word twice more:

> The way which from this dead and dark abode
>   Leads up to God,
> A way where you might tread the sun.

It is an image of transcendence. But at least as powerful in the seventeenth century was the idea of earth-bound pilgrimage.

II

In the unpretentious rusticity of Izaak Walton's *Compleat Angler* (1653), the inter-locutors, Viator the wayfarer and Piscator the angler (representing the Renaissance debate between action and contemplation), articulate what might be learnt to the benefit of one's moral life from virtuous undertakings in this world. Earlier in the century, Ben Jonson walked to Edinburgh to stay with the poet William Drummond – 'he is to write his foot pilgrimage hither, and to call it a discovery' – and they talked at length about poetry and life. And while imagery of elevation and aspirations to the transcendental, to Heaven's 'high palace hall', is pervasive in Milton's poetry – 'by steps we may ascend to God' – his most telling presentation of pilgrimage, at the end of *Paradise Lost*, is that of Adam and Eve setting out on the adventure of human existence on the 'subjected plain' of this fallen world:

> They, hand in hand, with wandering steps and slow,
> Through Eden took their solitary way.

It is a humanistic image and in Milton's treatment its implications are ambiguous, as those steps are of reluctant wanderers in the way. However, the restoration of their handedness (one of the central motifs in the poem – a type of correction of the relationship between humanity and God) gives direction to their pilgrimage through the 'world's wide wilderness'.

Wayfaring, for Milton, entailed warfaring. In poetic prose in the *Areopagitica* (1644), a principal text for freedom in the seventeenth century, he insists on the necessity of the quest to attain purity. The argument is as intellectual (Humanist) as it is spiritual (Christian), for Milton is arguing specifically against censorship:

> I cannot praise a fugitive and cloistered virtue, unexercised and
> unbreathed, that never sallies out and sees her adversary, but slinks out
> of the race where that immortal garland is to be run for, not without
> dust and heat. Assuredly, we bring not innocence into the world, we
> bring impurity much rather, that which purifies us is trial, and trial is
> by what is contrary.

As in *Paradise Lost*, the language is taken from epic diction. Similarly, the 'sage and serious' Edmund Spenser, as Milton called him, developed epic stories in *The Faerie Queene* to celebrate the attainment of such 'prizes' as Holiness and Temperance. But, ultimately, the heroic ideal in Milton's thought was not activity but passivity: 'They also serve', he concluded one of his sonnets, 'who only stand and wait'. The classical image of the victor in physical contests was replaced with 'plain heroic magnitude of mind' (as the Chorus says of the hero in *Samson Agonistes*). Adam, the ideal man of Milton's conception, recognises, after his conflict with the adversary (the meaning of 'Satan' in Hebrew), that true virtue consists in submission to God – an obedience that triumphs over the 'worldly-strong, and worldly-wise':

> . . . suffering for truth's sake
> Is fortitude to highest victory.

That Milton's own physical activity was severely restricted (he was blind and, at the Restoration, under threat of execution for his Cromwellian sympathies) adds a personal intensity to the praise of passive suffering and fortitude. In *Paradise Lost*, he rejects the classical models of such as 'the wrath / Of stern Achilles on his foe pursued' for an argument 'not less but more heroic': the attainment of righteousness, 'a Paradise within thee'.

Indeed, the identity of the true hero in *Paradise Lost* is often pondered, for there are several heroically conceived individuals. The epic poem, being an heroic undertaking itself, presents Milton as one of these. Unlike Homer and Virgil in their epics, Milton has an existence (in several autobiographical passages) within it. Milton declared (in the *Apology for Smectymnuus*) that he would become a 'true poem'. In *Paradise Lost*, we may say that he achieved this, as he overcomes the adversary of the arduousness of creativity in this most demanding of literary forms. It is the fulfilment of his pilgrimage, Humanistic and Christian, to the state he described as 'kingly': the triumph of artistry in this world and of faith in the next.

III

Along with the commitment to pilgrimage in life and learning in the seventeenth century, there was an extraordinary exploration and flourishing of artistic creativity, particularly in poetry and dramatic writing (Shakespeare's great tragedies and romantic comedies belong to the period 1601–9). The two principal 'schools' of earlier seventeenth-century poetry, the Metaphysical and Cavalier poets, derive from the writings of John Donne and Ben Jonson respectively. But the poetry of these schools, as of Donne and Jonson themselves, has much in common and, to modern readers, it may seem a fine point to separate Donne and his Metaphysical successors from Jonson and the 'sons of Ben'. The greatest differences, in fact, are to be found between the poetry of Donne and Jonson themselves. Later writers, like Marvell and Edmund Waller, may well combine the best of both. In Waller's 'Go, lovely rose!', we have Donne's directness of statement (as in 'The Indifferent') and Jonson's classical order and elegance:

> Go, lovely rose!
> Tell her that wastes her time and me
> That now she knows,
> When I resemble her to thee,   [resemble = compare]
> How sweet and fair she seems to be.
>
> Tell her that's young,
> And shuns to have her graces spied,
> That hadst thou sprung
> In deserts, where no men abide,
> Thou must have uncommended died.
>
> Small is the worth
> Of beauty from the light retired;

Bid her come forth,
Suffer herself to be desired,
And not blush so to be admired.

Then die! that she
The common fate of all things rare
May read in thee;
How small a part of time they share
That are so wondrous sweet and fair!

Here, the terms 'Metaphysical' and 'Cavalier', although in common usage in literary history, are both misleading. The former, from Greek, implies that this is poetry which is concerned only with matters above the physical world, with the intellect and the spirit. But as this and Donne's poetry plainly exemplify, the writing combines passionate and sensual experience with intellectual acuteness and spiritual insight.

'Metaphysical' was used in the later seventeenth and eighteenth centuries as a negative description. It focused attention on the tricks of argument – the witty element – of Metaphysical poetry and especially its concentration on minutiae of logical and pseudo-logical thought-processes: on the microcosmic world of individuals and the quest to pursue metaphors as far as imagination could take them. In Dryden's 'Discourse Concerning the Original and Progress of Satire' (1693), Donne is criticised because

he affects the metaphysics . . . and perplexes the minds of the fair sex with nice speculations of philosophy, when he should engage their hearts, and entertain them with the softnesses of love.

These speculations were, undeniably, components of Metaphysical poetry, but such critical accounts provided only partial assessments of its true range and character. This applied not only to Donne's poetry, but also to the work of George Herbert, Henry Vaughan and Richard Crashaw – to name the most prominent members of the 'school'.

Abraham Cowley (pronounced 'Cooley') was a Metaphysical writer who is not read today but who was regarded as representative of the tradition. He was the subject of one of Samuel Johnson's *Lives of the English Poets*, published in 1779–81, a century after Cowley's death. In that essay, Johnson sets out in detail his objections to the Metaphysical school and, in the process, provides a notable insight into the change of sensibility between the seventeenth and eighteenth centuries.

Johnson admits that the 'metaphysical poets were men of learning', but argues that instead of bringing their knowledge to bear on life, they confined their 'verses' to the display of their intellects and were particularly concerned to over-reach each other in such displays: 'to be singular in their thoughts'. He concedes that this project often produced striking ideas. But the more extraordinary the argument, the less 'natural' was the poetry. Stylistically, the eccentric arguments produced indecorous comparisons: 'the most heterogeneous ideas are yoked by violence together'. The unsatisfactory coexistence in one poem of diverse elements produced 'a kind of *discordia concors*; a combination of dissimilar images, or discovery of occult resemblances in things apparently unlike'. Donne is nonetheless praised as a man 'of a very extensive and various knowledge'. However, for Johnson, his poetry and that of his school fails the essential Johnsonian (and Augustan) test of a largeness and wholeness of presentation of life (or Nature, as they preferred to call it, including human nature).

A renewed appreciation of the Metaphysicals began in the Romantic movement with Coleridge's praise of Donne for those very qualities about which Dr Johnson was critical: 'wonder-exciting vigour, intenseness and peculiarity of thought, using at will the almost boundless stores of a capacious memory, and exercised on subjects where we have no right to expect it'. Praising Donne, he echoed Carew's tribute to the poet as the 'king' of the 'monarchy of wit'. In the twentieth century, Donne's rehabilitation in esteem was completed by T. S. Eliot in such essays as 'The Metaphysical Poets' (1921) and by substantial scholarly study of his achievement, begun by Herbert Grierson and continuing to the present.

■ SPECIAL STUDY 4

John Donne (1572–1631)

ABOUT THE AUTHOR

John Donne was born in London in 1572. Nothing is known of his early schooling, but he matriculated from Hart Hall, Oxford in 1584. He may have been at Cambridge, then in Europe, before he was admitted to Lincoln's Inn, in London, in 1592, to study law.

Donne joined Sir Walter Raleigh's expedition to Cadiz as a gentleman adventurer in 1596, and after taking part in the expedition to the Azores in 1597, he became secretary to Sir Thomas Egerton, the Lord Keeper. He was a Member of Parliament in 1601, but at the end of that year he secretly married Ann More, Egerton's niece. He was imprisoned for his elopement in 1602, and Egerton dismissed him from his service. The marriage was a fruitful one, but Donne had seriously hampered his public career by passionate action.

Over the next decade, Donne engaged in various polemical writings against the Catholicism into which he had been born and in 1611 he accompanied Sir Robert Drury to the Continent. He returned to England the following year and settled with his family in the Drury estate in Drury Lane. Donne was again a Member of Parliament in 1614 and in 1615 he was ordained deacon and priest in the Church of England, appointed a royal chaplain and made a Doctor of Divinity of the University of Cambridge.

After their twelfth child was stillborn, in 1616, Donne's wife died. He was in Germany in 1619–20 and in 1621 he was appointed Dean of St Paul's Cathedral, London. Donne was seriously ill in 1623, and more seriously still in 1630. The following year, on 31 March 1631, he died, survived by six of his twelve children.

DONNE'S POETRY

Certain misconceptions persist about Donne's poetry. One of these derives from the description of his art as 'metaphysical', suggesting that Donne's writing is a superficial and insincere display of ingenuity. A contrary misconception has also been prevalent: that Donne's love poems, especially the so-called songs and sonnets, are the direct expression of his unbridled sensuality.

The truth is a combination of these half-truths. In Donne's poetry, both secular and sacred, the head and the heart are married. In the way of seduction, for example, he is at once sexually forthright and argumentatively strenuous; in his addresses to God he is impassioned and, at the same time, theologically rigorous.

The essence of the genius of Donne's writing, however, is that in joining these and other opposing elements – Samuel Johnson's 'heterogeneous ideas' – he does not curb their distinctive impact. His emotive force lends passion to the argumentativeness, while the learning and reasoning (even when it is spurious) gives structure and direction to the emotions. The combination within one poem, for example, of religious and sexual imagery and references, can shed light on both domains.

We usually describe this hard-won facility – which, in Donne's hands, is made to look almost effortless – as 'wit', another term that has been misapplied in the reading of his work. Today, it suggests merely sophisticated comedy or shallowness. And while Donne's poetry has its share of humour and flippancy, the older and larger meaning of wit - acuteness of thought that is brilliantly realised – better encompasses his range of emotion and argument.

This diversity could scarcely be wider or richer. Renaissance man that he was, Donne delighted in the variety of human experience and the tension in the status of man, in the great chain of being, as a creature a little lower than the angels, a little higher than the beasts and partaking of the qualities of both. Donne's sensuality and piety are prominent in his poetry. Its captivating immediacy owes much to the extreme experiences he had known: the religious ardour of his recusant (Roman Catholic) childhood, his controversial elopement, the disappointments of his worldly career, and his profound faith as an Anglican priest in the last quarter of his life.

Donne's poetry is significant autobiographically, too. It is a record of his fulfilment of one of the expectations of a Renaissance man – that he should be able to turn his hand as deftly to the composition of a sonnet as to horsemanship and statecraft. This was the tradition of men like Sir Philip Sidney and Sir Walter Raleigh.

Yet, in the matter of Donne's best-known work, the love poems, the romantic idea that they are transcriptions of his experience as an Elizabethan Casanova has to be qualified. Certainly, he had been 'a great visitor of ladies' (as a contemporary testified), but it was also in his nature to become a conspicuously faithful and devoted husband and father. Donne's own contrast between Jack Donne the rake and Dr Donne the divine has been taken too literally. It is at least as likely that his love poems were written to impress his male friends at the Inns of Court, for their wittiness and bravado, as to seduce this or that young woman by their eroticism. And some of them at least – such as 'A Valediction: forbidding mourning' – could well have been written for his wife. They speak of a mature devotion.

Whatever their contemporary audience, the love poems would have made a strong impression as much for their scorn of the conventions of love poetry as for their fervent expressions of passion itself. For in matters of both style and subject, Donne's 'songs and sonnets' were radically innovative. For a start, they are rarely lyrical, as Donne himself observed: 'I sing not, siren like, to tempt; for I / Am harsh' ('To Mr S. B.'). Specifically, they broke with the traditions of the Petrarchan school.

In rejecting the Italian master, Donne was asserting an English self-confidence, reflecting the burgeoning national pride in the age of Shakespeare. As Carew remarks, in his elegy on Donne (1633), he 'opened us a mine / Of rich and pregnant fancy'. Donne's assertiveness is articulated in the dramatic immediacy of the settings of many of the poems, their Anglo-Saxon forthrightness of vocabulary and their vigorous rhythms. The theatricality of Donne's writing expressed the influence of English drama in its great epoch.

This stylistic innovation accompanied a new view of love. A modern equality between the sexes and – in several poems – a new earthiness emerge. Petrarch's Laura (or Sidney's Stella) was an idealised figure, pursued and celebrated by an adoring suitor. Her unattainable status ironically gave impetus to his devotion. In contrast, Donne argues that men and women are reciprocally sensual and idealistic. So, in a poem like 'The Indifferent', he views them both as promiscuous beings (overturning the Petrarchan

■ constancy of devotion), while in 'The Canonisation', where constancy has its apotheosis, both are equally saints in love.

However, Donne's disposal of Petrarch goes further than this. In many of his poems, he – not the lady or mistress – is the centre of attention. The lyrical, chivalric subordinate to the queenly Laura or Stella is replaced by the assertive, streetwise egotist with his racy declamation:

> I can love both fair and brown,
> Her whom abundance melts, and her whom want betrays,
> Her who loves loneness best, and her who masks and plays . . .
>
> I can love her and her, and you and you,
> I can love any, so she be not true.

'The Indifferent'

These self-celebratory sentiments are at the same time cynical and realistic. Yet Donne writes with apparently equal conviction of high Platonic devotion in 'The Ecstasy'. He delighted in exploring the extremes of the expression of love in poetry, relishing the literary possibilities. Accordingly, we should be wary of seeking the truth of Donne's view of love (let alone his own experience) in this or that poem. When he is most accomplished, it is possible that he is least sincere – as he said himself: 'I did best when I had least truth for my subjects' (letter to Sir Robert Carr). Although that statement, too, must be treated with reservation.

What is certain is that Donne's was a sensibility steeped in paradox and contradiction, as he recognised in one of his Holy Sonnets: 'Oh, to vex me, contraries meet in one'.

In his religious poetry, Donne is preoccupied with the issues of salvation and damnation: the so-called Last Things of a Christian's life – death, judgement, Heaven and Hell. For Donne (and his contemporaries) the prospect of being judged by God and consigned to an eternity of bliss or punishment at death were awful, literal truths. Like Hamlet, they were preoccupied with 'the dread of something after death, / The undiscovered country from whose bourn / No traveller returns'.

The original sin of Adam and Eve had perverted mankind from goodness, introducing an evil which had spread throughout human history. Yet God had provided the cure for sin in the saving work of his Son which was experienced by the faithful Christian in the gift of grace. Donne, so conscious of his sinfulness, all but despairs of his salvation. The desolation of his condition, and the thorough and violent purgation he desires to rectify his fallen nature, add a dramatic immediacy and vitality to the conventional Christian concern with virtue. He communicates something of its intensity even to the agnostic or atheistic modern reader.

■ SELECTED POEMS

THE FLEA

This poem contains several of the essential features we associate with Donne's love lyrics. While its subject matter is patently passionate – the speaker would make love to his lady – the structure of the poem is argumentative, using the action of the flea as a support for his thesis that intercourse is harmless. Further, the poem is set in a dramatic occasion, in the bedroom, where the lovers are debating; and it contains the dramatic action of the killing of the flea by the lady. Moreover, Donne brings several religious ideas and references into his language of eroticism. The speaker provides a sense of his mistress and himself as beings who are 'larger than life', of heroic, even mythological kind – as in the reference to their bed as their 'marriage temple'. The poem, that is to say, is an exercise in 'wit', not merely in the modern sense that it is entertaining and amusing, but that it is a complex and concentrated intellectual, argumentative, passionate, 'conceited' text, exploring an argument with zest, dramatising an occasion with intensity and ranging widely in references, sacred and secular.

The flea poem was conventional in the seventeenth century, for the flea was admired as a tiny creature that had access to the intimate parts of the beloved's body denied to the would-be lover. What is interesting in Donne's poem is how he gives this tradition unique life through his poetic strategies and vocabulary.

The first of these that we notice is the striking opening phrase, in the use of an imperative verb:

> Mark but this flea . . .

It is at once the beginning of an argument and a strongly emotive gesture. For good measure, the speaker repeats himself:

> . . . and mark in this.

His major premise is that if a mere flea might know the lady's body, why should not he, her lover, be invited to enjoy its delights. The flea has bitten him and her, so they are already intimately joined, for their lifebloods are mixed in the body of the insect. It is a kind of marriage, a sacred union:

> we'are met,
> And cloistered in these living walls of jet.

So far from being shameful, this is a consecration of their love. Yet she continues to resist him, and would smite the flea:

> Oh stay, three lives in one flea spare,
> Where we almost, nay more than married are.

■ They are 'more than married' because the flea's mixture of their blood has consummated their union.

For all the fun, Donne is making two important points. Generally, he is associating love with the ordinariness and realism of life (as represented by the flea), even as he makes extraordinary claims for its actions. Secondly, and more specifically, he is arguing for an equality, expressed in sexuality, between the man and the woman. This, too, is a new approach and an important aspect of Donne's innovativeness as a poet.

Nevertheless, the tone of the poem is extravagantly playful. The lady has acted and killed the flea. This trivial event is given epic, biblical proportions in a vocabulary of the crucifixion:

> Cruel and sudden, hast thou since
> Purpled thy nail, in blood of innocence?

And as the witty coup, at the conclusion of his argument, the speaker turns the event to his advantage. Does she feel weaker for the blood that she has lost to the flea – either physically, or in terms of her moral status? She replies in the negative. Nor, he suggests, will she feel any sense of loss after their love-making:

> Just so much honour, when thou yield'st to me,
> Will waste, as this flea's death took life from thee.

A poem of seduction, 'The Flea' is more importantly a poem that delights in its own existence as a witty exercise exploring the possibilities of its subject.

Question

Consider the religious vocabulary and imagery in this poem. How is it a vital component of the 'wit' of the piece?

A VALEDICTION: FORBIDDING MOURNING

The deathbed introduces 'A Valediction: forbidding mourning' as Donne alludes to the belief that the sign of a virtuous life was a serene and willing death. Such men 'pass mildly' and, indeed, 'whisper to their souls, to go'. The quietest opening to any of Donne's poems, this simile introduces a lyrical celebration of a mature and constant devotion. Though apparently morbid, it is not inappropriate, for the speaker is to commend a love that is virtuous and essentially spiritual. Moreover, the analogy includes the idea that each parting of true lovers is a little death, even though he is to argue, as the main thesis of the poem, that he and his lady are always metaphysically united though physically apart. Subtly present too is the idea that each act of intercourse shortens the participants' lives by a finite period.

■   Contrasting with his erotic verse, this poem of farewell (valediction) may
have been written to Donne's wife. Such sensuality as there is, in the
speaker's acknowledgement of 'eyes, lips, and hands', is subordinate to spiritual attraction, and speaks of a married love, definitely not of youthful lust-
fulness.

The 'Valediction' is also significant as a poem about love poetry.
Prominently, in the second stanza, Donne rejects Petrarchan commonplaces
of floods of tears and tempests of sighs and again uses religious imagery –
but, this time, not outrageously – to characterise a mature and transcendental devotion:

> 'Twere profanation of our joys
> To tell the laity our love.

Earthly-minded people are preoccupied with earthquake and flood as signs
of judgement and the decay of the world, but ignore the far more momentous movements of heavenly bodies. So, Petrarchan lovers, for all their
grandiose representation of their passions, are essentially sensualists bound
to this-worldliness:

> Dull sublunary lovers' love
> (Whose soul is sense) cannot admit
> Absence, because it doth remove
> Those things which elemented it.

In contrast, this love of the speaker and his lady is like an element refined to
such purity that it ceases to exist in physical terms and becomes a mystery,
even beyond their comprehension ('ourselves know not what it is'), 'like
gold to airy thinness beat'. Donne draws upon the process of alchemy, where
base commodities were supposedly turned to gold, but extends it: their love
is gold refined to such purity that it vanishes into air.

The closing three stanzas do not complete the argument; this has already
been achieved. They are a postscript in which Donne introduces another
conceit by which to explain his superlative devotion. He writes in the mode
of a philosopher arguing a proposition, and in the process evolves his most
famous conceit. It is a marvellous stroke of wit: an afterthought is superbly
wrought, showing the inexhaustible inspiration of the love he is celebrating.
If he and his beloved must be two souls, then:

> they are two so
> As stiff twin compasses are two.

This analogy is striking because of its oddity in comparing the conjunction of
lovers' souls to the design and operation of the cartographer's instrument.
Yet, like the lovers, the compass has both duality and unity. Further, properly

used, it describes a circle, which, for the Renaissance mind, was the symbol of perfection. But to crown the imagery is the realisation of the compass in action: she 'leans, and hearkens' after the roaming one (he). And Donne closes with an understated compliment, which is the more moving for being restrained and perfectly true to the facts of compass use:

> Thy firmness makes my circle just,
> And makes me end, where I begun.

Question

How does the language and technique of the poem convey the sense of a mature relationship?

OH MY BLACK SOUL!

This Holy Sonnet (or Divine Meditation) succinctly summarises the characteristics of Donne's religious poetry and his Christianity. The opening exclamation announces his honest recognition of the sin-laden state of his being. And urgency is immediately added to this apprehension as he notes that his current illness could well be fatal, bringing him shortly to judgement:

> now thou art summoned
> By sickness, death's herald, and champion.

The spectre of the Last Things haunts the experience he is describing.

Then, poet and worldly man that he is also, Donne embellishes his meditation with two similes from secular life: he is like a foreign traveller who has betrayed his country abroad and is terrified to return home, or like a convicted thief who wants to be released from prison, but when release is offered, in the form of execution, prefers to remain in gaol. Both similes suggest wretched mortal lives. But Donne is arguing that, for the sinner, prolonged suffering on earth is far preferable to what he fears of death.

In the sestet (as so often in his Holy Sonnets), Donne proffers the Christian solution to the problem posed in the octave. We can see, in this arrangement, how perfectly suited the sonnet form was to the character of the meditation, which is meant to progress from the realisation of the meditator's spiritual condition to the appreciation of God's response to it:

> Yet grace, if thou repent, thou canst not lack.

Theologically, Donne correctly observes that God's grace will absolve even the blackness of his soul. However, 'if thou repent' is the important phrase in this line. Donne rarely presents himself in a state of grace, but tentatively in the humble position of desiring it. And he closes the meditation in directions

■ to himself about becoming worthy. Notice the self-dramatisation, in the present tense, of this Christian discipline and the evolution of the colour conceit:

> Oh make thyself with holy mourning black,
> And red with blushing, as thou art with sin;
> Or wash thee in Christ's blood, which hath this might
> That being red, it dyes red souls to white.

The blackness of sin becomes that of mourning (sorrow for sin); the scarlet of evil becomes a red blush of regret; and the miracle of Christ's blood is that it changes the redness of sinful souls to a white purity. Donne also puns on 'dyes' and 'dies'. Through Christ's death, souls die to sin and are reborn to sinlessness.

Most importantly, the sonnet has progressed from 'black' to 'white', indicating that the meditation has achieved its purpose of transforming the poet's concentration on sin to contemplation of the release from it. Yet we should remember that at the heart of the sonnet is that contingency, 'if thou repent'. This is what Donne would desire, not what he has actually achieved.

BATTER MY HEART, THREE-PERSON'D GOD

This is Donne's noisiest poem. It contains a series of alliterated, onomatopoeic and violent verbs proclaiming the rigorous purgation he requires, thereby indicating the deep-seated sinfulness which demands such a purifying process. In fact, the extremity of the speaker's condition is captured in the opening phrase as he requests a battering, a rough physical motion, from the spiritual Trinity. This startling incongruity suggests the absolute separation of Donne from God even as it conveys his earnest desire to bridge it.

God is seen as the divine blacksmith who will take the misshapen metal of Donne's being and remake it in his refining fire. The idea, as so often in Donne's poetry, is paradoxical. He must be broken to become whole; that he might 'rise, and stand', God must 'o'erthrow' him.

Typically, Donne conflates religious and secular emotion in the poem's second analogy:

> I, like an usurped town, to another due,
> Labour to admit you, but oh, to no end.

He has been conquered by sin and animates his effort to resist the usurper in the forceful verb 'labour' and the cry of desolation, 'oh, to no end'. As an Anglican, Donne believed that reason, with grace, should assist the believer's progress to truth. But his mind has the habit of thwarting, rather than aiding his faith – as personification extends the conquest simile:

> Reason your viceroy in me, me should defend,
> But is captived, and proves weak or untrue.

There is the expected disjunction at the beginning of the sestet as a more positive demeanour is warmly evoked:

> Yet dearly I love you, and would be loved fain...

But again we notice that his status before God is contingent. And even more striking, in this sonnet, is his quick return to the original plea for a decisive separation from sin, culminating in the most extreme petition in all of Donne's religious poetry:

> Divorce me, untie, or break that knot again,
> Take me to you, imprison me, for I
> Except you enthral me, never shall be free,
> Nor ever chaste, except you ravish me.

In marked contrast to the assertive masculine persona of the love lyrics, the anguished penitent here calls on the Trinity to rape him. So profound is his impurity that it requires such a violent intervention by God to restore his soul. The poem closes, as it opened, in paradox, as intellectual acuteness is vivified by a clamour of powerful verbs.

Assignment

Read two or three more of Donne's Holy Sonnets, investigating the ways in which he uses the sonnet form to express his spiritual ideas and feelings. Focus closely on technical matters (such as the octave/sestet division) and the self-dramatisation of the persona.

GOOD FRIDAY, 1613. RIDING WESTWARD

This is one of the few poems by Donne which we can date with any certainty, because of its title. Interestingly, it was written two years before he took holy orders in the Church of England. This reminds us that religious concerns, in the Renaissance, preoccupied individuals as much during their secular lives as in their specifically religious vocations. The title focuses our attention on the most solemn day in the Christian calendar when the Church commemorates the crucifixion of Christ. It is typical of Donne to present himself in a situation or attitude of extremity, so we find him here, on this particular day, on horseback, riding away (westward) from God who was traditionally located in the east.

The wit of the poem is that while Donne notes that he has turned his back on God — and on this day, of all days — he meditates on what he might see if

■ he turned to Him. Further, he comes to realise that turning his back is appropriate, not for the purpose of ignoring God, but to submit to His purging 'corrections' (or punishments) which will free him from sin and enable him to look directly at God.

The poem begins in a detached, philosophical manner, like the major premise of an argument:

> Let man's soul be a sphere, and then, in this,
> The'intelligence that moves, devotion is,
> And as the other spheres, by being grown
> Subject to foreign motions, lose their own...
> Pleasure or business, so, our souls admit
> For their first mover, and are whirled by it.

As the planets ('spheres'), it was believed, were deflected from their courses by outside influences, so our souls are diverted by pleasure and business from the contemplation of God, and are made worldly by this off-course whirling (as Donne puns on 'world' and whirled'). Personalising the problem, Donne notes that his situation is an example of it:

> Hence is 't, that I am carried towards the West
> This day, when my soul's form bends towards the East.

Especially, we notice the verb 'carried' and the noun 'form'. That he is carried suggests that forces beyond the speaker's control are deflecting him. That he is riding on a horse, customarily associated, in Renaissance symbolism, with passion which needs to be bridled, is representative of his worldly self taking him from God and his religious duties. The 'form', in Plato's teaching, was the perfect expression of something. So Donne is being carried away from what his soul would incline to – the east, the dwelling-place of God.

Then Donne imagines the crucifixion itself – what he would see if he were travelling eastward rather than   westward, on Good Friday. In the typical manner of meditative poetry of this period, he looks closely at the physical aspects of the event, composing the place and situation (the *compositio loci* of the initial stages of a traditional meditation). Christ's flesh, for example, is 'ragg'd and torn'. Not worthy to look upon the dying God, he might focus on the grieving mother at the foot of the cross,

> Who was God's partner here, and furnished thus
> Half of that sacrifice which ransomed us.

So, as if in spite of itself, the poem has provided a meditation on the event by detailing what Donne does not see, because, of course, these images are in his mind even though his physical self is moving in the contrary direction:

> Though these things, as I ride, be from mine eye,
> They're present yet unto my memory.

The poem closes, as meditations traditionally do, with a prayer. Donne explains that he turns his back to the Saviour, not in ignorance, 'but to receive / Corrections, till thy mercies bid thee leave' (that is, 'until, through your mercy, you no longer need to punish me, in order to correct me, spiritually').

Donne's sense of his unworthiness is apparent: 'O think me worth thine anger', and he asks for a rigorous re-forming of his deformity (recalling that word from earlier in the poem, in the reference to the soul's 'form'):

> Burn off my rusts and my deformity;
> Restore thine image so much, by thy grace,
> That thou may'st know me, and I'll turn my face.

A poem that began in philosophical and scientific objectivity closes in personal intimacy, almost in the language of love.

Questions

1. 'In Donne's poetry, the mind and the heart, the intellect and the emotions, are intertwined.' Discuss, with reference to two or three poems.

2. 'Donne's religious poetry cannot speak to us today because most contemporary readers do not share his faith.' Is this true? Refer to two or three of the Holy Sonnets.

3. In 'Good Friday, 1613. Riding Westward', the poetry enacts what it would achieve – the speaker's union with God through meditation. Show how this happens.

IV

Of the other members of the Metaphysical tradition, George Herbert and Richard Crashaw are most worthy of note, as much for their distinctive voices as for their resemblance or indebtedness to the monarch of wit.

Herbert, whose mother Magdalen was one of Donne's courtly patrons, brings the wittiness of Metaphysical poetry to the service of Christianity, most notably in his sequence of poems *The Church*. It is a kind of anatomy of an individual's Christian pilgrimage and of Anglicanism – its liturgy, church architecture and spiritual ordinances and doctrine. The 'anatomy' is a closely detailed, systematic investigation of a phenomenon, and is another important mode of seventeenth-century writing. The most famous anatomy is on the subject of melancholy, by Burton. In anatomising his spirituality, Herbert is

not 'extreme, and scattring bright', either in argument or in imagery (unlike
Donne) – although there are notable exceptions to his reputation for temper-
ateness (as in 'The Collar' where the title plays on 'choler' or anger, one of
the four 'humours' of Renaissance medical theory). So we might wonder why
and how he is classified in the Metaphysical school and as a successor to
Donne.

Herbert is 'metaphysical' because of two elements that are strongly present
in the themes and structures of his poems: the element of argument, and the
component of sustained imagery. There is also the school's characteristic
element of self-dramatisation. The genius of Herbert's poetry is that qualities
such as these are – apparently effortlessly – incorporated into poems that exhale
simplicity. All their diverse elements are repeatedly resolved in harmonies of
faith and art. Herbert had a musical sensibility, and his collection of poems in
The Church is one of the most accomplished displays of metrical variety and facility in the language – only Tennyson (see Special Study 10) is comparable.
Musical metaphors constantly recur in his work as a sign of the progression that
he seeks from the disharmonies of sin to the perfect cadences of grace and
divine love.

Although Herbert's Christian persona is humble, he is also self-consciously a
Christian poet, in the meditative tradition, the explicitly theological component
of Metaphysical poetry. Seventeenth-century writers were interested in the
problem of bringing literary expertise and learning to a Christian subject
matter. There were the Books of Nature (the created world) and of Life (in
which those elected by God for salvation were enrolled) and there was the Book
of the Bible. What place could there be for the bookishness of Christian poetry?

In two poems, both entitled 'Jordan' (the biblical river, to be distinguished
from the two springs on Mount Helicon which were sources of pagan poetic
inspiration), Herbert confronts the problem of writing about Christian faith in
Renaissance poetry, with its classical sources and models. The first presents a
critique of the Metaphysical method:

JORDAN I

Who sayes that fictions onely and false hair
Become a verse? Is there in truth no beautie?
Is all good structure in a winding stair?
May no lines passe, except they do their dutie
            Not to a true, but painted chair?

Is it no verse, except enchanted groves
And sudden arbours shadow course-spunne lines?
Must purling streams refresh a lovers loves?
Must all be vail'd, while he that reades, divines,
            Catching the sense at two removes?

> Shepherds are honest people; let them sing:
> Riddle who list, for me, and pull for Prime: [Prime = a card game]
> I envie no mans nightingale or spring;
> Nor let them punish me with losse of rime,
>   Who plainly say, *My God, My King.*

Various fancies are enlisted: the intricacies of wit ('a winding stair'), the startling qualities similar to Donne's arresting openings and shocking allusions
('sudden arbours shadow course-spunne lines'), the obscure intellectuality
('catching the sense at two removes') and, above all, the complexity of the
Metaphysical method. These are mentioned only to be dismissed in preference
for plain speaking which is the literary sign of truth. But in its pursuit of plainness, 'Jordan (I)' is itself argumentative, with a series of propositions introduced
for refutation.

   More personally, in the second poem Herbert recalls his own Metaphysical
displays which he had brought to his Christian subject matter in his earliest
attempts to put his faith into verse:

> JORDAN II
> When first my lines of heav'nly joyes made mention,
> Such was their lustre, they did so excell,
> That I sought out quaint words, and trim invention;
> My thoughts began to burnish, sprout, and swell,
> Curling with metaphors a plain intention,
> Decking the sense, as if it were to sell.

A sense of creative frenzy in multiple witty strategies follows, including the
most common of Metaphysical puns in religious poetry, on 'sun' and 'Son':

> Thousands of notions in my brain did runne,
> Off 'ring their service, if I were not sped:
> I often blotted what I had begunne;
> This was not quick enough, and that was dead.
> Nothing could seem too rich to clothe the sunne,
> Much lesse those joyes which trample on his head.

As in other poems (most notably, 'The Collar'), where his intensifying energy of
perversity is checked by the friendly voice of wisdom, the unrestrained conceitedness of Metaphysical busy-ness must be set aside as the poet is charged to make
his writing conform with what is already manifestly written – the Word of God:

> As flames do work and winde, when they ascend,
> So did I weave my self into the sense.
> But while I bustled, I might heare a friend
> Whisper, *How wide is all this long pretence!*

> *There is in love a sweetnesse readie penn'd:*
> *Copie out onely that and save expense.*

God has the last word and, as always for Herbert, it is of love.

Two points need to be made about these two poems with their similar subjects. Firstly, the dedication to simplicity was conventional – whether in love poetry or poetry of the love of God. We have seen how Sidney declared his vulgarity and ignorance of literariness within the sophistication of his *Astrophil and Stella*. In *Paradise Lost*, a very complex work, Milton claims that his is an 'unpremeditated' poetry, inspired by God. He states that he is neither 'skilled nor studious' in traditional heroic writing, although he makes this comment after summarising its features in an accomplished synopsis.

Secondly, however, while Herbert's style is not merely plain, it is his essential genius to simplify, without ever reducing to the simplistic, the profound and humane phenomena of the complexities of doctrine and of the individual Christian's pilgrimage through worldliness to divinity. In doing this, he uses metaphors and small dramas of the spiritual life. Herbert achieves, thematically, the restraint, by truth, of mere metaphysical speculation and, aesthetically, the discipline of the metaphysical style by various kinds of plain speaking. One example is the parable (used most famously by Jesus in the New Testament), where a fictitious narrative conveys moral and spiritual teaching, as in this poem:

REDEMPTION
Having been tenant long to a rich Lord,
      Not thriving, I resolved to be bold,
      And make a suit unto him, to afford
A new small-rented lease, and cancell th'old.

In heaven at his manour I him sought:
      They told me there, that he was lately gone
      About some land, which he had dearly bought
Long since on earth, to take possession.

I straight return'd, and knowing his great birth,
      Sought him accordingly in great resorts;
      In cities, theatres, gardens, parks, and courts:
At length I heard a ragged noise and mirth

      Of theeves and murderers: there I him espied,
      Who straight, *Your suit is granted,* said, & died.

This sonnet is a parable which uses a circumstance of secular life (the re-negotiation of a lease on property) to explore an allegory of spiritual life. This is announced in the poem's title: the redemption from sin achieved by the sacrifice

of Christ on the cross. But the title also refers to the secular meaning of redemption: to buy back, as in a mercantile transaction.

The character of the poem is dramatic, from the second line where the
speaker determines to be 'bold'. He is dissatisfied with his agreement – 'not
thriving' – and wants to change the arrangement to something less grandiose.
Allegorically, there is the suggestion of acquiring humility. Not prospering in
faith, he must re-negotiate his relationship with God. This incites the speaker's
search for Him, which is misdirected – in Heaven, and among the wrong
circumstances on earth – showing that the relationship has not been an informed
one. The journey, however, is the necessary corrective of ignorance. Eventually
the landlord is found in unprepossessing company. Before the tenant had even
explained the purpose of his journey, or been given any conditions, the
land(Lord) speaks: 'Your suit is granted, said, & died'.

On the realistic level of the story of the parable, Herbert is making the point
that those who are usually the oppressors in society (such as landlords) may turn
out to be charitable. It is a surprising teaching, and is similar to those we find in
Jesus's parables, like that of the prodigal son who is gladly welcomed home by
his father in spite of his disreputable behaviour. On that level, the poem is a
moral fable. More importantly, of course, like the biblical parables themselves,
'Redemption' teaches that God, too, is a benevolent Father, near at hand, and
whose care for His children – to the extent of being prepared to die for them –
is absolute so long as they earnestly seek Him.

The poem has an autobiographical element, also: not only in its general
reflection of Herbert's faith, but in the reference to seeking God in the sumptu-
ous circumstances of 'cities, theatres, gardens, parks and courts'. Herbert knew
these urban domains well in his privileged young manhood. However, he found
God, if not precisely amongst 'theeves and murderers', in the rustic community
of Bemerton, near Salisbury, where he was the rector in the closing years of his
life.

All of these components of thought and artistry (and, no doubt, more) are
superbly compressed into this sonnet without it seeming congested. It has the
Metaphysical talent for making our minds work on several levels of argument
and allusion. Keeping the surprise of sudden death to the end is the consummation of the poem's dramatic strategy which gives impetus throughout to its
parable-like allegory.

The technique of delayed resolution is wittily applied again in another sonnet,
'Prayer':

> Prayer the Churches banquet, Angels age,
>> Gods breath in man returning to his birth,
>> The soul in paraphrase, heart in pilgrimage,
> The Christian plummet sounding heav'n and earth;

Engine against th' Almightie, sinners towre,
      Reversed thunder, Christ-side-piercing spear,
      The six-daies world transposing in an houre,
A kinde of tune, which all things heare and fear;

Softnesse, and peace, and joy, and love, and blisse,
      Exalted Manna, gladnesse of the best,
      Heaven in ordinarie, man well drest,
The milkie way, the bird of Paradise,

      Church-bels beyond the starres heard, the souls blood,
      The land of spices; something understood.

Here, the Renaissance delight in copiousness (although restrained by the discipline of the poem's form) is displayed in trying to define the subject. It is an intellectual enterprise, organised by quatrains, into different kinds of definitions. In the first, prayer is celebrated for, amongst other attributes, taking the heart on pilgrimage. In the second quatrain, prayer is still seen positively, but in more negative contexts: a prayer can be a weapon against God – a way of preventing his wrath. It is a means by which even the sinner can climb to heaven. At the heart of the poem is one of Herbert's numerous musical allusions: a prayer can restore harmony between God and man, transposing (like a key change) the six days of worldliness into the divinity of the sabbath. The most striking linguistic construction in the sonnet is the compound adjective, 'Christ-side-piercing', indicating that the prayer for redemption necessitated the crucifixion.

The many attributes of prayer means that there is no octave / sestet disjunction, apart from that between different registers of exaltation. This is at its highest in the third quatrain, only to be wittily restrained, as we expect a triumphant close of intellectual insight and are confronted instead with a failure of definition which is also the consummation of the praise of prayer. Prayer is immediately recognisable for what it is by those who use it: 'something understood'.

The poem, metaphysically, in its *discordia concors*, is an exercise of display. But it is ultimately controlled by that last phrase. Thirteen-and-a-half lines of inventive and, at times, exotic description amount to less than two words of plain speaking.

Sample question with guidelines

How does the following poem exemplify both Metaphysical qualities and the distinctive features of George Herbert's artistry?

VERTUE

Sweet day, so cool, so calm, so bright,
The bridall of the earth and skie:

The dew shall weep thy fall to night;
    For thou must die.

Sweet rose, whose hue angrie and brave
Bids the rash gazer wipe his eye:
Thy root is ever in its grave,
    And thou must die.
Sweet spring, full of sweet dayes and roses,
A box where sweets compacted lie;
My musick shows ye have your closes,
    And all must die.

Onely a sweet and vertuous soul,
Like season'd timber, never gives;
But though the whole world turn to coal,
    Then chiefly lives.

- The structure of the poem, like much Metaphysical poetry, is argumentative and concerned with definition. It is an intellectual exercise.
The poet defines 'vertue' by demonstrating what it is not. This is
a well-known strategy of argument. The complication of this
procedure is that he names several admired phenomena in nature
and, what is more, confers the qualities of sweetness upon them.
However, the refrain of the lyric, in the first three stanzas, indicates
that their sweetness, like their existence, is mutable: 'and must die'.
We also notice, in the third stanza, that sweetness has become over-
sweet through over-abundance, articulated linguistically here in
repetition.
- In contrast, when virtue enters the human soul, it gives it eternal life:
something sweeter than sweets. Herbert is distinguishing the human
creation from nature, however beautiful that may be, because of our
unique possession of this spiritual quality. He exaggerates the idea (a
Metaphysical characteristic) by arguing that at the very end of our lives
and the life of the world itself, the soul 'chiefly lives'.
- Also characteristic of Metaphysical poetry is the close attention to minutiae and the use of devices such as personification, as in this poem. There
is, moreover, the sharp distinction between the physical and transcendental worlds.
- 'Vertue' is also distinctly Herbertian. We notice, first, its lyrical order and
restraint and, in this context, the musical reference in line 11 – particularly in the self-conscious allusion to 'my musick' (that is, this very poem)
and its didactic quality. There is also the reference to rustic lore in the
simile 'like season'd timber'. For all his learning and literary culture,

Herbert enjoyed such allusions to the simplicities of rural life. It is another aspect of his plain speaking.

■ Most importantly, 'Vertue' is typically Herbertian in its concentration on a moral quality with profound spiritual implications. Virtue, for Herbert, is not merely good behaviour but implies the highest goodness of the soul which is synonymous with grace.

The poem, like so many in *The Church*, accumulates energy and intensity as it proceeds. In contrast with Donne, who often begins arrestingly, Herbert can start quietly and rise to a resonant 'close' or cadence, as anticipated in this poem by his reference to nature's 'closes' which are contrasted with eternity's endlessness. Wittily, this technique is paradoxical: rising to the eternal, with its open-endedness, at the end. Herbert's style, in its metrical finality, is nonetheless one of closure. But that is the genius of religious poetry at its best, to appear to constrain spirituality by language, while allowing it that freedom from all earthly (let alone, literary) constraints. Herbert's decisive close is also a sign of the finality of God's ordering of life, in this world and the next.

Question

'This poem is immediately recognisable as one of Herbert's.' Why might this be true? Refer in detail to matters both of theme and style.

THE PULLEY

When God at first made man,
Having a glasse of blessings standing by;
Let us (said he) poure on him all we can:
Let the worlds riches, which dispersed lie,
            Contract into a span.

So strength first made a way;
Then beautie flow'd, then wisdome, honour, pleasure:
When almost all was out, God made a stay,
Perceiving that alone of all his treasure
            Rest in the bottome lay.

            For if I should (said he)
Bestow this jewell also on my creature,
He would adore my gifts in stead of me,
And rest in Nature, not the God of Nature:
            So both should losers be.

> Yet let him keep the rest,
> But keep them with repining restlessnesse:
> Let him be rich and wearie, that at least,
> If goodnesse leade him not, yet wearinesse
> May tosse him to my breast.

V

The most peculiar manifestation of Metaphysical artistry is the poetry of Richard Crashaw. It expresses the character of the destination of his remarkable religious pilgrimage from a Puritan home, through Anglo-Catholicism at Cambridge (inconveniently, during the Civil War), to the whole-hearted embrace of the most floridly baroque manifestations of the Continental Counter-Reformation at the Italian shrine of the Virgin at Loreto, where he died.

His poetry is attuned to the ecstasies of mysticism, as expressed in the writings, for example, of one of his heroines of the spiritual life, the Spanish mystic, St Teresa of Avila. As a Metaphysical, Crashaw combines the diverse phenomena of the body and the soul. But as the only English baroque poet, these are at once discovered in their most fleshly and transcendental extremities and then precariously blended. So far from being decorous, Crashaw's is a most flamboyant artistry which is nonetheless ultimately restrained (like the baroque churches, paintings and sculptures) by doctrinal correctness. For all his aesthetic excess, Crashaw is theologically and devotionally impeccable under the authority of God and in the context of Counter-Reformation spirituality. He is a humble petitioner of the intercession of the saints – particularly female ones such as the Virgin, Mary Magdalen and St Teresa. He recounts St Teresa's autobiography in florid summary in 'The Flaming Heart', a title which summarises the combination of intense physical and spiritual experience to which he was irresistibly drawn. Crashaw's lines on Teresa's episode of being penetrated, in a vision, by the fiery sword of an angel, in his 'Hymn to Sainte Teresa' are, in both references and rhythm, evocative of divine eroticism:

> O how oft shalt thou complain
> Of a sweet and subtle PAIN.
> Of intolerable JOYES;
> Of a DEATH, in which who dyes
> Loves his death, and dyes again.
> And would for ever so be slain.
> And lives, and dyes; and knowes not why
> To live, but that he thus may never leave to DY.

As Milton was obsessed with hair, Crashaw was preoccupied with bodily fluids
– tears, milk and blood. In 'The Weeper', his poem on Mary Magdalen (the
former prostitute who became the Lord's devoted servant: a progression from
extreme physicality to impassioned spirituality which undoubtedly delighted
Crashaw), the penitent, with her weeping eyes following Christ, is portrayed in
this astonishing image:

> And now where're he strayes,
> Among the Galilean mountaines,
> Or more unwellcome wayes,
> He's follow'd by two faithfull fountaines;
> Two walking baths; two weeping motions;
> Portable, and compendious oceans.

Then, meditating on infant martyrs (children who have died for the faith),
Crashaw encourages them not to regret their departure from their mothers'
breasts (and their milk), for they are destined to be immersed in milkiness in
heavenly places:

> Goe smiling soules, your new built Cages breake,
> In heav'n you'l learne to sing ere here to speake,
> Nor let the milky fonts that bath your thirst,
>   Bee your delay;
> The place that calls you hence, is at the worst
>   Milke all the way.

And in 'On our crucified Lord, Naked and Bloody', Crashaw has a vision of
Christ after his crucifixion in which he sees him, not wrapped in linen, as the
gospels teach, but dressed in his own redeeming blood:

> Th' have left thee naked Lord, O that they had;
> This Garment too I would they had deny'd.
> Thee with thy selfe they have too richly clad,
> Opening the purple wardrobe of thy side.
> O never could bee found Garments too good
> For thee to weare, but these, of thine owne blood.

The 'purple wardrobe' is a good example of the extremity of Crashaw's
Metaphysical wit. It is at once logical (within the conceit of nakedness and dressing) and outré in its daring originality which almost reduces solemnity to a
grotesquerie, as in Samuel Butler's similar image of Eve coming 'from her closet
in [Adam's] side' in his satirical poem, Hudibras (1663). But, again, we should
note that Crashaw's poem (for all its peculiarities) is restrained within the
Christian tradition of devotion to the Crucified and the subject matter of the
Lord's Passion.

Question
Does the sensuousness of the spirituality of this poem by Crashaw aid or
obstruct his purpose of focusing the reader's attention on Christ's suffering?

ON THE WOUNDS OF OUR CRUCIFIED LORD
O these wakeful wounds of thine!
Are they mouths? or are they eyes?
Be they mouths, or be they eyne,   [eyne = eyes]
Each bleeding part some one supplies.

Lo! a mouth, whose full-bloomed lips
At too dear a rate are roses.
Lo! a bloodshot eye! that weeps
And many a cruel tear discloses.

O thou that on this foot hast laid
Many a kiss and many a tear,
Now thou shalt have all repaid,
Whatsoe'er thy charges were.

This foot hath got a mouth and lips
To pay the sweet sum of thy kisses;
To pay thy tears, an eye that weeps
Instead of tears such gems as this is.

The difference only this appears
(Nor can the change offend),
The debt is paid in ruby-tears
Which thou in pearls didst lend.

VI

Like 'Metaphysical', the term 'Cavalier', for the other important 'school' of
earlier seventeenth-century poetry, is misleading. It is a political rather than an
artistic classification, used to describe the swashbuckling royalists who
supported Charles I. As an adjective, it suggests an off-handed superciliousness
which does not characterise the finished qualities of the works of the poets who
generally are so named, such as Thomas Carew and Robert Herrick. Carew may
have been 'cavalier' in his personal behaviour, but his poetry is not, and Herrick's
apparent stylistic detachment does not conceal the occasional thematic seriousness beneath the suave surface of his poems.

The hero of the Cavaliers was Ben Jonson, whose poetry provides an interesting contrast with that of his contemporary, John Donne. Jonson could not

make up his mind about Donne's poetry, by turns admiring and criticising both its subjects and style. In his conversations with William Drummond in Scotland, Jonson remarked that Donne's 'Anniversary' (a commemoration of the deceased young girl, Elizabeth Drury) was 'profane and full of blasphemies' in its idealisation of her:

> that he told Mr Donne, if it had been written of the Virgin Mary it had been something.

With regard to Donne's Metaphysical manner of complexity, Jonson incorrectly predicted that Donne 'for not being understood, would perish'. But, conversely, he admitted that Donne was 'the first poet in the world, in some things'. However, one of these was not his management of metre: 'Donne, for not keeping of accent, deserved hanging'. Yet Jonson wrote a tribute to Donne almost free of ambiguity:

> Donne, the delight of Phoebus, and each Muse,
> Who, to thy one, all other brains refuse;
> Whose every work, of thy most early wit,
> Came forth example, and remains so, yet:
> Longer a-knowing, than most wits do live,
> And which no affection praise enough can give!
> To it, thy language, letters, arts, best life,
> Which might with half mankind maintain a strife.
> All which I meant to praise, and, yet, I would;
> But leave, because I cannot as I should.

The essential difference between the poets is related to the most important difference in English literature: between the classical and romantic temperaments. Donne's romantic extremity of attitude and rumbustious diction are the antithesis of the classical decorum of Jonson's utterance, as in this poem:

SONG: TO CELIA

> Drink to me, only, with thine eyes,
> And I will pledge with mine;
> Or leave a kiss but in the cup,
> And I'll not look for wine.
> The thirst, that from the soul doth rise,
> Doth ask a drink divine:
> But might I of Jove's nectar sup,
> I would not change for thine.
> I sent thee, late, a rosy wreath,
> Not so much honouring thee,
> As giving it a hope that there
> It could not withered be.

> But thou thereon didst only breathe,
> And sent'st it back to me:
> Since when it grows, and smells, I sweare,
> Not of itself, but thee.

This poem is a lyrical reworking of the Greek prose of Philostratus, and has been set to music in recognition of its melodiousness. That it is addressed 'to Celia', the heavenly one, indicates its idealising character.

More tellingly, Jonson brought qualities of classical restraint to poetry that is contrastingly personal and autobiographical, but which, again, draws inspiration from classical sources – as in this lamentation on the death of his son Benjamin (in Hebrew, 'child of the right hand'), who died on his birthday in 1603:

> Farewell, thou child of my right hand, and joy;
> My sin was too much hope of thee, loved boy,
> Seven years thou wert lent to me, and I thee pay,
> Exacted by thy fate, on the just day.
> O, could I lose all father, now. For why
> Will man lament the state he should envy?
> To have so soon 'scaped world's, and flesh's rage,
> And, if no other misery, yet age!
> Rest in soft peace, and, asked, say here doth lie
> Ben Jonson his best piece of poetry.
> For whose sake, henceforth, all his vows be such,
> As what he loves may never like too much.

The admirable control of the emotion of the poetry is secured by the objectifying references in its opening lines to the meaning of 'Benjamin', the biblical span of seven years and to the Day of Judgement. The heartfelt cry, 'O could I lose all father now!' is at once restrained by being framed by these allusions and by the universal reflection that immediately follows it (about the blessings of departure from this life), and made more forceful because of its exceptional quality in this poem.

Again, there is the sense of a personal presence in the petition, 'Rest in soft peace', but this is controlled by its Catholic liturgical model – *requiescat in pace*, 'rest in peace' (Jonson had converted to Catholicism in 1598) – while admitting the tenderness of 'soft' which is appropriate both to the speaker's grief and the body of a child. There is the subdued wit, too, of interpreting young Ben as the father's best work - a poem, as it were - and the perfect paradox in the resolution of his determination never again to become too attached to the things that are loved. Jonson borrowed the idea (as he borrowed so many others in his poems) from the first-century Roman poet, Martial, but the succinct expression of it is his own. John Dryden noted in 'An Essay of Dramatic Poesy' that Jonson was 'deeply conversant in the ancients, both Greek and Latin, and he borrowed boldly from them', but

> what would have been theft in other poets is only victory in him.

'On My First Son' is not merely polished, but to have achieved such finesse in the circumstances, without descending into sentimentality or – worse – allowing emotion to evaporate into literariness, is a testament to Jonson's poised artistry.

Confirming his skill in expressions of personal emotion is Jonson's similar poem, 'On My First Daughter':

> Here lies to each her parents' ruth,
> Mary, the daughter of their youth:
> Yet, all heaven's gifts, being heaven's due,
> It makes the father, less, to rue.
> At six months' end, she parted hence
> With safety of her innocence;
> Whose soul heaven's queen, (whose name she bears)
> In comfort of her mother's tears,
> Hath placed amongst her virgin train:
> Where, while that severed doth remain,
> This grave partakes the fleshly birth.
> Which cover lightly, gentle earth.

Again, the poet is indebted to Martial. This time it is for the petition at the end.

Sample question with guidelines

How successful is Jonson's combination of personal grief and the public expression of it in this lament for a child?

EPITAPH ON S. P.

Weep with me all you that read
This little story:
And know, for whom a tear you shed,
Death's self is sorry.
'Twas a child, that so did thrive
In grace, and feature,
As heaven and nature seemed to strive
Which owned the creature.
Years he numbered scarce thirteen
When Fates turned cruel,
Yet three filled zodiacs had he been

The stage's jewel;
And did act (what now we moan)
Old men so duly,
As, sooth, the Parcae thought him one,
He played so truly.
So, by error, to his fate
They all consented;
But viewing him since (alas, too late)
They have repented.
And have sought (to give new birth)
In baths to steep him;
But, being so much too good for earth,
Heaven vows to keep him.

Notes:
* Salomon Pavy was one of the Children of Queen Elizabeth's Chapel, an acting company. He had appeared in Jonson's play, *Cynthia's Revels*, but died a year later in 1602.
* The Parcae are the three Fates, one of their functions being to determine the length of lives.

■   The poem's beginning, with the imperative, onomatopoeic verb, 'Weep', strongly emphasises its qualities both as a personal lament and a work that would encourage others to participate in the lamentation, for the grief is profound in the untimely loss not only of a child, but of an exceptionally gifted one. The death of an actor, moreover, invites a certain theatricality of utterance in its commemoration. Jonson's beginning is appropriately dramatic. The poem is a performance.

■   That this is a 'little story' perpetuates the theatrical idea, but does not diminish the importance of the subject. The littleness is apt for a child and stresses the fact that this life-story was brief, sadly cut short. Even Death (usually personified as indifferent or cruel) is mourning the loss.

■   Next, Jonson explains his own grief, and why we should share it – combining personal, professional (as a playwright) and popular considerations in contemplating the boy's bodily and spiritual gifts, which made him both personally admirable and a success on the stage. Jonson's assessment of Salomon Pavy, in other words, is not only his own. Therefore, grief at the boy's death should be similarly shared.

■   With grim wit he notes that the child even played old men convincingly – too successfully, as it turned out, for the Fates thought he was what he was portraying, and took him. This quirky anecdote (which may just have behind it, tongue-in-cheek, the traditional criticisms of the theatre with regard to its mingling of fancy and fact) could be construed as inappropriate to the seriousness of the poem. But it is in the context of the literariness and theatricality of the boy's professional life, and therefore Jonson's

> association with him. The potential levity is subdued by the parenthesis '(what now we moan)' which is intensified by onomatopoeia. The Parcae, repenting of their mistake, would revive the boy in a magic bath.
>
> ■ In conclusion, Jonson disposes of these fancies. In the closing seriousness of the work he contemplates the fulfilment of the boy's goodness in heaven. Is the goodness there a reference to acting ability or to virtue more generally? Or is Jonson arguing that the very talent Salomon Pavy displayed on the stage was proof not only of artistry but of his saintly character?
>
> The poem succeeds in being both personal and public in its combination of private grief at the loss of the child and in reference to his loss from the stage. There is also the generally recognised grief at the death of one so young. The even rhythm and subdued vocabulary are also means for articulating personal grief publicly.

As in these poems in commemoration of dead children, Jonson's poems of address to living adults display his genius for discovering the appropriate register and timbre for his poetic voice. The verse-letter, 'Inviting a Friend to Supper', has a tone of moral seriousness or *gravitas* which is not over-serious because it counterbalances English hospitality (generous, but not flamboyant) and witty discrimination in the entertainment that will be provided. All of this is discovered in the context of genial friendship.

There is a note of unpretentious courtesy at the beginning as the speaker adopts the attitude of a humble petitioner for company, unworthy of 'such a guest'. There is nothing here of the over-reaching embellishment of arrogant Metaphysical wit. The catalogue of 'cates' or dishes that follows is as moderate as the 'pure cup of Canary wine' that will accompany the food and as the conversation that the speaker envisages:

> Nor shall our cups make any guilty men:
> But, at our parting, we will be, as when
> We innocently met. No simple word,
> That shall be uttered at our mirthful board,
> Shall make us sad next morning: or affright
> The liberty, that we'll enjoy tonight.

The purity of the wine is symbolic of the purity (but not puritanism) of the occasion.

Gravitas also characterises Jonson's celebration in 'To Penshurst', the country seat of the Sidney family in Kent. He begins by pointing out that the building is not 'built to envious show', but is part of the natural landscape which surrounds it and which provides it with sustenance: 'each bank doth yield thee conies [rabbits]'. The situation is, in the classical phrase, a *locus amoenus*, a location that, in this case, is doubly pleasant because it is both useful and beautiful.

As in the previous poem, 'To Penshurst' describes a focus of hospitality and generosity in human relations, but it is within the hierarchy of an ordered country estate ruled by a benevolent aristocracy:

> And though thy walls be of the country stone,
> They are reared with no man's ruin, no man's groan;
> There's none that dwell about them wish them down;
> But all come in, the farmer and the clown,
> And no one empty-handed, to salute
> Thy lord and lady, though they have no suit.   [suit = petition]

The propriety of Penshurst is guaranteed by the behaviour of the lord and the lady – 'a fortune in this age but rarely known', Jonson regretfully observes. Religious duties are not only performed but shape the lives of the place as virtue is passed on through the generations. Jonson is distinguishing the old Sidney family from the upstarts of modern times, with their 'proud, ambitious heaps'. The architectural proportions of Penshurst symbolise the decorum of its owners and both are reflected in the aesthetic order of this poem of commendation, which closes epigrammatically in another echo of Martial: 'their lords have built, but thy lord dwells'. The superficialities of the *nouveaux riches* and the cultivated inheritance of virtue are contrasted.

VII

Amongst Jonson's Cavalier successors, Robert Herrick called him 'Saint Ben' in 'His Prayer to Ben Jonson', asking for his 'aid' on his creative journey of literary pilgrimage:

> Make the way smooth for me
> When I, thy Herrick,
> Honouring thee, on my knee,
> Offer my lyric.
>
> Candles I'll give to thee
> And a new altar;
> And thou Saint Ben shalt be
> Writ in my psalter.

Yet Herrick, for all his indebtedness – expressed here with a little impertinence in the extended religious conceit – could speak memorably in his own voice, even in this poem on the well-worn theme of *carpe diem*, 'To the Virgins, to Make Much of Time':

Gather ye rosebuds while ye may,
Old time is still a-flying;
And this same flower that smiles today,
Tomorrow will be dying.

The glorious lamp of heaven, the sun,
The higher he's a-getting,
The sooner will his race be run,
And nearer he's to setting.

That age is best which is the first,
When youth and blood are warmer;
But being spent, the worse, and worst
Times still succeed the former.

Then be not coy, but use your time,
And while ye may, go marry;
For having lost but once your prime,
You may forever tarry.

The lyrical smoothness of Jonson, for which Herrick asked, is certainly there, but Herrick's voice is more intense (in the insistent 'worse, and worst') than his master's usually lyrical diction. And while the conventional subject of the poem is ever-present and it is equally conventional to speak of Herrick's happiness in his poetry – as he said of himself:

Jocund his muse was, but his life was chaste

– there are moments in his writing when a darker view emerges, literally and metaphorically:

Here we are all, by day; by night, we're hurled
By dreams, each one into a several world.

There is nothing 'cavalier' about this.

More typically, however, we note the absence of Jonson's *gravitas* from Herrick's poetry:

DELIGHT IN DISORDER
A sweet disorder in the dress
Kindles in clothes a wantonness.
A lawn about the shoulders thrown   [lawn = fine linen]
Into a fine distraction;
An erring lace, which here and there
Enthralls the crimson stomacher;
A cuff neglectful, and thereby

> Ribbons to flow confusedly;
> A winning wave, deserving note,
> In the tempestuous petticoat;
> A careless shoestring, in whose tie
> I see a wild civility:
> Do more bewitch me than when art
> Is too precise in every part.

The wit of this poem is that its description of disorder is perfectly ordered – even in the minute detail of the four syllables of 'distraction' – with a Jonsonian precision, 'in every part'.

Assignment

Compare and contrast several love poems by Donne and Jonson, with reference to 'romantic' and 'classical' elements of theme and style. You might begin with a comparison between 'The Canonization' by Donne and Jonson's 'A Celebration of Charis in Ten Lyric Pieces'.

The consummation of Renaissance and earlier seventeenth-century literature in English is the poetry of John Milton, and the culmination of his achievement is his epic, *Paradise Lost*, published in 1667. According to John Dryden, nothing less than a comparison with Homer and Virgil and the recognition of his superiority even to those masters can do justice to Milton's achievement and importance:

> Three poets, in three distant ages born,
> Greece, Italy, and England did adorn.
> The first in loftiness of thought surpassed,
> The next in majesty, in both the last:
> The force of Nature could no farther go;
> To make a third, she joined the former two.

We should conclude our study of these periods with an introduction to Milton's masterwork.

■ **SPECIAL STUDY 5**

John Milton (1608–74)

ABOUT THE AUTHOR

Milton was born in London in 1608. His father, also named John, was a scrivener (notary and conveyancer) and minor composer, who had been disinherited by his father for renouncing Roman Catholicism.

From 1615 to 1620, Milton attended St Paul's School under Alexander Gill, a classicist and one of the renowned Renaissance schoolmasters. He made friends with Charles Diodati, an Italian physician's son, who is the subject of several of Milton's poems.

Milton went up to Christ's College, Cambridge in 1625 and stayed there until 1632. In this period he wrote mainly Latin verse, but also his first great English poem, the Nativity Ode (Christmas, 1629). *L'Allegro* and *Il Penseroso* followed in 1631. Such an education would normally have led to ordination, but Milton's strain of nonconformity and his commitment to poetry prevented him from becoming a priest.

Extraordinarily, for a further six years, from 1632 to 1638, Milton spent his time at home, expanding his reading in several fields: literature, history, theology, philosophy, mathematics and music. He had decided to be a poet with a priestly function. Two major pieces were written in these years, the masque generally known as *Comus* (1634) and the pastoral elegy *Lycidas* (1637).

Milton travelled to Italy in 1638, visiting Florence, Rome and Naples, and meeting Galileo. He returned to England the next year and in 1640 planned to compose an Arthurian epic and also a dramatic work on the subject of the Fall of mankind, but these plans were set aside because of his commitment to the Revolution under Cromwell.

In 1642, Milton (aged 33) married Mary Powell (aged 17), with predictably unhappy consequences. The following year he wrote *The Doctrine and Discipline of Divorce*, arguing, radically, that mental incompatibility is a worse blight in marriage than adultery.

Another prose work, *Areopagitica*, defending freedom of thought in relation to publishing, appeared in 1644 and in the following year Milton and Mary were reconciled. In time, four children were born, three daughters surviving.

In 1649 Milton was made Secretary for Foreign Tongues in Cromwell's Council of State with the responsibility of putting the revolutionary propaganda into Latin for dissemination on the Continent. The next year he lost his sight in one eye and complete blindness followed in 1652. His wife died that same year.

Four years later, Milton married Katherine Woodcock and had a child by her in 1657. But the next year both mother and child died, as did Cromwell. In these harrowing personal circumstances, Milton began the long-delayed epic poem *Paradise Lost*, which took him seven years to write. During its composition, he also completed his theological study in prose, *De Doctrina Christiana*, and endured the restoration of the Monarchy and the Church in 1660. As a supporter of the regicides, he was under orders to be arrested and his books were burned. In 1661, Cromwell's body was exhumed and decapitated at Tyburn.

Milton was married, for the third time, in 1663, to Elizabeth Minshull. *Paradise Lost* was completed in 1665 and published in 1667. *Paradise Regained* and *Samson Agonistes* were published in 1670. Milton died in 1674 and was buried with his father at St Giles's, Cripplegate, in London.

Milton's day began at 4.30 a.m. (when he was read to from the Hebrew Bible). Then followed meditation, reading, a walk in the garden and the reception of friends and visitors. At 9 p.m. he had a glass of water and a pipe and went to bed where he wrote his poetry.

MILTON'S POETRY

Milton's poetry is influenced somewhat by the intellectuality we associate pre-eminently with Donne, and to a lesser extent with Herbert, but in at least two ways it should be differentiated from the Metaphysical school. First, there is none of the sheer playfulness of conceitedness which is such a feature of Donne's love lyrics. Certainly, Milton may toy with a concept and worry a poetic idea in the Metaphysical way, but the undertaking nearly always has an earnest point. Any witty display in Milton is part of a larger design with sober, even solemn implications.

Second, Milton's poetry, both in gesture and reference, is constantly inclining to large statements and cosmic utterances. He excelled at the sonnet – and one or two of his are justly celebrated as among the best in the language – but even here the tone is not one of intimacy but of grandeur. The differences between Milton and the Metaphysicals are most telling when his greatest work is compared with their best-known products. Milton is most himself in the midst of the awesome events and subject matter and the vast imagery of *Paradise Lost*, with its twelve books, while Donne finds his voice, most characteristically, in the little room of a meditation or a love lyric.

These contrasts in poetic styles reflect differences in temperament. Samuel Johnson, in his life of Milton, makes much of Milton's individuality and suggests that his pride and self-confidence would tolerate no restraint: he possessed a 'petulance impatient of control, and pride disdainful of superiority'. Johnson notes that Milton's ego predominated even when dealing with his family. He was not going to be subject to previous schools of liter-

■ ary thought and practice. 'He was naturally a thinker for himself', Johnson observes,

> confident of his own abilities and disdainful of help or hindrance.

Precisely because of his confidence in his unique talents, Milton was equal to the daunting task of undertaking the composition of *Paradise Lost*. It is the culmination of his career as a poet. For all the variety and accomplishment of his literary undertakings beforehand – including the Nativity Ode and the elegy *Lycidas* – we can see, in these works, the preparation for the great exercise of his learning, imagination and poetic artistry in the epic.

Milton admired Edmund Spenser, the author of the incomplete English Renaissance epic *The Faerie Queene*. He was determined both to fulfil the project of producing such a poem and, in the process, outstrip both Spenser's and the ancient poets' conception of the epic as a national work. He wanted to produce a poem that not only surveys the whole world and the condition of humanity from its creation, through the Fall to the advent of the Messiah, but one that ranges freely through Chaos, Heaven and Hell. Milton argues at the beginning of the poem that the purpose of *Paradise Lost* is to justify God's ways to men. But even though it is primarily a theological work, the poem is not only a presentation of the loss of innocence through Adam and Eve's disobedience to God and the means for redemption from our fallen condition. It is also a political poem as the 'paradise' that had been lost in Milton's lifetime was the Cromwellian Commonwealth. And the poem is deeply, often movingly, personal as Milton's regrets, such as his loss of sight, humanise the Christian doctrine. And that doctrine is essentially orthodox. Although Milton was fiercely partisan and, by the end of his life, idiosyncratic in his Protestantism, the theology of *Paradise Lost* is faithful to the central teachings of Christianity about creation, sin and salvation.

AN INTRODUCTION TO PARADISE LOST

The classical sources of the epic

The components of Milton's epic owe much to the classical epic poems. The first characteristic of classical epic – that it should concern the exploits of a hero of at least national importance, like Homer's Odysseus and Virgil's Aeneas – is more than fulfilled in *Paradise Lost*, where the protagonists have a cosmic, not merely a national significance. Furthermore, there are several heroically conceived participants in its action.

Secondly, the setting should be ample in scale. In antiquity, the Mediterranean Sea (as its name suggests) was at the centre of the known world and of sufficient amplitude for the performance of epic deeds. Milton, however, constantly striving to go beyond his classical models even as he reveals his debts to them, has the entire cosmic order for his setting.

■   Thirdly, epic deeds are expected of the hero. One of these, traditionally, was the arduous journey, such as the *Odyssey* recounts. Heroism in battle is another. In *Paradise Lost*, the conquest by the Son of God of the rebel angels in Book VI complies with this convention even as the scale of the warfare outstrips the dimensions of classical battle.

Fourthly, the gods take an active interest in the events. In *Paradise Lost*, God is the superintendent of the action and the angels – known technically as the 'machinery' of the poem – are His agents.

Milton's constant technique of drawing upon the epic conventions and then over-reaching them in scale is a sign of his conviction that whereas the classical authors were dealing with fictional tales, he is writing of the truth. Its larger significance calls forth the amplitude and universality of his epic.

The processes of the poem

In the opening lines of Book I of *Paradise Lost*, Milton refers to his 'great argument' and to asserting God's providence. But the arguments and assertions of the poem, which could be summarised in a few sentences, are not just baldly stated. Within the epic structure and through the epic conventions, Milton sets forth his thesis dramatically. For instance, at the end of most of its books there is suspenseful anticipation of the ensuing action. Book I, for example, concludes with a reference to the beginning of the great consult of the fallen angels, which is then set out in Book II.

The underpinning of the action throughout by a sense of the relentless cycle of days and nights gives a dramatic immediacy and potency to what would otherwise be the static setting-forth of a sequence of well-known events leading to an inevitable climax.

Further to the drama of the work is Milton's use of speeches. Traditionally epics abound in these, but we particularly note Milton's use of the soliloquy. We know that Satan is evil incarnate, but in the content and style of his speeches, particularly in his soliloquies, this evil is dramatised and, what is more, made to appear disturbingly human in its characteristics. Through this dramatic writing, Satan becomes more than a mere symbol of evil.

The subject of Paradise Lost

The theme of the poem is introduced in its title and set out in the opening lines:

> Of Man's first disobedience, and the fruit
> Of that forbidden tree, whose mortal taste
> Brought death into the world, and all our woe,
> With loss of Eden, till one greater Man

■   Restore us, and regain the blissful seat,
     Sing, heavenly Muse . . .

The subject of the poem is Original Sin and redemption from it. Milton's primary source is the first book of the Bible, Genesis. The Paradise which was lost was, literally, the place of innocence – Eden, which God had provided for mankind – and, metaphorically, the state of sinlessness in which Adam and Eve were originally created. The original sinful action was Eve's disobedience in eating the fruit of the Tree of the Knowledge of Good and Evil. God had commanded that neither she nor Adam should taste the apple. God had placed limits on their knowledge as the sign and guarantee of their correct relationship of submission to Him. Yet He had also given them free will, which included the possibility of disobedience to His commandments. Eve seduces Adam into similarly eating the forbidden fruit and both of them fall into sin. Accordingly, this event is known as the Fall and Milton indulges in extensive imagery of the decline from uprightness (physical and moral) to embellish this doctrine.

The title of *Paradise Lost*, as the opening lines of the poem indicate, is, in fact, inadequate to its subject matter. Milton's discussion of Original Sin includes a concern, from the very beginning of the epic, with its remedy: 'till one greater Man / Restore us'. This reference to Christ, the 'second Adam', introduces the teaching about the *felix culpa*, or 'fortunate fall', which is at the heart of Milton's purpose to 'justify the ways of God' to his readers. If Adam and Eve had not fallen, the opportunity would not have arisen for humanity to experience the saving grace of Christ's redemption.

Milton is not saying that Adam and Eve's sin is, in itself, pardonable. But what he insists upon in the poem is that, first, God created them free to choose obedience or disobedience, and, second, that God – after they chose wrongly – sent His beloved Son to redeem them. Having experienced evil – that is, alienation from God – they are more keenly appreciative of goodness than they had been even in Paradise. Much scholarly attention has been paid to the issue of whether the argument of the poem is true, or even valid. Others have claimed that what matters about *Paradise Lost* – as Lytton Strachey, for one, has argued – is not what Milton says but how he says it. Given the Christian argument of the poem, what is infinitely satisfying and endlessly surprising is the poetic resourcefulness that Milton brings to the epic subject matter.

The style of the poem

The language of *Paradise Lost* draws its inspiration from the epic nature of the undertaking and from Milton's dramatic impulse. It was an epic convention that heroic poetry ought to be ceremonial, elevated and sublime – befitting the momentous deeds and superhuman characters within it. Milton's fulfilment of this expectation has been one of the most controversial issues in literary criticism of the poem. T. S. Eliot, in a critique of the language of *Paradise Lost*, complained of Milton's artificial style and his alleged preference for the sound of words as opposed to their sense. 'I can enjoy the roll', Eliot writes of

> Cambula, seat of Cathain Can
> And Samarchand by Oxus, Temir's throne,
> To Paquin of Sinaean kings, and thence
> To Agra and Labor of great Mogul
> Down to the golden Chersonese, or where
> The Persian in Ecbatan sate, or since
> In Hispahan, or where the Russian Ksar
> On Mosco, or the Sultan in Bizance,
> Turchestan born...
>
> *Book XI, ll. 388ff.*

'and the rest of it, but I feel that this is not serious poetry, not poetry fully occupied about its business, but rather a solemn game'.

There is little sense in that passage as such, particularly when it is taken out of context. But there is both a crucial thematic purpose and an artistic logic in these lines. The appeal is to the ear – as Eliot, although critically, suggests. The exotic place names and those of their arcane rulers sound solemn and momentous, and it is appropriate that this impression is sustained throughout *Paradise Lost* as its subject is the most solemn and momentous imaginable – the divine destiny of humanity. But more importantly, this passage is thematically significant. Part of Milton's purpose is to present the collective experience of the human race, since its creation, and this catalogue (as in several others like it in the poem) assists the fulfilment of that goal.

Milton's vocabulary and syntax is substantially, but by no means exclusively, Latinate. We notice, for example, the frequent delaying of the verb in his grammatical structures (the principal verb in the opening verse-sentence, 'Sing', does not emerge until the fifth line) and the inversion of noun and adjective ('Angels numberless'). These techniques contribute to the elevated diction, giving it the dignity of style suitable to the 'great argument'.

Most striking, however, was Milton's bold innovation of the use of blank verse in a poem which celebrates the gift of free will. It was a 'charter of liberty' for him artistically, which expressed his commitment to the freedom, under God, of each individual. Although he was an admirer of Edmund Spenser, the sixteenth-century epic poet, Milton moved beyond the strict rhythmical and rhyming disciplines of the Spenserian stanza. He released himself from what he described as 'the troublesome and modern bondage of rhyming'.

■ *The opening to Book III*

We should now look at one of the most famous sections of *Paradise Lost*, the
invocation to light at the beginning of its third book:

> Hail, holy Light, offspring of Heav'n first-born,
> Or of th'Eternal coeternal beam
> May I express thee unblamed? Since God is light,
> And never but in unapproachéd light
> Dwelt from eternity, dwelt then in thee,
> Bright effluence of bright essence increate.
> Or hear'st thou rather pure ethereal stream,
> Whose fountain who shall tell? Before the sun,
> Before the heavens thou wert, and at the voice
> Of God, as with a mantle didst invest
> The rising world of waters dark and deep,
> Won from the void and formless infinite.
> Thee I revisit now with bolder wing,
> Escaped the Stygian pool, though long detained
> In that obscure sojourn, while in my flight
> Through utter and through middle darkness borne
> With other notes than to th' Orphéan lyre
> I sung of Chaos and eternal Night,
> Taught by the Heav'nly Muse to venture down
> The dark descent, and up to reascend,
> Though hard and rare. Thee I revisit safe,
> And feel thy sovran vital lamp; but thou
> Revisit'st not these eyes, that roll in vain
> To find thy piercing ray, and find no dawn.

One of the great simplicities of *Paradise Lost*, for all its complexities, is
Milton's use of the age-old metaphors of light and darkness as representative
of goodness and evil. Having spent the first two books of the epic in Hell,
Satan's dark domain, the reader now comes immediately into a strikingly
new situation, in the first phrase: 'Hail, holy Light'. Parallels and contrasts
characterise the story and technique of *Paradise Lost*, throughout its twelve
books. We have now moved to Heaven – appropriately, numerologically
speaking, in the third book, three being the number of the Holy Trinity of the
Christian Godhead (Father, Son and Spirit, contrasted later with the diabolical trinity of Satan, Sin and Death).

Milton notes that he is revisiting Light, having spent time in the 'Stygian pool'
of Hell. As such, he is calling on Light for further inspiration as he pursues his
solemn and stupendous task (stated at the beginning of the poem) of justifying
God's ways to men. So this passage is in the form of another invocation to his

■ 'Heavenly Muse'. This is not, of course, one of the Muses of classical literature, but akin to the wisdom of God. Thus we encounter another parallel in contrast.

His visit to the infernal regions of the underworld has classical as well as Biblical origins. Significantly, it is part of the presentation by the poet of himself as one undertaking heroic deeds. This personal dimension is an innovation in *Paradise Lost*. We do not find Homer, autobiographically, in his great epic poems of ancient Greece. But Milton is before us, struggling with the terrible blight of blindness, to compose his work. He becomes, thereby, one of the heroes of the poem as he records, pathetically, that his eyes, bereft of wondrous light, 'roll in vain/ To find thy piercing ray, and find no dawn'. The pathos deepens in the following lines:

> Thus with the year
> Seasons return; but not to me returns
> Day, or the sweet approach of ev'n or morn,
> Or sight of vernal bloom, or human face divine;
> But cloud instead, and ever-during dark
> Surrounds me, from the cheerful ways of men
> Cut off, and for the book of knowledge fair
> Presented with a universal blank
> Of Nature's works to me expunged and razed,
> And wisdom at one entrance quite shut out.
> So much the rather thou, celestial Light,
> Shine inward, and the mind through all her powers
> Irradiate, there plant eyes, all mist from thence
> Purge and disperse, that I may see and tell
> Of things invisible to mortal sight.

The qualities of the poetry deserve special attention here. One of the problems of reading *Paradise Lost* is that as we make our way through its vast design and thousands of lines, there is the temptation to read too quickly and not to concentrate closely on passages such as this which are, as it were, poems within the poem. We note the beautiful evocation of creation; the humane appreciation of the 'cheerful ways of men' (from one so often presented as a life-denying misanthropist), the cruel brusqueness of 'cut off' (at a line's beginning for further emphasis) – matched by the equal monosyllabic force of 'blank' (meaning 'blanc', as Milton's was, apparently, a milky blindness). And we also note, in yet another contrast, that Milton modulates to a further prayer or invocation to heavenly light in requesting that it should 'shine inward'. The Light of God is finally superior to the physical light of this world, and Milton closes the long verse-paragraph with the consolation that the negativity of his deprivation of sight may be turned to advantage – being blind to the physical world, he may see spiritual truth more keenly.

The thesis of *Paradise Lost*, at large, is a matter of deriving good out of evil – indeed, a greater good out of evil, through the sacrifice for sin of Christ which, Milton argues, is an even keener revelation of God's love for mankind than the original state of created innocence experienced by Adam and Eve in Eden. Here, we see this thesis personally expressed.

Assignment and question

Read either Book I or Book IX of *Paradise Lost*. To which matters of theme and style would you draw particular attention?

Question

Consider the following sonnet by Milton, on his blindness, written around 1652, some years before he began work on *Paradise Lost* and soon after he had become completely blind, and answer the questions which follow

> When I consider how my light is spent
> Ere half my days, in this dark world and wide,
> And that one talent which is death to hide
> Lodged with me useless, though my soul more bent
> To serve therewith my Maker, and present
> My true account, lest he returning chide;
> 'Doth God exact day-labour, light denied?'
> I fondly ask; but Patience to prevent   [fondly = foolishly]
> That murmur, soon replies, 'God doth not need
> Either man's work or his own gifts; who best
> Bear his mild yoke, they serve him best. His state
> Is kingly. Thousands at his bidding speed
> And post o'er land and ocean without rest:
> They also serve who only stand and wait'.

1. Why might the sonnet form be appropriate to this subject matter? (Think about, for example, its highly personal content and the need to discipline this.)
2. What theological points are being made in the poem? (Think about, for example, obedience to God – the representation of him as a king – and Milton's theory about the vanity of works in this world.)
3. Consider the use of enjambement in the poem. How and why is it effective?
4. What is the point of the contrast in the last verse-sentence?

The Restoration and Augustanism

THE ATTAINMENT OF LIMITED CLARITY

Richard Cromwell (Oliver's son) abdicated in 1659, after twenty years of civil strife, bringing an end to the Commonwealth. There was, inevitably, a strong national desire for the resumption of stable government in England. The restoration of the monarchy under Charles II, in 1660, was generally greeted with approval. The Church was also restored, with the re-establishment of Anglicanism in the place of the Puritans' Presbyterianism. In 1662, the Book of Common Prayer was reimposed as the national liturgy. Dissenting Protestants and Roman Catholics were effectively suppressed, both ecclesiastically and socially. Although there was a terrible plague in 1665 and the great fire in London in the following year – both interpreted as divine retribution for the debauchery of Charles II's court – the fortunes of England began to advance in this period to the extent that, within a century, she had become a world power.

While religious matters had been decisively settled, the political situation after the Restoration proved to be more volatile. Charles II held traditional views about the monarchy's superiority to parliament. Some politicians supported this concept and formed what came to be the Tory party. Others, who wanted a greater role for parliament, represented new commercial interests in the nation and a more progressive idea of the state. These were the Whigs.

The definitions of the two parties provided by Samuel Johnson in his *Dictionary of the English Language* (1755) indicate clearly his own political persuasion:

> TORY: One who adheres to the ancient constitution of the state, and the apostolical hierarchy of the Church of England, opposed to a whig.
>
> WHIG: The name of a faction.

The tension between them came to a head when Charles was succeeded by his brother, James II, who was a Catholic and who seemed to be set on establishing a Catholic succession to the English throne. The birth of his son in 1688 confirmed this fear. The people, who had wanted the restoration, now became very hostile to its regal representative.

157

The solution to the problem was found on the Continent where James's daughter, Mary, had married the prominent Dutch Protestant, William of Orange. The couple were invited to come to England and assume the throne. James moved to the religiously more congenial surroundings of France where he established his court, with the approval of Louis XIV, and perpetuated the Jacobite succession of 'pretenders' to the British crown.

In England, a constitutional monarchy was proclaimed under William and Mary, in the 'Glorious Revolution' – so different from the previous one, being peaceful and bloodless. The supremacy of parliament was ensured by the Bill of Rights of 1689 and English political life was ordered for nearly 150 years. The development of empire could proceed apace.

The succession to the throne was settled on Sophia, the Electress of Hanover, in 1701, because the heir to it, James II's daughter, Princess Anne, had no surviving children. Sophia was the granddaughter of James I and an undoubted Protestant. Anne succeeded William and Mary in 1702 and was herself, as the last Stuart monarch, succeeded by the Hanoverian kings, the three Georges. The long reign of George III takes us into the nineteenth century.

Queen Anne's sympathies, initially, were with the Whig party. However, she was a keen churchwoman, and in the last years of her reign she changed her allegiance to the party more inclined to support the established Church – the Tories. She was a patron of the arts, and writers enjoyed her largesse.

It was very different, however, under her successors. George I and George II were boorishly inartistic and preferred, moreover, to spend their time in Germany rather than in England. In this situation, the supremacy of Parliament was affirmed and abetted by the statesmanship of the Whig Prime Minister, Sir Robert Walpole. But he, like the Georges, was also a philistine. Writers could find little support in either the court or the government. They had to offer themselves to the publishers.

During the reign of George III (1760–1820), settled English life became disturbed, in spite of the growing prominence of the nation in world affairs. Increasingly, agitators demanded political reforms and sympathised with radical stirrings on the Continent which eventually produced the French Revolution in 1789. But George III was popular with his subjects, so that kind of uprising was avoided and internal troubles were subordinated to protracted warfare with France which began in 1793.

King George, unlike his predecessors, was also popular amongst writers, as James Boswell, Samuel Johnson's biographer, testifies:

> The accession of George the Third to the throne . . . opened a new
> and brighter prospect to men of literary merit, who had been
> honoured with no mark of royal favour in the preceding reign. His
> present Majesty's education in this country, as well as his taste and

beneficence, prompted him to be the patron of science and the arts; and early this year [1762] Johnson, having been represented to him as a very learned and good man, without any certain provision, his Majesty was pleased to grant him a pension of three hundred pounds a year.

I

During the Restoration, the movement towards the scientific interpretation of life which was initiated in the Renaissance gathered momentum. This was in reaction against the upheaval of the Civil War, which was perceived to be as much a religious conflict as a political one. Charles II established the Royal Society of London for the Improving of Natural Knowledge (known to this day as 'the Royal Society') in 1662, and this was a sign of the coming age.

God was not disposed of, but His intimate dealing with men and women in every aspect of their daily lives was replaced by the teachings of 'Deism'. This creed concentrated on God the Creator and, especially, on that part of His creation that could be experienced. The life of human beings in this world became the central concern of the age and, with that, convictions were nurtured about the need to live virtuous and wise social lives. James Boswell, interviewing the French philosopher Voltaire in 1764, came away with this report of the sage's Deistic theology:

> He expressed his veneration – his love – of the Supreme Being, and his entire resignation to the will of Him who is All-wise. He expressed his desire to resemble the Author of Goodness by being good himself. His sentiments go no farther. He does not inflame his mind with grand hopes of the immortality of the soul. He says it may be, but he knows nothing of it.

The obsessions with the individual's sinfulness, with judgement and punishment – and hence with the afterlife – were replaced by this more humanistic and rational religion. As good works abounded, pessimism about human nature was replaced by optimism, and the old preoccupation with Original Sin and Christ's redeeming sacrifice from it was accordingly diminished. Alexander Pope, as conservative in religion as he was in politics, ridiculed the new theology:

> Then unbelieving priests reformed the nation,
> And taught more pleasant methods of salvation.
> *An Essay on Criticism*, 1711

The newfound confidence in humanity's reasonableness and its capacity for goodness was not shared by Tory satirists such as Jonathan Swift and Pope. Swift, writing to Pope, rejected the definition of a man as *animal rationale* ('a rational animal'), preferring *animal rationis capax* ('an animal capable of reason'). The teaching that the proper study of humanity is humanity – 'no species of writing seems more worthy of cultivation than biography', wrote Samuel Johnson – implied that this was, nonetheless, a limited study, both in relation to the student's capacities and the subject.

The preoccupation with reason spawned a complementary sentimentality which begins to emerge in the middle of the eighteenth century and achieves its peak in the inspired irrationalities of Romanticism, early in the nineteenth century. Similarly, there also arose a resurgent spirituality in reaction to the dominant empirical, scientific and humanistic thought and morality of the Age of Reason. This movement was led by the two Wesley brothers, John and Charles, and was known as Methodism. It was notable for its enthusiasm, but, as its name suggests, there was a method in its emotionalism. Enthusiasm, however, was profoundly distrusted in the eighteenth century. It was defined by Dr Johnson in his *Dictionary* as 'a vain belief of private revelation; a vain confidence of divine favour or communication' and he gives Locke's judgement of it as an authority:

> Enthusiasm is founded neither on reason nor divine revelation, but rises from the conceits of a warmed or overweening brain.

And it was not until the nineteenth century that the Evangelical revival (of which Methodism was the first stage) and the following, counterbalancing Catholic ('Oxford') movement in the Anglican Church made a momentous impact, in combination with Romanticism, on national life and thought and literature.

In the eighteenth century, the dominant concern of English life and literature was what could be clearly seen and demonstrated to be true, while the limitations of that clarity were recognised – 'our business here is not to know all things, but those which concern our conduct', wrote John Locke. A principal text for this conviction is found in Pope's *An Essay on Criticism*:

> Be sure yourself and your own reach to know,
> How far your genius, taste, and learning go;
> Launch not beyond your depth, but be discreet,
> And mark that point where sense and dullness meet.
> Nature to all things fixed the limits fit,
> And wisely curbed proud man's pretending wit.

II

To describe the literature of this century-long period, we use, first, the term 'Restoration' (for the years immediately after 1660) – particularly in relation to the revival of drama, with the reopening of the theatres – and then 'Augustanism' or 'neo-classicism' for the later seventeenth century and the earlier portion of the eighteenth century, especially for poetry. 'Restoration literature' simply indicates the brief historical period to which it belongs. The idea of a new Augustan or neo-classical age, however, evokes the broad conception of itself which the period's political theorists, moralists and writers entertained – of its relationship to Augustan Rome and Periclean Athens. Rome under Augustus or Athens under Pericles were seen to be ideal societies in which political and moral conduct was exemplary and which, moreover, nurtured the creativity of talented citizens. Virgil, Horace and Ovid, for example, were the principal Augustan poets.

In England, neo-classicism or Augustanism drew its inspiration from continental Europe. But whereas in the Renaissance, Italy was the focus of artistic activity, neo-classicism thrived in France under Louis XIV. In eighteenth-century England, French literature and culture in general became the measure of excellence and good taste. Even so, England once again touched the imported European influences with its own distinctive characteristics and preserved a healthy contempt for French ways. 'Critic-learning flourished most in France', Pope observes, 'The rules a nation, born to serve, obeys'. The rigorous imitation by the French dramatists, for example, of the supposed classical 'unities' of time, place and action was subjected to unanswerable ridicule by Samuel Johnson in his 'Preface to Shakespeare'. Johnson did not enjoy the prospect of Englishmen in general being reduced 'to babble a dialect of France'. In contemplating finishing his dictionary by himself in three years, Johnson remarked on the fact that the *Dictionary* of the French Academy had taken forty scholars forty years to complete,

> forty times forty is sixteen hundred. As three to sixteen hundred, so is the proportion of an Englishman to a Frenchman.

There was a preference for clarity of argument and elegance of statement both in the thought of the time and in poetic theory and practice. These were the signs of reason and common sense, of political order and stability, of decorous behaviour. Classicism encouraged the concentration on general truths which could be derived from the universal experience of 'Nature', that central conception of eighteenth-century thought and art. No less than eleven definitions of it are given in Johnson's *Dictionary*, the most general being the fifth and tenth:

> The regular course of things.

> Sentiments or images adapted to nature, or conformable to truth and reality.

The Metaphysical interest in individual peculiarities, transcendental speculation and the appropriation of a 'conceited' style in which to express these intimations was firmly renounced. In *Mac Flecknoe* (1682), Dryden ridicules the Metaphysicals for dwelling in 'acrostic land' and directly criticises Herbert's poems, a few of which were shaped like the objects they described:

> There thou may'st wings display and altars raise,
> And torture one poor word ten thousand ways.

He had made the same point in *An Essay of Dramatic Poesy* (1668) where he treated of kinds of bad poetry.

Pope, in *An Essay on Criticism* similarly observed:

> In wit, as nature, what affects our hearts
> Is not the exactness of peculiar parts:
> 'Tis not a lip, or eye, we beauty call,
> But the joint force and full result of all . . .
>
> No single parts unequally surprise,
> All comes united to the admiring eyes:
> No monstrous height, or breadth, or length appear;
> The whole at once is bold and regular.

Dr Johnson repeatedly argues that the general condition of humanity ought to be the concern of writers:

> We are all prompted by the same motives, all deceived by the same fallacies, all animated by hope, obstructed by danger, entangled by desire, and seduced by pleasure.   (*Rambler*, 60)

Yet the poetic style of the eighteenth century – most famously, in the use of the rhyming couplet – is remarkably artificial, even though it reflects Nature. This apparent contradiction is the result of the Augustan fidelity to classical formality of statement (considered appropriate to represent universality) which repudiated the eccentricities and intricacies of earlier seventeenth-century wit. It developed the refined classicism of writers like Ben Jonson.

The great poets of the new age, Dryden and his successor, Pope, did not attempt the heroic scope of the epic which had been the apex of classical poetic composition. Dryden translated Virgil (1697), and between 1715 and 1726 Pope translated Homer. But the genius of their poetry is in its proximity to the moral issues of their times – most notably, in the form of satire (including the 'mock-epic', where the conventions of epic poetry are amusingly and scathingly applied to the more accessible matters of contemporary social concern).

Like the epic, lyrical poetry – essentially expressive of individual experience – underwent an eclipse in the milieu of earlier eighteenth-century life and letters. But in the rise of sentimentality and spirituality in mid-century, its voice re-emerged as a prelude to its superb recovery in Romanticism. A poem such as Thomas Gray's famous elegy in a country churchyard (1751) – celebrating melancholy solitude – presents a startling repudiation of the urban, sociable age of reason in which it was written:

> The curfew tolls the knell of parting day,
> The lowing herd wind slowly o'er the lea,
> The plowman homeward plods his weary way,
> And leaves the world to darkness and to me.

It is, in contrast, the impersonal poetic voice which strikes us in Dryden's poetry nearly a century before. In these stanzas from 'Annus Mirabilis' (the 'year of wonders', 1666, of the plague and fire), the poet is the chronicler of his times:

> Yet London, empress of the northern clime,
> By an high fate thou greatly didst expire;
> Great as the world's, which at the death of time
> Must fall, and rise a nobler frame by fire.
>
> As when some dire usurper Heaven provides,
> To scourge his country with a lawless sway:
> His birth, perhaps, some petty village hides,
> And sets his cradle out of fortune's way:
>
> Till fully ripe his swelling fate breaks out,
> And hurries him to mighty mischiefs on:
> His Prince, surprised at first, no ill could doubt,   [doubt = fear]
> And wants the power to meet it when 'tis known:
>
> Such was the rise of this prodigious fire,
> Which in mean buildings first obscurely bred,
> From thence did soon to open streets aspire,
> And straight to palaces and temples spread.

Unlike Gray's, this is impersonal, public poetry. The use of personification (here, of London) and of antithesis (for example, in 'Must fall, and rise ...') – both favourite devices of Augustan poets – adds a further externalising formality to a poetry that is already strictly disciplined in rhythm and rhyme. Dryden was striving to imitate the Virgilian 'heroic' stanza.

The poet's political persuasion is, however, implicitly present in the moral dimension of the work. In this example it is in the reference to purgation by fire (which is another of Dryden's classical allusions: to Ovid's *Metamorphoses*, where the purging of the world by that element is predicted). And the device of the extended simile or exemplum – familiar in epic poetry ('Annus Mirabilis' was published in the same year as *Paradise Lost*) – objectifies the didacticism even as it intensifies it. The comparison seems to be for poetic embellishment, yet it is an indirect indictment of Oliver Cromwell. The ambiguity of the stanzas, however, is that Dryden is arguing that, in a sense, the revolution was beneficial and Heaven-ordained. Just as a fire brings about rebuilding, so, out of the Civil War, London (and England) might emerge as 'a nobler frame'. That Cromwell is not named also assists the tendency to universalise in a poetry inspired by specific events at a particular time. Even the facts of the fourth stanza are not precise in detail as 'palaces and temples' are referred to, but not specified.

This generalising vein is also very evident in the opening lines of Dryden's two great satirical poems, *Absalom and Achitophel* and *Mac Flecknoe*. Faced with the difficulty of defending King Charles II, whose licentious court was notorious, Dryden – in the brilliant allegory in *Absalom* by which he compares that court to figures from the Old Testament – casts the king in the role of King David. That king is described in the Bible as 'a man after [God's] own heart', but, like Charles, he had numerous lovers:

> In pious times, ere priestcraft did begin,
> Before polygamy was made a sin;
> When man on many multiplied his kind,
> Ere one to one was cursedly confined;   [Ere = before]
> When nature prompted and no law denied
> Promiscuous use of concubine and bride;
> Then Israel's monarch after Heaven's own heart,   [Israel = England]
> His vigorous warmth did variously impart
> To wives and slaves . . .

Dryden was the principal initiator of this age of satirical poetry, and the numerous linguistic effects here provide the model. The opening phrase is (or appears to be) the introduction to an edifying narrative that was announced in the biblical title of the poem. Even the second phrase seems to be straightforward, for who can approve of 'priestcraft'? But the second line of the couplet introduces bathos, where the serious first line is undercut in retrospect, as polygamy is equated (through alliteration) with piety. It is a good joke, but it is not only whimsical; satire rarely is. Dryden is confronting the critics of Charles II and reminding them that there are biblical precedents for his behaviour, but at the same time he is criticising that behaviour.

Antitheses of alliteration give the poetry its impetus: there is the profusion of alliteration on 'm', 'man on many multiplied his kind' which symbolises that multiplication, while in the next line, in contrast, there is the indictment (assisted by alliteration on 'c') of being 'cursedly confined' to one partner in marriage. The alliteration of piety and polygamy is consummated with promiscuity in the sixth line, while the enjambement of lines 8 and 9 helps impart the 'vigorous warmth' by impelling the poetry beyond its line's length.

The most masterful passages in this masterly work are the portraits of the various figures involved in the controversy over the succession to the throne and the so-called Popish Plot. We can enjoy Dryden's portraiture even without detailed knowledge of the complex situation which inspired the poem. That of Zimri – who, in the allegory, represents George Villiers, duke of Buckingham –

can be read as representative not only of the historical individual and his political allegiance, but of a type of human being. Dryden himself said that 'the character of Zimri, in my *Absalom* is, in my opinion, worth the whole poem':

> A man so various, that he seemed to be
> Not one, but all mankind's epitome:
> Stiff in opinions, always in the wrong;
> Was everything by starts, and nothing long;
> But, in the course of one revolving moon,
> Was chymist, fiddler, statesman, and buffoon:
> Then all for women, painting, rhyming, drinking,
> Besides ten thousand freaks that died in thinking.
> Blest madman, who could every hour employ,
> With something new to wish, or to enjoy!

Again, but more starkly now, we notice the use of bathos in the second quoted couplet. In the first, it appears that Dryden is complimenting Buckingham as a Renaissance man. But the second shows that his variety is the sum of all mankind's stupidities. The catalogue, another favourite device of satirists in poetry and prose (Jonathan Swift makes skilful use of it in *Gulliver's Travels*, for example), is applied in this case to indicate the instability of Buckingham's character. For all the fun he has, Dryden is making a moral point. Such instability violates the cherished Augustan qualities of reason and common sense. It is the expression of fitful passions. The criticism is more telling for being conveyed through the ordered arrangement of Dryden's poetry. Buckingham's character is assassinated as much by the poet's style as by the substance of his ridicule.

Like all good satire, *Absalom and Achitophel* uses comic effects for serious purposes. Essentially, Dryden wants to persuade his reader to appreciate the value of order in the state. This is guaranteed by being faithful to traditional forms of government which have been tested and proved by time. The poem is a conservative manifesto which contains passages of political and social theory, the relevance of which is certainly not confined to the age in which it was written:

> What prudent men a settled throne would shake?
> For whatsoe'er their sufferings were before,
> That change they covet makes them suffer more.
> All other errors but disturb a state,
> But innovation is the blow of fate.
> If ancient fabrics nod, and threat to fall,
> To patch the flaws, and buttress up the wall,
> Thus far is duty: but here fix the mark;
> For all beyond it is to touch our ark.

> To change foundations, cast the frame anew,
> Is work for rebels, who base ends pursue,
> At once divine and human laws control,
> And mend the parts by ruin of the whole.
> The tampering world is subject to this curse,
> To physic their disease into a worse.

We notice, in particular, how the qualities of the poetic language bring this thesis to life. Theoretical ideas are given material expression. Kingship is 'a settled throne'; 'innovation' is like a 'blow'; conventions of government are compared to 'ancient fabrics' of buildings, which may 'nod' and need repair, but should not be demolished. At the heart of national life is, as it were, a sacred object, 'our ark', like the revered Ark of the Covenant of the Israelites, the chosen people of God. And the section closes with a reference to 'physic' or medicine in the familiar comparison of the body politic (an abstract idea) to the human body (a physical entity).

Mac Flecknoe similarly begins with a general comment. Its opening couplet is universal in reference and serious in tone:

> All human things are subject to decay,
> And when fate summons, monarchs must obey.

But, as it is a satirical poem, the bathos follows:

> This Flecknoe found, who, like Augustus...

Flecknoe was derided as a very poor Irish poet, so to include him in the context of the general truths of the opening couplet is incongruous enough, but Dryden goes further by comparing him to no less a figure than Augustus.

Once again, the matter of succession – this time, in literature rather than at court – has stirred Dryden. Mac Flecknoe is the son of Flecknoe – that is, his successor in poetic fame. Dryden has the playwright Thomas Shadwell in mind and it is important not only for our reading of this poem but for our interpretation of satire in general to note that Dryden and Shadwell had been on good terms. That is, satire should not always be read as seriously as its indictments appear to indicate and the focus on particular individuals does not always prove personal malice. In 'Verses on the Death of Dr. Swift', written by Swift himself, that accomplished satirist hoped that history's judgement of him and his works would be of this kind:

> Yet malice never was his aim;
> He lashed the vice, but spared the name;
> No individual could resent,
> Where thousands equally were meant.

But this is too good to be true – perhaps Swift is satirising those who want to be remembered for being more virtuous than they were. Nonetheless, it is possible to be over-serious about the genre and both its victims and victimisers, as we shall suggest in the reading of *The Rape of the Lock* in the following special study of Alexander Pope. Referring to his portrayal of Buckingham as Zimri in *Absalom and Achitophel*, Dryden remarked that 'it is not bloody, but it is ridiculous enough; and he for whom it was intended, was too witty to resent it as an injury'.

What is of most interest about satire, to the student of poetry, is how the particular style of poetic language, introduced by Dryden and perfected by Pope, is peculiarly appropriate for entertaining as well as instructing the reader. It investigates the weighty matters of politics and morality within the context of the Augustan understanding of them, and yet does so with elegant expressions and sharp wit without making those concerns trivial.

III

The Augustan style, in its satirical mode, is exemplified with admirable finesse in the poetry of Samuel Butler.

In his satire, *Hudibras* (1663), Butler denounces the recently ejected Puritans of whom Sir Hudibras (deriving, in literary terms, from a knightly figure in Spenser) is the embodiment. Butler thereby parodies both the seriousness of the Spenserian epic and of the Puritan cause, exposing its folly. The arrangement of the poem into cantos, with a preceding verse summary of the 'argument', immediately recalls *The Faerie Queene*, while the setting is specifically that of the Civil War:

> When civil fury first grew high,
> And men fell out, they knew not why;
> When hard words, jealousies, and fears
> Set folks together by the ears
> And made them fight, like mad or drunk
> For Dame Religion as for punk...   [punk = prostitute]

In the manner of satire, seriousness is represented comically. The political and theological disputes of the Revolution are dismissively assessed as incomprehensible – 'they knew not why' – and the grim details of the conflict are reduced to 'folks' being 'set ... together by the ears'. The war was engaged in by madmen and drunks who disputed as fiercely over their religious allegiances as they would over a whore. Religion appears, in debased personification, as a ridiculous figure from burlesque, 'Dame Religion', and is further debased by association with a 'punk' or prostitute. The use of slang gives the edge to the bathos and such sexual or other obscene references are a familiar component of satire for the purpose of debasement. Scatological allusions – to urination and defecation –

are also effective for the writer who would expose the bestial aspect of human life and thereby deflate humanity's pretensions. Swift and Pope regularly use them.

In Butler's style, we notice how the rhymes of his couplets assist his bathetic purposes. The word 'high' indicates elevation and significance, but it is forced to rhyme with 'why', querying its eminence. Then, 'fears' are serious enough, but when rhymed with 'ears', one of the more comical body parts, their seriousness is obliterated. The coupling of 'drunk' and 'punk' emphasises (in the sounds of the words as much as their references) the anarchic debauchery of the conflict, as Butler saw it. If we trace the couplets throughout *Hudibras* we will see numerous instances of the inventive use of rhyme for the purpose of debasing the enterprise of the Revolution and its protagonists in an amusing way. Again, the sound of words is crucial to the process of trivialisation, as in this description of Hudibras:

> Great on the bench, great in the saddle,
> That could as well bind o'er as swaddle.

'Saddle' and 'swaddle' echo other words of unheroic kind, like 'waddle'.

The comedy, however, is not merely frivolous. Butler exposes the irony of warfare which is conducted in the name of Christianity – supposedly a religion of love and peace – and the peculiar awfulness of civil war, where a nation is set against itself. Hudibras personifies these evils, as in this portrayal of his belligerent religiosity:

> For his Religion, it was fit
> To match his learning and his wit;
> 'Twas Presbyterian true blue;
> For he was of that stubborn crew
> Of errant saints whom all men grant
> To be the true church militant;
> Such as do build their faith upon
> The holy text of pike and gun;
> Decide all controversies by
> Infallible artillery;
> And prove their doctrine orthodox
> By apostolic blows and knocks;
> Call fire, and sword, and desolation,
> A godly-thorough-reformation.

We see how the rhymes of the couplets in these crisp lines are crucial to the process of sarcastic ridicule: the Puritans' faith is founded 'upon' the holy text of 'pike and gun'. That they are 'orthodox' is shown by the 'knocks' or blows that they inflict. The Parliamentarians' destruction of Anglican churches and their ornaments, which they deemed a 'reformation', is judged by Butler to be a 'desolation' as the antithesis in the rhyme indicates the juxtaposition of the holy idea and the disgraceful reality.

The brevity and succinctness of both the couplet form and the phrases within it are essential to communicating the authoritative and decisive judgement which characterises Augustan satirical poetry. 'Infallible artillery' is an excellent example of this devastating ability of Butler and the other Tory satirists to indict and reject, with finality, their opponents. The phrase is doubly successful: firstly, it implies a contradiction in terms – spiritual certainty combined with (and enforced by) violent weaponry – and secondly, it very wittily borrows terminology from the arch-enemy of the Presbyterians, Roman Catholicism, to describe the Puritans' sense of their absolute and exclusive access to theological truth: 'infallible'.

Butler is most agitated, however, by the moralism and inhumanity of the Puritans. He had observed them closely when he worked as a clerk for Puritan justices of the peace during the Commonwealth, and we see them, too, in his collective caricature, which includes (as often in satire) a comparison with animals:

> A sect, whose chief devotion lies
> In odd, perverse antipathies;
> In falling out with that or this,
> And finding somewhat still amiss;
> More peevish, cross, and splenetic
> Than dog distract or monkey sick.

The particular observations and judgements, moreover, do not obscure Butler's general satire. His argument, in *Hudibras*, is against irrationality and in favour of common sense. That, for him, was the guarantee of peace and (in the Augustan way) the summit of wisdom.

■ SPECIAL STUDY 6

Alexander Pope (1688–1744)

ABOUT THE AUTHOR

Alexander Pope was born in London, to elderly parents, on 21 May 1688. A few years later the family moved to Binfield, in Windsor Forest. From about 1705, Pope began to become known in London literary society and his *Pastorals* were published in 1709.

His *Essay on Criticism* was published in 1711 and much praised, and the first version of *The Rape of the Lock* came out the following year. By this time, Pope had met Jonathan Swift. The enlarged version of *The Rape of the Lock* was

■ published in 1714 and 3000 copies were sold in four days. Pope began his translation of Homer's *Iliad* in 1715, but it received much criticism. He persisted with the project, however, and moved on to the *Odyssey*. Pope's Homeric translation took several years.

His family moved back to London, to Chiswick, in 1716.

In 1725 Pope published his edition of Shakespeare in six volumes, and Swift twice visited him, in 1726 and 1727. The mock-epic poem *The Dunciad* appeared in three books in 1728, establishing Pope as a major verse-satirist. It was not until the 1740s, just before Pope's death, that the complete *Dunciad*, with a fourth book, was finished. In the intervening years, Pope continued his literary efforts. The *Essay on Man* of 1733–4, for example, made his reputation as a philosophical poet.

Pope died on 30 May 1744.

POPE'S POETRY

Pope was excluded from a public career because he was a Roman Catholic. He had to make his living solely by literature and, in this respect, he is unique in his times. His translations of Homer's epics made him a small fortune and allowed him to live comfortably by the Thames on five acres of land.

Pope was, however, the victim both of recurring ill-health and of a stunted deformity, attributed to tuberculosis of the spine. This, combined with his Catholicism, detached him from those about him who were both successful in their careers and able-bodied. It was undoubtedly a spur to his satirical assessment of humanity.

Through his association with the Tory satirists such as Swift, Pope became a brilliant critic of the moral and cultural decadence which the Tories blamed on the Whigs, under Sir Robert Walpole. Both individuals and society at large, including the literary world, were subjected to his satirical scrutiny in poetry.

Pope's mastery of the rhyming couplet proves his genius as a stylist. And, in addition to applying it to satirical subjects, it is important to note the variety of topics to which he could adapt its rigorous discipline and the flex-ibility he could discover within the form. In *Windsor Forest*, it expresses his celebration of an idealised pastoral world; in the *Essay on Criticism*, it is used didactically; in the *Essay on Man*, philosophically, and in various verse-letters (or epistles), morally. If the rhyming couplet is most appropriate to Pope's satire, it should be noted that there is much variety within that constraint, from the light-heartedness of *The Rape of the Lock* to the grim vision of *The Dunciad*.

No other poet of the eighteenth century exhibits the mastery and variety of accomplishment we find in Pope's work. Swift celebrated his friend's achievement, in these lines of mock jealousy, in 1731:

In Pope I cannot read a line,
But with a sigh I wish it mine:
When he can in one couplet fix
More sense than I can do in six,
It gives me such a jealous fit,
I cry, 'Pox take him and his wit!'

THE RAPE OF THE LOCK

The circumstances of the composition of the poem are well documented. John Caryll, known to many Catholics of Pope's time, was concerned about an estrangement between two Catholic families: the Petres and the Fermors. Robert, Lord Petre had cut a lock of Arabella Fermor's hair, and, as she was offended, Caryll asked Pope to 'laugh them together' again in poetry. The poet produced the early, two-canto version which was published in 1712. Two years later, he published the poem again but this time it was enlarged by such additions as the card game and the sylphs and gnomes, the mock-epic 'machinery'.

The Rape of the Lock is a mock-epic poem, not because it mocks epic, but because it uses numerous epic conventions absurdly to mock social conventions and human behaviour. It is most obviously a mock epic in terms of the vast difference between its insignificant subject matter (focused on the tiny lock of hair) and the solemn importance of the usual preoccupations of epic – as in *Paradise Lost*. The wit of the poem, however, is that while it is hilarious, in its reduction of great things to small – a battle to a card-game, for instance – there are important moral teachings and reflections on human life. Byron believed that Pope was the 'great moral poet of all times'. Maynard Mack, Pope's modern biographer, observes that even in this incandescent poem,

> he can remind us of the inexorable conditions of life, death, and self-giving that not even the most glittering civilization can afford to ignore.[1]

The process by which we are reminded, however, is that of satire. Through laughing at foibles wittily exposed, we both pause to admire the artistry of the representations and to consider the more serious implications of the events and characters before us.

Title and introduction

The title refers to Lord Petre's removal of a lock of Arabella Fermor's hair. 'Rape' did not only have a sexual connotation in the eighteenth century, but more generally referred to taking or carrying off by force. Sexual violation is

---

1. *Alexander Pope: A Life* (New Haven, CT: Yale University Press, 1985), p. 257.

nonetheless implicit in the term and relates, here, to the atmosphere of eroticism which is undeniably present in the poem.

The epigraph, from the Roman poet Martial translates as 'I was unwilling, Belinda, to ravish your locks; but I rejoice to have conceded this to your prayers'.

The prose address is to 'Mrs' – that is, mistress (used generally for adult women, married or not) – Arabella Fermor, whom Pope did not know and probably had never seen. He explains details of the poem, particularly the difficult concept of the 'machinery' or supernatural agents he has introduced. The explanation is tongue-in-cheek, because while it appears to be a genuine introduction, Pope, in providing it, is in fact indicating the ignorance of the lady and her kind: 'I know how disagreeable it is to make use of hard Words before a Lady'. This becomes one of the serious subjects of his comic satire: how society women of the time occupy themselves with trivialities. This address is a satire itself of the dedication in prose and the associated conventions which it mimicks.

Canto I

In the manner of Dryden, Pope begins with a couplet of incontestable wisdom:

> What dire Offence from am'rous Causes springs,
> What Mighty Contests rise from trivial things...

which is not only a shrewd comment on life but a possible text for this poem which, while appearing trivial, as 'an heroic-comical' work, may yet reveal serious aspects of social and human experience.

The familiar bathos occurs in the third line as the generalisation is abruptly curtailed by the reference to Pope's friend: 'This Verse to Caryll, Muse! is due'. It is given in the context of an address to the muse of epic poetry, which is usually invoked at the beginning of such a work. Important as Homer and Virgil were as sources for Pope, it is Milton's epic *Paradise Lost* which is used most extensively in this parody of the literary conventions and language of that elevated genre.

The incantatory address to the muse – 'Say ... / Oh say' – presents the affectation of urgency and significance in the poet's demand for elucidation on a vital matter. But the subject of his query is the motivation of a lord to cut off Belinda's hair. Again, we note the technique of bathos as greatness and triviality are juxtaposed.

Throughout *Paradise Lost*, Milton uses imagery of the waxing and waning of the sun and of light and darkness to accompany the progress of the narrative and as a form of judgement on its components. When the sun is ascending, for example, God's purposes are in the ascendant. Darkness is Satan's

■ domain. Similarly – but ludicrously dissimilarly, given the context – Pope imitates the same narrative impulse and metaphor:

> Sol thro' white Curtains shot a tim'rous Ray,
> And op'd those Eyes that must eclipse the Day.

The second line of this couplet contains a paradox in the antithesis. So beautiful are Belinda's eyes that, once they are opened, the morning light is eclipsed. In epic, paradox is the sign of profound mystery. Here it is diminished to describe the mock-heroine's physical attractiveness, at once light-giving and blindingly light-denying.

The undercurrent of social criticism, which seldom rises to the surface of the poem but is nonetheless present as a component of it, is revealed in the conservative satirist's criticism of the moral laxity of his time:

> And sleepless Lovers, just at Twelve, awake.

Pope's restraint prevents him from dwelling on this disreputable behaviour, as lust and sloth are neatly combined in a line. It is a restraint based on his commitment in this poem to retain a light touch throughout.

Ominously, the bell rings 'thrice'. In epic, triplicity of action is portentous, but here it is merely the bell signalling the time to rise. Belinda has had a dream, another important component of epic poetry: Eve has a dream in *Paradise Lost*, in which she foresees her evil actions. Dreams contain visions and warnings, and Belinda has received hers from the sylph, Ariel. His presence introduces another vital element of epic, the participation of supernatural beings. Pope has Milton's angels specifically in mind here and, like Milton, he enjoys the lore of angels, in particular the ability of angels to

> Assume what Sexes and what Shapes they please.

This directly recalls the fallen angel Satan in *Paradise Lost*, who takes a variety of forms to insinuate himself into Eden. But again, in noting the similarity, we are made conscious of the preposterous disparity. Satan's duplicity leads to Original Sin and the downfall of the human race. The purpose of Ariel is to guard Belinda as she makes her way

> In Courtly Balls, and Midnight Masquerades.

The phrase has a Miltonic echo – of the epic poet's critique of 'wanton ball and midnight mask' – and again we discern the undercurrent of Pope's social criticism of the frivolity of society. In another memorable phrase he captures and denounces the inconstancy and puerility of amorous young women in this milieu:

> They shift the moving Toyshop of their Heart.

■ At such moments the poem transcends its frivolous occasion, and even its historical and cultural setting, to pass a comment on human nature.

Belinda, unwisely, takes no notice of the sylph's warning:

Beware of all, but most beware of Man!'

She wakes and 'all the Vision vanish'd' from her head.

The first canto closes with a passage that is one of the triumphs of Pope's artistry. In traditional epic, the arming of the hero as he prepares for battle is a standard episode. Belinda, the hero of this mock-epic piece, puts on her armour in this passage as she prepares to enter into the contests of flirtation and dalliance. The language is ceremonial and religious, as Belinda 'begins the sacred Rites of Pride' at her dressing-table. The verse-paragraph can be read in two ways: as a humorous parody or as an indictment of vanity. Enjoying the catalogue, as Augustan satirists do, Pope notes that on her table, Belinda has

Puffs, Powders, Patches, Bibles, Billet-doux.

It seems a random observation, but it is highly organised. The alliteration on 'p' binds those first three collections of objects together, equating them. However, the next alliteration startlingly binds bibles and love-letters together. Further to Pope's brilliance here is to have 'Bibles' in plural. Belinda collects copies of the holy book, we can imagine, for its various bindings. Perhaps she is concerned with the outward appearance of things, including – most importantly – herself, or perhaps the number of bibles helps (so she imagines) to affirm her non-existent piety.

Appropriating the solemnity of the epic voice, Pope announces:

Now awful Beauty puts on all its Arms

and the canto closes, like the books of *Paradise Lost*, suspensefully. With the heroine armed, we are now impelled to read on to learn of her fate in the crucial activity of an epic tale, the battle.

Canto II

Belinda goes forth to conquest, in all her finery. Pope notes that she wears a cross, for adornment rather than as the expression of spiritual commitment. For this reason, it is an object

Which Jews might kiss – and Infidels adore'.

Again, as with the 'Bibles' in Canto I, we can see the seriousness beneath the jesting, but once more Pope does not labour the point. Merriment is quickly resumed:

Her lively Looks a sprightly Mind disclose,
Quick as her Eyes . . .

■ Three-quarters of the couplet is complimentary, but then comes the bathos:

> …and as unfix'd as those.

The device of antithesis, which is crucial to giving the couplet its air of finality, is demonstrated in several lines in this passage:

> Favours to none, to all she Smiles extends,
> Oft she rejects, but never once offends.

Pope closes the verse-paragraph with a linguistically bathetic gesture:

> If to her share some female Errors fall,
> Look on her Face, and you'll forget 'em all.

Argumentatively, this is precisely poised between condemnation and praise. There is something to be said for bewitching beauty even if it is the deceptive facade of vacuity or folly.

The subject of the conflict, the lock, is then described in exquisite detail by this visual poet, who was a painter as well as a writer. The Baron will assault Belinda for her lock, and with the triplicity associated in epic with momentous action, Pope notes:

> He saw, he wish'd, and to the Prize aspir'd.

Belinda's guardian angel is justifiably apprehensive and calls his angel-hosts to her defence. There follows his address to these diaphanous warriors in parody of Satan's speech to the fallen angels in Hell in *Paradise Lost*. The speech begins with a mock-epic catalogue:

> Ye Sylphs and Sylphids, to your Chief give Ear,
> Fays, Fairies, Genii, Elves, and Daemons hear!

He charges them to defend women's honour, in particular Belinda's. The battle speech has a series of splendid antitheses which present a society of moral anarchy where the loss of chastity ('Diana's Law') is only as serious as the cracking of a China Jar:

> Or stain her Honour, or her new Brocade,
> Forget her Pray'rs, or miss a Masquerade,
> Or lose her Heart, or Necklace, at a Ball…

Ariel himself will guard the lock and the canto closes with the suspense heightened further:

> With beating Hearts the dire Event they wait,
> Anxious, and trembling for the Birth of Fate.

■ *Canto III*

The dreadful assault occurs in the middle of the poem. The setting, at
Hampton Court, is specified in contemporary terms in the opening lines of
this canto, with its wry indictment of Britain's statesmen who

> oft the Fall foredoom
> Of foreign tyrants, and of Nymphs at home.

Queen Anne, ambiguously regarded by the Tory satirists, does not escape
Pope's wicked wit. At the palace, the great ruler

> Does sometimes Counsel take – and sometimes Tea.

The caesura prepares us for the bathos.

In a famous caricature of the *beau monde*, the social world of the 'beautiful
people', Pope exposes their superficiality with sarcastic venom:

> In various Talk th'instructive hours they past,
> Who gave the Ball, or paid the Visit last:
> One speaks the glory of the British Queen,
> And one describes a charming Indian Screen.

The paragraph closes with a gesture of superb dismissiveness:

> Snuff, or the Fan, supply each Pause of Chat,
> With singing, laughing, ogling, and all that.

At this point in the poem, Pope's satire is most obviously directed at serious
social criticism, particularly in this indictment of eighteenth-century justice:

> The hungry judges soon the Sentence sign,
> And Wretches hang that jury-men may Dine.

Nonetheless, the action of the poem remains his principal concern. Like the
narrative in *Paradise Lost*, it is impelled by the process of the day, now declining into night, the signal that dastardly deeds are imminent.

Pope adapts the epic conventions of the macrocosm to the microcosm of
his situation here by comparing a battle to a card-game at which Belinda
appears to be triumphant. Hers is like the voice of God at the creation of
light:

> The skilful Nymph reviews her Force with Care;
> Let Spades be Trumps! she said, and Trumps they were.

The Baron's forces, however, are formidable, and on the 'Velvet Plain' of the
card-table/battlefield,

> Throngs promiscuous strow the level Green.

The inversion of adjective and noun is Miltonic (as is the latinate 'promiscuous') and, so too, is the exemplum which follows:

> Thus when dispers'd a routed Army runs
> Of Asia's Troops, and Africk's Sable Sons.

Pope's contemporaries, knowing Milton intimately, would have been as stunned as they were delighted by these bold misappropriations of his manner.

The Baron seizes his opportunity and in a paradoxically mysterious and portentous action, takes the scissors and cuts off the lock:

> The Peer now spreads the glitt'ring Forfex wide
> T'inclose the Lock; now joins it, to divide.

At this point, we remember the opening of the poem where it was contended that from trivial events momentous consequences may flow. We may similarly remember that at the heart of the action of *Paradise Lost* is the simple action of apple-eating. And as in that epic, where nature groans at the violation of God's decree, so here there are immediate cosmic consequences:

> Then flash'd the living Lightning from her Eyes,
> And screams of Horror rend th'affrighted Skies.

Canto IV

Pope can elicit great variety from the discipline of the rhyming couplet. It can be seen here in the incantatory negatives of the opening verse-paragraph of this canto. As always in good poetry, the stylistic device accompanies a thematic purpose. The negativity is appropriate to the melancholy that Belinda experiences after the 'rape' of her lock by the Baron.

In place of Ariel, his antithesis Umbriel exercises supernatural power over the heroine. He is the spirit of darkness, as the poem has now entered night, and he journeys to the underworld, in fulfilment of another common feature of the epic, returning to cure Belinda of the melancholy 'Vapours' of spleen. This produces 'more than mortal Ire' in Belinda. She demands satisfaction and, in a miniature caricature, Pope presents the eighteenth-century fop whom Belinda asks to avenge her rape. It is a descriptive gem:

> (Sir Plume, of Amber Snuff-box justly vain,
> And the nice Conduct of a clouded Cane)
> With earnest Eyes, and round unthinking Face,
> He first the Snuff-box open'd, then the Case,
> And thus broke out – 'My Lord, why, what the Devil?
> Z-ds! damn the Lock! 'fore God, you must be civil!

Plague on't! 'tis past a jest – nay prithee, Pox!
Give her the hair' – he spoke, and rapp'd his Box.

Belinda now realises that she should have heeded Ariel's warnings – 'in mystic Visions, now believ'd too late!'

Canto V

In this concluding section, Pope introduces Clarissa to comment on what has happened. Her name suggests that she sees clearly and Pope, writing about her inclusion, noted that her speech would

open more clearly the MORAL of the poem, in a parody of the speech of Sarpedon to Glaucus in Homer.

The speech is crucial to our assessment of the tone and purpose of *The Rape of the Lock*. Clarissa's teaching is certainly true to the spirit of Augustanism:

How vain are all these Glories, all our Pains,
Unless good Sense preserve what beauty gains.

But it is indecorous in the circumstances because it is moralistic (bearing the same relation to morality as religiosity bears to religion). As well as being a parody of Homer, it is a parody of itself. Pope's note, with 'MORAL' capitalised, laughs at its inclusion, and when Clarissa finishes, her speech is met with the same response as Satan's 'victory' speech in Hell after he has arranged the Fall of Adam and Eve:

So spoke the Dame, but no Applause ensu'd.

Belinda and her supporters begin to wreak vengeance on the Baron and his, as we hear the motion of the elaborate women's fashions of the early eighteenth century in some phrases of vivid onomatopoeia:

Fans clap, Silks russle, and tough Whalebones crack.

In a hilarious exemplum, Pope compares their angry engagement with the Gods' warfare in Homer: 'all Olympus rings with loud Alarms'. Instead of gunpowder, she assaults her oppressor with snuff, which has never been better described than as 'the pungent Grains of titillating Dust'. She will stab him with her hairpin.

In sympathy with Belinda's victory, the cries go up:

Restore the Lock! the vaulted Roofs rebound

and in a comparison at once ludicrous (in the conflation of tragedy with comedy) and apt (for it is another instance of how trivial objects – in this case a handkerchief, in another an apple – can cause mighty suffering), Belinda's appeal is compared to that of Shakespeare's tragic hero:

> Not fierce Othello in so loud a Strain
> Roar'd for the Handkerchief that caus'd his Pain.

Such allusions are Pope's way of preventing us from absolutely dismissing his story as being as frivolous as the people and the incident it describes and recounts.

However, the lock once lost, like virginity, cannot be restored. Rather, it is taken by the sylphs to Heaven, to add 'new Glory to the shining Sphere'. The poem closes affirmatively in light, like *Paradise Lost*, its principal source.

Questions

1. 'It is Pope's poetic performance in the context of the subject matter of *The Rape of the Lock* which is captivating: the morality is too fitful to be engaging and the story could not be slighter.' Is this a fair assessment of the poem?

2. '*The Rape of the Lock* demonstrates the variety and flexibility of Augustan poetry, in spite or because of its rigid metrical and rhyming conventions.' Do you agree? Refer closely to two or three passages in the poem.

SPECIAL STUDY 7

Anne Finch, Countess of Winchilsea (1661–1720)

ABOUT THE AUTHOR

Admired by Alexander Pope, who also encouraged her to publish her poetry, Anne Kingsmill Finch is probably the best woman poet in England before the nineteenth century. The daughter of Sir William Kingsmill, who died soon after her birth but left her well provided for, Anne lost her mother three years later and was brought up initially by her paternal grandmother, Bridget, Lady Kingsmill, who also vigorously ensured Anne's education, which after Lady Kingsmill's death was completed under the care of her uncle, William Haslewood. Anne Kingsmill grew up familiar with the classics, Greek and Roman mythology, and with the Bible – both families (Kingsmills and Haslewoods) being devout Anglicans.

They were also supporters of the Stuart royal family, so Anne went to court in 1682 as a Maid of Honour to the wife of James, Duke of York (later

■ King James II). This domain provided further intellectual stimulation for her and she also met her future husband (Heneage Finch) here. They married in 1684, beginning a successful and happy partnership.

Both Heneage and Anne refused to take the oath to the new monarchs, William and Mary, who had assumed the throne after the bloodless revolution of 1688, brought about by James II's conversion to Roman Catholicism. So, in this bitter dispute, they took the side of the 'Nonjurors' and Jacobites (supporters of James, exiled in France). This period of acute anxiety for the Finches changed the character of Anne's poetry. As she was often depressed, its colours became darker.

Exiled in the country, they yearned to return to London. This became possible after the deaths of both James and William and the accession of Queen Anne, daughter of James II in 1702.

Anne Finch had published some of her poetry, anonymously, as early as 1691. 'The Spleen', also published anonymously, appeared in 1701 to a favourable reception. However, with the changing political situation, she was able to publish a volume of 86 poems in 1713 (although initially anonymous, subsequent editions carried her name).

In 1712, the Earl of Winchilsea died and Heneage came into the earldom and Anne became Countess of Winchilsea. The title brought little happiness to the couple as there were financial and legal problems associated with it. As well, when Queen Anne died in 1714, a Whig government, hostile to the Nonjurors and Jacobites, came into power and the Finches were again under suspicion. The following year, Anne became seriously ill and the remainder of her life was a decline to her death in 1720. Her husband noted in his obituary that

> To draw her Ladyship's just Character, requires a masterly Pen like her own (She being a fine Writer, and an excellent Poet).

SELECTED POEMS

FRIENDSHIP BETWEEN EPHELIA AND ARDELIA

In this dialogue, Finch uses a name, 'Ardelia', which she sometimes used to refer to herself. The debate is about friendship, so we immediately note the Augustan quality of the work in the preoccupation with this moral quality and the desire to understand it more profoundly:

> *Ephelia*. What Friendship is, Ardelia show.
> *Ardelia*. 'Tis to love, as I love you.

Not content with this emotive response, Ephelia continues the inquiry:

> This account, so short (tho' kind)
> Suits not my inquiring mind.

> Therefore farther now repeat:
> What is Friendship when complete?

We see the definite emphasis on the intellectual value and meaning of the term, as we might expect in the Age of Reason. Like Pope, although a critic of her times (and, in politics and religion, definitely set against its dominant movements), Finch also reflects its deeper cultural emphases.

Ardelia, pressed into definition, provides one, with an air of completeness:

> 'Tis to share all joy and grief;
> 'Tis to lend all due relief
> From the tongue, the heart, the hand;
> 'Tis to mortgage house and land;
> For a friend be sold a slave;
> 'Tis to die upon a grave,
> If a friend therein do lie.

The problem now, in this passionate outpouring of friendship's devotion and sacrifices unto death, is that Ephelia finds it all too impassioned, incredible and conventional:

> This indeed, tho' carried high,
> This, tho' more than e'er was done
> Underneath the rolling sun,
> This has all been said before.
> Can Ardelia say no more?

Here is the nub of the problem and the insight which this slight poem gives into major issues of its time. The problem with Ardelia's definition is that, for all the high esteem in which it enshrines friendship, the experience of life shows that the idea and the reality are very different. All of this has 'been said before', but never 'done'.

The empirical temper of the Age of Reason is discerned in this riposte, as well as the tendency to depression in Anne Finch's poetry and life. To expect Ardelia to say anything more, after this, is grimly witty and we are not surprised that she can only repeat her initial declaration:

> Words indeed no more can show:
> But 'tis to love, as I love you.

Ephelia is left unsatisfied, intellectually; although, emotionally, she should be pleased. Beneath the smooth surface and balanced diction we sense a quiet desperation.

> ### Question
> Why is the dialogue form appropriate and effective in this poem?

ADAM POSED

    Could our first father, at his toilsome plow,
    Thorns in his path, and labor on his brow,
    Clothed only in a rude, unpolished skin,
    Could he a vain fantastic nymph have seen,
    In all her airs, in all her antic graces,
    Her various fashions, and more various faces;
    How had it posed that skill, which late assigned
    Just appellation to each several kind!
    A right idea of the sight to frame;
    T'have guessed from what new element she came;
    T'have hit the wav'ring form, or giv'n this thing a name.

The intellectual characteristics of Finch's poetry are again exemplified here. She adopts a querying stance, as in her inquiry about friendship in the previous poem, but this time with a satirical subtext in reference to the artificiality of social life in Restoration England. We are immediately reminded of Pope's similar satire of women in *The Rape of the Lock* (see Special Study 6). Yet the comedic element is not as obvious here. The criticism is less light-hearted, possibly because it is being made by a woman herself.

Finch takes us back to the first human being, Adam, in the Garden of Eden in the book of Genesis, and to the particular incident (*Genesis* 2:19) when he named the creatures. In other words, Finch is implying that the 'vain fantastic nymph' she has in mind is a kind of subhuman beast who, if she had appeared before Adam along with the animals, would have posed a difficulty for him in finding a name for her. This is savage enough, but we need to note that Adam himself is presented as a 'rude, unpolished' individual. This is doubly effective. First, in the style of the noble savage, he is admired for being a plain, undecorated rural man; but also, the comparison is marked between his simplicity (the original state of humanity) and what has become of the human race subsequently, as embodied by the 'nymph':

    In all her airs, in all her antic graces;
    Her various fashions, and more various faces.

The emphasis is on the unnatural character of this representation of contemporary womanhood. While everything else in creation comes (so it was believed) from the four elements – air, earth, water and fire – she is made out of a new element. Adam would have been puzzled to identify this but, further, would have found it difficult to have kept her still to study her, because of her 'wav'ring form' (suggesting both physical and moral instability) and so would have been at a loss to give 'this thing' a name. Notice the further dehumanisation in 'this thing'.

The conception is witty, in the satirical way, but we might wonder if this is a humorous exercise at all (satire is meant to laugh us into a consciousness of seriousness). Is it more savage than playful?

Question

Why – if at all – is the sex of the 'thing' significant? Think about reasons why Finch may or may not have written in the same way about men of the *beau monde*.

TO DEATH
O King of terrors, whose unbounded sway
All that have life must certainly obey;
The King, the Priest, the Prophet, all are thine,
Nor would ev'n God (in flesh) thy stroke decline.
My name is on thy roll, and sure I must
Increase thy gloomy kingdom in the dust.
My soul at this no apprehension feels,
But trembles at thy swords, thy racks, thy wheels;
Thy scorching fevers, which distract the sense,
And snatch us raving, unprepared, from hence;
At thy contagious darts, that wound the heads
Of weeping friends, who wait at dying beds.
Spare these, and let thy time be when it will;
My bus'ness is to die, and thine to kill.
Gently thy fatal scepter on me lay,
And take to thy cold arms, insensibly, thy prey.

This is an unusual poem by the standards of Augustan writing and reminds us that Finch, like the Tory satirists such as Pope and Swift, was at odds with the prevailing creeds of her time. A key word is 'sense'. The new Age of Reason was putting great value on sense. Finch notes that Death, which is inescapable, violates sense, through the sheer physical violence of its visitation. We are snatched, 'raving', from our sensible equilibrium.

From the beginning of the poem, indeed, we seem to be reading a work more from the age of Donne than from the Age of Reason. Personifying Death – to make his presence even more immediate and terrifying (as Donne

■ did in his famous sonnet 'Death, be not proud...') – Finch notes that he is a 'King of terrors' to whom even earthly kings must submit. Her references, in the fourth line, to the Incarnation and Crucifixion of Christ are also unusual in the poetry of her time which, as in contemporary society, preferred to focus on the moral rather than the theological teachings of Christianity.

Finch's much reported tendency to depression seems to be reflected in her reference to 'thy gloomy kingdom in the dust' to which she knows she will be consigned. A faithful Christian, she hastily points out that this does not make her spiritually fearful, but her soul 'trembles' at the prospect of Death's physical pains and for the grief of her mourning friends.

The poem closes – like so many meditative poems from the early seventeenth century – with a prayer. Here, it is to Death, with a request that he should be merciful to her friends and to her:

> Gently thy fatal scepter on me lay,
> And take to thy cold arms, insensibly, thy prey.

It is a chilling close, certainly, as she is reduced to a hunted creature. The prayer for the 'weeping friends' does give the poem a certain element of the social quality of the age in which Finch lived.

Question

Compare this poem with John Donne's 'Death, be not proud...' of nearly a century before. How are they similar? How are they different? (Be careful to refer to matters of language-use as well as thematic issues.)

THE SPLEEN: A PINDARIC POEM

This longer poem was the most popular of Finch's poems in her lifetime. Its subject was a malady she knew well. Deriving from the organ of that name, spleen was a combination of depression, melancholy, bad temper, hypochondria and various other nervous ailments. The subtitle refers the reader to the Greek poet Pindar, author of odes combining lyricism with elevated subject matter.

As in other poems we have considered, Finch again presents herself as an inquirer, seeking to understand the essence of her subject:

> What art thou, Spleen, which ev'ry thing dost ape?

The opening question also refers to the habit of people pretending to be afflicted by the disorders of spleen, as she later argues that individuals can blame spleen for a range of afflictions. Prior to spleen was Original Sin itself.

As was typical of the Tory satirists, Finch will not eliminate this initial, universal, disabling affliction from her account of humanity. Spleen is merely sin's 'dull attendant'.

Yet, as a victim of depression, she does not underestimate its malignant influence, as it spreads its 'gloomy terrors'. She also entertains some of the (to us) crazy remedies for spleen, such as the belief that, having been induced by sweet smells, foul odours could dispel it:

> Some offensive scent thy pow'rs appease,
> And pleasure we resign for short, and nauseous ease.

The use here, and elsewhere, in the poem of an oxymoron emphasises the prevailing idea of the particular perversity of spleen.

At the heart of the poem, having considered others, male and female, in various conditions of life who come under spleen's influence, Finch becomes personal:

> O'er me alas! thou dost too much prevail:
> I feel thy force, while I against thee rail;
> I feel my verse decay, and my cramped numbers fail.
> Through thy black jaundice I all objects see,
> As dark, and terrible as thee,
> My lines decried, and my employment thought
> An useless folly, or presumptuous fault.

While it might not be surprising that, in a poem, Finch should reflect upon spleen's bad influence on her writing, the fact that she particularises spleen's disabling effect on that activity, while referring to her general suffering from it, shows how important her poetry was to her and how she sought approval, as a woman (and perhaps also as a Nonjuror and Jacobite) who wrote poetry for publication.

The closing sixty lines of the poem return to the malady at large and its widespread pollution of humanity's physical and moral lives.

'The Spleen' shows Finch's masterly control of a subject, providing an anatomy of it, cataloguing its various features and its range of victims, including her personal experience but not allowing that to dominate, drawing us into the mores of her time and with a rare subtlety conveying (in several examples) precisely what it must be like to suffer this affliction. Here, oxymorons are used again:

> Music but soothes thee, if too sweetly sad,
> And if too light, but turns thee gaily mad.

Assignments

1. Identify the oxymorons and ambiguities Finch associates with spleen and relate these to her general presentation of the malady in this poem.
2. Compare Finch's representation of spleen with Pope's 'gloomy Cave of Spleen' and his portrayal of Umbriel in Canto IV of *The Rape of the Lock*. What similarities and differences would you note?

A Nocturnal Reverie

In this imaginative work, Finch takes us into the romantic worlds of night and dream. The opening lines, with the repetition of the phrase 'in such a night' and words such as 'mysterious' conjure a poetic spell of enchantment. The natural environment is evoked with a beautiful delicacy, 'where the sleepy cowslip sheltered grows'. The night-time world is preferable to daytime. Beauties such as the Countess of Salisbury are even more beautiful by its light, and aromas, prevented by the sun from coming forth, now sweeten the air. Buildings are more impressive and worthy of reverence by night, and animals may appear, unhindered and unafraid:

> When the loosed horse now, as his pasture leads,
> Comes slowly grazing through th' adjoining meads,
> Whose stealing pace, and lengthened shade we fear,
> Till torn-up forage in his teeth we hear:
> When nibbling sheep at large pursue their food,
> An unmolested kine rechew the cud;   [kine = cattle]
> When curlews cry beneath the village walls   [curlew = bird like a sandpiper]
> And to her straggling brood the partridge calls;
> Their shortlived jubilee the creatures keep,
> Which but endures, whilst tyrant man does sleep.

This extraordinary vision of liberated animals, freed (for a time, by night) from the tyranny of their masters has been interpreted by Germaine Greer (who judges the poem to be 'Winchilsea's most significant achievement') as a remarkable presentation of 'high-born ladies rambling amongst the animals in the fields at night' which thereby advances the notion that the women, too, are 'unmolested only when man sleeps'. Greer recognises, of course, that the 'tyrant man' from whom the animals are temporarily freed is not necessarily gender-specific, but her argument that the addition of women to this 'carnival of the animals' encourages a feminist reading of the work is certainly persuasive.[2] Equally striking, in an era well before the beginning of a cultural

---

2. *Slip-Shod Sibyls* (London: Viking, 1995), pp. 245–6.

consciousness about animal welfare, in the later nineteenth century, is this vision of animal liberation.

In its closing lines, the poem reveals a characteristic desire by Finch to celebrate freedom from the cares and concerns of daily (and daytime) life which this nocturnal reverie has afforded her:

> In such a night let me abroad remain,
> Till morning breaks, and all's confused again;
> Our cares, our toils, our clamors are renewed,
> Or pleasures, seldom reached, again pursued.

Such a desire for escape, coupled with an appreciation of the beauties of nature and the creatures, is a principal reason why Finch has often been presented as a precursor of the Romantic poets of the nineteenth century, particularly Wordsworth (who appreciated her). But her style (for example) is markedly different – in the use, for instance, of the rhyming couplet, which gives a neatness and precision to her observations markedly different from the freer-flowing discourse of the Romantics, reinforcing a sense of processes of thought (in the Augustan way), rather than the outpourings of emotion we are more likely to associate with those later poets.

Assignment

Look closely at the adjectives in this poem. How are they crucial to conveying its tone and meaning?

THE INTRODUCTION

'The Introduction' might also have been entitled an 'Apology', in the sense of a defence of women poets and of Finch herself. She begins with a recognition that the public response to her 'lines' would be bound to be negative once it was recognised that they were 'by a woman writ':

> Did I, my lines intend for public view,
> How many censures, would their faults pursue,
> Some would, because such words they do affect,
> Cry they're insipid, empty, uncorrect . . .
> Alas! a woman that attempts the pen,
> Such an intruder on the rights of men,
> Such a presumptuous creature, is esteemed,
> The fault can by no virtue be redeemed.

Composition of poetry, she continues, is deemed unwomanly: writing, reading or thinking 'would cloud our beauty'. Such endeavours would take a woman beyond her highest position in society: 'the dull manage of a servile house'.

Poetry of personal complaint is often more interesting for what it complains about and what it tells us about the person complaining than as poetry itself. This is certainly the case here, as Finch reminds us of the prejudices against women in any kind of intellectual activity and is obviously speaking from her own heartfelt experience.

The poetry itself becomes more engaging, as poetry, in the second verse-paragraph, when Finch cleverly draws upon biblical examples of women poets, in the holy virgins who completed the divine hymn accompanying the return of the Ark of the Covenant to Jerusalem, the female chorus who declared the wondrous acts of David, and Deborah, the fourth judge of Israel, author of a song of praise. It is interesting that Finch confines herself to the Old Testament and does not cite the example of the Virgin Mary as a poet and singer (in the 'Magnificat') in the New Testament. This may have been considered a too-daring, even blasphemous comparison.

Finch summarises the story of Deborah who 'triumphs with a song' and

> Then, to the peaceful, shady palm withdraws.

In imitation of such retirement, the poem closes with Finch's instruction to her Muse:

> Be cautioned then my Muse, and still retired;
> Nor be despised, aiming to be admired;
> Conscious of wants, still with contracted wing,
> To some few friends, and to thy sorrows sing;
> For groves of laurel thou wert never meant;
> Be dark enough thy shades, and be thou there content.

Yet the tone is not one of contentment but frustration, as this melancholy fate is described.

Questions
1. Why is the choice of biblical precedents effective here?
2. Do you find the personal element of the poem too intrusive?

IV

By the middle of the eighteenth century, sentiment, sensibility, enthusiasm and spirituality appear in English poetry. They counterbalance the emphasis on rationality and sense (which had in turn taken the place of what was regarded as the fanaticism which had produced the Civil War in the seventeenth century). The urban and social milieux of the lives and writings of the Tory satirists were also complemented by a new interest in the natural world and in individuality. James Thomson's very popular series of poems on *The Seasons* (collected as such in 1730) established the taste for the poetic description of nature. It focused on individual details of the landscape and its creatures in the different seasons, and on the evidence these provide of God's presence in the world. In Thomson's evocation of dawn in 'Autumn', the personification of morning represents the divine design of creation:

> The lengthened night elapsed, the morning shines
> Serene, in all her dewy beauty bright,
> Unfolding fair the last autumnal day.
> And now the morning sun dispels the fog;
> The rigid hoarfrost melts before his beam;
> And, hung on every spray, on every blade
> Of grass, the myriad dewdrops twinkle round.

It is a mistake, however, to read such passages as proto-Romantic, anticipating the nineteenth-century poetry of natural description. These lines are at least as reminiscent of Milton as they are prophetic of Wordsworth. Especially, we note the ordered quality of nature presented here, reflected in the orderly style of the poetry. The couplet has gone, but the polished rhythm and rhyme present a certain idealisation of the scene. There is detachment, too, as the speaker observes rather than participates in the location he is describing. Nonetheless, his close attention to the minute details of the scene provides an interesting contrast with Samuel Johnson's dictum that the poet 'does not number the streaks of the tulip'.

With regard to individuality, the life of the scholarly recluse Thomas Gray presents an exception to the eighteenth-century preoccupation with sociability. The Romantic attraction to solitude may be dimly anticipated in Gray's representations of his aloneness, but in the famous 'Elegy Written in a Country Churchyard', and other poems, Gray moves from his personal intimations to general truths. Gray dispenses with the satirical style to become more lyrical and less shy of the presentation of the speaker's emotions, even if these are, eventually, validated in terms of their universality.

In 'Ode on a Distant Prospect of Eton College' (1747), Gray views the college (where he had been educated) from the distance of both space and time. The epigraph in Greek forms a characteristically gloomy subtitle to the work: 'I am a man: sufficient reason for being miserable'. This introduces the melancholy tone, contrasting in its intimacy with the formal concept of an ode which is written from a position of detachment.

Yet the opening stanza is detached, highly formal – ode-like – and unquestionably Augustan in its use of personification and the idealised pastoral setting:

> Ye distant spires, ye antique towers,
> That crown the watery glade,
> Where grateful Science still adores
> Her Henry's holy shade;   [Henry = King Henry VI, founder of Eton]
> And ye, that from the stately brow
> Of Windsor's heights the expanse below
> Of grove, of lawn, of mead survey,
> Whose turf, whose shade, whose flowers among
> Wanders the hoary Thames along
> His silver-winding way.

There is a change of tone, however, in the second stanza as nostalgia for child-hood (which becomes a prominent Romantic theme) brings intimate emotion into poetry that was formerly intellectual and objective:

> Ah happy hills, ah pleasing shade,
> Ah fields beloved in vain,
> Where once my careless childhood strayed
> A stranger yet to pain!
> I feel the gales, that from ye blow,
> A momentary bliss bestow,
> As waving fresh their gladsome wing,
> My weary soul they seem to soothe,
> And, redolent of joy and youth,
> To breathe a second spring.

The speaker may be characterised as a world-weary adult, reminiscing about a childhood he has idealised, and his emotions of sadness may seem more conven-tional than real. However, there is an insistence here on the individual ('my care-less childhood', 'I feel', 'My weary soul') and on the intensity of his feelings of pain and weariness that is unusual, in its confessional character, in the Augustan context.

As if conscious of how strongly he evokes personal emotion, Gray retreats to artificiality in the third stanza – which was famously ridiculed by Dr Johnson:

> Say, Father Thames, for thou hast seen
> Full many a sprightly race
> Disporting on thy margent green
> The paths of pleasure trace,
> Who foremost now delight to cleave
> With pliant arm thy glassy wave?
> The captive linnet which enthrall?

> What idle progeny succeed
> To chase the rolling circle's speed,
> Or urge the flying ball?

Johnson commented:

> His supplication to Father Thames, to tell him who drives the hoop or
> tosses the ball, is useless and puerile. Father Thames has no better
> means of knowing than himself.

Yet even this heavy-handed personification and the arch request of Father
Thames includes an active, keenly observed series of images of youthful vitality.
The sequence of verbs is superbly animated: 'delight to cleave', 'enthrall',
'succeed / To chase' – the chase being of speed itself – and they 'urge' the ball
that is already 'flying', having, as it were, its own impetus (and not merely being
tossed, as Johnson claims).

The fourth stanza provides a psychological study as it conveys the disposition
of the kind of boy Gray had probably been: serious-minded, inhibited, apprehensive:

> While some on earnest business bent
> Their murmuring labours ply
> 'Gainst graver hours, that bring constraint
> To sweeten liberty:
> Some bold adventurers disdain
> The limits of their little reign,
> And unknown regions dare descry:
> Still as they run they look behind,
> They hear a voice in every wind,
> And snatch a fearful joy.

The concluding oxymoron brings the complex mystery of psychology into
focus.

The negative aspects of the experiences do not contradict the positive thesis
that childhood and schooldays are blessed. Gray does not deny that melancholy
will be known within that environment, but it quickly passes under the pressure
of youth's innate optimism:

> Gay hope is theirs by fancy fed,
> Less pleasing when possessed;
> The tear forgot as soon as shed,
> The sunshine of the breast:
> Theirs buxom health of rosy hue,
> Wild wit, invention ever new,
> And lively cheer of vigour born;

> The thoughtless day, the easy night,
> The spirits pure, the slumbers light,
> That fly the approach of dawn.

The second half of the poem balances this happiness with the despair which adulthood and the mature experience of life bring: 'black Misfortune's baleful train!' These are impersonal stanzas in a series of personified evils that pass before us like a medieval procession of sins, but the poet gives each evil an immediacy which speaks of personal suffering. He uses vivid adjectives to describe each blight of human existence, and fervid verbs to animate them:

> These shall the fury Passions tear,
> The vultures of the mind,
> Disdainful Anger, pallid Fear,
> And Shame that skulks behind;
> Or pining Love shall waste their youth,
> Or jealousy with rankling tooth,
> That inly gnaws the secret heart,
> And Envy wan, and faded Care,
> Grim-visaged comfortless Despair,
> And Sorrow's piercing dart.

The classical epigraph to the poem is justified in this and the final stanza. At his distance from the young Etonians, Gray would not oppress them with his knowledge of life's miseries, even as he recognises that their joyfulness is both short-lived and expressive of their ignorance of what lies before them:

> To each his sufferings: all are men,
> Condemned alike to groan;
> The tender for another's pain,
> The unfeeling for his own.
> Yet ah! why should they know their fate?
> Since sorrow never comes too late,
> And happiness too swiftly flies.
> Thought would destroy their paradise.
> No more; where ignorance is bliss,
> 'Tis folly to be wise.

The Ode is not only a philosophical poem: it is not another *Essay on Man*. It is an exploration of emotional and psychological states which is intensified and animated by the speaker's individual experience of them. This personal element is not overstated – it is barely present (only in the second stanza, explicitly). But it is undeniably there in this poetry of 'sensibility', defined by Dr Johnson as 'quickness of sensation; quickness of perception; delicacy', which marks an important movement away from that of 'sense'. It retains qualities of the Augustan style, and prepares the way for Romanticism.

Sample questions with guidelines

1. What qualities of Augustan poetry does the following elegy by Dryden display?

TO THE MEMORY OF MR OLDHAM

Farewell, too little, and too lately known,
Whom I began to think and call my own:
For sure our souls were near allied, and thine
Cast in the same poetic mould with mine.
One common note on either lyre did strike,
And knaves and fools we both abhorred alike.
To the same goal did both our studies drive;
The last set out the soonest did arrive.
Thus Nisus fell upon the slippery place,
While his young friend performed and won the race.
O early ripe! to thy abundant store
What could advancing age have added more?
It might (what nature never gives the young)
Have taught the numbers of thy native tongue.   [numbers = metre]
But satire needs not those, and wit will shine
Through the harsh cadence of a rugged line.
A noble error, and but seldom made,
When poets are by too much force betrayed.
Thy generous fruits, though gathered ere their prime,
Still showed a quickness; and maturing time
But mellows what we write to the dull sweets of rhyme.
Once more, hail and farewell; farewell, thou young,
But ah too short, Marcellus of our tongue;
Thy brows with ivy, and with laurels bound;
But fate and gloomy night encompass thee around.

Notes:
• John Oldham (1653–83) was a satirical poet.
• In Virgil, Nisus slipped when he was about to win a race.
• Marcellus, the nephew of the Roman emperor Augustus, although destined for rule, died at the age of twenty.

■ The poem is an elegy – a work of commemoration for a dead man and, in this case, for one who died young and full of promise. However, it is written with the restraint of the strict rhyming couplet form (apart from the triplet, towards the end) and with several classical references to make it objective. Even the culminating salutation, 'hail and farewell', is a direct translation of Catullus's conclusion to his elegy to his brother: 'ave atque vale'. These restraints are appropriate to the memory of one whom, as Dryden confesses at the beginning, he had come to know only recently: 'too little, and too lately known'.

■ The Augustan restraint of the poem – its reasonable grief – is assisted by the presence of a third entity, apart from the speaker and Oldham. This is poetry, the activity which drew the two men together: 'to the same goal did both our studies drive'. Dryden is referring, particularly, to sharing the same kind of poetry – satirical verse: 'knaves and fools we both abhorred alike'. This is a dominant mode of Augustan literature.

But we also notice what is absent from the poem, and that is theological consolation. It is pertinent to compare this poem with Milton's great elegy on a young scholar, 'Lycidas', with its theological and ecclesiastical concerns.

■ Although they were both satirists, this work in which Dryden commemorates Oldham and his poetry is elegiac, apart from its passing reference to 'knaves and fools' and its description of the satirical mode with its 'harsh cadence of a rugged line'. With the exception of the word 'rugged', there is nothing harsh about that description. The elegant polish of Augustan poetic diction prevails.

■ Yet it would be a mistake (as it is an error in the presentation of Augustanism in general) to neglect the warmth of emotion in appreciation of the restrained poise. In the exclamations, 'O early ripe!' and 'ah too short' there is a heartfelt recognition of the sadness of youthful talent annihilated. In the caesura, in line 22, we hear a break in the voice, emblematic of lament, and the poem closes darkly indeed in imagery that is almost 'gothic' in its doom-laden tone:

> But fate and gloomy night encompass thee around.

Again, we note the absence of transcendentalism and the limitations of clarity, as Oldham is consigned to the darkness.

■ The final impression, however, is of the simplicity of this poem. In particular, classical allusions are woven into it with ease and an air of inevitability. The wit of comparing Oldham to Marcellus seems to be Metaphysical in its extremity, until we recognise that there is a parallel in earlier comparisons of poetic craftsmanship to classical feats of valour, such as Nisus's race. The poem is a perfect specimen of the poetic treatment of a subject; this is eminently reasonable as it is a lament for a poet.

2. What qualities of the 'poetry of sensibility' are revealed in this short ode by William Collins?

ODE WRITTEN IN THE BEGINNING OF THE YEAR 1746
How sleep the brave who sink to rest
By all their country's wishes blest!
When Spring, with dewy fingers cold,
Returns to deck their hallowed mould,
She there shall dress a sweeter sod
Than Fancy's feet have ever trod.
By fairy hands their knell is rung,
By forms unseen their dirge is sung;
There Honour comes, a pilgrim grey,
To bless the turf that wraps their clay,
And Freedom shall awhile repair,
To dwell a weeping hermit there!

Note:
• The 'brave' to whom Collins refers are assumed to be those who defended England in 1745 against the Scotch Jacobites.

■ The poem, as well as being an ode, is also an elegy. Consequently, as it is a work of mourning, it conveys the emotion of grief. Nonetheless, this is to a degree restrained by the poet excluding a personal presence or voice, represented by 'I'. The poem is concerned with national sentiment rather than personal sorrow.

■ The reference to Spring, although formally personified in the manner of Augustan poetry, introduces nature into the poem and allows the phrase of vivid description - 'with dewy fingers cold'. This is reminiscent of the immediacy with which the poets of sensibility convey the details of the natural world.

■ The word 'sod' is not the easiest to incorporate into a poem. Yet the oxymoron in 'sweeter sod', the alliteration on 's' and the strong rhyme with 'trod' preserve poetic decorum while Collins, once again, brings us very close to nature. He prefers the sweetness of the earth, in the grave-yard, to the artificial locations which Fancy describes. There is a common-sensical element in that observation.

■ But the poem, in its second stanza, enters the world of imagination, of 'Fancy'. The presentation of the supernatural is one characteristic of the poetry of sensibility. The divine is not usually presented in an orthodox Christian way, but in terms of heterodox intimations of the spiritual world: 'fairy hands', 'forms unseen'.

■ To conclude, Collins brings personified Honour and Freedom to the
graveyard. As these figures are seen, they prefigure character-types which
are popular in Romantic poetry – a pilgrim and a hermit. Both are solitaries who commune with the eternal. And the poem closes on a note
of sensibility as the hermit, Freedom, is seen weeping over the loss of the
brave.

Questions

1. What qualities of Augustanism can be found in this portrait of Cardinal
   Wolsey, Lord Chancellor of Henry VIII, by Samuel Johnson in 'The Vanity
   of Human Wishes'? Refer to both the matter of the section and the
   characteristics of the poetic language.

> In full-blown dignity, see Wolsey stand,
> Law in his voice, and fortune in his hand:
> To him the church, the realm, their powers consign,
> Through him the rays of regal bounty shine;
> Turned by his nod the stream of honour flows,
> His smile alone security bestows:
> Still to new heights his restless wishes tower,
> Claim leads to claim, and power advances power;
> Till conquest unresisted ceased to please,
> And rights submitted, left him none to seize.
> At length his sovereign frowns – the train of state
> Mark the keen glance, and watch the sign to hate.
> Where'er he turns, he meets a stranger's eye,
> His suppliants scorn him, and his followers fly;
> At once is lost the pride of awful state,
> The golden canopy, the glittering plate,
> The regal palace, the luxurious board,
> The liveried army, and the menial lord.
> With age, with cares, with maladies oppressed,
> He seeks the refuge of monastic rest.
> Grief aids disease, remembered folly stings,
> And his last sighs reproach the faith of kings.

2. What qualities of the poetry of sensibility can be found in these lines from
   the opening section of Oliver Goldsmith's *The Deserted Village* (1770)?

> Sweet Auburn! loveliest village of the plain,
> Where health and plenty cheered the labouring swain,

Where smiling spring its earliest visit paid,
And parting summer's lingering blooms delayed:
Dear lovely bowers of innocence and ease,
Seats of my youth, when every sport could please,
How often have I loitered o'er thy green
Where humble happiness endeared each scene;
How often have I paused on every charm,
The sheltered cot, the cultivated farm,
The never-failing brook, the busy mill,
The decent church that topped the neighbouring hill,
The hawthorn bush, with seats beneath the shade,
For talking age and whispering lovers made . . .

Romanticism

9

IN PRAISE OF IMAGINATION

The Romantic Movement of the nineteenth century was a reaction against the eighteenth-century Age of Reason. The so-called Enlightenment was roundly repudiated, as we find in the scornful lines below of 1796 by William Blake, the first English Romantic poet. Voltaire, Rousseau and Newton, champions of reason and science, are sneeringly dismissed in the praise of the mysterious divinity of creation:

> Mock on, Mock on, Voltaire, Rousseau;
> Mock on, Mock on, 'tis all in vain.
> You throw the sand against the wind,
> And the wind blows it back again;
>
> And every sand becomes a Gem
> Reflected in the beams divine;
> Blown back, they blind the mocking Eye,
> But still in Israel's paths they shine.
>
> The Atoms of Democritus
> And Newton's Particles of light
> Are sands upon the Red sea shore,
> Where Israel's tents do shine so bright.

Romanticism found its expression in all the arts, and in the political and social turmoil of European history from the period of the French Revolution in 1789.

As neo-classicism in England had taken its cue from France, so radical thought about the structure and condition of English society was also inspired, at this time, by the French experience. The Declaration of the Rights of Man in France and the storming of the Bastille, where political prisoners were held, encouraged English radicals to believe that a democratic republic could also be established in Britain. Tom Paine defended the French Revolution in his *Rights of Man* (1791–2), although, more moderately, William Godwin, in his *Inquiry concerning*

Political Justice (1793), proposed an evolutionary rather than a revolutionary model for the equal distribution of wealth. For the young idealists of this time it was as if a new age of freedom was dawning. Its spirit is exhilaratingly captured in William Wordsworth's lines from the eleventh book of *The Prelude*:

> Bliss was it in that dawn to be alive,
> But to be young was very Heaven!

Within a decade, however, a strong reaction against the Revolution and its consequences had set in, as in Wordsworth's presentation of his own disappointment (if not complete disillusionment) in the second book of *The Prelude*:

> in this time
> Of dereliction and dismay, I yet
> Despair not of our Nature, but retain
> A more than Roman confidence, a faith
> That fails not, in all sorrow my support.

However, Shelley, thirty years on, preserved the revolutionary hope in his sonnet 'England in 1819':

> a glorious Phantom may
> Burst, to illumine our tempestuous day.

A concern for the living and working conditions of the poor, both those who remained in agricultural employment and the burgeoning masses in the factory towns, is fundamental to the liberal political thinking of the period and an important theme in Romantic literature. The urgency of the concern can be attributed to the speed of the momentous social change, in Britain in these years, from an agricultural to an industrial economy. The suffering of the workers in industry was not only physical but spiritual. And it was this aspect of the Industrial Revolution which particularly agitated the Romantic poets. One of Blake's searing indictments of the conditions of the urban poor is found in his poem on the city that was becoming the great centre of the new age and of its most powerful empire:

> LONDON
> I wander thro' each charter'd street,
> Near where the charter'd Thames does flow,
> And mark in every face I meet
> Marks of weakness, marks of woe.
>
> In every cry of every Man,
> In every Infant's cry of fear,
> In every voice, in every ban,
> The mind-forg'd manacles I hear·

How the Chimney-sweeper's cry
Every blackning Church appalls,
And the hapless Soldier's sigh
Runs in blood down Palace walls.

But most thro' midnight streets I hear
How the youthful Harlot's curse
Blasts the new-born Infant's tear,
And blights with plagues the Marriage hearse.

Blake's reference to the 'hapless soldier', in this poem of 1794, refers to the recruitment for the long war against France which began after France invaded the Rhineland and the Netherlands. This aggression, combined with the execution of the French royal family and the violence of the Reign of Terror under Robespierre, quickly curbed English enthusiasm for revolutionary political and social change. Strict laws were imposed to prevent public agitation for reform.

The end of the war with France came triumphantly in the victory over Napoleon at Waterloo in 1815. In these years, from 1811 to 1820, known as 'the Regency period', the Prince of Wales acted as regent for his father, George III, who was judged insane and, on his death, the prince became George IV. It is the period of Jane Austen's novels, which reflect the comfortable and elegant lives of the country gentry and all but ignore the momentous events taking place elsewhere in the nation and internationally.

For the urban working class, it was a very different story. There was an industrial depression, after Waterloo, caused by the demobilisation of the troops and a fall in demand for manufactured items. This intensified the dissatisfaction of the workers with their generally appalling conditions and, in 1819, at organised rallies, they demanded the reform of Parliament so that their interests might be represented. A large meeting at St Peter's Fields, Manchester, was broken up by troops. Nine demonstrators were killed and hundreds were injured. This became known as the Peterloo Massacre (after Waterloo). In the next decade, the demand for reform gained the support of the middle classes and some of the Whigs. After continuing turmoil, the first Reform Bill was passed in 1832. The vote was extended, although not as far as the working class. But the process towards universal adult suffrage, for men and, much later, women, had been set in motion.

In 1837, Queen Victoria ascended the throne and the Victorian Age, which was to last for the rest of the century, began.

I

The contradiction of Augustanism by Romanticism is apparent in numerous aspects of its literature. In his essay on 'Mr. Wordsworth' (1825), William Hazlitt noted the poet's rejection of the forms and formalities of neo-classical poetry:

The Ode and Epode, the Strophe and Antistrophe, he laughs to scorn. The harp of Homer, the trump of Pindar and of Alcaeus are still. The decencies of costume, the decorations of vanity are stripped off.

Most importantly, the Romantics overturned the concentration on good sense and reason, which had dominated the subject matter and style of neo-classical poetry. Essentially, they focused on the imagination and, in particular, on the individual's imaginative capacity. Especially, they affirmed the poet's genius. Wordsworth, in his preface to the *Lyrical Ballads*, which he and his close friend and literary collaborator Samuel Taylor Coleridge published first in 1798, then in 1800 and, finally, in 1802, declares that a poet is

> endued with more lively sensibility, more enthusiasm and tenderness .
> . . has a greater knowledge of human nature, and a more comprehen-
> sive soul, than are supposed to be common among mankind . . . the
> poet is chiefly distinguished from other men by a greater promptness
> to think and feel without immediate external excitement, and a
> greater power in expressing such thoughts and feelings as are
> produced in him in that manner.

While thinking and thoughts are present, we particularly note Wordsworth's reference to feeling and feelings. The combination of ideas and emotion leads to an intensified 'state of excitement', which is itself passionate, emotional. It was, Coleridge writes in the *Biographia Literaria* (1817), 'the union of deep feeling with profound thought'.

The significance of feelings had been discerned in the later eighteenth-century poetry of sensibility, but in the theory and practice of the Romantic poets, emotion is not only validated but the poet's distinctive experience and communication of it is praised:

> As high as we have mounted in delight
> In our dejection do we sink as low.
>   Wordsworth, 'Resolution and Independence'

Certainly Wordsworth, who sympathised with the liberal political and social thought of this time (although he became increasingly conservative later), is at pains to argue that the poet's

> passions and thoughts and feelings are the general passions and
> thoughts and feelings of men.

But the imagination of the poet is such that these general experiences are given heightened expression, not in artificial forms – like the poetic diction of the Augustans which Wordsworth rejected – but in a language as close as possible to ordinary speech, yet nonetheless poetic. Wordsworth restored to English poetry its natural, quasi-conversational rhythm of blank verse as in these lines from the 'Prospectus' to *The Recluse*:

> And I am conscious of affecting thoughts
> And dear remembrances, whose presence soothes
> Or elevates the Mind, intent to weigh
> The good and evil of our mortal state.

Yet while the mode is accessible, the ideas are erudite. And Coleridge, in his response to his friend's theory, in the *Biographia* repudiated the equation Wordsworth had tried to establish between poetic language and ordinary speech. 'Rustic life', he insisted, was 'especially unfavourable to the formation of a human diction'. The 'best parts of language' are the 'products of philosophers, not clowns [rural folk] or shepherds'.

However, it is not only the concentration on imagination and emotion that distinguishes Romanticism from the preceding age. In its detail we can plainly see the complete revolution in thought and feeling which Romantic art advocated and achieved. Especially significant is how the attention is directed away from the urban, social domain to the world of nature. This, too, had been anticipated by the poets of sensibility, but their evocations of the natural world retained traces of the constraints and formalities of pastoral.

The Romantics, radically, celebrated nature for its wildness and enjoyed associating their ecstatic emotions with its spontaneity and vitality, in both literature and the visual arts. Coleridge, in 'This Lime-Tree Bower My Prison' (1797), imagines his friends on a ramble through the countryside, near his cottage. They

> Wander in gladness, and wind down, perchance,
> To that still roaring dell, of which I told;
> The roaring dell, o'erwooded, narrow, deep,
> And only speckled by the mid-day sun;
> Where its slim trunk the ash from rock to rock
> Flings arching like a bridge – that branchless ash,
> Unsunned and damp, whose few poor yellow leaves
> Ne'er tremble in the gale, yet tremble still
> Fanned by the waterfall!

Nature, as Coleridge presents it here, is vividly alive in all its components, as the liveliness is aurally communicated in the repeated onomatopoeia of 'roaring' and in the visual immediacy of 'tremble'. The journey of his friends (Wordsworth and his sister Dorothy and Charles Lamb), as imagined by Coleridge, who was confined at home, is a text for one of the principal purposes of Romantic poetry. The poet describes for the reader what he hopes his friends will encounter. He has the same desire that we might experience nature as he has, and be transported by the experience:

> So my friend
> Struck with deep joy may stand, as I have stood,
> Silent with swimming sense; yea, gazing round
> On the wide landscape, gaze till all doth seem
> Less gross than bodily; and of such hues
> As veil the Almighty Spirit, when yet he makes
> Spirits perceive his presence.

Yet, ironically (and amusingly), good friend as he was of Coleridge, Lamb had no time at all for the Romantics' obsession with nature:

> I don't much care if I never see a mountain in my life. I have passed all my days in London, until I have formed as many and intense social attachments as any of you mountaineers can have done with dead Nature.

And Coleridge's lines are at least as much a celebration of what Coleridge has experienced – and therefore of himself, as a man of rarefied sensitivity and a poet – as they are of the hope that others might be similarly moved. This is a manifestation of the motif of the 'egotistical sublime' (in John Keats's phrase) in Romantic poetry, which is one of its profoundest paradoxes. For this artistry, which is so concerned with the condition of humanity, is also noteworthy for its self-centredness, its celebration of the eccentricity and idiosyncrasy of the poet and the artist. Coleridge's most ecstatic presentation of the Romantic conception of the poet, almost as a divinity, concludes his 'Kubla Khan':

> Beware! Beware!
> His flashing eyes, his floating hair!
> Weave a circle round him thrice,
> And close your eyes with holy dread,
> For he on honeydew hath fed,
> And drunk the milk of Paradise.

In striking contrast, the untutored and uncorrupted association of rural folk with the natural world is central to the celebration of nature in Romantic poetry. Wordsworth's Simon Lee, 'The Old Huntsman', and his leech-gatherer in 'Resolution and Independence', are praised in the spirit of the poet's creed that we should let nature be our teacher and renounce formal scholarly learning. This can be seen in these lines (ironic, from one who was to produce many books) from 'The Tables Turned' (1798):

> Books! 'tis a dull and endless strife:
> Come, hear the woodland linnet,
> How sweet his music! on my life,
> There's more of wisdom in it.

The Romantic sage rejects the learning of the 'sages':

> One impulse from a vernal wood
> May teach you more of man,
> Of moral evil and of good,
> Than all the sages can.

This cult of rusticity of the early Romantics was satirised by Thomas Love Peacock in 'The Four Ages of Poetry' (1820). This essay is best known for provoking Shelley's splendid 'Defence of Poetry', but is also important as a reminder that the Romantics' literary contemporaries were not necessarily supporters of their theories:

> To read the promiscuous rubbish of the present time . . . is to substitute the worse for the better variety of the same mode of enjoyment . . . The highest inspirations of poetry [today] are resolvable into three ingredients: the rant of unregulated passion, the whining of exaggerated feeling, and the cant of factitious sentiment . . . the poet is wallowing in the rubbish of departed ignorance, and raking up the ashes of dead savages to find gewgaws and rattles for the grown babies of the age . . . Mr Wordsworth picks up village legends from old women and sextons, and Mr Coleridge, to the valuable information acquired from similar sources, superadds the dreams of crazy theologians and the mysticisms of German metaphysics.

Even Byron, whose life seems to be the very pattern of Romanticism, had considerable reservations about his contemporaries' achievements, believing that the last great poet was the neo-classical Pope:

> Thou shalt believe in Milton, Dryden, Pope;
> Thou shalt not set up Wordsworth, Coleridge, Southey;
> Because the first is crazed beyond all hope,
> The second drunk, the third so quaint and mouthy.

The rustic elements of Wordsworth's poems are scoffed at:

> 'Peddlers', and 'Boats', and 'Wagons'! Oh! ye shades
> Of Pope and Dryden, are we come to this?

The desire for a return to simplicity after a century of intellectuality is one explanation of the Romantic cults of rusticity, youth and childhood. In Blake's sets of songs of 'Innocence' (several of which have their negative parallels in his songs of 'Experience', or adulthood), the purity of childhood is reflected in the lyrical simplicity of the poetry which, nonetheless, is not itself innocent of Blake's urgent social concerns:

THE CHIMNEY SWEEPER
When my mother died I was very young,
And my father sold me while yet my tongue
Could scarcely cry "weep! 'weep! 'weep! 'weep!'
So your chimneys I sweep & in soot I sleep.

The adult world of experience brings evil and corruption into human life in all its aspects. Blake was a visionary and social reformer inspired with a religious fervour that was as transcendental as it was applicable to the terrestrial circumstances of the Industrial Revolution in England. However, he was severely critical of organised religion and, in particular, its prohibitions, which inhibited what he regarded as natural behaviour, especially sexual expression. The Church is implicated in 'The Garden of Love' (1794), from the *Songs of Experience*, in an anti-Romantic oppression of the spirit and the flesh:

THE GARDEN OF LOVE
I went to the Garden of Love,
And saw what I never had seen:
A Chapel was built in the midst,
Where I used to play on the green.

And the gates of this Chapel were shut,
And 'Thou shalt not' writ over the door;
So I turn'd to the Garden of Love,
That so many sweet flowers bore,

And I saw it was filled with graves,
And tomb-stones where flowers should be;
And Priests in black gowns were walking their rounds,
And binding with briars my joys & desires.

But Blake could conceive of a world in which adults retained the virtues of innocence, and this is merrily celebrated in 'The Ecchoing Green', where

Old John with white hair
Does laugh away care,
Sitting under the oak,
Among the old folk.
They laugh at our play,
And soon they all say:
'Such, such were the joys,
When we all, girls & boys,
In our youth-time were seen,
On the Ecchoing Green'.

Assignment

Compare the 'Nurse's Song' from the *Songs of Innocence* with the 'Nurse's Song' in the *Songs of Experience*. Note the differences in the poetry which reflect the differences between Innocence and Experience. Describe those different states as Blake presents them in these poems.

Childhood is crucial, too, to Wordsworth and Coleridge. For the previous Age of Reason, in contrast, a child was only an incomplete adult. In *The Prelude*, Wordsworth's long autobiographical work (although, in a sense, all his poems are autobiography), the growth of his mind and spirit is seen to have its source in his earliest years:

> I remember well
> That once, while yet my inexperienced hand
> Could scarcely hold a bridle, with proud hopes
> I mounted, and we journied towards the hills.

His inexperience is the attribute which gives to that pleasure its uninhibited naturalness. Such is the value of childhood innocence that it should cast its influence over all our lives. Wordsworth's convictions grow into a philosophical paradox – and it is a paradox itself that a concern with childhood simplicity should produce a metaphysical system – which produces a text for his great ode on immortality (see Special Study 8), initially encountered at the end of this short lyric of 1802:

> My heart leaps up when I behold
>   A rainbow in the sky:
> So was it when my life began;
> So is it now I am a man;
> So be it when I shall grow old,
>   Or let me die!
> The Child is father of the Man;
> And I could wish my days to be
> Bound each to each by natural piety.

For all the naturalness of childhood, as Blake and Wordsworth present it, the child in Romantic poetry is also a symbol of the new age of Romanticism which they had brought to birth.

Coleridge, in his meditative poem, 'Frost at Midnight' (1798), both describes his own childhood and pronounces a blessing on the 'Dear Babe' asleep beside him, in his cottage, at this late hour. The baby symbolises new life and hope. Its 'gentle breathings', synonymous with divine inspiration,

> Fill up the interspersed vacancies
> And momentary pauses of the thought.

They are a token of the life-force of nature which unobtrusively but uninterruptedly continues while our mental processes are fitful. Coleridge is ecstatic in contemplation of his child, his creation:

> My babe so beautiful! it thrills my heart
> With tender gladness, thus to look at thee.

The baby, a prototypical Romantic, will not be schooled unhappily, like his father, in London – 'in the great City pent' (as Coleridge writes elsewhere) – under the oppressive authority of 'the stern preceptor'. Rather,

> thou shalt learn far other lore,
> And in far other scenes!

The child's education will take place in the school of nature:

> But thou, my babe! shalt wander like a breeze
> By lakes and sandy shores, beneath the crags
> Of ancient mountain, and beneath the clouds
> Which image in their bulk both lakes and shores
> And mountain crags.

That the child (in a simile) should wander 'like a breeze' suggests both its unity with nature and, in that particular comparison, its freedom. Unity and harmony are further conveyed in Coleridge's perception of the mirroring, in the clouds, of earth's formations.

Always the philosopher, Coleridge indicates that such a bond with creation is not merely naturalistic or emotional, but metaphysical and religious:

> so shalt thou see and hear
> The lovely shapes and sounds intelligible
> Of that eternal language, which thy God
> Utters . . .

This vision expands into a statement of the Romantic doctrine of pantheism, the idea of the presence of the divine in all of the natural order:

> . . .who from eternity doth teach
> Himself in all, and all things in himself.
> Great universal Teacher! he shall mould
> Thy spirit, and by giving make it ask.

In the form of an argument or thesis, the poem's concluding verse-paragraph begins with 'Therefore', as Coleridge finishes bestowing his blessing of a Romantic future on the baby:

> all seasons shall be sweet to thee.

He gives us brief pictures of those seasons, each delightful in its own characteristics:

> Whether the summer clothe the general earth
> With greenness, or the redbreast sit and sing
> Betwixt the tufts of snow on the bare branch
> Of mossy apple-tree . . .
>   . . .whether the eave-drops fall
> Heard only in the trances of the blast,
> Or if the secret ministry of frost
> Shall hang them up in silent icicles,
> Quietly shining to the quiet Moon.

In this gentle close, Coleridge reveals his careful observation of creation, but also his symbolic, poet's interpretation of it. Some 'eave-drops' will fall, but others will be saved by frost, in its secret ministry, to be given the beautiful structure of the icicle, shining by moonlight and, in turn, in reciprocity, to the moon. That action of the frost and the icicle that is formed and its luminous character are images of the unity and harmony of the natural world into which Coleridge would incorporate a new, reborn humanity, represented in this poem by the 'Dear Babe'.

II

The first Romantic poets' celebration of childhood is accompanied by their moral vision. When Wordsworth writes, in 'The Two April Mornings', that he came upon a beautiful girl one morning and that 'to see a child so very fair, / It was a pure delight!' he is not only conveying his appreciation of her physical beauty, but morally he perceives that that beauty was the expression of her purity. Wordsworth saw his role as a poet as a warning voice against the social and spiritual depravity of his age. In this, he associated himself with Spenser and Milton, the great moralists in poetry in the English tradition. This depravity had its literary expression, he wrote, in 'frantic novels, sickly and stupid German tragedies, and deluges of idle and extravagant stories in verse'. Readers displayed a 'degrading thirst after outrageous stimulation'. He would 'counteract' that decadence with the celebration of the stimuli which the natural world provides. In response to these, his readers will discover in themselves 'certain inherent and indestructible qualities of the human mind'. The term 'innocence', in the Blakean sense, might serve as a summary of these.

Wordsworth places emphasis on what he describes, in *Michael*, as 'the pleasure which there is in life itself', and which Coleridge defines as 'joy' (for example, in 'Dejection: An Ode'). This needs to be associated with the moral vision of Romanticism: the 'apt admonishment' which nature, for those who are attuned to it, provides. But as we speak of morality, and particularly of Wordsworth's association with Milton and the 'Puritan' tradition, it is important to distinguish it from moralism. Certainly, in Wordsworth's 'Ode to Duty', beginning 'Stern Daughter of the Voice of God!' and in the famous sonnet, 'Milton! thou should'st be living at this hour . . .' the voice is bracingly didactic. As Milton was the great defender of freedom in his morally strenuous poetry and prose, Wordsworth's constant celebration of pleasure is combined with his stern utterances to produce a positive rather than a merely censorious moral vision.

This is most apparent in his thesis of the 'spots of time' (enunciated in the twelfth book of *The Prelude*) where the experience of the commonplace reveals momentous truths in epiphanies. The freedom of the imagination, exercised in this way, produces the profound and lasting pleasure of the exaltation of the spirit:

> In trivial occupations, and the round
> Of ordinary intercourse, our minds
> Are nourished and invisibly repaired;
> A virtue by which pleasure is inhanced,
> That penetrates, enables us to mount,
> When high, more high, and lifts us up when fallen.
> This efficacious Spirit chiefly lurks
> Among those passages of life that give
> Profoundest knowledge how and to what point
> The mind is lord and master – outward sense
> The obedient Servant of her will.

With these various ideas about early Romantic poetry in general and Wordsworth's concerns in particular, we should turn to a closer examination of his artistry.

■ SPECIAL STUDY 8

William Wordsworth (1770–1850)

ABOUT THE AUTHOR

Wordsworth was born in Cockermouth in Cumbria, in the north of the Lake District, on 7 April 1770, the son of an attorney. The earliest record of his poetry dates from 1785, before he went up to St John's College, Cambridge, from which he graduated in 1791. After a walking tour of the Alps, Wordsworth spent a year in Paris in 1792, where he had an affair with Annette Vallon and their daughter Caroline was born. Returning to England, Wordsworth visited Tintern Abbey in 1793.

In 1795, Wordsworth met Samuel Taylor Coleridge, the beginning of the most famous of Romantic artistic collaborations. Together, the poets published *Lyrical Ballads* in 1798, but the volume received an unenthusiastic reception. The 'Lucy' poems followed and, in 1799, Wordsworth settled with his sister Dorothy in Dove Cottage, Grasmere, in the Lake District. He and Annette had amicably agreed not to pursue their relationship and, in 1802, Wordsworth married a childhood friend, Mary Hutchinson, and their son was born the following year.

While Wordsworth had settled permanently in the rural beauty of Grasmere, he was a constant traveller in Britain and Europe, and his poetic activity continued throughout his long life. In 1843 he was made Poet Laureate.

Over the years, Wordsworth's early radicalism in politics was replaced by conservatism. His later poetry seems less inspired than his earlier work which was revolutionary in style and theme and which introduced Romanticism into English poetry.

PREFACE TO *LYRICAL BALLADS*

The most important source for Wordsworth's ideas on poetry – apart from his poems themselves – is the Preface to the second edition of *Lyrical Ballads* which he wrote in 1800. Here, Wordsworth asserts that his poetry will be based on 'the real language of men in a state of vivid sensation'. He further argues that 'all good poetry is the spontaneous overflow of powerful feelings' and that

> Poetry is the breath and finer spirit of all knowledge; it is the impas-
> sioned expression which is in the countenance of all Science.

These principles establish Wordsworth's conviction that poetry springs from the spirit of human nature; in other words, it should convey, with unique power, those feelings that bind the human race together. He also believed that poetry is the quintessence of the expression of our perceptions about life. 'The Poet thinks and feels in the spirit of human passions', he continues; but he also suggests that, in the process of giving these artistic expression, the poet will meditate on their meaning: poems originate in 'emotion recol-lected in tranquillity'.

This Preface, one of the seminal documents of Romanticism, stresses the significance of feelings and emotions in art and claims an inspired role for the poet. It also emphasises the reaction against the consequences of the Industrial Revolution – such as 'the increasing accumulation of men in cities' – which will only be remedied, in Wordsworth's view, by a recovery of the passions of the human spirit, such as poetry embodies and expresses; for it is 'the image of man and nature'.

Also of interest in the Preface is the attention Wordsworth pays to the matter of 'poetic diction'. Because he wants poetry to recall the 'real language of men', he contends that strict rules about metre and rhyme (which were in use in the eighteenth century) needed to be relaxed, so that poems might more realistically reflect our passions and thoughts.

Ultimately, he wants poetry to please, through conveying the truths of life:

> the Poet, singing a song in which all human beings join with him, rejoices in the presence of truth as our visible friend and hourly companion.

SELECTED POEMS

TINTERN ABBEY

This poem, usually known by the abbreviated title above, is misleadingly so called. For the work is scarcely about the ruins of the old church at all, although Wordsworth – like all Romantics – rejoiced in the air of mystery and spirituality evoked by such scenes. 'Tintern Abbey' focuses on the natural beauty of the surrounding area and Wordsworth's and his sister's relationship with it.

The poem opens with a characteristic Romantic and Wordsworthian gesture of recollection and nostalgia for the past:

> Five years have past; five summers, with the length
> Of five long winters!

The remembrance is of a natural scene which is notable for its sublimity. The 'mountain-springs' are 'rolling' and the cliffs 'steep and lofty'. The scene is 'wild secluded'. Wordsworth thus claims our attention and stirs our imagination by evoking such an arresting sight. However, this poem has modulating descriptions and moods. Soon a quieter and more accessible, almost domestic scene is discerned within the grander landscape:

> These plots of cottage-ground, these orchard-tufts . . .

Man has settled here, but he has not violated Nature. Rather, his dwellings and cultivation are attuned to it:

> Once again I see
> These hedge-rows, hardly hedge-rows, little lines

■   Of sportive wood run wild: these pastoral farms,
        Green to the very door.

To close the first verse-paragraph, he imagines that the peaceful scene might
be perfected by the presence of a hermit in the nearby woods. Such solitaries
stirred the Romantic fancy, for they communed, in solitude, with the eternal.

Wordsworth becomes philosophical next, as he entertains the Platonic
theory of the 'forms': the perfect ideas of qualities and quantities. His
memory of Nature has sustained him while engulfed by 'the din / Of towns
and cities'. Typically, Wordsworth argues that such recollection has elevated
his moral being:

    …that best portion of a good man's life

and, ultimately, his spiritual sense:

    …that serene and blessed mood,
    In which the affections gently lead us on
    … we are laid asleep
    In body, and become a living soul.

The poem, like so many Romantic texts, testifies to the unique power of the
poet's sensibility. The reader is not so much invited to participate in the experience as to admire the profundity of Wordsworth's emotions. Time and again,
the poetry concentrates on 'I', as in Wordsworth's recollection of his childhood:

        when like a roe
    I bounded o'er the mountains.

For all the Romantic idealisation of childhood as a time of supposed innocence and spontaneity, it is interesting that Wordsworth dissociates himself
from those 'coarser pleasures' which he yet describes so vividly in these lines.
Maturity has brought a wider interpretation, which he reveals in the context
of pantheistic writing – the sense of 'a presence'

    Whose dwelling is the light of setting suns,
    And the round ocean and the living air,
    And the blue sky, and in the mind of man.

The poem closes in celebration of Wordsworth's sister Dorothy, who reminds
the poet of his bond with the natural world. As a 'worshipper of Nature', he
calls down a blessing upon her and recalls his opening lines in the closing
resonant exclamation.

'Tintern Abbey' is a highly structured work thematically, but technically it
flows with all the naturalness of an elevated conversation, as Wordsworth
reveals the abundant inspiration he has received from this beautiful location.

■
Question
How does Wordsworth persuade us of the unity of humanity and nature
– and the benefits which flow from that – in this poem?

ODE: INTIMATIONS OF IMMORTALITY

This formal poem gives a philosophical interpretation of the Romantic
preoccupation with childhood, especially in its fifth stanza where
Wordsworth summarises the Platonic doctrine of pre-existence:

> Our birth is but a sleep and a forgetting.

On coming into this world, a baby possesses vestiges of the eternal realm
whence it came:

> Not in entire forgetfulness,
> And not in utter nakedness,
> But trailing clouds of glory do we come
> From God, who is our home.

As our earthly life proceeds, however, we lose sight of our immortality,
which fades 'into the light of common day'.

The poem begins with Wordsworth in despair of recovering his sense of
the 'celestial light' in which even common sights had once been 'apparelled'.
To emphasise his feeling of dispossession, he writes deliberately uninspired
poetry in the second stanza. His suggestion is that, without communion with
the immortal idea of life and nature, creative inspiration, too, will falter:

> The Rainbow comes and goes,
> And lovely is the Rose.

His grieving thoughts, however, are relieved by the experience he recounts
in another poem, 'Resolution and Independence'. Its composition, 'a timely
utterance', encouraged him to believe that he still possessed the soul to love
nature and the power to write about it with insight into eternal truth:

> The cataracts blow their trumpets from the steep;
> No more shall grief of mine the season wrong;
> I hear the Echoes through the mountains throng.

This is suitably triumphant poetry as his earlier melancholy mood is eradi-
cated.

In exultation, Wordsworth writes a hymn of praise to nature in the fourth
stanza, but disconcertingly, at its end, the sense of fleeting inspiration comes
upon him once again:

■
>   Whither is fled the visionary gleam?
>   Where is it now, the glory and the dream?

These questions prompt the philosophical answer, in stanza 5, to which we have referred. Stanzas 6 and 7 extend the idea of the intrusion of worldliness upon immortality. Wordsworth's genius is such that he writes as magnificently of these negative influences as of the glimpses, or intimations, of eternity he praises.

Earth is only our foster-mother – our true home is elsewhere. All that we undertake in our mortal lives amounts to an ever-changing series of roles, 'dialogues of business, love, or strife', like an actor's career, and ends, unedifyingly, in 'palsied Age'.

The antithesis of this depressing and absurd process, which Wordsworth describes with a Shakespearean mixture of venom and comedy, is the life of the soul, which the Child symbolises as that 'best Philosopher':

>   Mighty Prophet! Seer blest!
>   On whom those truths do rest,
>   Which we are toiling all our lives to find.

As in 'Tintern Abbey', Wordsworth is not simplistically suggesting that if one could become a baby again, the meaning of life would be instantly clarified. Certainly, his thoughts of 'past years' are a joy to him, as he announces in the arresting opening of stanza 9 - but these are not so much his recollection of 'the simple creed / Of childhood', as his

>   obstinate questionings
>   Of sense and outward things.

His intellect, as much as his emotions and his soul, has revealed to him the truths of life. Intimations of the eternal give us a source of solace and inspiration, no matter how far removed our circumstances may appear to be from that domain. Wordsworth argues this with great beauty, in a geographical metaphor:

>   Hence in a season of calm weather
>   Though inland far we be,
>   Our Souls have sight of that immortal sea
>   Which brought us hither,
>   Can in a moment travel thither,
>   And see the Children sport upon the shore,
>   And hear the mighty waters rolling evermore.

Tranquillity, nature, the spiritual dimension and the pure innocence of childhood and the sublime are powerfully combined in these lines of exultant praise.

■   The closing stanzas reiterate and expand this theme, as the poem concludes – for all its universalising tendencies – on a note as personal as its opening. Even the most unprepossessing bloom in nature stimulates Wordsworth to ponder the religious and philosophic explanation of all being:

> To me the meanest flower that blows can give
> Thoughts that do often lie too deep for tears.

Question

How (and how successfully) does Wordsworth combine thought and feeling in this poem?

COMPOSED UPON WESTMINSTER BRIDGE

It is surprising that a Romantic poet should take the great urban centre of London as a subject for celebration. When Wordsworth's contemporary, William Blake, writes of London, in his poem of that name, he presents a terrifying indictment of it as a centre of corruption and cruelty. But we notice that in Wordsworth's sonnet he is talking of the sleeping city at sunrise, before it comes to life. His sister Dorothy recounts how her brother got his inspiration for the poem in her entry in the 'Grasmere Journals' for Thursday, 29 July 1802:

> It was a beautiful morning. The City, St. Paul's, with the River and a
> multitude of little Boats, made a most beautiful sight as we crossed
> Westminster Bridge. The houses were not overhung by their cloud of
> smoke and they were spread out endlessly, yet the sun shone so
> brightly with such a pure light that there was even something like the
> purity of one of nature's own grand spectacles.

As the poet writes, all of the city's elements are attuned to nature:

> Open unto the fields, and to the sky.

Yet it is a scene from which humanity is absent. The 'ships, towers, domes, theatres, and temples' are 'silent, bare' and 'the very houses seem asleep'. The modern metropolis is strangely primeval:

> Never did sun more beautifully steep
> In his first splendour, valley, rock, or hill.

Again, it is the effect of the scene upon Wordsworth that is most moving, and indicative of his acute sensibility. Only the dull spirit could neglect 'a sight so touching in its majesty', and this worshipper of nature now confesses that 'ne'er saw I, never felt, a calm so deep' as the emotion he experienced in this vision of London.

We should notice, finally, the mounting enthusiasm of the speaker's mood, as the language reveals it. The octave of the sonnet is declarative, but restrained in diction. But in the succeeding sestet, the exclamations (especially 'Dear God!') convey an effusion of ecstasy that brings the poem to a resounding close.

Question

How does Wordsworth animate the formal characteristics of the sonnet to convey his feelings as well as his ideas in this poem?

CHILDHOOD (THE PRELUDE)

The Prelude has the subtitle 'Growth of a Poet's Mind: An Autobiographical Poem'. In the passage from the first book (which consists of an introduction and a discourse on 'Childhood and Schooltime'), Wordsworth explains his mature love of nature in terms of his first experience as a child 'in that beloved Vale'. Through verbs, he vividly communicates his youthful vigour:

> 'twas my joy
> With store of springes o'er my shoulder hung
> To range the open heights...
> Scudding away from snare to snare.

Yet the picture is not without its less innocent elements: he stole prey from hunters' traps, but – always alert to the moral dimensions of his actions – he sensed nature's disapproval:

> I heard among the solitary hills
> Low breathings coming after me.

This section is splendidly visual, too, as is Wordsworth's evocation of his hazardous expeditions to the raven's nest: 'on the perilous ridge I hung alone'.

In portraying the variety of his youthful impulses and activities, Wordsworth reflects that we are the harmonious sum of our discordant parts, by virtue of 'a dark/ Inscrutable workmanship'. He praises nature for fashioning his moral being with a combination of admonitions and delights.

The anecdote of his evening's sailing in an 'elfin pinnace' is delicately described in an atmosphere of expectation and mystery. It shows how Wordsworth was educated in the awe he always retained of the natural world which, in his pantheism, leads to his praise of the 'Wisdom and Spirit of the universe!'

These intimations in solitude are balanced with the joy of company – 'in games / Confederate' – but after Wordsworth's return from that tumult he is most himself in solitary communion with the divine in nature:

> I stood and watched
> Till all was tranquil as a dreamless sleep.

It is experiences such as this, indeed, which inspire his greatest poetry.

Questions

1. To what extent is Wordsworth's teaching that 'all good poetry is the spontaneous overflow of powerful feelings' true of his own poems? Refer to two or three poems.
2. 'Wordsworth's poetry of nature is not natural; it is idealised, philosophical.' Do you agree? Refer to two or three poems.

III

The focus of Romantic thought and poetic practice was the emotion of love. 'To be beloved is all I need', writes Coleridge in 'The Pains of Sleep', 'and whom I love, I love indeed'. In our reading of Romantic poetry, we encounter numerous songs of praise to this most passionate of human experiences. The emotion, however, is often discovered in the context of disappointment and failure in love, and the suffering which it can cause: 'our sweetest songs', wrote Shelley, 'are those that tell of saddest thought'. 'The sadness of life', in George Moore's words, 'is the joy of art'. The intensity of these negative experiences, of course, is further testimony to love's power, as in these lines of Byron:

> When we two parted
> In silence and tears,
> Half broken-hearted
> To sever for years,
> Pale grew thy cheek and cold,
> Colder thy kiss;
> Truly that hour foretold
> Sorrow to this.

The idealisation of love in the person of the beloved, even in the context of recording her disdain and the distress that that causes, reminds us of the source of the term 'Romanticism' in the 'Romance' period of the Middle Ages, where the poetic expression of the chivalric code of love, *fin amor*, produced lyrics of a similarly celebratory kind. We turn to Byron again:

> She walks in beauty, like the night
> Of cloudless climes and starry skies;
> And all that's best of dark and bright
> Meet in her aspect and her eyes:
> Thus mellowed to that tender light
> Which heaven to gaudy day denies.

The poet's detailed account of the beloved's physical beauty also recalls the medieval convention of the blazon in which the mistress's physical charms were named, as the poem concludes in a line resonant with the idealistic impulse of Romantic love:

> And on that cheek, and o'er that brow,
> So soft, so calm, yet eloquent,
> The smiles that win, the tints that glow,
> But tell of days in goodness spent,
> A mind at peace with all below,
> A heart whose love is innocent!

In Romantic poetry, love can also be less transcendental and more sensual. In Coleridge's exotic image in 'Kubla Khan', for example, quasi-religious idealisation earlier in the work is replaced by the pagan outpouring of a 'woman wailing for her demon lover'. But his concluding portrayal of femininity as the symbol of music and song is more moderate:

> A damsel with a dulcimer
> In a vision once I saw:
> It was an Abyssinian maid,
> And on her dulcimer she played,
> Singing of Mount Abora.

And Coleridge's concerns for his friends, such as Wordsworth ('O friend! my comforter and guide!') and Charles Lamb – 'my gentle-hearted Charles!' – includes platonic affection as well as passionate devotion. Wordsworth's loving evocations of his sister Dorothy are yet another version of Romantic love, as is the Romantic writers' embrace of humanity in general.

Various forms of devotion for a human being are at the heart of Romantic artistry. A great poem of this period which expresses such devotion is Percy Bysshe Shelley's *Adonais*, a lament in memory of the poet John Keats, whom Shelley regarded as 'among the writers of the highest genius who have adorned our age':

> I weep for Adonais – he is dead!
> O, weep for Adonais! though our tears
> Thaw not the frost which binds so dear a head!

Shelley's grief is both for his friend and the type of poet which Keats represented. The name 'Adonais' is a version of 'Adonis', the beautiful youth of classical legend. Shelley (like Milton in *Lycidas*, another lament for the death of a young man of accomplishment) appropriates the convention of pastoral elegy in the idealisation of the man he is mourning.

Yet, amongst the many paradoxes of Romanticism is the contrary celebration of solitude in its poetry. Wordsworth writes, in the second book of *The Prelude*:

> for I would walk alone
> Under the quiet stars, and at that time
> Have felt whate'er there is of power in sound
> To breathe an elevated mood, by form
> Or Image unprofaned.

Again, this can be ambiguous (as we shall see in Special Study 9 on Keats, in his sonnet, 'Bright star!. . .') where solitude is interpreted as loneliness. Yet in Shelley's fragment on the moon, where this interpretation is proposed, the moon's companionlessness inspires a rare beauty of utterance which invests the experience with a certain lyrical relish:

> Art thou pale for weariness
> Of climbing heaven and gazing on the earth,
> Wandering companionless
> Among the stars that have a different birth –
> And ever changing, like a joyless eye
> That finds no object worth its constancy?

Shelley imagines that the moon is experiencing melancholy (in the so-called 'pathetic fallacy' familiar in Romantic poetry, whereby human emotions are ascribed to nature and its elements). Yet this same melancholy is satisfying to contemplate in terms of the deep emotion which loneliness can produce. Then, in *Alastor: or The Spirit of Solitude*, Shelley recognises the alienation of the solitary state, yet praises it for facilitating a vision of humanity and creation which is able to see its totality and lovingly transform it by that knowledge. This is not possible, Shelley writes in the preface to the poem, for 'those unforeseeing multitudes who constitute ... the lasting misery and loneliness of the world'. But it is the poet's special vocation. Byron reflected (in *Childe Harold's Pilgrimage*) that 'to fly from, need not be to hate, mankind':

> Is it not better, then, to be alone,

> And love earth only for its earthly sake?. . .
> Is it not better thus our lives to wear,
> Than join the crushing crowds, doomed to inflict or bear?

And nowhere does Shelley express that solitary, visionary being more ecstatically than in the soaring stanzas of 'To a Skylark'. In this poem, the bird is the symbol of the spirit of poetry and of self-animated and self-fulfilled artistry, of nature transubstantiated:

> Hail to thee, blithe Spirit!
> Bird thou never wert —
> That from Heaven, or near it,
> Pourest thy full heart
> In profuse strains of unpremeditated art.
>
> Higher still and higher
> From the earth thou springest
> Like a cloud of fire;
> The blue deep thou wingest,
> And singing still dost soar, and soaring ever singest.

Yet the skylark's aloneness, its soaring solitude, communicates truths to the poets who, in turn, convey them to humanity. Ultimately, thereby, it is implicated in that expression of boundless love:

> Teach me half the gladness
> That thy brain must know,
> Such harmonious madness
> From my lips would flow
> The world should listen then — as I am listening now.

Sample question with guidelines

What characteristics of Romantic thought and practice would you identify in the following poem by Shelley?

MUTABILITY

We are as clouds that veil the midnight moon;
How restlessly they speed, and gleam, and quiver,
Streaking the darkness radiantly! — yet soon
Night closes round, and they are lost for ever:

Or like forgotten lyres, whose dissonant strings
Give various response to each varying blast,
To whose frail frame no second motion brings

One mood or modulation like the last.

We rest. – A dream has power to poison sleep;
We rise. – One wandering thought pollutes the day;
We feel, conceive or reason, laugh or weep;
Embrace fond woe, or cast our cares away:

It is the same! - For, be it joy or sorrow,
The path of its departure still is free:
Man's yesterday may ne'er be like his morrow;
Nought may endure but Mutability.

■ Wordsworth has a poem with the same title, which suggests the importance of the concept of change and decay for the Romantic poets. It is a
negative perception about life and the human condition which stirs
strong emotions – most notably despair which arises out of the sense of
the futility of existence. The poem's subject, in other words, is characteristically Romantic in its emotionally charged concentration on human
experience.

■ The opening simile compares our condition with nature's behaviour. It is
not merely intellectually satisfying to note that we are like fleeting clouds.
It is a beautiful visual image and, set in the mystery of night and in the
heavens, conveys the sense of a process that is irreversible and inevitable.
The ambiguity of Shelley's presentation of a phenomenon which is at
once lovely yet representative of the experience of unhappiness of the
knowledge of life and its processes is characteristically Romantic.

■ The musical allusion in the second stanza to lyres, or wind harps, suggests
the ambiguity of beauty that is thwarted, but more darkly now, in the
reference to the breezes as 'each varying blast'. The strong noun contradicts the musical allusion and symbolises the dissonance of life. In
contrast, the weakness of the 'frail frame' of the instrument (ourselves)
shows the ineffectual resistance which humanity presents to nature's
laws.

■ Even sleep has its terrors. And waking is like a nightmare. The sense of
the pain of life and, in particular, how thought can poison our beings, is
strikingly Romantic. But Shelley does not find consolation in emotion.
Rather, he discerns our oscillating moods as 'we feel ... laugh, or weep'. In
particular, we notice the oxymoron of 'fond woe', sadness lovingly
nurtured. It is a familiar Romantic notion.

■ The argument of the poem closes paradoxically: it may be the case that
all that remains is change. This is a harrowing speculation which is well
justified by the examples in each stanza. Yet Shelley conveys a certain
pragmatism as he makes his observation. The conditional 'may' (repeated)

softens the blow, but does not emasculate it. The poem is a poised combination of reasoned meditation on an age-old theme (see, for example, Edmund Spenser's cantos of 'Mutabilitie' from the sixteenth century) and a general view of human emotion. These elements of the poem give it its distinctive Romantic character.

Question

What characteristics of Romantic poetry would you identify in this lyric by Thomas Moore?

> Believe me, if all those endearing young charms,
> Which I gaze on so fondly today,
> Were to change by tomorrow, and fleet in my arms,
> Like fairy-gifts fading away,
> Thou wouldst still be adored, as this moment thou art,
> Let thy loveliness fade as it will,
> And around the dear ruin each wish of my heart
> Would entwine itself verdantly still.
>
> It is not while beauty and youth are thine own,
> And thy cheeks unprofaned by a tear
> That the fervour and faith of a soul can be known,
> To which time will but make thee more dear;
> No, the heart that has truly loved never forgets,
> But as truly loves on to the close,
> As the sunflower turns on her god, when he sets,
> The same look which she turned when he rose.

IV

In the context of the Romantics' fascination with the Middle Ages of faith and the 'Gothic', there is, in their poetry, an emphasis on the visionary ability of the artist. The poet is not only a maker (which is the derivation, from Greek, of the word), but a seer.

The Gothic spirit persisted throughout the nineteenth century, and was expressed in architecture and painting as well as literature. It was a reaction against the present and modernity. The first scene of Byron's dramatic poem *Manfred* is set in 'a Gothic gallery' and De Quincey recalls, with delight, that Coleridge described to him Piranesi's paintings of 'vast Gothic halls'.

The Romantic revival of medievalism, aesthetically and, to a degree, spiritually, provides an interesting contrast with the Romantic recovery of enthusiasm for the natural world, although in a poem like Wordsworth's 'Tintern Abbey', the two are combined. Both reactionary impulses had the same source – a rejection of industrialisation and urbanisation. And in both cases the favoured domains were presented selectively and idealistically. Like everyone under the spell of nostalgia, the Romantics tended to view the past (as well as rural life and folk) through rose-tinted spectacles.

The Romantic appreciation of the medieval worldview was contemporary with and very influential upon the great religious revivals of the early nineteenth century which persisted for 100 years, like the Gothic aesthetic which they appropriated (in church architecture and interior design, liturgy and vestments). The two movements in Anglicanism in England – the Evangelical ('low church') and Oxford ('high church' or Anglo-Catholic) – emphasised the recovery of supernatural religion in contradiction of the rationalistic Deism of the eighteenth century.

Wordsworth gradually brought himself into conformity with doctrinal Christianity, most notably in his *Ecclesiastical Sonnets*. Yet Romanticism, in its visionary and even its Gothic dimensions, avoided orthodoxy and dogmatic formulae. But it warmly praised the religious spirit: the transcendence of reason. Even professed atheists such as Shelley convey supernatural intimations, especially when contemplating nature, as in these lines on the sublimity of the Swiss Alps:

MONT BLANC
Lines Written in the Vale of Chamouni

The everlasting universe of things
Flows through the mind, and rolls its rapid waves,
Now dark – now glittering – now reflecting gloom –
Now lending splendour, where from secret springs
The source of human thought its tribute brings
Of waters, – with a sound but half its own.
Such as a feeble brook will oft assume
In the wild woods, among the mountains lone,
Where waterfalls around it leap forever,
Where woods and winds contend, and a vast river
Over its rocks ceaselessly bursts and raves.

And Coleridge's pantheism – although, again, not strictly orthodox – is also close to Christian teaching about the presence of God in His creation. Later in the nineteenth century, this idea was given orthodox expression in Gerard Manley Hopkins's sacramental reading of the natural world in his poetry.

For the second generation of Romantic poets, most notably Shelley and Keats, their artistry became their religion. The moral dimension of

Wordsworth's and Coleridge's poetry finds no place in their work. Shelley was careful to point out in a footnote to his 'Choruses from *Hellas*', where he deals with the problem of evil, that it should not be supposed 'that I mean to dogmatise upon a subject', while in the Preface to *Prometheus Unbound* he announces that 'didactic poetry is my abhorrence'. Nonetheless, both his and Keats's poetry is didactic in the sense that they teach that the beauty of artistry is the highest truth, as Keats wrote in the opening line of *Endymion*, in his most famous utterance:

> A thing of beauty is a joy for ever.

Similarly, in the 'Ode on a Grecian Urn', the urn affirms that 'Beauty is truth, truth beauty' and that this is all that human beings need to know: it is the sum of wisdom.

Wordsworth and Keats nonetheless shared a high view of the poet's vocation. The poet, as a priest of the Imagination, was a visionary who saw uniquely into the eternal truth of things and who therefore had the inspiration to give beautiful expression to that truth. Both would have agreed with Shelley's teaching that the poets are 'the unacknowledged legislators of the World'.

Assignment

Explore the 'gothic' dimension of Romanticism in poetry, the 'gothic novel' and the nineteenth-century revival of religion. This was a popular 'school' of writing in the nineteenth century, drawing upon the fascination with medieval culture and religion, especially its more bizarre supernatural manifestations. How would you define the 'gothic'? What are its characteristics and how is it revealed in literary terms?

SPECIAL STUDY 9

John Keats (1795–1821)

ABOUT THE AUTHOR

Born in London and apprenticed, at fifteen, to an apothecary, Keats trained as a surgeon. He qualified, but preferred a literary career. He joined the Romantic circle of William Hazlitt and Leigh Hunt and met his fellow-poet, Shelley, in Hunt's house. Hunt printed some of Keats's early poems, such as the sonnet on Chapman's Homer, which appeared in 1816. Keats published his poems, with Shelley's help, in 1817. In 1819 he wrote 'Bright star!. . .', 'La Belle Dame . . .' and the great Odes. Meantime, he had fallen in love with

■ Fanny Brawne, but by 1820 Keats was seriously ill with tuberculosis.
He sailed for Italy in September 1820, reaching Rome in November, and
died there in February 1821. Shelley famously lamented his friend's early
death in the elegy *Adonais*.

SELECTED POEMS

BRIGHT STAR!. . .
In this sonnet, Keats appeals for the constancy of love, inspired by the vigi-
lant heavenly body. He would be 'steadfast as thou art'. He calls on the star
in consciously religious language to evoke the sense of his communion with
a mystical presence. Yet that he requires constancy – and he uses a stolid word
('steadfast') to describe the star's condition – suggests both that he is incon-
stant and that the constancy he requires would be very different from the
star's.

The parenthesis, of which the remaining seven lines of the octave consist,
reveals that Keats wants steadfastness on his own terms, not those of the
'bright star'. He beautifully characterises the star's constancy, even as he
dissociates himself from its qualities:

Not in lone splendour hung aloft the night.

The ambiguity of Keats's strategy is evident here in the sounds of words, as
well as their sense. The adjective 'lone' has a moan in it and qualifies the
grandeur of 'splendour'. The sound of 'hung', as well as its disturbing associations with death, is more chilling than alluring. Most importantly, the star is
a watcher of the night, rather than a participant in its mysteries, 'with eternal
lids apart'. This is a passionless steadfastness. The participle 'gazing' emphasises the idea of a distant watcher rather than a participant in nature's daily
and seasonal processes.

Brilliantly, the poetry of the octave is syntactically suspended, like the star.
Keats is a master of the controlled artistry required in a sonnet. He deliberately chose this disciplined form in a poem on constancy. The sonnet's
constancy and purposefulness enact artistically what he would require
personally.

The suspension of the syntax is splendidly released at the beginning of the
sestet:

No – yet still steadfast, still unchangeable.

Keats repeats the negative to affirm his difference from the bright star. He
would be 'steadfast', but in the utterly different circumstance of an active
participant in erotic love:

Pillowed upon my fair love's ripening breast.

■ How different is this sensuous language from that applied to the subjects of the star's contemplation! The verbs merit special attention. The participle 'pillowed' immediately evokes the intimacy of his beloved and 'ripening' celebrates her reciprocity. 'To feel' has a tactile immediacy which is extended in the gentle cadence of 'its soft swell and fall'. This is not sleep and stillness, but as the oxymoron declares, 'a sweet unrest', a delicious passion. So far from being 'steadfast', in the way of the bright star, Keats's speaker would enjoy the wonderful restlessness of love-making.

If such constant love is not possible, he would gladly 'swoon to death'. Even dying, in this context, borrows its language from the vocabulary of passion.

Question

How, in this poem, does Keats achieve the contrast between the largeness of the moon and its cosmic functions and the intimacy of human love? (Look closely at vocabulary and rhythm.)

ON FIRST LOOKING INTO CHAPMAN'S HOMER

The title of this sonnet is an important part of the poem's meaning. George Chapman was a contemporary of Shakespeare, and Keats is referring to his first encounter with Chapman's translation of the Greek epic poet Homer, whose *Odyssey* was the classical account of a hero's mighty triumphs. We note, particularly, that Keats writes 'on first looking' – showing, again, how we need to be attentive to every word as we study poetry. In other words, the impact of Chapman's translation (and thereby the impact of Homer himself) was immediate. The revelation of the great poet's world of imagination, through Chapman's skilful translation of the ancient Greek into English, was instantaneously wondrous. Such is the unique power of poetry, Keats is implying, in a poem that we see is about three poets: Homer, Chapman and Keats. Homer inspired Chapman who inspired Keats. As always, we are alert, too, to what is absent from the poem: the suggestion that we might similarly be inspired on opening Chapman's Homer. We could infer this, from the sonnet, but it is not explicitly there. Keats is recounting his own, possibly unique communion with great poets of the past. Arguably, the poem is showing that only those of heightened poetic sensibility are susceptible to this rarefied inspiration.

The analogy which is pursued throughout the sonnet is that between physical exploration and metaphysical journeying. When Keats begins,

> Much have I traveled in the realms of gold,
> And many goodly states and kingdoms seen . . .

he is referring, of course, to his 'travelling' through the great books of literature. More precisely, he links the analogy to the travelling of Homer's Odysseus, in the Mediterranean, both by reference to 'many western islands' and the allusion to the Greek Apollo, god of poetic inspiration. Further, he imitates Homer in the use of a compound epithet (common in Homer's poetry itself, in such phrases as 'the wine-dark sea') when he introduces him into the sonnet as 'deep-browed Homer'. This wittiness emphasises the literariness of the journeying analogy, for Homer is presented as if he were the ruler of 'one wide expanse' of territory, to be encountered by such travellers as Odysseus. This 'demesne', however, is the world of poetic imagination.

Certainly, Keats would have heard of Homer before, but had not completed the usual classical education of the university men of the time (such as Wordsworth and Coleridge), so was unschooled in Greek. Hence his comment that he had 'been told' about Homer's genius and his praise of Chapman's translation for making Homer accessible:

> Yet did I never breathe its pure serene   [serene = atmosphere]
> Till I heard Chapman speak out loud and bold.

The sestet of the sonnet describes the impact of that first encounter, bringing the analogy with exploration to its magnificent conclusion:

> Then felt I like some watcher of the skies
> When a new planet swims into his ken;
> Or like stout Cortez when with eagle eyes
> He stared at the Pacific – and all his men
> Looked at each other with a wild surmise –
> Silent, upon a peak in Darien.

It is the combination of emotions which is the secret of the power of the poetry here. First, generally, there is feeling ('Then felt I...'); next, a sense of wonderment and surprise as a patient 'watcher of the skies' finds 'a new planet' swimming into his knowledge; then there is a kind of dumbstruck and awestruck astonishment, like that European explorer must have experienced who first saw the Pacific Ocean (not Cortez, but Balboa), leading to 'a wild surmise' (as the geographical implications of what has been discovered begin to register); and, finally, an almost religious reverence before the mighty sight: 'Silent, upon a peak in Darien'.

Essentially, Keats is showing that Chapman, through the skill of his translation, speaking out 'loud and bold', opened a whole new world of literary experience and imagination for him. It is one of the great compliments in poetry. In writing about it so splendidly, in the geographical analogy, Keats is also indicating, in the character of his own writing, that he is not only an admirer of Homer but has incorporated the spirit of his poetry into his own.

Question

How do the sounds of the poetry, in this sonnet, communicate the ideas and emotions of the poet?

LA BELLE DAME SANS MERCI: A BALLAD

As its subtitle indicates, this is a ballad and an excellent example of the music of Keats's poetry: from the lyrical stanzaic form, the lilting ballad metre, the refrain-like repetition of phrases, the incantatory use of 'And', to the rhyming second and fourth lines of each stanza.

The poem blends two preoccupations of Romanticism: the chivalric world of the Romance period in the Middle Ages and the tendency to melancholy, especially as the result of love. For the Romantics, the pain of love could be as thrilling as its satisfaction.

Here, the beloved is a 'faery's child', and we need to remember that the domain of fairy in medieval times could be evil. She is not a Tinkerbell. Her very wildness, however, excites the speaker's passion.

It is important to note that Keats does not enclose the knight's speech in inverted commas, and therefore deliberately entertains the notion of himself as the knight. Imaginatively, he becomes that Romantic lover:

> O what can ail thee, knight-at-arms,
> Alone and palely loitering?

The musicality of the vocabulary here is palpable: there is a wail in 'ail' and a moan in 'alone', which increase the sense of misery evoked by the visual image. In the truncated last lines of the stanzas, where the iambic metre is disturbed, Keats marvellously conveys the air of finality attending the death of passion: 'and the harvest's done'.

The flowers of the third stanza are linked with feminine purity, but here the lily is mixed with anguish and the rose, like the sedge, is withering. As we have seen, the Romantics enjoyed associating human emotions with states in nature.

Of the faery's child herself, Keats's most memorable description refers to her wildness – the adjective 'wild' is repeated several times. In the fifth stanza, as a knight from Romance should do, he engages in love's service, presenting her with gifts of adornment. She very quickly submits to her lover, in an eroticism which overturns the idealism usually associated with chivalric love:

> She looked at me as she did love,
> And made sweet moan.

This reconstruction of the tradition alerts us to the idea that this love is not secure, for all the abandon of its participants. The first sign of disease in their bond appears in the seventh stanza, where her declaration 'I love thee true' is, nonetheless, in 'language strange'.

The source of this is the fact that she is a fairy and he is mortal. Hence her sorrow in stanza eight, for their love cannot last:

> . . . there she wept and sighed full sore.

The disparity of their conditions leads to a destructive passion in which she must consume her suitors, as the knight discovers in his dream (another important Romantic phenomenon).

The poem is balanced between the unconstrained joy of their love and the price that had to be paid for it. Is he saying, then, that such love should not be indulged? It is more likely that this poem should be read as a thrilling evocation of forbidden passion, than as a warning against it, despite its debilitating consequences.

Question

How and why is Keats's choice of the ballad form suitable to the subject matter of this poem?

ODE TO A NIGHTINGALE

In the formal utterance of an ode, Keats enunciates many of the convictions of Romanticism. He even reminds us of the source of the term 'Romanticism' in the second stanza of this poem, in his reference to 'Provençal song'. For inspiration, the Romantics looked back to medieval times, and a focus of their nostalgia was the troubadour poetry of old France, such as found in Provence. 'Romance' was the vernacular language of that region and period. It was derived from Latin, as its name suggests, though different from it.

The nightingale, for Keats, is at once the singing bird of nature – a creature of the night which sings most beautifully in the breeding season – and a symbol of the Romantic poet who was drawn to the mystery of night and the celebration of passion.

In hearing its song, Keats is like one drugged in ecstasy: 'being too happy in thine happiness'. Here we see Keats in a familiar attitude, of extremity. Whether in pain or joy, he is discovered at the most extreme point of that experience. Most of all he admires the 'full-throated ease' of the nightingale's song: its poetry comes unhaltingly, triumphantly, as all poets wish theirs would do.

In Keats's plea for the same unplanned and abundant inspiration, he juxtaposes the frigid north with the fecund south. He would travel to Provence or to the very home of the muses in Greece, to drink from their fountain:

> With beaded bubbles winking at the brim,
> And purple-stained mouth.

It is a pagan image of satiety which changes into a glad renunciation of worldliness like that which concludes 'Bright star!':

> and leave the world unseen,
> And with thee fade away into the forest dim.

The reasons for Keats's infertility in song are given in the next stanza, although, ironically, he writes an inspired poetry about his difficulties in composition. We notice, in particular, that thought is considered one of the pains of life. As Keats remarked famously in one of his letters:

> O for a Life of sensations rather than of Thoughts!

Keats's speaker would fly invisibly to a realm beyond the restrictions of the 'dull brain' to commune with the spirit of artistic creation in the enchanted forest of the imagination:

> While thou art pouring forth thy soul abroad
> In such an ecstasy!

Compared to the immortal bird, he is but a 'sod'. The thud of that word marks a clear distinction between the music of poetic immortality and the mortally prosaic domain of our aspirations to the spontaneity and beauty of nature's artistry.

For Keats, it is song or poetry that redeems the world. He imagines that the biblical Ruth, desolate in a foreign country, was soothed by the nightingale's song, and that in the realm of faery, as in ancient days, the fears and dangers of life and all its tragedy could be charmed away by poetic artistry.

In the concluding stanza, the poet must bid farewell to the bird and the fancies which have temporarily consoled him. Exquisitely, Keats records the disappearance of the nightingale's song, in a graded distancing:

> Past the near meadows, over the still stream,
> Up the hill-side; and now 'tis buried deep
> In the next valley-glades.

What is true in life, he asks finally: what we envisage in moments of inspiration, or our ordinary existence? It is a rhetorical question. For Keats, the truth of experience belongs to the moments of inspiration and imagination.

> ## Question
> Trace the language and imagery of escape in this poem. What is the essence of its effectiveness?

ODE ON MELANCHOLY

It is the arresting opening line of this ode which strikes us, initially, with its succession of negatives:

> No, no, go not to Lethe, neither twist
> Wolf's-bane . . .

Keats catalogues the methods by which one might annihilate the despair of melancholy. But all of these would lead to utter destruction. Do not go to Lethe (or Hades), he argues; avoid Proserpine, the Queen of Hell, and yew-berries from the graveyard, and beetles, moths and owls, synonymous with darkness, death and burial. This gruesome list supports the view of Keats's poetry that relates it to Shakespeare and the Elizabethan–Jacobean world. These lines have a Donnean quality, yet the conclusion of the first stanza is perfectly Romantic: self-annihilation would destroy the experience of 'wakeful anguish'. Like the 'sweet unrest' of 'Bright star!', the passion of melancholy should be consciously known; savoured indeed.

In the style of a prescription – and this, too, has a distinctly Elizabethan and Jacobean flavour – Keats provides a cure for melancholy in the second stanza. It is to transport oneself to the other extreme of experience: exultant joy. We notice the sensuous immediacy of the verbs which dramatise such a wholehearted abandon:

> . . . glut thy sorrow on a morning rose.

And the process climaxes in some violent love-making that is straight out of Donne:

> Or if thy mistress some rich anger shows,
> Emprison her soft hand, and let her rave,
> And feed deep, deep upon her peerless eyes.

The drama of this writing contrasts perfectly with the listlessness of melancholy.

For all Keats's concentration on emotion in this poem, its organisation is strictly argumentative. Like Donne, he combines passion and thought. The first stanza introduces the thesis: melancholy exists, and is a dastardly afflic-tion, encouraging suicidal thoughts. The second stanza provides the antidote in an antithesis: melancholy may be banished by joy. The third stanza,

■ predictably, is a synthesis: melancholy dwells with the very means of its
banishment:

> Ay, in the very temple of Delight
> Veiled Melancholy has her sovran shrine.

The emphasis, in Romanticism, on eccentric, extreme experience is beautifully represented here as Keats argues that melancholy will only be known by
those whose sensibilities are sufficiently refined to experience ecstasy. Only
he

> whose strenuous tongue
> Can burst Joy's grape against his palate fine

will similarly know the 'wakeful anguish of the soul'. As elsewhere in his
poetry, Keats combines passion and its consequences realistically, for all the
adornment of his language. Emotions are ephemeral – joy and pleasure must
die (as in 'La Belle Dame sans Merci') but Keats is not arguing that, therefore
they should not be experienced.

Melancholy, personified in this ode, is female, as Keats closes by noting
her victory over him:

> His soul shall taste the sadness of her might,
> And be among her cloudly trophies hung.

Her spoils of victory are 'cloudy' because they have to do with ethereal
qualities: the soul and spirit of man.

Question
How does the framework of argument in this poem strengthen Keats's
presentation of powerful emotion?

Assignment
Make a study of the verbs in this poem. How are the ideas of the poem
advanced through Keats's use of them?

ODE ON A GRECIAN URN
In the classical form of the ode, Keats concentrates, in this poem, on the
classical object, and the ancient Greek scene depicted on it:

> O Attic shape! Fair attitude! With brede   [brede = woven pattern]

Of marble men and maidens overwrought.

The symmetry and beauty of the urn emblematise the self-conscious construction of the poem Keats has written about it.

It appears to be a poem about the timelessness of art by one who often writes of the mortality and mutability of life. Keats would even transcend such art as is known in life for a higher form:

Heard melodies are sweet, but those unheard
Are sweeter . . .

He attempts, in fact, to achieve the impossible: a supernatural artistry, a toneless music:

therefore, ye soft pipes, play on;
Not to the sensual ear, but, more endeared,
Pipe to the spirit ditties of no tone.

Similarly, he describes youth and love without their concomitant qualities of age and melancholy, catching love just before it comes to climax and freezing it there. Already, we are becoming suspicious of the ideal world portrayed on the urn:

Bold Lover, never, never canst thou kiss,
Though winning near the goal . . .

What kind of love is this, without kisses and bliss? Certainly, it is 'all breathing human passion far above', but the important word there is 'breathing'. It is breathless, lifeless, like the ashes urns often contained.

What is the scene depicted on the urn? Keats reveals its details with a painterly succinctness and a Miltonic resonance in his description of the sacrificial beast: 'And all her silken flanks with garlands dressed'. Again, this is ambiguous. The pagan scene is beautiful, but its focus is death – of the heifer, and of the town that has been deserted:

thy streets for evermore
Will silent be; and not a soul to tell
Why thou art desolate . . .

If Keats truly believed – as he appears to be arguing – that the supersensual world was to be preferred, that unheard melodies are sweeter than heard ones, then we might be persuaded that he would prefer a love permanently unfulfilled, a town bereft of its life for ever, and 'marble men and maidens' to human beings of flesh and blood.

The fifth stanza clarifies the difficulty of this apparently puzzling poem. Its central exclamation, 'Cold Pastoral!' indisputably dissociates Keats from the

■ teaching he appears to have been promoting. The urn depicts the pastoral world of ancient Greece, but it is as frigid as death. The concept of pastoral, in literature, usually recalls ideas of warmth and emotion. Keats's adjective 'Cold' is strikingly contradictory.

Certainly, the urn is finally addressed as a 'friend to man', because it speaks of the eternal, but that is a tepid compliment in comparison with the almost hysterical address in the third stanza ('Ah, happy, happy boughs. . . . / happy love! more happy, happy love!'). The poem, as it proceeds, discloses Keats's detachment from the urn's supersensual lifelessness.

The final lines have proved the most troublesome in Keats's poetry for we have no copy of them in Keats's hand and, in 1820, two editions with opposing punctuation appeared – one enclosing 'Beauty is truth, truth beauty' in inverted commas, the other not: one suggesting that the urn gives utterance to the equation only, with Keats affirming its teaching in the final lines, the other suggesting that both lines might be the urn's.

The excessive attention to these lines has obscured the importance of the crucial phrase in the stanza, and the poem as a whole: 'Cold Pastoral!' As we have suggested, the lines may be punctuated with just the identification of beauty with truth in inverted commas, or the two lines in their entirety thus enclosed. For Keats believes in the identification, and its sufficiency for life – so whether the urn gives utterance to it, or he does, is inconsequential. What matters is that the poem as a whole shows that the urn's presentation of this truth is insufficient. For truth and beauty, for Keats, were discovered and revealed in the sensual experience of life and art.

Question
What is the significance, in the context of the argument of the poem as a whole, of the phrase 'Cold Pastoral!'?

TO AUTUMN
This hymn of praise varies the typical Romantic concentration on Spring, as Keats reminds us in the third stanza that Autumn has its 'music' too.

In the first stanza, he conveys the fecundity of the season in a series of verbs which convey the sense of nature at the extremity of her bounty: 'to load and bless', 'to bend', 'fill', 'to swell... and plump', 'to set budding more', 'o'er-brimmed'. This is sensuous poetry as Keats refers to the 'clammy cells' of the bees; and it is musical in the opening, engaging alliteration:

Season of mists and mellow fruitfulness.

■ This is extended in the second line in 'bosom-friend' and 'maturing' and in the humming and buzzing sounds of the last three lines, evocative of bees.

In the personification of Autumn, in the second stanza, we have a pagan figure of jocular, somewhat slovenly, and benign intoxication. She is 'careless' – casual and carefree – and in the wake of a successful harvest, is unconcerned in her reaping.

The details in these two stanzas (as in the third to come) make it clear that this is an English autumn: the 'thatch-eves' and 'cottage-trees', the Anglo-Saxon simplicity of much of the vocabulary, the 'cider-press', which we can easily imagine in Somerset, and the bird-life, such as the robin of English winters.

Nowhere is the music of Keats's poetry, the intensity of his vision and the air of mystery which he loves to convey, better combined than in the closing lines of this poem. The music abides in the onomatopoeia: 'a wailful choir', the *mourning* gnats, the *bleating* lambs, the singing hedge-crickets, the *whistling* of the robin and the *twittering* of the swallows. All of these sounds are orchestrated in a song of praise to Autumn, which nonetheless acknowledges its transience. With exemplary poise, Keats balances the air of foreboding at the end – the gathering swallows – with the bright song of the robin heralding winter.

Assignment

'Passionate he may be, but Keats's speaker is also thoughtful and philosophical, giving argumentative strength and purpose to his emotional outpourings.' Do you agree? Refer to two or three poems.

Victorianism

10

FAITH AND DOUBT

The Victorian Age took its name from the long-reigning monarch, Queen Victoria, who ascended the throne in 1837 and died in 1901. However, this term is misleading for several reasons. First, it suggests that that period of more than sixty years was monochrome in its characteristics, whereas it was a time of extraordinary variety and development in English life and human experience at large. Further, 'Victorianism' implies that the personal convictions and temperament of the Queen expressed her subjects' interpretations of and responses to life. In fact, as Lytton Strachey argues in his biography of Victoria (1921), the monarch was a very imperfect representation of the age that bears her name.

Victorianism is the story of unprecedented developments and turbulent complexity in the intellectual, moral and cultural lives of society and of individuals. Yet the Queen preserved the characteristics of her singular personality through more than eighty years of existence, as Strachey observes:

> the girl, the wife, the aged woman, were the same: vitality,
> conscientiousness, pride and simplicity were hers to the latest hour.

In particular, her straightforward religious beliefs contrast markedly with the furious engagement between theological doctrines and scientific theories, of faith and doubt, during her reign. And while the nation's affection for Victoria was clearly demonstrated in the jubilees of her final years, she had endured long periods of profound unpopularity, as in her reclusive existence during her mourning for her consort Prince Albert, who died in 1861. When she later appeared to have become friendly with her Scottish servant, John Brown, this relationship was the subject (as Strachey notes) of 'ribald jests'.

The understanding of the Victorian Age and the appreciation of its literature in the twentieth century has been seriously hampered by the caricatures of Victorianism (such as those of the Queen herself as, for example, the dumpy, sour-faced 'widow at Windsor'). These were enthusiastically promoted by the first post-Victorian generation which was anxious to liberate itself from the repressive aspects of Victorian life, and keen to blame that heritage of national self-confidence for the tragic bloodbath of the First World War. This generation was impatient to forge a new society that would embody the antitheses of the shortcomings of its predecessor.

The problem with this reaction (like many reactions, an over-reaction) is that it constructed a substantially critical image of the previous age which produced further distortions. Only the negative aspects of this image were heeded by subsequent generations. The best example, in literature, of this misreading of history and the responses to it is to be found in the customary presentation and interpretation of Lytton Strachey's study of several *Eminent Victorians*, published in 1918.

Strachey's highly entertaining biographical essays on Cardinal Manning, Florence Nightingale, Dr Arnold and General Gordon are nearly always cited as proof of the Edwardian and Georgian generations' repudiation of their Victorian forebears for their religious hypocrisy, self-righteous priggishness and vainglory. Certainly, Strachey's portraits are largely negative appraisals. His bitterness is often apparent – as in the essay on Dr Arnold, the model of the Victorian headmaster and the father of the poet and critic, Matthew Arnold. This is the least objective of the four biographies. But it is a superficial reading of *Eminent Victorians* (and an over-simplification of Strachey's and many of his contemporaries' attitudes to the age of their birth and upbringing) to see the work only as character assassination designed to destroy the reputation of the society which produced and canonised these eminences.

Strachey's generation failed to notice that while he was deconstructing the Victorian idolisation of its heroes, he was simultaneously constructing their extraordinary individuality. *Eminent Victorians* is as much a testament to the vitality and eccentricity of the age as a set of debunking caricatures. Indeed, Strachey's general view of Victorianism in his essay on Thomas Carlyle (1928) shows the inadequacy of the representation of his interpretation of the age as merely negative and of the conception of Victorianism which persisted for most of the twentieth century. It was

> an age of barbarism and prudery, of nobility and cheapness, of satisfac-
> tion and desperation; an age in which all the outlines were tremen-
> dous and all the details sordid; when gas jets struggled feebly through
> the circumambient fog, when the hour of dinner might be at any
> moment between two and six, when the doses of rhubarb were peri-
> odic and gigantic, when pet dogs threw themselves out of upper
> storey windows, when cooks reeled drunk in areas, when one sat for
> hours with one's feet in dirty straw dragged along the street by
> horses, when an antimacassar was on every chair and the baths were
> minute tin circles, and the beds were full of bugs and disasters.

Strachey's emphasis is on the Dickensian oddity, the perversity and peculiarity of the period. Aspects of it were disgusting, certainly, but it was amusing and fascinating too.[1]

I

Those several decades were bound together by the period's commitment to change and progress. 'This wondrous mankind', Carlyle wrote in 1831, on the brink of the new age, 'is advancing somewhither'. As the advances appeared, self-confidence flourished too, along with its less attractive manifestations. Tennyson wrote in 'Locksley Hall' of a hope in the triumph of humanity over daunting adversity:

> For I dipped into the future, far as human eye could see,
> Saw the Vision of the world, and all the wonder that would be . . .
>
> Heard the heavens fill with shouting, and there rained a ghastly dew
> From the nations' airy navies grappling in the central blue;
>
> Far along the world-wide whisper of the south wind rushing warm,
> With the standards of the people plunging through the thunderstorm;
>
> Till the war drum throbbed no longer, and the battle flags were furled
> In the Parliament of man, the Federation of the world.

While his idealism was not finally justified, Britain nonetheless secured its place as the world's premier imperial power during the Victorian Age and London became the centre of the civilised world, its population trebling to more than six million during Victoria's reign. The transition from an agricultural to an industrial economy was completed, and slowly but relentlessly, economic prosperity was accompanied by a gradual extension of voting rights to all the people. The working conditions of the lower classes, especially in the mines and factories, were improved through parliamentary representation and legislation. The second Reform Bill of 1867 extended the franchise to the working class. Tennyson captures the spirit of the age precisely (if in technically inaccurate imagery, from the new railway):

> Not in vain the distance beacons. Forward, forward let us range,
> Let the great world spin forever down the ringing grooves of change.

The formidable historian of the period, Macaulay, saw signs of the 'natural progress of society' everywhere. The accomplishments of Victorian technology were stupendously celebrated in the Great Exhibition in London in 1851. A decade later, Benjamin Disraeli, statesman and novelist, romantic eccentric and

---

1. For a detailed discusson of Strachey's attitude to the Victorians and Victorianism, and his work at large, see my *Lytton Strachey* (New York: Edwin Mellen 1995).

confidant of the Queen, reflected that 'it is a privilege to live in this age of rapid and brilliant events'. Undoubtedly it is difficult, even with a more detached evaluation of Victorian achievements, to reconcile the spirit of the time with the modern dismissal of Victorianism as stolid, stuffy and complacent. The Victorians may well have become so in their latter days, and this is scarcely surprising given their accomplishment and prosperity. But a stronger impulse for a longer period was their sense of excitement at the prospect of a constantly improving world for humanity, both in material and spiritual terms.

Any tendencies to complacency were smartly checked by the numerous controversialists of this age of self-scrutiny. John Ruskin, in 'The Storm-Cloud of the Nineteenth Century' (1884), describes and criticises the pollution of the atmosphere by the poisonous smoke from industry in such as Manchester's 'devil darkness'. For him, the exploitation of factory workers in that environment was a 'slave trade . . . much more cruel . . . than that which we have so long been endeavouring to put down'. In *Culture and Anarchy* (1869), Matthew Arnold ridicules the shortcomings of society in each of its classes – Barbarians, Philistines and Populace – and in *The Function of Criticism* (1864) he provided a vignette of Victorian urban reality in his reference to dismal Nottinghamshire: 'the gloom, the smoke, the cold, the strangled illegitimate child!' The corruption of institutions and the grinding poverty which produced such suffering for millions are also exposed in the novels of Charles Dickens such as *Hard Times* (1854), in which Coketown is based on Preston, a centre of cotton manufacturing in Lancashire.

For the Victorians, material and spiritual well-being came to be interdependent. Their conception of spiritual improvement was substantially focused on the amelioration of domestic and working conditions. This would raise the standards of moral life. Works of social philanthropy and charity are hallmarks of Victorianism. While some of this charity was sanctimonious, mean-spirited and almost as terrible as the blights it was meant to cure (as we see in the Evangelical charity school in Charlotte Bronte's *Jane Eyre*), it is again a gross distortion of the humanitarian spirit of the age only to present it critically. Florence Nightingale's reform of nursing, the founding of societies for the prevention of cruelty to animals and the poet Christina Rossetti's work amongst 'fallen women' were characteristic demonstrations of the Victorian social conscience, with its Christian origins.

In 'Up-Hill' (1858), Christina Rossetti (see Special Study 11) provides a vignette of the Victorian commitment to moral strenuousness, with its Christian apotheosis, combined with the exhaustion of its pursuit:

> Does the road wind up-hill all the way?
> >Yes, to the very end.
> Will the day's journey take the whole long day?
> >From morn to night, my friend.

With her profound faith, unlike many of her contemporaries, Rossetti had no doubts about eternity. As she and the Victorian Age grew older, her world-weariness intensified. These tormented lines of 1881 provide a sharp critique of the optimism of Victorianism and our conception of the Victorians' self-satisfaction:

> I am sick of foresight and of memory,
> I am sick of all I have and all I see,
> I am sick of self, and there is nothing new;
> Oh weary impatient patience of my lot! –
>   Thus with myself: how fares it, Friends, with you?

II

The revivals of faith early in the nineteenth century, in the Evangelical and Oxford Movements, came under increasing challenge during the Victorian Age, both from within Christian studies and outside in scientific discovery. The Victorian period was, as Tennyson described it, a 'recklessly speculative age'.

The so-called 'Higher Criticism' of the Bible originated in Germany and brought the holy text under scholarly scrutiny. It revealed that the scriptures, just like other literary texts, had evolved historically, and that the received canonical books should not necessarily be read either literally or as the products of their supposed authors. What had been considered infallible was called into question in this process. Ironically, this questioning was attuned to that very spirit of progress which those Victorians who had retained their faith tended to interpret as God-ordained, as one of their hymns proclaimed:

> God is working his purpose out as year succeeds to year,
> God is working his purpose out and the time is drawing near;
> Nearer and nearer draws the time, the time that shall surely be,
> When the earth shall be filled with the glory of God as the waters
>   cover the sea.

In the Higher Criticism, the foundations of the faith of countless Christians were shaken, particularly in the Protestant and Anglican Churches which based their teachings on the inerrancy of the Bible.

Faith was further destabilised when these new textual uncertainties about divine truth were combined with scientific evidence, such as Sir Charles Lyell's *Principles of Geology* (1830) which established the aeons-old age of the earth. The Bible had taught, if read literally, that the world was created a mere 6000 years ago. The crisis of belief caused by geological research is personalised in Edmund Gosse's *Father and Son* (1907), where the breach between the generations of faith and doubt in Victorianism is recounted. The author's father, Philip, was both a renowned zoologist and a member of the Plymouth Brethren, a fundamentalist

Christian sect. Incapable of letting sleeping dogmas lie, as the son wittily observes, he was reduced to reconciling his fidelity to scientific truth and biblical teaching by arguing that God 'hid the fossils in the rocks in order to tempt geologists into infidelity'. In other words, faith on this reckoning was believing what you knew to be untrue.

Charles Darwin's evolutionary theories, propounded in *The Origin of Species* (1859) and *The Descent of Man* (1871), were equally damaging. He argued that instead of the originally sinless Adam and Eve in the Garden of Eden (as the book of Genesis taught),

> our ancestor was a hairy quadruped furnished with a tail and pointed ears, probably arboreal in his habits . . . man is the codescendant with other mammals of a common progenitor.

If this were true, man did not – as the Churches maintained – have a privileged place as the pinnacle of the earthly creation, as the image of God, but was merely part of an age-old biological process of the survival of the fittest. Rather than being a little lower than the angels, man was somewhat more developed than the ape. The theory was a devastating critique of the 'egotistical sublime' of the Romantics and destroyed the Christian vocations of many. Walter Pater, who was to become the theorist of aestheticism, abandoned his intentions to become an Anglican priest when he studied Darwin's theories at Oxford. Darwin asserted, with reference to contemporary anecdotes of the dignity of animal behaviour, that

> for my own part I would as soon be descended from that heroic little monkey, who braved his dreaded enemy in order to save the life of his keeper; or from that old baboon who, descending from the mountains, carried away in triumph his young comrade from a crowd of astonished dogs – as from a savage who delights to torture his enemies, offers up bloody sacrifices, practices infanticide without remorse, treats his wives like slaves, knows no decency, and is haunted by the grossest superstitions.

That 'savage' was not necessarily in the jungle. He could be found in the 'civilised' Victorian cities.

Negative interpretations of the human condition, of course, were at least as old as Christianity, but the prospect of immortality compensated for the pains of this world. However, confidence in eternal life was another casualty of Victorian 'agnosticism', a term originally coined by one of the leading scientific controversialists of the time, Thomas Henry Huxley. He argued, in *Science and Culture* (1880), that 'nature is the expression of a definite order with which nothing interferes' and by 'nothing' he meant God. This non-interference included our lives beyond (or rather in) the grave, as the words that Huxley wrote for his tombstone indicate – although with the contingency of agnosticism rather than the certainty of atheism:

> Be not afraid, ye waiting hearts that weep
> For still he giveth His beloved sleep,
> And if an endless sleep He wills, so best.

The irony of this inscription is that it draws upon the language of the Bible, even though it questions its teachings about the resurrection of the body. It also capitalises the pronoun references to the Deity whose existence Huxley doubted. Swinburne was more direct when he observed, in 'The Garden of Proserpine' (1866), that:

> no life lives forever;
> That dead men rise up never;
> That even the weariest river
> Winds somewhere safe to sea.

That last is an image of oblivion at the end of life, after 'this short day', as Walter Pater called it, 'of frost and sun', in which the only pleasure and fulfilment we can enjoy derive from 'getting as many pulsations as possible into the given time'.

The Victorians came to concentrate less on eternity and more on the utilitarian improvement of the lot of humanity in this world. John Stuart Mill's philosophy of Utilitarianism was based on the principle that the criterion of morality was the greatest happiness of the greatest number. This would produce a heaven on earth – in William Morris's phrase, an earthly paradise. Yet the afterlife continued to vex the Victorians. The most popular poem of the age, *In Memoriam*, is an extended meditation on the subject (see Special Study 10 of Tennyson). Although they were, as Arnold reflected, 'light half-believers of our casual creeds', the materialism of Utilitarianism could not satisfy the spiritual yearnings of a people still influenced by the spirit if not the beliefs of Christianity and Romanticism.

Carlyle and Arnold, although critical of ecclesiastical and doctrinal formulations, wanted to keep that religious spirit alive, but outside the Churches. Carlyle advocated a 'Natural Supernaturalism'. Thomas Huxley reflected that he 'led me to know that a deep sense of religion was compatible with the entire absence of theology'. Arnold believed that poetry could provide the sustenance formerly supplied by Christian teaching and worship. His theory is another example of the Victorian dissociation between the generations: the faith in Christianity of Dr Arnold was supplanted by the faith in poetry of his son. The poet, Matthew Arnold argued, 'saw life steadily, and saw it whole'. He could speak both 'to the need in man for conduct, and to the need in him for beauty'. In *The Study of Poetry* (1880), he said that 'most of what now passes with us for religion and philosophy will be replaced with poetry'.

In the life and writings of Arnold's friend Arthur Hugh Clough – the 'Thyrsis' of Arnold's pastoral elegy about him – we find expressed the central dilemma of Clough's life and of Victorianism at large: the conflict between faith and doubt. In Clough's poem, 'Say Not the Struggle Nought Availeth' (1849), this torment is vividly captured in an extended metaphor from warfare – of spiritual, intellectual and emotional conflict:

> Say not the struggle nought availeth,
> The labour and the wounds are vain,
> The enemy faints not, nor faileth,
> And as things have been they remain.
>
> If hopes were dupes, fears may be liars;
> It may be, in yon smoke concealed,
> Your comrades chase e'en now the fliers,
> And, but for you, possess the field.

Addressed as much to himself as to the reader, these lines are an incitement to go into battle against the enemy (which are the old beliefs that have entrapped humanity). The recognition that the struggle is futile indicates how momentous it is. But we should not be thwarted by fears which may be lies. Yet he confesses that hopes for a new order of existence, free from this oppressor, may be dupes. This is certainly a doubtful state of mind that is being presented. It is akin to that described by his friend Matthew Arnold in the 'Stanzas from the Grande Chartreuse':

> Wandering between two worlds, one dead,
> The other powerless to be born.

The future cannot be clearly discerned: 'in yon smoke concealed', like the result of a furious battle. Yet Clough has the sense that his comrades – others who have challenged the old armoury of dogma with the force of scepticism – are pursuing the remnants of the fleeing alien from the field of the world. Clough does not underestimate the painstaking slowness of the campaign, now represented in a changed metaphor of the sea:

> For while the tired waves, vainly breaking,
> Seem here no painful inch to gain,
> Far back, through creeks and inlets making,
> Comes silent, flooding in, the main.

And in a third metaphor, expanding the imagery of the rising sun as synonymous with the truth of God, he closes in a cadence of muted optimism as the west is seen to be also bright with light:

> And not by eastern windows only,
> When daylight comes, comes in the light,

> In front, the sun climbs slow, how slowly,
> But westward, look, the land is bright.

This visual image of a world vested with light, both in the east and in the west, represents a pervasive truth that is earth-centred.

The same conviction, but in a more affirmative context and with a musical analogy, is found at the conclusion of Robert Browning's dramatic monologue 'Abt Vogler'. The musician-priest, who had gladly offered his artistry to God, is equally content to abide on the plane of ordinary existence:

> Well, it is earth with me; silence resumes her reign:
> I will be patient and proud, and soberly acquiesce.
> Give me the keys. I feel for the common chord again,
> Sliding by semitones, till I sink to the minor – yes,
> And I blunt it into a ninth, and I stand on alien ground,
> Surveying awhile the heights I rolled from into the deep;
> Which, hark, I have dared and done, for my resting place is found,
> The C Major of this life: so, now I will try to sleep.

But Victorian confidence, such as this, was always being undermined by apprehensions and anxieties. In 'Prospice' (that is, 'look forward'), Browning does look forward and discovers that an old enemy resists resolution into the harmonies of 'this life':

> Fear death? – to feel the fog in my throat,
> The mist in my face,
> When the snows begin, and the blasts denote
> I am nearing the place,
> The power of the night, the press of the storm,
> The post of the foe;
> Where he stands, the Arch Fear in a visible form,
> Yet the strong man must go.

For all their commitment to change and progress, the Victorians were profoundly aware of the ultimately ephemeral character of human enterprises and existence. In yet another paradox of their age, this self-confident, forward-looking people were much preoccupied with death.

III

The revaluation of the Victorian Age in all its dimensions – in particular in a renewed appreciation of its rich and diverse literature – continues today. The scorn of Victorian poetry – and especially that of the poet laureate Alfred, Lord Tennyson – in the early twentieth century was part of the larger rejection of Romanticism, which was seen to have been reduced to the so-called Decadence of the 1890s. The enervating sense of *fin de siècle*, the end of an era, was accompanied by the insistence (in the writings of Walter Pater and Oscar Wilde, for example) on 'art for art's sake', the self-indulgent cult of the beautiful as opposed to the useful and the edifying. This last generation of the Victorians had rejected Matthew Arnold's theory that 'poetry is at bottom a criticism of life':

> that the greatness of a poet lies in his powerful and beautiful application of ideas to life – to the question: How to live.

For the dissipated Swinburne, the aural appeal of poetic language was at least as important as anything it had to say about our lives:

> There lived a singer in France of old
> By the tideless dolorous midland sea.
> In a land of sand and ruin and gold
> There shone one woman, and none but she.

For Wilde (in the Preface to *The Picture of Dorian Gray*),

> There is no such thing as a moral or an immoral book. Books are well written, or badly written. That is all.

Aestheticism was easy to ridicule, as Gilbert and Sullivan demonstrated in their operetta *Patience* (1881), a satire of its narcissism:

> If you're anxious for to shine in the high aesthetic line as a man of
>   culture rare,
> You must get up all the germs of the transcendental terms, and plant
>   them everywhere.
> You must lie upon the daisies and discourse in novel phrases of your
>   complicated state of mind,
> The meaning doesn't matter if it's only idle chatter of a transcendental
>   kind.

The contemporary popularity of Gilbert and Sullivan's operettas, humorous verse (such as Edward Lear's), nonsense (like Lewis Carroll's) and of the comedy of the music hall reveals how limited were succeeding ages' portrayal of Victorianism as an era of dour solemnity.

As with the interpretation of Victorianism as a whole, the early Modernist poets and critics (see Chapter 11) presented readings of their Victorian predecessors that advanced their own quest to make poetry new by contradicting the worst aspects of the prevailing literary fashions. It was a highly successful campaign, assisted by the First World War (1914–18) when the Romantic, Victorian and Edwardian worldviews were finally rendered untenable.

The Modernists focused on what they regarded as the lurid emotionalism or the tedious didacticism of the worst Victorian poetry. They disliked its loose style and the obsession with length of utterance (a poetic expression, they argued, of the Victorian preoccupation with size). In prose, the succinctness of Strachey's biographical essays is a critique of the gargantuan, two-volumed Victorian biographies. For the literary artists of the early twentieth century, Victorianism (and its afterglow, Edwardianism) represented a bloated and then exhausted Romanticism.

In truth, Victorian artistry was as vigorous and various as Victorian life. In Tennyson's poetry, to which we turn now, the preoccupations and dilemmas of Victorianism are most fully represented in the context of an artistry of remarkable accomplishment and variety – a characteristic product of the age.

■ SPECIAL STUDY 10

Alfred, Lord Tennyson (1809–92)

ABOUT THE AUTHOR

Tennyson was born in 1809 at Somersby, in Lincolnshire, where his father was the rector. His early education, in a village school, was supplemented by music lessons and the classical languages and literature which he learned from his father. In these childhood experiences, we find important sources for his later poetry – its musicality and classical subjects. Tennyson attended Louth Grammar School, unhappily, from 1816 to 1820.

Aged just fourteen, Tennyson's experiments with poetry included a three-act blank-verse comedy *The Devil and the Lady*. His first printed poems appeared in 1827 when he also began his university studies at Trinity College, Cambridge. He was strikingly handsome – over six feet tall, with an imposing head and long flowing hair: every inch the Romantic idea of the poet. In the year behind him at Trinity was Arthur Henry Hallam. A deep friendship was formed between them but was abruptly curtailed when Hallam died in 1833. This had a profound effect on Tennyson and on his poetry. *In Memoriam*, his most popular poem, was dedicated to Hallam's memory. It established his reputation as the 'Poet of the People'.

After a troubled fourteen-year engagement, Tennyson married Emily Sellwood (his brother's wife's sister) in 1850, by which time his reputation as the successor of Wordsworth as the great English poet was secure and confirmed by the Poet Laureateship. Also in 1850, Tennyson published his masterwork *In Memoriam*, which had been written over the seventeen years since Hallam's death.

Tennyson's other famous poems, such as 'The Lady of Shalott' and 'The Lotos-Eaters', belong to his young manhood in the 1830s, while 'Crossing the Bar', written in 1889, comes from the twilight of his life.

Tennyson and his wife had two sons, Hallam (named after his dead friend) and Lionel (who died before his father, another grief in Tennyson's life). In the wake of this, sadness and ill-health dogged the poet's last years. Tennyson died on 6 October 1892. His widow and surviving son collaborated on the *Memoir* of his life (published in 1897).

SELECTED POEMS

THE LADY OF SHALOTT

In the Romantic tradition, to which Victorianism and Tennyson's poetry belong, the preoccupation with the past, and in particular the 'Romance' period of the Middle Ages, provided a variety of subjects for imaginative and artistic escape from the present. Consequently, distant times and places were idealised. Tennyson was especially drawn to the legendary English medieval world of King Arthur and his court, which is the setting of this poem. The Victorians saw this age in colourful, picturesque but also heroic terms: it was a time of passionate love and noble deeds.

The setting of the poem is carefully described by Tennyson in Part I. The poet presents the scene like a painter, with attention to detail, colour and the attitudes of the people, 'gazing where the lilies blow'. It is an idealised, dream-like world which moves more slowly than real life, or more delicately:

> Little breezes dusk and shiver...
> The shallop flitteth silken-sail'd.

The rhythmic pulse of the poetry catches this mixture of the languid and the ethereal perfectly, and is assisted by an abundance of alliteration. Tennyson appeals both to our eye and ear.

The section closes with a quality that Victorians loved in their literature – mystery:

> the reaper weary,
> Piling sheaves in uplands airy,
> Listening, whispers, ''Tis the fairy
> Lady of Shalott'.

Who is this mysterious Lady? Part II provides the answer, as she is seen to be an artist who is detached from life and dedicated to creating beautiful objects. But her story is made more dramatic by the curse that will fall upon her if she engages directly with reality and looks 'down to Camelot'. She must glean her subjects for her art from what appears to her in a mirror. Therefore, what she produces in tapestry is the reflection of a reflection:

> Sometimes a troop of damsels glad,
> An abbot on an ambling pad.

■ The irony of this is that the 'real' world, as Tennyson evokes it here, is as artificial as the tapestry the lady is weaving.

Central to Romantic poetry was the theme of love, both disappointment in love and satisfaction with it. In her dedication to art, and her separation from life, the lady is without love ('she hath no loyal knight and true') and her frustration closes the second part:

> when the moon was overhead,
> Came two young lovers lately wed,
> 'I am half sick of shadows', said
> The Lady of Shalott.

Tennyson achieves a magnificent tonal contrast in the next section – the juxtaposition of the largely feminine world of Parts I and II with this masculine intrusion in Part III. Contemplation gives way to action, on the spirited arrival of Sir Lancelot:

> A bow-shot from her bower-eaves,
> He rode between the barley-sheaves.

Nothing could be more different from the delicate dream-like setting which opened the poem. Yet Tennyson retains the same rhyming and rhythmic patterns. It is his vocabulary, especially his verbs ('rode', 'rung', 'flow'd', and so on) and the alliteration on 'b' that bring this passionate and active force so vividly before us. And the Lady catches its spirit, as this emphatic language indicates:

> She left the web, she left the loom,
> She made three paces thro' the room.

But the consequence is fatal:

> Out flew the web and floated wide;
> The mirror crack'd from side to side;
> 'The curse is come upon me', cried
> The Lady of Shalott.

Tennyson is exploring the conflict between the worlds of the artist and of 'real' life, of action and contemplation, of the spirit and of passion, of masculinity and femininity. He communicates his own sense of the tension between his vocation as a poet, set apart, and an obligation to be involved in society. That the artist, in isolation, will always be a mysterious figure in the world is indicated in the last part of the poem, as the knights and burghers watch the body of the Lady floating by uncomprehendingly. Lancelot, for whom she had made this sacrifice, notes her beauty and prays for her, but dispassionately.

Question
How do the sounds of this poem assist its sense?

THE LOTOS-EATERS

The Lotophagi, or Lotos-Eaters, were people who fed on a fruit – the lotos
– which had the effect of making them lose all desire to return to their native
countries. In the ninth book of his epic poem, *The Odyssey,* Homer records
Odysseus's reaction to the change which overcame those of his men who had
explored Lotos-land:

> All they now wished for was to stay where they were with the lotos-
> eaters, to browse on the lotos, and to forget that they had a home to
> return to. I had to use force to bring them back to the ships and they
> wept on the way.

The idea of antiquity (as of the Middle Ages) in the nineteenth century was
idealised, both in terms of its setting and the lives and actions of its people.
The magical Lotos-land and its spellbound inhabitants were perfect subjects
for such romanticisation:

> The charmèd sunset linger'd low adown
> In the red West . . .
> And round about the keel with faces pale,
> Dark faces pale against that rosy flame,
> The mild-eyed melancholy Lotos-eaters came.

The prelude to the poem, before the Choric Song, casts the spell of lotos-life
which is a retreat from all the obligations of country, family and work. Those
three elements were central to Victorian moral teaching, and here they are
decisively rejected by the mariners:

> We will return no more.

This separation from their former existence indicates a transcendence of
mortal life into a paradise of rest and beauty. They will not transcend death,
finally; but in the meantime they can know something of heaven. They argue
strongly to be suspended from duty now. This suggests that they doubt the
prospect of an eternal reward in the future, after doing good works all their
lives:

> Death is the end of life; ah, why
> Should life all labour be?

The Victorians were troubled by such questioning of Christian teachings of
eternal compensation for earthly exertions and sufferings. Some turned to a

■ paganism of which this poem is an early, subtle, but undeniably sensuous expression:

> . . . propt on beds of amaranth and moly,
> How sweet (while warm airs lull us, blowing lowly)
> With half-dropt eyelid still.

The intoxication of pleasure is graphically conveyed through a combination of alliteration, onomatopoeia and visual detail, and the desire for escape from the tedium of daily existence is passionately expressed.

However, the idle sailors do not escape the claims of their former lives. Indeed, in the even-numbered stanzas in the chorus, that other world is presented – most tellingly in stanza 6:

> Dear is the memory of our wedded lives.

But the last even-numbered stanza, which closes the poem, expresses their resolution to remain in Lotos-land, unlike Odysseus's mariners who were forced to return to their ships:

> Oh rest ye, brother mariners, we will not wander more.

They are carefree, and will be 'careless of mankind', which is seen to exist in 'wasted lands' and blighted with every evil. Individual lives are absurdities, signifying nothing: 'like a tale of little meaning'. The emphatic repetition: 'surely, surely, slumber is more sweet than toil' focuses on the Romantic desire for escape and pleasure. This opposed the Victorian ethic of work and duty, and patriotic and familial obligation.

Assignment

Read Tennyson's poem 'Ulysses' – the Latin name for Odysseus – for its contrasting celebration of heroic activity: 'To strive, to seek, to find, and not to yield'. Together, 'Ulysses' and 'The Lotos-Eaters' represent an important tension in Tennysonian and Victorian thought. Discuss and describe this with detailed reference to the poems.

FROM IN MEMORIAM

As the title and dedication of this work indicate, the essential theme of *In Memoriam*, uniting all its elements, is immortality.

Dark house . . .

Tennyson is referring here to the home of the Hallam family in London's Wimpole Street. It is 'dark', both literally and metaphorically, at daybreak

■ and in mourning for Arthur Hallam's death. The most striking feature of the poem is Tennyson's presentation of the urban streetscape in all its unloveliness. It perfectly reflects his depressed mood but also realistically describes this world at that time of day – its unattractive sounds ('the noise of life') and ugly appearance:

> And ghastly thro' the drizzling rain
> On the bald street breaks the blank day.

Tennyson here anticipates the Modernist presentation of the urban wasteland in poetry in the early twentieth century, as in the poems of T. S. Eliot (see Special Study 13). We should also notice the contrast between friendliness in the past ('where my heart was used to beat / So quickly, waiting for a hand') and friendlessness now, in a powerful simile at the heart of the poem:

> And like a guilty thing I creep
> At earliest morning to the door.

Yet the climax of the poem is undeniably in its last line, both visually and aurally, in that arresting alliteration on 'b'.

Oh yet we trust . . .

In his essay on *In Memoriam*, Eliot argued that the poem should be admired not for 'the quality of its faith, but because of the quality of its doubt ... a very intense experience'.

In this lyric, Tennyson expands from the particular occasion of his grief over his friend's death, to raise the question of the purpose of life and the existence of a benevolent Creator God. Certainly, the emphasis of the poetry here is on doubt, as in the use of the vague 'somehow' in the opening line and the accumulation of the evils which we find in our world:

> pangs of nature, sins of will,
> Defects of doubt, and taints of blood.

The speaker confesses that we have no ultimate certainties – 'we know not anything' – and all that we can do is hope

> that good shall fall
> At last – far off – at last, to all,
> And every winter change to spring.

But this pious sentiment is dismissed, in the closing stanza, as a mere 'dream' by one who is infantile in the knowledge of eternal truth, and – like a baby – incapable of uttering words of hope, able only to wail in anguish:

> An infant crying for the light:
> And with no language but a cry.

■ The Victorian crisis of faith is movingly summarised in this lyric and the one that follows it.

The wish . . .

Here, Tennyson – after questioning the purpose of life on earth – expresses a concern with the afterlife in eternity. He wishes that every individual life is valuable and may not 'fail beyond the grave'. Yet the evidence of nature seems to indicate that while species are important to her, single lives are expendable: he finds, for example, in an analogy with human existence,

> that of fifty seeds,
> She often brings but one to bear.

The evidence of nature conflicts with the Christian idea of God nurturing each individual. So, 'I falter where I firmly trod'. In striking self-dramatisation, the speaker is presented

> falling with my weight of cares
> Upon the great world's altar-stairs
> That slope thro' darkness up to God.

The 'darkness' here is symbolic of the inscrutable character of God's purposes. The intensity of Tennyson's plight is articulated in directly physical and tactile terms, in the last stanza. Now his doubt is patently stronger than his religious convictions (even as he wanted those to be true):

> I stretch lame hands of faith, and grope,
> And gather dust and chaff, and call
> To what I feel is Lord of all,
> And faintly trust the larger hope.

Notice the depersonalisation of God – 'to what I feel'. The pronoun represents the Victorians' dislocation from traditional ideas of God, which was abetted by contemporary scientific theories and discoveries (about, for example, evolution) and textual criticism of the Bible that meant that intelligent men and women could no longer believe that every word of it was the literal, inspired truth.

By night we lingered . . .

Tennyson's gift for scene-setting inspires the first four stanzas of the poem. The scene is initially appealing, but has darker, more ambiguous appearances as it unfolds. The 'woolly breasts and beaded eyes' of the bats are unsettling, and while the glimmering of the 'white kine', or cattle, is attractive, there is something mysterious and even sinister about the personified trees which

■ 'laid their dark arms about the field'. In the fifth stanza, the speaker is left alone in this mysterious atmosphere.

His loneliness is passionate – 'a hunger seized my heart' – and summons vivid memories of an unnamed 'dead man', until in a mystical experience

> The living soul was flash'd on mine.

Yet, this union is fleeting, for it is dispelled by Tennyson's scepticism about the experience of the supernatural:

> At length my trance
> Was cancell'd, stricken thro' with doubt.

The closing quarter of the poem recalls the opening scene both in its details and the ambiguity of its evaluation of nature's appearances. The speaker wins back the world of time and space with expressions that are at once beautiful and gross. He uses overly luxurious adjectives – 'the full-foliaged elms' and 'the heavy-folded rose' – and aggressively demonstrative verbs: 'swung' and 'flung'. Yet the close is surprisingly affirmative: the speaker values his recollections of immortality but also gladly accepts the new life of the present and the future: 'to broaden into boundless day'.

Assignment

Read more widely in *In Memoriam*. Select three or four poems on the basis of the contrasting and distinctive poetic techniques they display and describe them in detail.

CROSSING THE BAR

Written at the end of his life, this poem is not a declaration of certain faith by Tennyson after a life of doubt. It is a prayer for a peaceful passage from time to timelessness, and an expression of hope that God and eternity do indeed exist, on the other side of death.

Tennyson uses a nautical metaphor throughout (the 'bar' being a sand-bar at the mouth of a harbour) and draws on the ancient ideas of the sea both as our true home and as synonymous with immortality. Like many of his fellow Victorians, the speaker can no longer assent to a doctrinal and dogmatic Christianity, so he is not certain that he will see God. However, he retains the desire for faith and resurrection to eternal life:

> For tho' from out our bourne of Time and Place
> The flood may bear me far,
> I hope to see my Pilot face to face
> When I have crost the bar.

■ The most significant words here are 'may' and 'hope'. It is poetry of contingency, not certainty.

> ## Questions
> 1. 'The concern with immortality is most urgent in Tennyson's most vivid writing.' Do you agree? Refer to two or three poems.
> 2. 'It is through his imagery that Tennyson most tellingly conveys his ideas and emotions.' Is this true? Refer closely to two poems.

IV

Two features of Victorian poetry are of vital interest to its students: the relationship between it and the Romantic poetry of the earlier nineteenth century, and the variety and abundance of poetic subjects and forms which reflect the complexities of the age itself:

> the confusion of the present time is great [Matthew Arnold wrote in 1853], the multitude of voices, counselling different things, bewildering, the number of existing works capable of attracting a young writer's attention, and of becoming his models, immense.

The broad similarities between Romantic and Victorian poetry are clear. The Romantics' emphasis on the emotions persists in the Victorians' work. The world of nature and the nostalgic impulse – Tennyson's 'passion of the past' – remain. In Arnold's 'Scholar Gypsy', the rustic seventeenth-century life of the student who had forsaken Oxford for 'a gypsy crew' and 'roamed the world with that wild brotherhood' is romantically idealised as an indictment of modernity. The idea of the poet as a visionary and seer, as well as an inspired maker, continues even into the early modern period. W. B. Yeats, for example, referred to himself as a Romantic as late as 1931 (see Special Study 12).

The conversational and lyrical voices of Romantic poetry are heard again in Victorianism, yet with variations. There are, for example, the dramatic monologues of Browning and the bewitching musicality of Tennyson, as in this song from *The Princess*, where the sounds and the sense are one:

> Sweet and low, sweet and low,
> Wind of the western sea,
> Low, low, breathe and blow,
> Wind of the western sea!
> Over the rolling waters go,

Come from the dying moon, and blow,
Blow him again to me;
While my little one, while my pretty one, sleeps.

The poetry of Gerard Manley Hopkins was very different, but in many thematic aspects it, too, was quintessentially Victorian. He used dramatically forceful 'sprung rhythm' and unprecedented intensity to evoke the natural world as the sacrament of God. His poems were so in advance of their time, stylistically, that Hopkins's editor, Robert Bridges, assumed that there could be no audience for them until 1918. By then Hopkins had been dead for thirty years and the pioneering Modernists had begun to cultivate readers' tastes beyond Victorian aesthetics.

The Victorians' view of the Romantic poets could be ambiguous. Matthew Arnold placed Wordsworth in the same class as Shakespeare and Milton and superior to all others:

I say that Wordsworth seems to me to have left a body of poetical work superior in power, in interest, in the qualities which give enduring freshness, to that which any of the others has left.

Yet, when he considers Romantic poetry at large – including Wordsworth's – he argues that

the English poetry of the first quarter of this century, with plenty of energy, plenty of creative force, did not know enough. This makes Byron so empty of matter, Shelley so incoherent, Wordsworth even, profound as he is, yet so wanting in completeness and variety.

Keats is savagely criticised for neglecting his themes while pursuing 'vivid and picturesque turns of expression'.

Other Victorians simply laughed at the Romantics, as Lewis Carroll does in 'The White Knight's Song' in *Through the Looking-Glass* (1856). This is a hilarious parody of Wordsworth's solemn poem in celebration of the wisdom of leech-gatherers, 'Resolution and Independence':

. . . And now, if e'er by chance I put
My fingers into glue,
Or madly squeeze a right-hand foot
Into a left-hand shoe,
Or if I drop upon my toe
A very heavy weight,
I weep, for it reminds me so
Of that old man I used to know –
Whose look was mild, whose speech was slow,
Whose hair was whiter than the snow,

> Whose face was very like a crow,
> With eyes, like cinders, all aglow,
> Who seemed distracted with his woe,
> Who rocked his body to and fro,
> And muttered mumblingly and low,
> As if his mouth was full of dough,
> Who snorted like a buffalo –
> That summer evening long ago
> A-sitting on a gate.

Serious Victorian poets intensified Romantic themes and styles. Arnold interpreted this as a concentration of the Romantic expansion of ideas and artistry. One of the most striking aspects of this phenomenon, which also looks forward to a major element in twentieth-century writing, is the presentation of the psychological dimension of personal experience in poetry. The Romantic concern with the self has an externality about it, as in Wordsworth's exultant lyric:

> I wandered lonely as a cloud
> That floats on high o'er vales and hills.
> When all at once I saw a crowd,
> A host of golden daffodils;
> Beside the lake, beneath the trees,
> Fluttering and dancing in the breeze.

In contrast, the internal, psychological element in this poem by Emily Brontë is dominant, for all its external references:

> I'm happiest when most away
> I can bear my soul from its home of clay
> On a windy night when the moon is bright
> And the eye can wander through the worlds of light –
> When I am not and none beside –
> Nor earth nor sea nor cloudless sky
> But only spirit wandering wide
> Through infinite immensity.

The landscape of the spirit that Brontë describes is at once more intimate and more generalised ('infinite immensity') than Wordsworth's. The particularity of Wordsworth's location in the natural world and of the experience it excited contrasts with the arbitrariness of Brontë's gesture to that domain – 'nor earth nor sea nor cloudless sky' – as she disengages herself from physicality and mortality. Wordsworth's emotional sympathy with nature is very different from Brontë's psychological dissociation from it, in spite of the points of similarity between the poems: their lyricism and the presentation of the speaker, in both cases, as a wanderer. It is the character of the wandering in these works that marks a difference between the Romantic and Victorian sensibilities.

In Victorian love poetry, too, passion's immediacy is there, but not with the uninhibited exhilaration of the Romantics (which they could experience even when they were bemoaning love's cruelty and absence). Victorian love poetry is not merely a domesticated form of its Romantic models. It is fraught with new anxieties and, again, the psychological investigation of love's processes and, particularly, its disease.

George Meredith's sequence of fifty sixteen-line sonnets, *Modern Love* (1862), both reflects the trials of his own experience of marital unhappiness and a concentration of and departure from Romantic love poetry, thematically and stylistically, as in the first poem in the sequence:

> By this he knew she wept with waking eyes:
> That, at his hand's light quiver by her head,
> The strange low sobs that shook their common bed
> Were called into her with a sharp surprise,
> And strangled mute, like little gaping snakes,
> Dreadfully venomous to him. She lay
> Stone-still, and the long darkness flowed away
> With muffled pulses. Then, as midnight makes
> Her giant heart of Memory and Tears
> Drink the pale dry silence, and so beat
> Sleep's heavy measure, they from head to feet
> Were moveless, looking through their dead black years
> By vain regret scrawled over the blank wall.
> Like sculptured effigies they might be seen
> Upon their marriage tomb, the sword between;
> Each wishing for the sword that severs all.

It is not merely that the 'love' described here is loveless and passionless that makes the poem substantially unromantic. Its beginning, indeed, is reminiscent of Romanticism in Meredith's concentration on the woman's suffering, the man's tender if futile attempt to approach or console her, from which she recoils. But the psycho-drama of the poem projects the experience beyond the idealised waxing and waning of Romantic devotion and sensuality. The strangeness to which the poet refers is the agitated perplexity of their failed union, represented by 'their common bed', and the punitive details of their estrangement, 'like little gaping snakes', which have poisoned their relationship. The minuteness of the detailed observations – 'his hand's light quiver', and so on – is a poetic equivalent of the detail of the contemporary Pre-Raphaelite school of painting which revealed the interior lives of its subjects.

Meredith's quasi-Romantic reference to the Memory and Tears of midnight's 'giant heart' is displaced by the realities of 'sleep's heavy measure' and of the emotion of 'vain regret' – a limited response to a limited love. The concluding medieval imagery, of stone figures representing those entombed below, has a Gothic quality, but the modernity of the love, described before, renders the Romanticism of the allusion grotesque. Indeed, the concluding image is as much a commentary on the departure of that cult of love as it is an indication of the cold disengagement of this married pair.

Not that the Victorians (contrary to contemporary caricatures of them) were incapable of sensuousness and of expressing it in their poetry. But their sensuality was markedly different from its Romantic variety. In Dante Gabriel Rossetti's *House of Life*, this sonnet of married love is more erotic, in its protracted intensity of sexual allusion, than anything in Romantic love poetry:

> At length their long kiss severed, with sweet smart:
> And as the last slow sudden drops are shed
> From sparkling eaves when all the storm has fled,
> So singly flagged the pulses of each heart.
> Their bosoms sundered, with the opening start
> Of married flowers to either side outspread
> From the knit stem; yet still their mouths, burnt red,
> Fawned on each other where they lay apart.
>
> Sleep sank them lower than the tide of dreams,
> And their dreams watched them sink, and slid away.
> Slowly their souls swam up again, through gleams
> Of watered light and dull drowned waifs of day;
> Till from some wonder of new woods and streams
> He woke, and wondered more: for there she lay.

Passion has been consummated, but the assessment of the aftermath is disturbing rather than affirmative. The wonder that the speaker experiences is amazement mixed with displeasure in post-coital emotion. But the imagery of destruction and death throughout the poem links sensuality and morbidity with an intensity that is peculiarly (even unpleasantly) Victorian.

Sample question with guidelines

What is distinctively Victorian about this poem by Elizabeth Barrett Browning from her *Sonnets from the Portuguese* (1845–7)?

> When our two souls stand up erect and strong,
> Face to face, silent, drawing nigh and nigher,

Until the lengthening wings break into fire
At either curvèd point – what bitter wrong
Can the earth do to us, that we should not long
Be here contented? Think. In mounting higher,
The angels would press on us and aspire
To drop some golden orb of perfect song
Into our deep, dear silence. Let us stay
Rather on earth, Belovèd, – where the unfit
Contrarious moods of men recoil away
And isolate pure spirits, and permit
A place to stand and love in for a day,
With darkness and the death-hour rounding it.

■ The sonnet is concerned with love and the passion between the two
   lovers (the *Sonnets from the Portuguese* describe the poet's love for
   Robert Browning). At the beginning, there is a sense of the stark determination of their bond, which is soulful but also assertively physical: 'erect
   and strong'. This gives intensity and particularity ('Face to face') to their
   Romantic love. It is a quality of much Victorian love poetry.
■ The striking imagery of their transformation into angelic beings – 'lengthening wings break into fire' – emphasises the transcendental quality of
   their passion. The preoccupation of the Victorians with the religious
   dimension of experience has been introduced.
■ That spiritual quality would elevate them beyond the 'bitter wrong' that
   the world might inflict upon them. It appears to confirm a desire for
   Romantic escape. But the impulse is arrested by the imperative verb,
   'Think'. An intellectual rigour will scrutinise this soaring tendency.
■ To become ethereal would transform their unique shared being – 'our
   deep, dear silence'. They would be required to participate in the heavenly
   chorus, its 'perfect song'. The speaker would rather remain on earth – a
   determination that is characteristically Victorian, in its commitment to
   reality and its suspicion about supernatural fancies.
■ The poet closes with an evocation of Victorian life – 'the unfit /
   Contrarious moods of men' – which they will, nonetheless, be able to
   withstand because they have been purified by their love. However, with a
   further Victorian emphasis, the speaker acknowledges that that supreme
   happiness will probably be fleeting and will certainly be terminated by
   death:

   A place to stand and love in for a day,
   With darkness and the death-hour rounding it.

Question

What distinctive concerns of Victorianism are expressed in this poem by William Ernest Henley?

INVICTUS   [Invictus = unconquered]

Out of the night that covers me,
Black as the Pit from pole to pole,
I thank whatever gods may be
For my unconquerable soul.
In the fell clutch of circumstance
I have not winced nor cried aloud.
Under the bludgeoning of chance
My head is bloody, but unbowed.
Beyond this place of wrath and tears
Looms but the Horror of the shade,
And yet the menace of the years
Finds, and shall find, me unafraid.
It matters not how strait the gate,
How charged with punishments the scroll,
I am the master of my fate;
I am the captain of my soul.

Assignment

Read some of the American poets of the Victorian era, such as Ralph Waldo Emerson, Walt Whitman and Emily Dickinson. Investigate the similarities between their poetry, in theme and style, to that of the English Victorians. Do you discern a distinctive American voice?

■ SPECIAL STUDY 11

Christina Rossetti (1830–94)

ABOUT THE AUTHOR

Regarded by many as the finest woman poet of the nineteenth century, Christina Rossetti, of Italian ancestry, was born in London, the sister of the poet and painter Dante Gabriel Rossetti. She was educated at home by her mother, with whom she lived all her life. Devoutly religious, her Anglicanism was in the High Church tradition, emphasising Catholic beliefs and practices. Her sister Maria became an Anglican nun.

■ Rossetti's first poems were published anonymously in 1850. Her long narrative poem 'Goblin Market' (the subject of considerable, ongoing interpretation) was the major work in her first significant collection, published in 1866.

Rossetti writes with consummate facility in a variety of poetic forms, such as the sonnet and the ballad. Her poem 'In the bleak mid-winter', set to music by Gustav Holst, has become one of the best loved of English Christmas carols. Many influences are discernible in her poetry: the Bible and the Fathers of the Church, Plato and Dante, and, of course, poets in the English tradition, especially from the Renaissance (such as George Herbert) and the Romantic movement of the earlier nineteenth century.

Wistful regret over unrequited love is one of Rossetti's major themes, in addition to religious subjects – her last collection of poems was *The Face of the Deep: A Devotional Commentary on the Apocalypse* (1892) – and a recurring motif is a steadfast determination to transcend the disappointments of life, both through moral and religious strenuousness and the very act of writing, in poetry, so beautifully about the trials and triumphs of human existence. Speaking usually in a personal voice, Rossetti also touches on universal themes. She extracts a kind of joy out of her pains, through poetry, and a degree of fulfilment in her expression of the inadequacies of life's experiences.

SELECTED POEMS

SONG

The title of the poem (written in December 1848) indicates its lyrical character. This introduces the irony of the work. The singer is doubly unhappy – she is meditating on her death and also on the prospect that her beloved may not remember her when she is gone. Yet these reflections provoke a song and one, furthermore, that is crisp and resolute, not melancholy or protracted. Rossetti's biographer, Georgina Battiscombe, rightly warns us against deducing autobiographical fact from such works, but we might disagree with her assessment of the poem as 'more like a poetic exercise than an expression of heartfelt emotion'.[2]

The opening is almost shocking in its monosyllabic directness:

> When I am dead . . .

and the alliteration of 'dead' with 'dearest' which follows neatly juxtaposes the conflicting emotions of love and the death of love (and life) which form the poem's subject. The speaker rejects 'sad songs' from her beloved and will not sing in this manner now. Her succession of negatives reveals a determination not to be mourned:

---

2. *Christina Rossetti* (London: Constable, 1981), p. 65.

■   Plant thou no roses at my head,
        Nor shady cypress tree.

There is the suspicion, however, that she protests too much. Enlisting the
rose and cypress to reject them, they nonetheless are deeply appealing and
we may sense that she is regretting their absence even as she demands it. Is
this a method for dealing with disappointment by anticipating it and devalu-
ing the circumstances which can stir it? Sufficient, she claims, will be the
green grass above her simple grave and the wet dewdrops which fall upon it.
They represent nature's tears. The rose and the cypress, placed there by
human agency, may not be natural, for all their beauty. Beneath this discrimination is the idea that the love she has known may not be genuine, so she
would prefer no gestures of mourning from that quarter, rather than merely
conventional ones. This idea is reinforced in the closing lines of the first
stanza:

        And if thou wilt, remember,
        And if thou wilt, forget.

The emphasis (in the repetition) on the beloved's will seems to suggest that
she recognises that she has no power over his emotions – and certainly not
once she is dead. It is a poor compliment to her 'dearest' but a way of registering a one-sided love. (We note, incidentally, that he is not named and no
details at all are given about him.)

    The self-centredness of the poetry strikes us in the second stanza with the
prevalence of the first-person pronoun. And, again, her resolution dominates
in the choice of 'shall' (rather than 'will'):

        I shall not see the shadows,
        I shall not feel the rain;
        I shall not hear the nightingale
        Sing on, as if in pain . . .

There is exultation here, won out of apparent defeat. It is not only an individual's *cri de coeur*, nor is it only an expression of relief that love's pains are
over. It is the joyful announcement of blessed release from the tribulations of
life. In this way (as so often in Rossetti's writing), what seems so personal is,
in fact, universal in its significance.

    Specifically, the singer locates herself in an eternal domain (of dream and
twilight) freed from the mutability and mortality of life in this world: 'that
doth not rise nor set'. Again, we can see this as simply positive, but lurking
beneath that apparent praise we may discern a certain unsatisfactoriness with
a twilight life of dream, as we may also find the repetition of the determined
'I shall' slightly over-pitched in its exultation.

■ The poem closes in wry recollection of her gift, as it were, to her dearest at the end of the first stanza, where she said he may choose to remember her or forget her. So, too, she, in the grave, may have the same blessing:

> Haply I may remember,
> And haply may forget.

'Happily' is heard in 'haply', but we wonder how happy, in the end, is the life- and love-renouncing teaching of this poem.

Question

How is this poem not only (or merely) personal in its teaching?

REMEMBER

Although written ten years later than 'Song', this sonnet focuses on the same themes of love, death and remembrance, with a similar mode of address to the beloved and a determination to deal with the prospect of being forgotten in death and what this implies about the quality of love during one's life. So the poem indicates that these are abiding concerns of Rossetti. Yet a different love seems to be being spoken of here – one in which a greater degree of mutuality is discerned. In a sense, though, this makes the recognition that it, too, will end with her death and that, again, she can envisage being forgotten all the more devastating.

She begins, in the imperative voice, demanding (or, we might say, plead- ing for) remembrance once she has died. Unlike 'Song', the reference to death (usually surrounded in mystery and euphemism in Victorian discourse) is less direct here:

> Remember me when I am gone away,
> Gone far away into the silent land.

The opening quatrain of the sonnet concludes with images of physical contact (and reciprocity) in their love and an exquisite vignette of the reluctant lover's departure:

> When you can no more hold me by the hand,
> Nor I half turn to go yet turning stay.

One of the marks of Rossetti's artistry is her ability so simply to convey such a complex motion and emotion. It is one of the ways she reminds us of George Herbert.

This love had an earthly future (implying marriage), with plans mutually discussed. At her death, she can only ask for remembrance, as the plans will

■ remain unfulfilled: 'you understand / It will be late to counsel then or pray'.

In Rossetti's skilful mastery of the sonnet form, she divides the octave from the concluding sestet by juxtaposing futurity with pastness. The octave turned about the idea of her future death; the sestet (while still in the future tense) focuses on her beloved's response once that event has occurred. Its opening line is striking in its pragmatism and common sense:

> Yet if you should forget me for a while
> And afterwards remember . . .

This would almost be comical if it were not so clear-sighted and, finally, terrible. Is this really what human love can amount to – a fitful remembrance in the wake of reciprocated passion and plans for a lifetime together? It is in this way that the poem is a more disturbing assessment of love than 'Song'.

In the closing lines, death is a matter of 'darkness and corruption' of the body (there is 'dreaming through the twilight' of 'Song' here). As the beloved thinks of her, thus, she can only hope that some remains of his regard for her survive: 'a vestige of the thoughts that once I had'. Like 'Song' in this case, however, we are once again in the domain of a poor compliment. Cannot human love survive the departure of the beloved's body? Is it mostly a physical phenomenon? Sanely facing this reality, she concludes with a perfect mixture of grimness and generosity (registering the ambivalence, at large, of her assessment of love):

> Better by far you should forget and smile
> Than that you should remember and be sad.

Question

Look closely at Rossetti's use of the sonnet form here. How has she used its distinctive characteristics to her advantage?

UP-HILL

Here, Christina Rossetti displays her mastery of the stanzaic lyric. 'Up-hill', in fact, is a perfect representation of the essential thematic requirement of stanzaic poetry – that each stanza should have its own, self-contained subject yet be linked to the evolving argument of the poem at large. In the first stanza, she introduces the metaphors of the winding, uphill road and the 24-hour day for the daunting experience of a lifetime in this world. She also introduces the device of question-and-answer which binds each stanza to the others, throughout. The journey is arduous spatially, and protracted temporally:

Does the road wind up-hill all the way?
Yes, to the very end.
Will the journey take the whole long day?
From morn to night, my friend.

The second stanza, contrastingly, poses the question of a reward for such strenuous journeying. Metaphorical again, this is representative of the conclusion of all lives in death – a destination that cannot be missed, unlike other goals on our journeys through life. Interestingly, as elsewhere in her poetry, death is seen as a blessed release from the tedious demands of human existence:

But is there for the night a resting-place?
A roof for when the slow dark hours begin.
May not the darkness hide it from my face?
You cannot miss that inn.

These two stanzas have focused on the individual's wayfaring in this world. The third stanza, having its own integrity, but linked to the others, introduces the idea of others journeying on life's pilgrimage:

Shall I meet other wayfarers at night?
Those who have gone before.
Then must I knock, or call when just in sight?
They will not keep you standing at that door.

By this stage in the poem, its religious and biblical implications and references are becoming clear. Specifically, the idea of Christ as the way (and the truth and the life) and the image of the Saviour, standing at the door and knocking (the subject of the most famous of Victorian religious paintings, 'The Light of the World', painted by Dante Gabriel Rossetti's friend William Holman Hunt) are now apparent. The poet is describing the human pilgrim's entry into Heaven. The blessings of eternity, accordingly, are the subject of the final stanza:

Shall I find comfort, travel-sore and weak?
Of labour you shall find the sum.
Will there be beds for me and all who seek?
Yea, beds for all who come.

This splendid poem combines biblical language and ideas, literary allegory (reminiscent, in small, of John Bunyan's *Pilgrim's Progress* and numerous other writers and texts in this tradition), Rossetti's distinctive idea of the weari-someness of life in this world with her counterbalancing faith in the rewards of eternity (generously available to all who seek – no Calvinist restrictions to

the Elect!), in the context of a restrained and carefully modulated metaphorical elaboration of thought through four perfectly self-contained but astutely
linked stanzas.

Questions

1. What similarities and differences do you notice between the representations of love in 'Song' and 'Remember'? To what extent are these
   dependent upon the poet's use of a lyrical form in one poem, and the
   sonnet in the other?

2. To what extent do you agree that Christina Rossetti is a poet of
   universal human emotions? Or do you find her worldview, as
   expressed in her poems, more notable for its individuality, even eccentricity?

3. Look carefully at the details of the metaphorical writing in 'Up-Hill'.
   How would you account for all of these in the evolving narrative of
   the poem?

4. Georgina Battiscombe notes that '"Up-hill" appeals to a wide variety
   of readers and it has remained a steady favourite, to be found today
   in many anthologies'.[3] Why do you think this is so?

---

3. Battiscombe, p.99.

Modernism

'MAKE IT NEW'

Modernism was the dominant aesthetic movement of the earlier twentieth century. It is often considered to be a thorough critique and repudiation of Romanticism in general and Victorianism in particular. Now that Modernism is no longer modern, however, we are able to evaluate the ideas and artistic expression of the Modernists from a distance. We can see that Modernism included modified elements of characteristics which are associated with the Romanticism they professed to find so revolting.

First, Modernist poets were as inclined as Wordsworth or Shelley to see themselves in detachment from and criticism of their society. W. B. Yeats, the Irish poet who called himself the 'last Romantic' and who we might also describe as the first Modernist, located himself, literally and metaphorically, in a solitary tower (Thoor Ballylee), set apart from ordinary human existence. Similarly, T. S. Eliot, whether in the guise of Prufrock in his 'Love Song' or Tiresias in *The Waste Land*, is a lonely commentator on the mores of his age. The Romantic motifs of solitude and loneliness persist in Modernist poetry in the distinctively twentieth-century condition of alienation.

Secondly, the Modernists share the Romantics' desire to escape to distant and idealised worlds. As Coleridge dreamt of Xanadu and Tennyson of Lotos-land and King Arthur's court, Ezra Pound wrote of oriental Cathay and D. H. Lawrence mused, in prose and poetry, on 'luxurious' Etruscan places. Yeats would journey to Byzantium and Eliot yearned for the life-giving rain of distant, eastern Himavant which will not fall in the decayed infertility of modern Western civilisation. He also idealised the earlier seventeenth century not only for its literature but for its social order, as the Romantics and Victorians were nostalgic for the Middle Ages.

The dissimilarities of these similarities, however, indicate the newness of Modernism. In the Romantic poets' celebration of isolation, the mood was usually one of elevation and exhilaration, even in the experience of melancholy. In Modernist poetry, however, the isolated condition of the men and women portrayed is usually seen as part of a collective experience of spiritual despair and emotional dissociation in the passionless and soulless wasteland of their post-industrial society. Yeats descends from his tower and notes the fingers fumbling in a 'greasy till' ('September 1913') and Eliot, while fastidiously preserving his detachment, observes the sordid realities of metropolitan life, such as the unromantic sexuality of modern love in the sexual engagement of the typist and the 'young man carbuncular' in the third section of *The Waste Land*.

The Romantics escaped from the present by contemplating past ages and distant worlds. Imaginatively, a writer such as Tennyson all but lived his life in the past and encouraged his readers to do the same. The mellifluousness of his aural appeal –

> The moan of doves in immemorial elms,
> And murmuring of innumerable bees –

transported his readers to a Lotos-land of the imagination. His was a poetry of 'gutless swooning', William Faulkner alleged in *Light in August* (1932), 'full of sapless trees and dehydrated lusts'.

> *It is better than praying without having to bother to think aloud. It is like listening in a cathedral to a eunuch chanting in a language which he does not even need to not understand.*

The Modernists wanted to confront the present rather than to escape from it. They used contrasts with past ages as measures of the decline of the twentieth century. Their cyclic interpretation of history, whether derived from Vico or Spengler (in *The Decline of the West*), saw the twentieth century as the beginning of a new age, antithetical to the 2000 years of the Christian era. 'Romantic Ireland's dead and gone', Yeats wrote (again, in 'September 1913'), 'it's with O'Leary in the grave'. Eliot, in a sharp visual comparison, contrasted the ceremonious beauty of the social intercourse of the Virgin Queen with the debauchery of the modern Thames 'maidens' in the third section of *The Waste Land*.

The Modernists confronted modernity, and that is what sets their artistry apart from the dominant modes of nineteenth-century poetry. There is, however, a source of Modernism in the nineteenth-century realistic novel, but unlike the realists in prose, Modernist poets used the resonance of imagery and symbolism. A more direct source from the nineteenth century, in fact, was the poetry of the Frenchman Charles Baudelaire, in his *Fleurs du Mal* (*The Flowers of Evil*, 1857) where the ordinary and sordid Parisian cityscape is given a surreal quality. He had already inspired Oscar Wilde in the aestheticism of the 1890s, which was as much a prelude to Modernism as the death-throes of Romanticism.

Where the Romantics retreated to a rural scene, Modernist poets focused on the urban environment. Although they were repelled by the city, writers such as

Pound, Eliot and Joyce, like Paul Morel at the close of D. H. Lawrence's *Sons and Lovers*, were drawn irresistibly to it. The dehumanising metropolis was the microcosm of twentieth-century existence, as Eliot writes in *Preludes*. He used his familiar imagery of anonymous, disembodied body parts to represent the fragmentation of the modern personality or sensibility:

> One thinks of all the hands
> That are raising dingy shades
> In a thousand furnished rooms.

And the city, for all its faults, was crucial in practical terms to the development of Modernism. After the First World War, the concentration of artists in Paris and London facilitated the cross-fertilisation of their ideas. The movement being fostered in these large centres of teeming life was essentially that of a coterie, an elite, generated and sustained by a highly educated and cultivated class of writers and readers. Before the war, Yeats had appointed Ezra Pound as his secretary in London, and Pound also acted as a kind of literary agent for the unknown Eliot and edited his Modernist masterwork *The Waste Land*, which Eliot dedicated to him as *il miglior fabbro* – 'the better craftsman'. Even a section of London was colonised by, and has given its name to, one of the artistic groups related to Modernism: Bloomsbury. Writers such as Virginia Woolf and Lytton Strachey were prominent members of the Bloomsbury Group.

Modernism was a metropolitan, cosmopolitan phenomenon. But it was not a popular movement. Much of the early publication of Modernist works, which were themselves erudite and allusive, took place in 'highbrow' journals with small circulations. Joyce's *Ulysses* was serialised in the *Little Review* from 1918 to 1920, before being published as a book in 1922. Yet Modernism sought to express the spirit of the new age of democracy. Joyce's poetic *Finnegans Wake*, the successor to *Ulysses*, deals with the ordinary life of Dublin – with washerwomen, for example – but its complexity has confined its readership to literary scholars.

The dating of the beginning of the movement need not be precise, but D. H. Lawrence and Virginia Woolf both presented suggestions. Woolf proposed December 1910, when King Edward VII and the Edwardian era (the vulgar afterglow of Victorianism) came to an end. With devastating simplicity, she believed that at that time 'human nature changed':

> all human relations shifted – those between masters and servants, husbands and wives, parents and children. And when human relations change there is at the same time a change in religion, conduct, politics, literature.

D. H. Lawrence, in *Kangaroo,* his Australian novel, prefers a later date:

> It was in [1915] the old world ended . . .

that is, the time which Thomas Hardy referred to as 'the breaking of nations', the dismemberment of Europe during the Great War.

I

The First World War of 1914–18, a period which also included the Irish uprising of 1916 and the Russian revolution of 1917, is the decisive historical phenomenon in the development of Modernism. Yeats's *Responsibilities* collection was published in 1914. In it, he dedicates himself and his poetry to giving voice to the new world that was emerging out of Victorianism and Edwardianism. The first of D. H. Lawrence's 'new' novels, *The Rainbow*, which introduced a startling frankness into the discussion of sexual relationships, appeared in 1915. T. S. Eliot's collection, *Prufrock and Other Observations*, was published in 1917. It included poems that had been written as early as 1910 challenging both the conventional subject matter and style of contemporary post-Victorian poetry. And Lytton Strachey's *Eminent Victorians*, scrutinising and denouncing Victorian reputations, was published in 1918.

The Great War, in which nearly nine million lives were lost, was the shocking and tragic beginning of the age of violence and carnage, on an international scale, persisting into the twenty-first century. Literature, and poetry in particular, was bound to register both the cosmic and personal impact of this horror on contemporary society and on individuals. In Eliot's poetry, there is both the probing of personal psychological and emotional disturbance and the broader evocation of societal and cultural decay, as in the opening verse-paragraph of 'Gerontion' (meaning 'little old man') of 1920:

> Here I am, an old man in a dry month,
> Being read to by a boy, waiting for rain.
> I was neither at the hot gates
> Nor fought in the warm rain
> Nor knee deep in the salt marsh, heaving a cutlass,
> Bitten by flies, fought.
> My house is a decayed house,
> And the Jew squats on the window-sill, the owner,
> Spawned in some estaminet of Antwerp,
> Blistered in Brussels, patched and peeled in London.

This poem represents the European and personal consequences of the conflict. However, the most immediate manifestation of this cruel new world was in the poems written during the war by those English soldiers who had experienced the nightmare of trench warfare against the Germans in France, on the 'Western front'.

The Romantic ideals of heroism and patriotism were assaulted by Siegfried Sassoon, Ivor Gurney, Isaac Rosenberg and Wilfred Owen, who had experienced the realities of battle. Their poems shockingly contradicted the official propaganda about the conflict as a noble venture – as it had been envisaged by Rupert Brooke, for example, in his war sonnets at the beginning of the hostilities:

> If I should die, think only this of me:
> That there's some corner of a foreign field
> That is forever England. There shall be
> In that rich earth a richer dust concealed;
> A dust whom England bore, shaped, made aware,
> Gave, once, her flowers to love, her ways to roam,
> A body of England's, breathing English air,
> Washed by the rivers, blest by suns of home.
> And think, this heart, all evil shed away,
> A pulse in the Eternal mind, no less
> Gives somewhere back the thoughts by England given;
> Her sights and sounds; dreams happy as her day;
> And laughter, learnt of friends; and gentleness,
> In hearts at peace, under an English heaven.

The blithe spirit of this work was replaced by poetry of a very different kind, as the fighting wore on and the casualties mounted. Wilfrid Owen wrote the sonnet 'Anthem for Doomed Youth' in 1917, by which time Rupert Brooke and the serene world he represented in his life, his person and his poetry, had been buried for ever:

> What passing-bells for these who die as cattle?
> – Only the monstrous anger of the guns.
> Only the stuttering rifles' rapid rattle
> Can patter out their hasty orisons.   [orisons = prayers]
> No mockeries now for them; no prayers nor bells;
> Nor any voice of mourning save the choirs, –
> The shrill, demented choirs of wailing shells;
> And bugles calling for them from sad shires.
>
> What candles may be held to speed them all?
> Not in the hands of boys but in their eyes
> Shall shine the holy glimmers of goodbyes.
> The pallor of girls' brows shall be their pall;
> Their flowers the tenderness of patient minds,
> And each slow dusk a drawing-down of blinds.

The title, appearing to promise an 'anthem', is deliberately ironic. An anthem is usually a prolonged song of praise, such as a patriotic writer might have penned for a nation's fighting heroes. It also has religious connotations, as part of a service – perhaps of commemoration of the dead, such as occurred in Britain during and after the Great War. Owen, in presenting such a brief utterance as an 'anthem', strikingly disappoints such expectations and thereby emphasises his point that there is nothing to celebrate in his subject.

Further to the negative persuasion of the poem is the adjective 'doomed'. Everything about that word is disquieting: its gloomy sound – the two d's reverberate, like a bell, and its 'oo' is aurally hollow (and visually, in print on the page, it seems to gape at the reader like two eyes with nothing behind them) – and its sense of an overwhelming fate that mere humans cannot reverse. The tragic implications of the title are strengthened because it is youth that is 'doomed'. Age is doomed to death by virtue of its years. But it is a perversity of circumstances for youth to be so brutally truncated.

In the poem itself, Owen strictly observes the conventions of the sonnet. We notice the principal division into octave and sestet, the use of subdivision into quatrains (three four-line sections), which is emphasised by the orderly rhyming pattern, and the concluding couplet. The discipline of the form restrains (and thereby intensifies) the passion of the ideas in the poem.

The slaughter of young men in the war is so inhuman that any idea of their humanity is stripped from them and they 'die as cattle'. The question in the opening line is rhetorical, for the dignity of the 'passing-bell' (in the parish church, tolling to inform the community that one of their number is dying) has itself passed, in the dehumanisation of this situation. To accompany their deaths, the young men only have the percussion of the guns and rifles. Owen closes his first quatrain in noisy onomatopoeia. The quick firing of the rifles is like hasty prayers, stammered out over the dead. Onomatopoeia is present again in 'shrill' and 'wailing' as the shells of battle provide the only choirs to sing these soldiers to their rest.

Echoing the opening line of the poem, the sestet similarly begins with a question. This marks a further stage in the progress of dead youth's fate and gives a new emphasis in the poetry. Owen now asks who will pray for the souls of these lost ones and wish them 'God-speed' on their spiritual journey:

> What candles may be held to speed them all?

The weeping eyes and pallid brows of their friends and family at home will keep them in remembrance. In the place of wreaths, there will be the memories kept in minds which patiently hope for a reunion beyond the grave and, in the meantime, there is at 'each slow dusk a drawing-down of blinds'. This moving image of closure aptly closes the sonnet. Like the conclusion to the octave, where the lads' rural origins were noted, this is another English touch in the poem, referring not only to drawing blinds at evening, but to the old custom of drawing down the blinds in a house of mourning.

The most remarkable feature of this poem is its combination of bitterness and poignancy: Owen's direct and forceful criticism of the brutality of war and his 'tenderness' in contemplating the loved ones of the 'doomed youth'. Both emotions could easily have become uncontrolled. Owen's mastery of the sonnet form prevents such a lapse.

The anti-war poets of the First World War brought a new reality into poetry, of a disturbing contemporary kind. Theirs was a crucial contribution to Modernism, displaying its commitment to confronting modernity with the facts of contemporary life. Their subject matter, nonetheless, was limited. Philip Larkin insisted that Owen's poetry, for example, is not only concerned with the Great War, 'but all war':

> not particular suffering but all suffering; not particular waste but all waste.

Yet our minds inevitably turn to the First World War when we read their poems. And while no one regrets the mastery of traditional poetic forms which they display, their exploration of the possibilities of form was also limited.

Assignment

Read Wilfred Owen's 'Dulce et Decorum Est'. What aspects of theme and technique would you identify as 'Modernist' in it?

II

The most important feature of Modernist poetry is its innovative style, fulfilling the urgent imperative of Ezra Pound, emphatically capitalised, to 'MAKE IT NEW'. Outmoded ways of writing, in particular the lyrical and discursive voices of nineteenth-century poetry, were discarded in order to discover and pursue a technique suited to the new subjects which the Modernists were addressing. An unlovely world demanded an abrasive new voice and the confrontational aspect of the project called for immediacy and succinctness. Pound, the principal theorist of the movement, had promoted these new ideas with a didactic voice in *Poetry* magazine in 1913:

> Use no superfluous word, no adjective which does not reveal something . . . Go in fear of abstractions. Do not tell in mediocre verse what has already been done in good prose.

However, although traditional poetic diction is rejected, a clear distinction between prose and poetry is maintained and the priority of poetry is affirmed. The Modernists avoided abstractions, but they did not commit themselves absolutely to the concrete. Rather they pursued the imagistic and symbolic use of language, as in the opening lines of Eliot's 'Rhapsody on a Windy Night',

where he evokes a nightmarish scene at the Romantic midnight hour of visionary revelation, but then confronts the reader, in two similes, with surrealistic
images of derangement, the poetic rearrangement of reality:

> Twelve o'clock.
> Along the reaches of the street
> Held in a lunar synthesis,
> Whispering lunar incantations
> Dissolve the floors of memory
> And all its clear relations,
> Its divisions and precisions.
> Every street-lamp that I pass
> Beats like a fatalistic drum,
> And through the spaces of the dark
> Midnight shakes the memory
> As a madman shakes a dead geranium.

Pound declared that the image 'presents an intellectual and emotional complex
in an instant of time' because it resists paraphrase, suggesting rather than telling
(as in the formerly popular narrative poetry and moralistic verse of
Victorianism). The image, an inspired insight, is also found in prose, in the
'epiphanies' of James Joyce who described the technique as a 'revelation of the
whatness of a thing'. Such things could include everyday objects: 'the soul of the
commonest object . . . seems to us radiant'. This intense combination of realism
and a quasi-supernatural aura is reminiscent of the theory of 'thisness' proposed
by the proto-Modernist Gerard Manley Hopkins in the nineteenth century. Both
Joyce and Hopkins were Jesuit-educated. They drew philosophical inspiration
for their aesthetic principles from medieval Catholic writers who, like them,
believed that the individual integrity of created things revealed their divine
origin. In Hopkins's case, it was Duns Scotus, in Joyce's, William of Occam.
Such indebtedness reveals one of the paradoxes of Modernism: the combination
of traditional learning and the exercise of the individual talent.

   As the French Imagistes were influential on the Modernists, so were the
Symbolistes. In literature, the symbol needs larger scope than a single poem
usually allows. As the characteristic Modernist poem is a short work (even *The
Waste Land* can be read as a series of fragments, emblematising the fragmented
world it describes and denounces), symbols in Modernism tend to be developed
through a series of poems. Yeats's golden bird in 'Sailing to Byzantium' reappears
in the later 'Byzantium' which Yeats wrote in order to further elucidate the ideas
about art and the artist that the bird represents, as in this stanza:

Miracle, bird or golden handiwork,
More miracle than bird or handiwork,
Planted on the starlit golden bough,
Can like the cocks of Hades crow,
Or, by the moon embittered, scorn aloud
In glory of changeless metal
Common bird or petal
And all complexities of mire and blood.

The bird, in other words, symbolises inspired craftsmanship and creativity. It has an eternal quality which transcends (scorns) the order under the moon which is yet vividly present in that last line as Yeats indicates the tension in his own thought between those two domains.

The rose and the swan are also important symbols in Yeats's poetry with romantic and classical origins and significance. Yeats gathers diverse influences to produce a heterodox Modernism, even while he displays in his poetry a sustained commitment to the Modernist creed of making poetry new (most strikingly in his *Responsibilities* collection of 1914). Yeats nonetheless retains to the end the resonances of his artistic genesis in Romantic literature (such as the work of Blake and Shelley) and combines all of this with his essential Irishness:

UNDER BEN BULBEN   [a mountain in western Ireland]

Swear by what the sages spoke
Round the Mareotic Lake   [an ancient site of contemplation in Egypt]
That the Witch of Atlas knew,   [*The Witch of Atlas* by Shelley]
Spoke and set the cocks a-crow.

Swear by those horsemen, by those women
Complexion and form prove superhuman,
That pale, long-visaged company
That air in immortality
Completeness of their passions won:
Now they ride the wintry dawn
Where Ben Bulben sets the scene . . .

The wistful, Pre-Raphaelitism of the Celtic twilight – 'that pale, long-visaged company' – has, in contrast, the strenuous superhumanity of horsemen and women and the 'completeness of their passion'. The specific setting of Sligo – 'where Ben Bulben sets the scene' – invests the vision of the past with a present particularity: Romanticism and Modernism meet.

SPECIAL STUDY 12

William Butler Yeats (1865–1939)

ABOUT THE AUTHOR

Yeats was born in Dublin in 1865, the eldest son of the painter J. B. Yeats. He attended the Godolphin School in Hammersmith, London and also the High School, Dublin. He studied for three years at the School of Art in Dublin but abandoned art in favour of literature, editing William Blake's poetry for publication in 1893.

Yeats became involved in the Irish nationalist movement and helped create the Irish theatre. His play *The Countess Cathleen* was performed in Dublin in 1899. Yeats had already published collections of poetry on ancient Irish themes, such as *The Celtic Twilight* of 1893. Other volumes followed, but Yeats gradually divested himself of his preoccupation with the Romantic past of Ireland and the lush lyricism in which he expressed it. The most significant group of poems in his thematic and artistic development was the *Responsibilities* collection of 1914.

In 1917, Yeats married Georgie Hyde-Lees and he formulated his system of symbolism in *A Vision* of 1925. This influenced several subsequent collections of poems.

Yeats served as a senator of the Irish Free State from 1922 to 1928 and received the Nobel Prize for Literature in 1923. He died in France in 1939.

FROM ROMANTICISM TO MODERNISM

The greatest Irish poet and a monumental figure in twentieth-century literature, Yeats presents a series of contradictions, both in his life and his work. The most important of these is that between his Romanticism and his Modernism.

Yeats saw himself as one of the 'last Romantics', and there is abundant evidence of the influence of Romanticism in his early life and work. Much of this, for example, is devoted to the celebration of Irish myth and legend, of the supernatural and pastoral worlds. Yeats's conception of himself was as a bard and a visionary. These subjects and these ideas about his vocation all belong to the nineteenth-century Romantic view of poetry and the poet. Lyricism dominates Yeats's early writing.

By the accident of the date of his birth, however, Yeats lived into the modern age, which had arrived violently in the First World War and, more locally, in the equally turbulent civil war in Ireland in the same years. Yeats realised that he needed to speak of and to this new world, in a different style and with a subject matter relevant to it. He put the Celtic twilight behind him, and the lyrical style he had used to evoke it, and began to write a poetry that confronted contemporary life in more argumentative language.

■   Yet he retained his idea of the poet as a solitary and a visionary, so his later work continues to present the artist as an acutely experiencing being who has a unique ability to perceive and convey the truth.

Another contradiction in Yeats's life and achievement concerns his relationship with Ireland. Although he was often a patriotic poet, he could be scathing in his criticism of his country and countrymen. While he supported Irish independence from Britain, for example, he was appalled by the violence which achieved it and by the unheroic personalities of the revolutionaries. Yeats admired the hierarchical, aristocratic ordering of society in previous ages. He never ceased to yearn for that dignity and ceremoniousness.

A further tension in Yeats is that between the active and contemplative lives. On his father's side, there was a strong tradition of devotion to the arts and spirituality; while in his mother's family, the heritage was of vigorous action. Yeats admired both approaches and argues, as much in self-persuasion as to convince the reader, for the value of the meditative way (which must be the poet's vocation) in several poems.

The accomplishment of Yeats's developing style and the extraordinary variety of his voice are without parallel in twentieth-century poetry. He is characteristically rhetorical, symbolistic and hieratic. But he can be comic, self-deprecating and earthy, because human life, for Yeats, was a combination of the supernatural and the natural.

SELECTED POEMS

EASTER 1916

This poem is in commemoration of the uprising of the Irish Republicans in Dublin during Easter week, 1916. It is rich in ambiguity and reveals the complexity of Yeats's response to Ireland in general and the Republican cause itself. Yeats contended elsewhere that we make poetry out of the 'quarrel with ourselves', and his ambiguous assessment here is focused in the refrain of the poem:

All changed, changed utterly;
A terrible beauty is born.

Yeats was temperamentally and politically opposed to revolution, but here he was confronted with a cause dear to his countrymen's hearts. Also, several people he admired and loved – such as the Countess Markiewicz and Maud Gonne – were passionately involved. Hence his oxymoron: 'a terrible beauty'.

He begins by evoking the settled, pre-revolutionary urban life of Dubliners and the politeness of their social rituals, in which he participated. Yet he registers the sense that these outward forms were a ceremony of little

■ substance – 'polite meaningless words' – like play-acting: 'where motley is worn'. For beneath the pleasantries was lurking a desire for change and freedom.

Yeats writes in his elegiac mode (after the execution of the leaders of the revolt), which is splendidly elaborated in several poems (such as 'In Memory of Major Robert Gregory' and 'Beautiful Lofty Things'). The poet portrays, in the second verse-paragraph, a series of friends and associates who had been caught up in the all-changing fervour: the Countess (formerly Constance Gore-Booth of County Sligo), Patrick Pearse (whose school Yeats had visited), Thomas MacDonagh, a budding poet, and Major John MacBride, the 'lout' who married Maud Gonne.

Again, Yeats's ambiguity of assessment is dominant. In the heat of revolution, these spirits are consumed. The 'casual comedy' of their ordinary lives has been sacrificed. 'Transformed' is as pointedly paradoxical as 'changed', and 'utterly' dauntingly indicates the impossibility of a reversal of fortune.

Yeats interprets their revolutionary zeal in surprisingly natural terms when he compares the rebellious band to a stone troubling 'the living stream'. This provides a startling contrast between the urban setting of the events and the countryside and rural life he loved. The very verb 'to trouble' brings a negative evaluation to bear upon the stone's function, yet Yeats concedes that change is at the heart of nature and its elements:

> Minute by minute they change.

The living stream, a symbol of life, will constantly have its serenity disturbed – by horse and rider, the clouds, birds and the stone itself. Yet, in a skilful modulation from this imagery, Yeats indicates that

> Too long a sacrifice
> Can make a stone of the heart.

The revolutionaries' impassioned zeal unto death is questioned: 'was it needless death after all?' Yet Yeats is also suggesting that their quick and sudden deaths took them while they were at the peak of their fervour, before they had become hardened by their convictions. He also refers obliquely to the way in which her revolutionary commitments made Maud Gonne stony, as it were, in the face of Yeats's great love for her. So the poet poses the question, and is clearly uncertain of the answer. He can only observe:

> We know their dream; enough
> To know they dreamed and are dead.

However, that they were people of dream and vision would commend them to Yeats. He names the heroes with his characteristic self-consciousness of his role as the bard of Ireland, its national poet:

■   I write it out in a verse.

The most memorable stylistic device in the poem is the use of the caesura in the refrain: 'are changed, changed utterly'. That mid-line pause is at once evocative of an emotional break in the voice and pregnant with the emphasis that falls on the repeated 'changed', as the reader is challenged to ponder the 'change' which is then ambiguously defined as 'a terrible beauty'. The organisation of the refrain, in other words, combines the appeal to the emotions which is conventional in elegy, with Yeats's querying assessment of this sacrifice.

Question
How would you demonstrate and explain the ambiguity of the poem?

THE SECOND COMING
'The Second Coming' was written in the wake of the First World War, the Irish uprising and the Bolshevik revolution in Russia and is one of the most powerful indictments, in poetry, of the modern age. Yeats sees this breaking of nations as anarchy, the repudiation of all authority. The second image of the poem – 'the falcon cannot hear the falconer' – suggests not only the absence of authority, but the violent destructiveness (represented by the uncontrolled falcon) which follows without it. While observing the horror of anarchy, Yeats paradoxically diminishes its significance by calling it 'mere'   a word that sneers at it, both in sense and sound. It is at once tumultuous and mean, and its results are catastrophic:

> The blood-dimmed tide is loosed, and everywhere
> The ceremony of innocence is drowned.

Yeats's preference for an ordered, ceremonious society is clear in that memorable phrase, but he does not acquit the rulers and aristocrats from responsibility for these debacles:

> The best lack all conviction, while the worst
> Are full of passionate intensity.

By 'the best' he also means the artists and thinkers.

Yeats's view of the destruction of order in Europe was held by many of his contemporaries. For them, the anarchy of the times was apocalyptic, heralding a new age:

> Surely some revelation is at hand;
> Surely the Second Coming is at hand.

■ Here, Yeats reflects the Christian teaching that such breaking of nations would signal the end of the world, the Second Coming of Christ and the Last Judgement. However, the Second Coming he envisages is not Christian but pagan:

> The Second Coming! Hardly are those words out
> When a vast image out of *Spiritus Mundi*
> Troubles my sight . . .

Yeats's speaker is clearly before us now as a visionary and a prophet, roles which Yeats associated with the poet's calling. His vision is of a troubling world-spirit, not a benign heavenly being, which is coming to life to bring in a new age. It is in the form of the Egyptian sphinx:

> . . . somewhere in sands of the desert
> A shape with lion body and the head of a man,
> A gaze blank and pitiless as the sun,
> Is moving its slow thighs, while all about it
> Reel shadows of the indignant desert birds.

There is nothing attractive about this birth, it is gross and sensual, and (most alarmingly) the being is indestructible, as the vultures recognise. Christianity, having replaced the pagan order, must now give way to its resurrection.

The vision is horrifying yet brief – 'the darkness drops again' – but it has been a revelation to Yeats:

> now I know
> That twenty centuries of stony sleep
> Were vexed to nightmare by a rocking cradle.

The new pagan, anarchic world, he argues, is the result of 2000 years of Christian suppression of the pagan. This conforms with Yeats's view of the waxing and waning of the natural and supernatural, in individuals and civilisations. Brilliantly blending the two antithetical worldviews, he has the spirit of the sphinx, some indefinable 'rough beast', about to begin its epoch, slouching 'towards Bethlehem to be born'.

The power of 'The Second Coming' is cumulative, as meaning and sound gather force, line by line, and bear down, like the beast of paganism on Bethlehem, upon 'slouches' – that ugly, but unforgettable verb.

Question

How does the language of the poem convey the awfulness of the new order which the poet foretells?

■ SAILING TO BYZANTIUM

It is generally agreed that in the collection of poems *The Tower* (1928) Yeats's genius reaches a peak of maturity and accomplishment. 'Sailing to Byzantium' is perhaps the most famous work in that collection. It is a poem of escape from the present time and place to an idealised location in the past – ancient Byzantium. To this extent it is a Romantic poem, both in the yearning for an idyllic existence and in the celebration of an exotic world in which to pursue it. It is also Romantic in the high status Yeats gives to artist and poet.

The poem begins, however, in detached reference to Ireland, in the present, as Yeats's speaker finds himself, now an old man, out of tune with the youthful vitality about him. One of the many tensions in Yeats's later poetry is that between youth and age. As a Romantic, he raged against the passing of the years and the decay of his body.

The first stanza, ironically, is perhaps the best in the poem, for Yeats writes vigorously and vividly about the world to which he no longer belongs:

> The young
> In one another's arms, birds in the trees
> – Those dying generations – at their song,
> The salmon-falls, the mackerel-crowded seas.

He emphasises the mortality of this natural world: the singing birds will die, along with everything else that is begotten and born. Yet we sense that that 'sensual music' still captivates him, in spite of the fact that its allure diverts us from 'monuments of unageing intellect'.

Yeats has set himself a difficult task in this poem, for while he often explores the tension between mortality and immortality, here he must celebrate the triumph of eternity over time, in the context of art. His strategy is to satirise his own decaying condition, as a scarecrow –

> An aged man is but a paltry thing,
> A tattered coat upon a stick

– and to celebrate the world of timeless beauty by giving it a precise location in time and space in Byzantium which is so far removed from the present as to assume eternal significance:

> . . . therefore I have sailed the seas and come
> To the holy city of Byzantium.

In the third stanza, he invokes the spirits of the place, who are wise men, and asks them to instruct his soul in their supersensual lore so that, as a poet, he might sing of eternal truths:

> . . . be the singing-masters of my soul.

■ But, again, it is the presentation of mortality that makes the more compelling poetry:

> Consume my heart away; sick with desire
> And fastened to a dying animal
> It knows not what it is; and gather me
> Into the artifice of eternity.

Like the 'monuments of unageing intellect', the 'artifice of eternity' is less striking as poetry than Yeats's descriptions of the state he would renounce.

In the final stanza, he specifies the form that he would take, having shrugged off the scarecrow mantle of mortality. It is a golden singing bird, in the court of the Emperor, which has the gift, in compelling song, to tell of all times: 'Of what is past, or passing, or to come'. Yeats's idea of the poet as visionary is recalled here. With the 'lords and ladies' about, we remember his celebration of aristocratic and hierarchical civilisation, and the system of courtly patronage of artists, which Yeats enjoyed in a small way in the home of Lady Augusta Gregory.

'Sailing to Byzantium' is a splendidly controlled utterance, in which Yeats's mastery of the spacious stanza, one of the features of his later work, is clearly evident.

Question

Do you agree that Yeats writes more compellingly, here, of the world he would renounce than of that he hopes will receive him? Why might such a judgement of the poem be made?

Among School Children

This is a poetic exploration of oppositions which haunted Yeats's thought. The poem begins in the mundane setting of a modern classroom, with Yeats, the Irish senator ('a sixty-year-old smiling public man') inspecting the girls' work. Thus the first of several tensions is established: between youth and age, masculinity and femininity. Further, in the second stanza, the speaker's public role is contrasted with his private imaginative speculations:

> I dream of a Ledaean body.

Among these children, he is thinking of Helen (daughter of Leda) and also (as always in such a reference) of his unattained Helen, Maud Gonne. The contrast between youth and age is pursued here, too, as he now imagines Maud Gonne as an old woman:

bent
Above a sinking fire.

He commemorates a momentary unity he enjoyed with her as Maud's anecdote of her schooldays (a 'trivial event') struck a chord in his own experience, and they blended

Into the yolk and white of the one shell.

Next, in this sequence of antitheses, Yeats thinks of that girlish Maud and wonders if the splendid creature knew (as the girls about him know) the ordinariness of life: 'every paddler's heritage'. This puts the senator, on his official visit, into the romantic frenzy of his younger manhood:

And thereupon my heart is driven wild:
She stands before me as a living child.

On the brink of sensuous physicality, the writing suddenly changes to the opposite domains of the aesthetic and the spiritual. He now imagines his idealised beloved in terms of the delicate, supersensual painting of the Italian fourteenth century, such as Fra Angelico's (far removed, indeed, in another antithesis, from twentieth-century Ireland). There, the physical became ethereal:

Hollow of cheek as though it drank the wind.

He would console himself with such arcane spirituality now that his own physical strength and handsomeness have waned, and he has been reduced, in comic self-mockery, to 'a comfortable kind of old scarecrow'.

The second half of the poem interprets these musings philosophically as the tension between the physical, intellectual and spiritual interpretations of life is explored. Thinking of his own mother (in stanza 5), Yeats wonders if she (or any mother) would assess the pain of childbirth positively, if she could see her child in its dotage – 'with sixty or more winters on its head'. The rhetorical question requires no answer.

Recalling the classical philosophers' contradictory speculations about the meaning and character of existence, Yeats masterfully summarises Platonic, Aristotelian and Pythagorean teachings in the sixth stanza. In Plato's philosophy, this world and its elements ('nature') were undervalued as poor imitations of the supernatural Forms; Aristotle, on the contrary, was too earth-bound and is amusingly presented here chastising his young pupil Alexander the Great:

Solider Aristotle played the taws
Upon the bottom of a king of kings . . .

and the musical Pythagoras is pictured fingering the harmonies of the spheres to an audience of 'careless Muses'. These once influential interpreters of life and their philosophies are now, like Yeats himself, with his complex theories, just scarecrows:

> Old clothes upon old sticks to scare a bird.

How, then, are these tensions between youth and age, men and women, the physical, intellectual and spiritual worlds to be resolved, if not in religion and philosophy? In the closing stanzas, Yeats celebrates his conviction that only art can satisfy his yearning for the absolute, for it combines, in a unique unity, the mortal and the supernatural.

The images which nuns worship are superior to those adored by mothers (their children), for these physical objects are also representative of the divine. But they do not decline into decrepitude – they 'keep a marble or a bronze repose'. They are not passionless – 'they too break hearts' – but coming from God, though fashioned by artists' hands, they are immortal, and Yeats invokes them:

> O Presences
> That passion, piety or affection knows,
> And that all heavenly glory symbolise –
> O self-born mockers of man's enterprise.

The resonant declaration of the closing stanza is a statement of Yeats's artistic faith. Unlike the labour of childbirth with its depressing consequences in our mortality, the labour of creation in art is, paradoxically, 'blossoming or dancing'. Moreover, this artistry is impersonal, for it is divinely inspired; and it is not intellectual or philosophical (coming out of 'blear-eyed wisdom'), but spiritual. Finally, it has a totality about it, in all its elements: like the magnificent chestnut tree in its blossoming (the artistry, in nature, of God's workmanship); or in a beautifully executed dance, where the dancer and the dance become as one: a perfect image of the resolution and consummation of humanity in artistic creation.

Questions

1. 'Yeats's poetry is an exploration of tensions.' Do you agree? Refer to two or three poems.
2. 'For all his constant remaking of his ideas and artistry, throughout his career, Yeats remains, to the end, a Romantic. He was, Ezra Pound wrote, "a sort of great dim figure with its associations set in the past".' Do you agree? Refer to several poems.

III

The variety of Modernist poetry is as notable as the principles which its practitioners have in common. Although Ezra Pound – the midwife, as it were, of Modernism – was closely associated with both Yeats and Eliot, his entrepreneurial and editorial functions were complemented by his own poetic creativity in works in which he speaks in his own distinctive voice.

Like Yeats, Pound had much to discard before his career as a Modernist could begin. His early poetry had been influenced by his university study in America of the Romance languages. He indicated his renunciation of these lyrical and often lengthy poems – which he had been publishing in the first decade of the century – in 'Salutation the Second', in the journal *Poetry* in April 1913.

'I come from an American suburb', Pound reflected,

> where both parents are really foreigners, i.e. one from New York and
> one from Wisconsin. The suburb has no roots, no centre of life. I
> imitate Browning. At a tender age London critics scare me out of frank
> and transparent imitation.

London was the crucial corrective. Yet in his poem 'Salutation the Third', in Wyndham Lews's *Blast* in 1914, Pound presents an appropriately angry diatribe against the bourgeois smugness of much of London life and its generally debased literary standards. He reveals the Modernist ambivalence about the city.

His *Cantos* are Pound's great work. They span the best part of half a century, beginning in 1918. They are uneven poems, for Pound's characteristic Modernist concern with the decline of the West was bound up with a denunciation of its banking system. So large stretches of the *Cantos* are given over to minute investigation of the economic and monetary structures of China during the dynasties, Italy in the Renaissance and America in the twentieth century. It is uninviting material. More accessible is a poem of the period of Pound's earliest work on the Cantos, *Homage to Sextus Propertius* (1917).

Pound was not destined to be the great poet of Modernism. But he was largely responsible for producing him. As Wyndham Lewis recalled,

> Mr Eliot was lifted out of his lunar alley-ways and fin-de-siècle
> nocturnes into a massive region of verbal creation in contact with that
> astonishing didactic intelligence.

That 'intelligence' was Pound's, manifested, for example, in his editing of Eliot's masterwork of Modernism, *The Waste Land*.

T. S. Eliot (1888–1965)

ABOUT THE AUTHOR

Thomas Stearns Eliot was born in St Louis, Missouri, in the United States. His family's origins, however, were in New England and, even further back, in England itself. Early in his life, Eliot experienced an acute sense of root-lessness in America and as his education proceeded, he had an intellectual, as well as an emotional, desire to return to the old world, with its history and traditions.

Accordingly, he travelled to France, England and Germany in the years before the First World War. His family had hoped that he would become a philosopher, and his studies at Harvard and Oxford had prepared him for this academic career. But Eliot was more interested in literature, and having settled in England, at some distance from family pressure, he began his career as a poet in earnest in 1915. The same year, he married an Englishwoman, Vivien Haigh-Wood, a relationship that brought them both much unhappi-ness but which was an inspiration for his poetry.

Eliot took out British citizenship in 1927 and joined the Church of England. As the decades passed, he became the most distinguished of contemporary men of letters, receiving the Nobel Prize in 1948.

A REVOLUTION IN POETRY

No one would have supposed, when Eliot's poetry first appeared in print, that such a status was in store for him. To the readers of poetry early in the century, who had been used to the lyricism and beauty of Romantic verse, Eliot's art was scandalously unpoetic. He is one of the great innovators in English literature. Eliot believed that the Romantic worldview had been exhausted and that the twentieth century required a poetry of its own, to express its distinctive concerns and speak to its people of the realities of their lives. He deliberately and provocatively produced a new poetry that contra-dicted all the expectations of Romanticism.

The Romantic cults of youth, idealism and loveliness, for example, were disposed of. The personae of Eliot's poems, such as Prufrock, are character-istically middle-aged and world-weary. So far from being idealistic, they are pessimists, tending to despair. The beautiful settings and heroic action of much Romantic poetry is similarly rejected. Eliot's usual scenario is the urban desolation of the modern metropolis – London, for instance, as in his most famous poem *The Waste Land* (1922). The human activities he portrays are typically trivial, demeaning, even sordid. Heroism is replaced by anti-heroism; love by loathing, indifference or mechanical lust.

■   The transcendentalism and spirituality of Romanticism is also discounted. Although Eliot embraced Christianity in middle age, in his early poetry he is sceptical about any religious panacea for the tragedy and meaninglessness of modern life. Even in his later Christian period, he is never evangelistic and seldom assured in faith. For Eliot, religious experience was always a matter of 'hints and guesses', brief and fleeting insights into God's love and the salvation from suffering that it could bring.

SELECTED POEMS

PRELUDES

The title of this collection of short poems suggests brief works of a lyrical kind, and, stylistically, Eliot is less adventurous here than in his other early poetry. However, the uneven line lengths and the random rhyme scheme subtly alert us to a poetry that is dislocating itself from the musicality of conventional lyricism. Yet this is not conversational or prosaic writing, by any means. Notice Eliot's use of an insistent incantatory rhythm in the third Prelude:

> You tossed a blanket from the bed,
> You lay upon your back, and waited;
> You dozed . . .

There is an implied accusation in that pointed emphasis on 'you' – unsettling, if we take it personally. But the second prelude is regular, almost lilting in its metre. Its message, however, is strikingly at odds with its smoothness.

Where these *Preludes* are most innovative is in their subject matter. If we think of the sweetness of one of Chopin's Preludes for the piano (as, ironically, Eliot may have intended us to do), these are surprisingly sour in comparison. The setting is the urban wasteland at its least attractive. A 'winter evening' (Prelude I) suggests sterility and death – 'the burnt-out ends of smoky days'. The leaves are 'withered' and even the man-made creation is derelict: 'broken blinds and chimney-pots'. As so often in Eliot, the populous city is, paradoxically, a place of loneliness, too, as noted here in the 'lonely cab-horse'.

The separate final line offers a glimmer of hope in this despairing world:

> And then the lighting of the lamps.

The glow of gaslight, although artificial, provides some alleviation of the gloom, but scarcely enough to redeem it.

In the time-scheme of the sequence, the second Prelude focuses on morning, but it is as bereft of loveliness and consolation as the desolate night. Daybreak brings a time of illusions and hypocrisies:

■   With the other masquerades
    That time resumes . . .

and a vision of tedium extending across the entire city: 'In a thousand
furnished rooms'.

This is a characteristic reference by Eliot to rootlessness and dispossession, to the fragmentation of home and family. We notice also the fastidious
detachment of the formal construction, 'One thinks of all the hands'. Eliot's
speaker is a detached observer, examining, dissecting, assessing modern life.

From the impersonal close of the second Prelude, Eliot changes to an intimate portrayal and address in the third. The person his speaker addresses is
representative, nonetheless, of contemporary men and women:

> You curled the papers from your hair,
> Or clasped the yellow soles of feet
> In the palms of both soiled hands.

From the evil domain of nightmare – 'the thousand sordid images / Of which
your soul was constituted' – the figure must rise to face the waking nightmare of daily life: 'such a vision of the street / As the street hardly under-
stands'. The yellowness, a favourite colour in Eliot's poems, indicates
jaundice: physical and metaphysical decay.

The closing Prelude retains this personal dimension of reference at first,
as the modern man steps out for the day's office work and returns (in lines
of punctuated rhythm, like a futile march):

> ...trampled by insistent feet
> At four and five and six o'clock.

This is the soul-destroying treadmill of the modern mercantile and industrial
world that Eliot was to know at first hand, as a bank clerk in the City of
London:

> And short square fingers stuffing pipes,
> And evening newspapers, and eyes
> Assured of certain certainties.

Tenderly, however, the penultimate stroke of this Prelude reveals the poet's
sympathies for modern human beings who have found themselves in this
Hell:

> I am moved by fancies that are curled
> Around these images, and cling:
> The notion of some infinitely gentle
> Infinitely suffering thing.

But the close of *Preludes*, importantly, returns to his earlier detachment. This is the way the world is. With the inevitability of old women going about their timeless tasks, human existence is set on its fatalistic course.

These poems are vignettes of modern life rather than sustained analyses of the kind Eliot offers in longer works. They expand from realism to surrealism ('His soul stretched tight across the skies / That fade behind a city block'), and from the universal to the specific ('You tossed a blanket from the bed'). And the notes of lyricism cleverly intensify the sordidness of the scenario by their very inappropriateness to their subject matter.

> **Question**
> How are connections, thematic and technical, between the 'Preludes' established, and what is the accumulating tone and effect of the sequence?

THE LOVE SONG OF J. ALFRED PRUFROCK

The key to the ironic theme of this poem is given in its title. What follows is neither a song nor a celebration of love. It is a dramatic monologue about the frustrations of unfulfilled passion. This irony is anticipated and intensified in the name of the supposed singer, with its formality and the suggestion of prudery (Pru-) and effeminacy (-frock).

In the opening verse-paragraph, Eliot locates his speaker in a night-time cityscape. As in *Preludes*, this is a rootless world of 'one night cheap hotels'. Nonetheless, Prufrock is sufficiently animated to go visiting and to encourage the reader to accompany him. He sets out for an alluringly cultured and feminine destination:

> In the room the women come and go
> Talking of Michelangelo.

This couplet is a haunting refrain, full of promise but ultimately disillusioning. It describes an ambience where Prufrock will confront his inadequacies, rather than find fulfilment.

The jaundiced world of modernity, enclosing Prufrock, is beautifully evoked in the feline imagery of the second verse-paragraph:

> The yellow fog that rubs its back upon the window-panes . . .

And the speaker's obsession with time is captured with equal effectiveness in lines where Eliot has 'time' incessantly repeated, like a clock ticking:

> There will be time to murder and create . . .
> Time for you and time for me.

This world is bound to temporality and, so, to mortality.

■   Prufrock's status as a disappointed and decaying Romantic is mercilessly exposed in the anxieties of a middle-aged man:

(They will say: 'How his hair is growing thin!').

This exposure easily becomes satirical as a being so insignificant and unprepossessing wonders:
Do I dare
Disturb the universe?

Yet the poem reveals Prufrock's self-knowledge too, and the despair that has produced. Essentially, Prufrock is the victim of lovelessness. Unlovely and unloved, he is incapable of devising a strategy to ameliorate his desolation: 'how should I presume? . . . how should I begin?'

He is haunted, too, by the larger matter of the meaning of life and his incapacity to interpret it. He cannot find the answer to the 'overwhelming question' of existence. Unlike the tragic heroes who see into the heart of things, and their own hearts, he is not 'Prince Hamlet, nor was meant to be'. Even his suffering is inconsequential and absurd.

The monologue closes in a lyrical fantasy of sensual romance – Prufrock's vision of the mermaids – but its final line relegates this experience to the illusory and transitory domain of dream:

We have lingered in the chambers of the sea
By sea-girls wreathed with seaweed red and brown
Till human voices wake us, and we drown.

Of the several refrain-like lines in this poem, Prufrock's repeated question 'would it have been worthwhile?' is the most important. For this is a poetry of the futility of life and of the frustration of human passion. Like Hamlet, to this degree, Prufrock sees how 'weary, stale, flat, and unprofitable' are the 'uses of this world'.

Prufrock is one of Eliot's several questors. But his journey only confirms his judgement that life is an endless round of trivial events, a perpetual disappointment of affection, sordid and terrifying: 'In short, I was afraid'.

However, the poetry conveying these grim truths has a remarkable variety and vitality. Confidently and memorably, Eliot catalogues details of contemporary manners and dress, notes meticulously the appearances of femininity, presents an urban location vividly, and elicits a complex response to his speaker from the reader. We laugh at Prufrock and despise him, but we also sympathise with him as the complications of his plight unfold, are universalised and begin to resemble our own.

Question

Why is the use of the dramatic monologue, in this poem, so effective in conveying the poet's concerns?

PORTRAIT OF A LADY

In this duologue, we note the lack of rapport between the two speakers: the young man and the older woman. It is another examination by Eliot of the failure of love. The poem's title is not ironic, for this work has the detachment of art and the female figure is a woman of cultivation. But the epigraph, with its reference to fornication, is strikingly (and deliberately) inappropriate.

While Eliot calls their talk a 'conversation', her speeches are met not by the man's reciprocal response, but by his meditated satire and cynicism. To her refined but also hysterical outpourings, his mind responds with 'a dull tom-tom' (which possibly includes a pun on the poet's first name). He is utterly out of tune with her intentions.

The satirical component of the portrait is most obvious in the second section when the lady, expostulating on the meaning of life, strangles a lilac in her hands. Eliot is at his most cynical in these lines:

'And youth is cruel, and has no remorse
And smiles at situations which it cannot see'.
I smile, of course,
And go on drinking tea.

The clipped quality of the rhyme perfectly catches his glib indifference to her overheated advances.

Yet, by the middle of the poem, we begin to see that the portrait of the lady is also a portrait of the young man. While her precious romanticism is being mocked, his aloofness – 'I keep my countenance, / I remain self-possessed' – is similarly scrutinised.

He acknowledges that in his very self-regard he is incapable of responding to another's love for him. Even the manifestations of less rarefied passion – 'some worn-out common song' – leave him cold: these are 'things that other people have desired'.

We notice that the poem begins (as *Prufrock* did) in the sterile depths of winter, moves to spring in its second section, but returns to autumn and winter in the third. The experience, in other words, is enclosed by seasonal imagery of decay. Moreover, Eliot's visual depiction of the interior of her home ('an atmosphere of Juliet's tomb'), though beautiful in its detail, is also claustrophobic and emblematic of death.

■ The indictment of the woman may seem to us, by the end of the poem, to be less savage than the speaker's own self-criticism:

I feel like one who smiles, and turning shall remark
Suddenly, his expression in a glass.
My self-possession gutters; we are really in the dark.

She may be pathetic, but he is callous. After much wry satire at her expense, he wonders, finally, whether she is not the better human being for having such feelings, however misdirected: 'Would she not have the advantage, after all?' And who is he to mock her?

And should I have the right to smile?

Question

How is the idea of the lady as representative of Romanticism conveyed and Romanticism, thereby, evaluated?

JOURNEY OF THE MAGI

This is the first of Eliot's Christian poems, but it is important to recognise that it expresses the difficulty of the Christian way. It is not a statement (let alone a celebration) of conversion.

Eliot takes as his subject the biblical story of the pilgrimage of the wise men to the Christ child, but he modernises it and so, in a sense, reverses it. The worldly-wise men of today, who have abandoned Christianity, must rediscover its central truth, as represented by the holy infant. En route, they will endure the scenes of Christ's passion and death which Eliot captures in a series of images from the scriptural narrative, here strikingly poeticised. The 'three trees on the low sky', for example, represent the Crucifixion. This makes the journey more difficult for the modern pilgrims than for the original Magi, for the humanistic twentieth century has supposed that the Christian story has been superseded.

The difficulty of the quest is particularised in the opening verse-paragraph in a setting redolent of the Holy Land. Eliot's language, appropriately, recalls that of the Bible – in particular, the Authorised Version of 1611 – as in the incantatory use of 'And'. His opening quotation is from a sermon by the seventeenth-century Anglican bishop Lancelot Andrewes, who was one of the translators of that version.

In the course of their journey, the Magi encounter 'a temperate valley'. This is a very significant moment in Eliot's poetry as a whole, for although this fertile location contains disquieting scenes from the Lord's suffering, the

■ fact that the setting is lush contrasts sharply with Eliot's earlier landscapes and cityscapes, with their dry sterility – most memorably in his long poem *The Waste Land*.

Yet, taken as a whole, the middle section of 'Journey of the Magi' is at best ambiguous and it closes, as the Magi arrive at the end of their journey, in a pointedly prosaic flatness of utterance:

it was (you may say) satisfactory.

The reason for this bland diction is that the Wise Men, although having reached their destination, find the implications of the experience disturbing rather than exhilarating. They realise the difficulty of what is yet before them: their responsibility to act upon what they have seen. We should also note that 'satisfactory' is, as well, a technical term from theology. Eliot is pointing out that the birth of Christ and his death are a 'satisfaction' for sins – that is, they are sufficient to redeem them.

In the closing verse-paragraph, the singular and more personal voice of one of them is still trying, years later, to come to terms with the experience. The 'Birth', which marked the beginning of his faith, was not joyful, but 'hard and bitter agony'. As he has had to return to his worldly existence, with its alienation from Christian truth, he is engaged in a constant struggle to develop his original insight. He prays for 'another death' – that is, for a further (and more decisive) death to worldliness that would enable him to advance further on his spiritual journey.

'Journey of the Magi' is a poem about faith, certainly. But it is most importantly about the first tentative steps in belief, and it emphasises the difficulties of growing in the love of God in an unbelieving age preoccupied with lesser idols. Eliot completes his temporal reversal of the scriptural story by calling the modern, post-Christian civilisation, 'the old dispensation' – a phrase first used for the pre-Christian world from which the original Magi came.

Question
How does the language of this poem indicate the difficulty of the journey of faith for 'wise' men?

FOUR QUARTETS (an introduction)
After 'Journey of the Magi' came Eliot's six-part religious poem 'Ash-Wednesday, 1930', written over the years from 1927 to 1930. As indicated by its title, taken from the first day of the Christian penitential season of Lent, the poem is a meditation on the need to turn from sin to God. It is a

lyrical prayer for forgiveness, most moving and beautiful, perhaps, in its representation of the mysterious Virgin-like figure who moves through it – a symbol of hope and spiritual regeneration in the wasted land of modernity.

Eliot's last major poetic work (apart from verse-drama, which preoccupied him for the next thirty years) was *Four Quartets*, written from 1936 to 1942. These four poems, beginning with 'Burnt Norton' which was written without the idea of a sequence, are essentially philosophical meditations, with significant religious (specifically Catholic-Christian) implications and ruminations about poetry and its ability to speak of and to its time about matters – in particular, spiritual matters – which are alien to its culture. The last three *Quartets* were written during the Second World War – specifically, during its early years when the prospects for victory, in Britain, were not good. This temporal urgency intensifies the sense of despair and difficulty in the spiritual life.

As the collective title of the *Quartets* implies, music provided inspiration for Eliot in their composition. The arrangement of each poem conforms loosely to the classical sonata, with the introduction of 'subjects' (that is, themes) and their recapitulation and a version of the brisk scherzo movement in the fourth section of each poem. Also, more generally, as music is the most abstract of the arts, so the *Quartets* are particularly abstract poetry, recalling in their opening lines, for example, Eliot's own training as a philosopher:

> Time present and time past
> Are both perhaps present in time future
> And time future contained in time past.

This subject introduces the principal theme of the poems: the tension between time and timelessness and the need to be alert and open to the transcendence of time while in a time-bound world. Eliot develops a symbol for this timelessness:

> At the still point of the turning world. Neither flesh nor fleshless;
> Neither from nor towards; at the still point, there the dance is.
>
> 'Burnt Norton'

In terms of Christian theology, the intersection of time with timelessness was at the Incarnation when the word of God was made flesh in Christ. Eliot does not underestimate the difficulty of coming to an understanding of such ideas:

> The hint half guessed, the gift half understood, is Incarnation.
> Here the impossible union
> Of spheres of existence is actual,
> Here the past and future
> Are conquered, and reconciled . . .
>
> 'The Dry Salvages'

■ The poems are by no means only philosophical and theological, however. As their titles indicate, they are firmly located in the physical world – in three locations in England, and one in America: the Dry Salvages, a small group of rocks, Eliot's note tells us, off the north-east coast of Cape Ann, Massachusetts. Eliot knew the place well in his youth. As a keen sailor, he recognised the value of such seamarks in the turbulent Atlantic. The Dry Salvages were a particular still point. And Eliot writes beautifully, in each of the poems, about the four classical elements of air, earth, water and fire (respectively). Here is his representation of the Atlantic in the third *Quartet*:

> The sea has many voices,
> Many gods and many voices.
> The salt is on the briar rose,
> The fog is in the fir trees.
> The sea howl
> And the sea yelp, are different voices
> Often together heard: the whine in the rigging,
> The menace and caress of wave that breaks on water,
> The distant rote in the granite teeth,
> And the wailing warning from the approaching headland
> Are all sea voices.

Most important, however, are the extended meditations, usually in the fifth, final section of each *Quartet*, on the tension between the words poets must use and the Word (of God). Once again we encounter Eliot's distinctive Modernist voice and concerns. He is committed to making poetic language new:

> So here I am, in the middle way, having had twenty years –
> Twenty years largely wasted, the years of *l'entre deux guerres* –   [between
>   the two wars
> Trying to learn to use words, and every attempt
> Is a wholly new start . . .
>
>   'East Coker'

He is committed to finding a language that will speak of eternal truths that are ever new:

> Words strain,
> Crack and sometimes break, under the burden,
> Under the tension, slip, slide, perish,
> Decay with imprecision, will not stay in place,
> Will not stay still....
>
>   'Burnt Norton'

He by no means despairs of the undertaking, as he reflects on the finished poem in the last *Quartet*, where

> every phrase
> And sentence that is right (where every word is at home,
> Taking its place to support the others,
> The word neither diffident nor ostentatious,
> An easy commerce of the old and the new,
> The common word exact without vulgarity,
> The formal word precise but not pedantic,
> The complete consort dancing together).
>
> 'Little Gidding'

Four Quartets is one of those poems which stays with the reader through life, to be returned to time and again, with a new appreciation of its depth and breadth of meaning on each re-reading.

Questions

1. 'Eliot's most striking achievement is to produce images and symbols for the conditions of the modern world, both its external manifestations and the psychological condition of its inhabitants.' Do you agree? Refer to two or three poems.

2. 'Eliot's poetry has its own "poetic" qualities, of rhythm and resonance, for example, which modify, by their inventiveness, the despair of his worldview.' Is this true? Refer to two or three poems.

Assignments

1. Find the recording of T. S. Eliot reading *The Waste Land* and follow it with a text of the poem. Eliot claimed that genuine poetry could communicate before it was fully understood. Is this your experience in listening to his reading of the poem? What ideas and emotions were communicated?

2. Read *Four Quartets* through, silently, without seeking to understand the meaning of each word or reference. Then begin a lifetime's appreciation of the poem by making a close study of the first *Quartet*, 'Burnt Norton', with the aid of a good critical guide, paying particular attention to the different characteristics of poetic style in (and within) the five sections of that *Quartet*. What is the effect of these variations?

After Modernism 12

In the generations since Modernist poetry flourished in the 1920s, there has been a remarkable variety of responses to and rejections of its precepts and practices. Generally speaking, poets of the later twentieth century affirmed their individualistic creativity in a range of styles, from a new formality (usually, however, idiosyncratic) to the most experimental of forms, from a childlike simplicity to an elusive complexity of utterance. Increasingly, the contributions of poets from North America and elsewhere in the English-speaking world further enriched and diversified the tradition.

A survey of poetry since Modernism (that is, roughly speaking, since the Second World War) reveals the astonishing fertility of poetic craftsmanship in mid-century and beyond, in spite of increasing apprehensions (in those years of the burgeoning intrusion of television into everyone's daily life) that the culture of reading was dying or even dead. Yet that post-war culture, with regard to the reception and appreciation of poetry in particular, was undergoing significant changes which had their sources in Modernism and its complexities.

The extent to which poetry was ever a popular art-form can be debated. Now, although more poetry is being read than ever before – in fulfilment of the requirements of school curricula and because of the ever-increasing numbers of students, since the 1950s, completing high school to matriculation – it has probably never been less popular, in the sense of readers, in general, taking poems to their hearts for life, and reading poetry voluntarily for pleasure (let alone reciting it from memory – once a common social activity). Because of the persistence of poetry in school syllabuses, throughout the Western world, poetry as a subject to be studied – and poems as texts to be interpreted, rather than enjoyed – has (very regrettably) become the dominating idea of poetry today. Poetic works suitable for this study need to be complex. Naturally, poets write for the audience they are most likely to reach. If the general, popular audience ceases to exist for the 'simpler' kinds of poetry, then that poetry will cease to be written.

That an audience can still be found for such poetry is demonstrated in the

297

career of the English poet, Pam Ayres (1947–). Moreover, in her case, the original oral tradition of verse has reasserted itself. Beginning by reading her poetry at a folk club in Oxfordshire, then going on local BBC radio, Ayres reached a national audience in 1975 when she appeared on BBC television and she has subsequently toured the world with her one-woman poetry show. It is her delivery of her poetry, with her distinctive accent, as much as the poetry itself which has been the essence of her success. Ayres has published six collections of her poems and at the end of the twentieth century she was the fifth best-selling poet in Britain. Her poems are concerned with everyday life and are usually a comic interpretation of it, as in her best-known poem 'I wish I'd looked after me teeth'. It remains to be seen if her humorous verse comes to be appreciated (and anthologised) for its wit in the way of Edward Lear or whether she is more accurately assessed as a comedian who happens to speak in poetry.

An example of a 'serious' poem which has captured the popular imagination is 'Funeral Blues' from 'Twelve Songs' by W. H. Auden (1907–73). Because of its recitation in the film, FourWeddings and a Funeral (1994), it has become one of the best-known poems of recent years:

FUNERAL BLUES
Stop all the clocks, cut off the telephone,
Prevent the dog from barking with a juicy bone,
Silence the pianos and with muffled drum
Bring out the coffin, let the mourners come.

Let aeroplanes circle moaning overhead
Scribbling on the sky the message He Is Dead,
Put crepe bows round the white necks of the public doves,
Let the traffic policeman wear black cotton gloves.

He was my North, my South, my East and West,
My working week and my Sunday rest,
My noon, my midnight, my talk, my song;
I thought that love would last for ever: I was wrong.

The stars are not wanted now; put out every one;
Pack up the moon and dismantle the sun;
Pour away the ocean and sweep up the wood;
For nothing now can ever come to any good.

People use it at funerals of their own family members and friends and it is regularly found on cards to be sent to the bereaved. It is a rare case, in the modern age, of a serious poem gaining popular status in the culture, and the irony of this achievement is that, before it had been used in the film, it was not one of Auden's well-known poems. (A similar situation has occurred in relation to T. S. Eliot and the use of his light-hearted *Old Possum's Book of Practical Cats* in the musical *Cats*. Millions today know some of Eliot's lines about these various felines who have never even heard of *The Waste Land* or *Four Quartets*.)

The extraordinary popularity of 'Funeral Blues' has explicable and inexplicable elements. Understandable is its appeal because of its use in a very popular film; that it focuses on a universally familiar human emotion – the dreadful sense of loss at the death of a lover and partner; that it is brief and lyrical, with some striking images that make it memorable, but a vocabulary that is simple, without one 'difficult' word or abstruse phrase which would present an obstacle to any literate person. What is extraordinary is that, both in the film and the personal circumstances of the poet who wrote it, the poem is explicitly about the death of a homosexual lover (yet the poem has been as warmly embraced by heterosexuals and we could just as easily imagine it being read by a woman as a man); the apparent simplicity is in fact complicated by several surreal images ('Pack up the moon...' and so on, with which, it might be supposed, 'ordinary' readers would not 'identify') and, more generally – and very encouragingly – that in a supposedly unpoetic age, people of all ages and circumstances have taken this poem to their hearts.

This may indicate that the future popularity of poetry could be secured if people first encounter it through the popular media of film and television rather than be expected to read it (let alone study it) in the printed form. This would take us back to the original way in which poetry, as an oral art, was transmitted.

> **Question**
> How would you account for the popularity of 'Funeral Blues'? (Focus on both thematic and linguistic aspects of the poem. If possible, view its use in the funeral in the film.)

The difficulty of much modern poetry (whether Modernist or more recent) and, arguably, the abandonment (by many poets) of regular rhythm and rhyme, and the tendency of contemporary poetry – as of 'serious' literature at large – to present a critical even despairing rather than celebratory attitude to life, have had negative consequences in terms of its popular reception. T. S. Eliot argued that modern poetry had to be 'difficult' because it reflected the complexities of modern life. While various reactions to Eliot's principles and practice attempted to correct what many interpreted as a lamentable divorce between poetry and 'the people', the poetry written under the influence of this reaction (such as Philip Larkin's, from the 1950s onwards) has failed to significantly recapture a popular readership for verse. The usual persona of Larkin's poetry, a sexually dysfunctional, loveless and ageing provincial middle-aged man, pessimistic about the future of his culture and society, is perhaps not the most alluring of subjects. It would seem that poetry is now destined to be a coterie interest of the specialised literary community and, during the years they are required to study it, of high-school students.

Assignment

Do you agree that poetry is now largely understood to be an academic subject rather than an important component of individuals' cultural and life experiences and personal memory-store? What evidence would you cite for and against this idea?

I

In emphasising the impact of Modernism – and its influence over the twentieth century at large – we could overlook the persistence of the contrary, Romantic tradition in the works of several significant twentieth-century poets. One of these is the American Robert Frost (1874–1963). In the following poem (of 1923), the traditional lyrical character of Frost's art is clearly evident.

STOPPING BY WOODS ON A SNOWY EVENING
Whose woods these are I think I know.
His house is in the village though;
He will not see me stopping here
To watch his woods fill up with snow.

My little horse must think it queer
To stop without a farmhouse near
Between the woods and frozen lake
The darkest evening of the year.

He gives his harness bells a shake
To ask if there is some mistake.
The only other sound's the sweep
Of easy wind and downy flake.

The woods are lovely, dark and deep,
But I have promises to keep,
And miles to go before I sleep,
And miles to go before I sleep.

This is poetry that is disciplined in rhythm and rhyme; it is fit to be sung and, therefore, 'lyrical'. Yet the work's technical organisation is not simplistic. The rhyming pattern is arranged to give the last stanza a finality which is the result of an accumulation of rhymes. In particular, we notice that the last word of the third line of each of stanzas 1 to 3 introduces the dominant rhyme for the following stanza: 'here', in stanza 1, looks forward to the rhymes of 'queer', 'near' and 'year' in stanza 2, and so on. In the concluding stanza, however, all the lines rhyme, perfectly closing the poem. This cadence is further ensured by the repetition of lines at the very end.

Similarly controlled is the work's metrical, or rhythm, pattern. There are four lilting 'feet' per line, which at once suggest movement, appropriate to a horse-ride, but are also in tension with the stillness of 'stopping'.

The speaker's experience is of solitude and the evening. These two elements in the poem, along with the beautiful natural setting, combine to make it distinctively Romantic in quality. This is not poetry engaging with the modern industrial and urban world, as poetry was beginning to do when Frost was first published, early in the twentieth century, nor with its anxieties and complexities. It is writing devoted to the spirit of escape from that populous and ugly environment. The Romantic artists found solace in nature and, typically, in solitude.

We note that Frost emphasises his dissociation from other human beings: there is not a 'farmhouse near', and his experience is in the deep dark of midwinter – he sees no one and cannot be seen by anyone. The 'little horse' adds to this sense of pleasant communion with nature, 'the woods and frozen lake', introducing a light-hearted touch in this essentially happy poem:

> He gives his harness bells a shake
> To ask if there is some mistake.

The conclusion of the poem, however, modifies the happiness of the preceding stanzas. While reaffirming his appreciation of these tranquil moments in nature – 'the woods are lovely, dark and deep' – Frost submits to the demands of his ordinary duties: 'but I have promises to keep' and resumes his journey:

> And miles to go before I sleep,
> And miles to go before I sleep.

The repetition represents at once the tedium of travel before him and its rhythmic motion on horse-back.

The poem symbolises the contrast between action and contemplation. In the Romantic tradition, Frost inclines to the tranquillity of meditation on nature and the enjoyment of the pleasures of the senses which it excites. He finds the business of ordinary life less inspiring and moving, even as he acknowledges that he must pursue it. The Romantic worldview and the demands of daily existence are held in a tension.

More eccentric was the poetry of John Betjeman (1906–84), who was taught by T. S. Eliot as a schoolboy, admired him personally and intellectually and shared his religious faith, but who deliberately set himself against the 'school' of poetry which Eliot had founded. The eccentricity consists in Betjeman's wilful determination to contradict the precepts of Modernism. So far from evoking the cosmopolitan world of the present, Betjeman focuses on the details of suburban and provincial life – in poems like 'Death in Leamington', set in the Warwickshire resort of Leamington Spa, and 'East Anglian Bathe' – frequently yearning for an idealised past. The writing is lyrical, stanzaic, immediately comprehensible, easily memorised, evocative of and appealing to straightforward emotions of nostalgia, sadness and uncomplicated happiness:

> Oh when the early morning at the seaside
> Took us with hurrying steps from Horsey Mere
> To see the whistling bent-grass on the leeside
> And then the tumbled breaker-line appear . . .
> > 'East Anglian Bathe'

It is poetry which celebrates life and falls easily on the ear, yet in its often directly autobiographical way it may only speak directly to readers who have either shared the kind of experiences Betjeman knew or wished they had. It is possible that its very accessibility – sometimes bordering on a kind of smugness and twee cosiness – is as alienating for many readers as it is appealing for others. In his biography of Betjeman, Bevis Hillier points out that the kind of poetry Betjeman wrote was not entirely eccentric nor 'a sudden strange throw-back – a Newbolt from the blue, as it were – but part of an identifiable *recent* tradition' of lyrical poetry touching on 'train journeys, typists, gas meters and Southend Pier'.[1] But of the several names he lists in evidence of this 'tradition', only Betjeman's has survived.

II

Many poets imbibed the principles of Modernism but, being selective in their appropriation, put their own stamp on its characteristics. In the next generation of poets, W. H. Auden – a friend of Betjeman and eventually published by Eliot (at Faber and Faber) – is notable for pursuing the engagement with contemporary thought and experience of the Modernists, but developing his own extraordinary body of imagery and suppleness of rhythmical expression. We have already looked at the lyricism of his lullaby 'Lay your sleeping head . . . ' and the song-like wistfulness of 'Funeral Blues', but Auden ranged widely from tight stanzaic forms (such as 'As I Walked Out One Evening'), the high rhetoric of the ode-like elegy 'In Memory of W. B. Yeats', the meditative complexity of 'In Praise of Limestone', the commemorative, political discourse of 'Spain 1937', and the deceptively conversational philosophy of 'Musée des Beaux Arts' (1940).

---

1. *Young Betjeman* (London: John Murray, 1988), p. 342.

The style of this last poem perfectly mirrors its subject matter. Auden is viewing suffering, even tragedy, as part of life, rather than exceptional. So the language and rhythms of the poem are prose-like. Yet the subtle syntactic energy which animates the language early in the poem, through the use of 'how' three times, gives an accumulative impetus to the writing. This persists in the echo 'anyhow', in the eleventh line, elevating the conversational mode to poetry.

Suffering may have an eternal significance – like the blood of the martyrs – but (Auden argues) the great painters of the Renaissance understood that it takes place in the midst of life and often in the most unprepossessing circumstances: 'Anyhow in a corner, some untidy spot'. To make his point explicit, Auden focuses typically on a tale (as painted by Pieter Bruegel, the sixteenth-century Belgian artist) with moral implications. He introduces *The Fall of Icarus* in an arbitrary way – 'In Brueghel's *Icarus*, for instance' – which is appropriate to his idea of the randomness of suffering.

Icarus disobeyed his father Daedalus and flew so high on their escape from Crete that his wax wings melted and he plunged to his death. The victim of vanity and foolhardiness, he tumbles headlong into a calm estuary; neither shepherd nor ploughman on the verdant promontory notice, and the galleon sails on out to sea. Looking at the painting – which, like so many of Bruegel's, is crowded – we have to search for the disappearing legs of Icarus in the bottom right-hand corner. The ploughman, the shepherd and the galleon are of far more interest than the ostensible subject of the work.

Auden deftly captures the disposition of the painting in his closing lines, but whether his teaching is the same as Bruegel's is debatable. The painter is pronouncing a severe judgement on Icarus for pride followed by a literal fall, consigning him to insignificance in comparison with the worthy, if commonplace activities of life. If this is 'suffering', it is self-induced and deserved.

Auden's canvas, as it were, is broader. He is talking of suffering in general. To turn away from a foolish boy falling from the sky is a kind of wisdom – the ploughman is right to get on with his work. But indifference to suffering in the lives of the undeserving is at best ignorance (like children, not recognising its implications, or the torturer's horse, incapable of understanding its master's actions) and at worst unspeakable.

Assignment

Find a reproduction of Bruegel's painting and consider Auden's poem with reference to it. Do painting and text convey the same 'messages' to you?

III

In the increasing individuality and eccentricity of modern poetry, the voice of absurdity – a kind of lunacy in response to the madness of modern life, mani festing itself in the breakdown of language into gibberish – is sometimes heard. Again, this was anticipated by the Modernists. In the third section of *The Waste Land*, fractured, neurotic experience finds its expression in broken vocalised fragments of speech:

> Twit twit twit
> Jug jug jug jug jug jug
> So rudely for'd.
> Tereu

In the poetry of Stevie Smith (1902–71) – and the childish line-drawings she used to accompany it – a kind of infantile nightmare stands for contemporary individuals' response to human existence. Here, the style of nursery rhyme is absurdly appropriated to the debate about the death of God:

> OUR BOG IS DOOD
> Our Bog is dood, our Bog is dood,
> They lisped in accents mild,
> But when I asked them to explain
> They grew a little wild.
> How do you know your Bog is dood
> My darling little child?
>
> We know because we wish it so
> That is enough, they cried.
> And straight within each infant eye
> Stood up the flame of pride,
> And if you do not think it so
> You shall be crucified.
>
> Then tell me, darling little ones,
> What's dood, suppose Bog is?
> Just what we think, the answer came,
> Just what we think it is.
> They bowed their heads.
> Our Bog is ours
> And we are wholly his.
>
> But when they raised them up again
> They had forgotten me
> Each one upon each other glared
> In pride and misery

For what was dood, and what their Bog
They never could agree.

Oh sweet it was to leave them then,
And sweeter not to see,
And sweetest of all to walk alone
Beside the encroaching sea,
The sea that soon should drown them all,
That never yet drowned me.

(1950)

Like Emily Dickinson, Stevie Smith's enjoyment of hymns in her childhood nurtured her appreciation of lyrical poetry. She drew upon this in her own writing, as in this poem, with its insistent rhythm and simplicities of diction, both of which are to be found in children's hymns. She did not, however, retain her childhood faith in Christianity, although she remained intensely interested in it, and many of her poems, lyrical and otherwise, are debates with the Church over matters of doctrine. In adulthood, her hopes were transferred to death, which is often personified in her work. She beseeched him, as if he were a lover, to come and take her from her life and human life in general, which, in her usual assessment, is seen as a trial of suffering, without the promise either of redemption or of eternity.

In this poem, Smith's curious mixture of a childlike simplicity of utterance with concerns of a profound kind is announced in the title and the opening line. The twice repeated 'Our Bog is dood' calls out for interpretation even as it is clearly, on one level, either baby-talk or nonsense. The ill-formed words initially make us think of 'our dog is dead' – as children might mangle that expression. But the capitalisation of 'Bog' and the recollection that 'God' is 'dog' backwards, achieves an engagement between theological controversy and infantile discourse (with, perhaps, a satirical comment embedded in that conjunction). By discovering it amongst children and in their inarticulate enunciation of the concept, Smith is indicating the futility of pondering the matter and the puerility of their insistence on the statement. It is something that cannot be resolved decisively for it is beyond human knowledge:

How do you know your Bog is dood
My darling little child?

The pride of the assurance is criticised next and the punitive judgement of these atheistic totalitarians (who would have indicted Christianity and the Churches for their dogmatism) is ridiculed pointedly. The punishment they dispense is the same as that inflicted on Christ:

And if you do not think it so
You shall be crucified.

While Smith was an agnostic, she is as critical of those who absolutely deny God's existence as she could be of those who unquestioningly affirmed it. Who or what is this 'Bog' that the strident children claim is dead?

> Just what we think, the answer came,
> Just what we think it is.

They have pronounced the death of a God of their own creation. It is the essence of their subjective childishness, and, furthermore, each child has a different Bog – an idol that has been raised up and then destroyed. Paradoxically, it is themselves in their egocentricity, and this nurtures their hostility towards each other and their own unhappiness:

> Each one upon each other glared
> In pride and misery.

They do not even understand what death is: 'what was dood' (and there is an implied rhyme here, characteristically in Smith's writing, with 'good'). So they are ignorant both of God and death, even as they loudly proclaim the death of God; their ignorance is linguistically emblematised in their vague enunciation: 'Our Bog is dood'. The bog itself suggests that they have been in a mire of confusion.

The closing stanza differentiates the speaker from these infants who represent contemporary adults. In a familiar image in Smith's poetry, the speaker is seen to be relishing her aloneness: 'Oh sweet it was to leave them then'. There is the vision, too, of the encroaching sea which will 'drown them all'. This is synonymous with a death (unlike that of God) which is certain: human mortality. In her own triumph, the speaker concludes that it 'never yet drowned me'. She is not suggesting that she is immune from death. Rather, she will exalt in it, whereas these proud ones must face the horrible contradiction of annihilation.

The poem's sing-song rhythm and rhyme accurately conveys the immaturity of the adult-infants.

IV

Further to the maintenance of a song-like voice in the midst of the prosaic cacophany of twentieth-century life was the resonant, song-like writing of Dylan Thomas (1914-53), bringing his prodigious Welsh musicality of utterance and a delight in poetic form to a poetic environment dominated by formlessness and unlovely sounds, as in the poem 'Do Not Go Gentle Into That Good Night'.

Referring to the personal source of this poem in a letter to Princess Caetani on 28 May 1951, Thomas observed:

> The only person I can't show the little enclosed poem to is, of course, my father, who doesn't know he's dying.

The poem was published in November 1951 and Thomas's father died a year later.

Dealing with a matter of intense, profound and immediate emotional significance, Thomas disciplined his subject in the choice of the strict French form of the *villanelle*, requiring nineteen lines based on two rhymes. These are introduced in the first two lines in 'night' and 'day'. Then the sequence of complementary third lines of each stanza is concluded in the last, when they are brought together, decisively resolving the work and affirming the double imperative of the son's address. The technical accomplishment of the poem is astounding, and the more so for not ostentatiously calling attention to itself, but for being the perfect choice of style for the theme.

The difference in tone between the two refrains is that between the gentleness and raging to which they refer. Although the speaker urges his father not to 'go gentle into that good night', the accents and sounds of that petition are subdued, and the night, after all, is 'good'. Wisely, Thomas has chosen this less insistent imperative to begin his address. Having introduced the idea of resistance, even as he acknowledges the inevitability of acquiescence (he may not go gently, but he will go), he then calls for a more assertive, indeed angry complaint 'against the dying of the light'. This imperative is not only stronger in the choice and repetition of 'rage', but in the explicit reference to 'dying'.

While the poem has its source in Thomas's personal situation, it is the balance of personal and impersonal elements, in addition to its technical formality, which both restrains and universalises the emotion. There are several impersonal gestures – notably, at the beginning:

> Old age should burn and rave at close of day

as 'rave' prepares us for the more direct address of 'rage' in the next line. Then there is the catalogue of kinds of men (all of which, we can imagine, Thomas's father has been): 'Good men', 'Wild men' and 'Grave men'. These broad gestures put the intimacy of 'And you, my father' into the context of universal humanity which shares the common experience of death.

Thomas effectively communicates the various ideas and emotions which the subject invites. The common modern notion that form inhibits the expression of feeling is not only disproved here. Thomas demonstrates that form, organising feeling, intensifies its expression.

■ SPECIAL STUDY 14

Robert Lowell (1917–77)

ABOUT THE AUTHOR

One of the most influential American poets of the mid-twentieth century, Lowell was born into an aristocratic Bostonian family. However, early in life he began that rebellion against his upbringing which developed into a pronounced hostility. Much of Lowell's poetry takes his biography as his subject matter as he defines his selfhood in terms of his rejection of family convictions and conventions.

His first collection of poems, *Lord Weary's Castle*, appeared in 1946, after the Second World War, during which Lowell had converted to Catholicism, became a conscientious objector and made the first of a series of unhappy marriages. The novelty and savagery of the poetry was compared by critics at the time to that of T. S. Eliot's revolutionary poems, on his generation, thirty years before.

However, the most important development in Lowell's career occurred in the mid-1950s when he began to discard the formality of his earlier poetry for a more conversational, less referential verse. He moved away from the objective classical tradition into a markedly subjective mode, most famously exemplified in *Life Studies*. This established Lowell as the pre-eminent writer of 'confessional' verse, the style which has dominated poetry since the 1960s. In this kind of writing, the poet is committed to self-revelation, but strives, in the process, to convey a larger interpretation of contemporary life. Lowell's *Life Studies* are both studies of his life (and that of his family) and of the modern American culture and society in his generation.

It is important to note that Lowell's criticism of others also includes satire of himself and that the spare, apparently conversational style of his writing is very carefully crafted.

SELECTED POEMS FROM *LIFE STUDIES*

GRANDPARENTS

In this poem, Lowell violently juxtaposes personal reminiscence with comically grandiose allusions – the old order of his grandparents' rustic New England farm is compared to the *Ancien Régime* in France before the Revolution. This technique restrains his recollections of his grandparents from becoming sentimental. Yet the bitterness which Lowell brings, for example, to his accounts of his parents, elsewhere in *Life Studies*, is absent from this poem, as he recalls his grandparents with a certain affection.

'Grandparents', however, is not merely personal. In his minute observation of the paraphernalia and rituals of their existence, Lowell presents a culture and generation of the later nineteenth and early twentieth century which has now gone for ever. Such details as the Pierce Arrow automobile garaged in a horse stall, the road that is dusty and unsealed, and Grandmother's touring veil for motoring, place the time of his grandparents' old age, in transition from the old world to the new.

The first verse-paragraph, enclosed by the lines 'They're altogether other-worldly now' and 'They're all gone into a world of light' (adapted from the seventeenth-century poet Henry Vaughan to emphasise the pastness of his grandparents and their civilisation), give the poem an elegiac quality. There is also a touch of humour as Grandmother, heavily garbed, is seen ludicrously as a Mohammedan and Grandfather, like a slapstick comedian, waving his stick.

Yet the intrusion of Lowell himself, first in his 'throw-away and shaggy span / of adolescence' and then, more rudely, in his acquisitive declaration 'the farm's my own', dispels the decorum of the elegy. This is further assaulted at the beginning of the second verse-paragraph in Lowell's repeated (but now exclaimed) use of the phrase. The poet's self-presentation, combined with self-criticism, now dominates. To accompany Lowell's char-acteristic sense of the futility of his life, the evocation of his grandparents now becomes more critical. Theirs was a world, Lowell suggests, that attempted to conceal the unpleasantness of reality. *Life Studies*, as the title indicates, unmasks it.

Yet the closing verse-paragraph is affectionate towards its subject. Here, Lowell melodramatically overstates his sentiment to make it objective and, in the use of an earthy and vividly visual verb, to modify sadness: 'Tears smut my fingers'. When we remember that this is the adult Lowell imploring and weeping, there is something pathetic here as well. Lowell's dissociation from his family (and his guilt about it) appears in the last lines as his grandparents' past is again associated with events of world significance, such as the Bolshevik Revolution of 1917, the year of his birth, and he is suggesting that this was the birth of the modern world also. As so often in this collection, the personal experience is associated with matters of great moment and, thereby, it is at once comically minimised and objectified.

Question

Look at Lowell's use of verbs in this poem. Why and how are they so effective in conveying his meaning?

MEMORIES OF WEST STREET AND LEPKE

This poem of reminiscence is based on Lowell's imprisonment as a conscien-tious objector in 1943, when he served five months in New York's West

■ Street Jail. But the poem does not begin with memories. Rather, in a clever stroke in the opening lines, Lowell introduces the idea of a metaphorical imprisonment in the present, by which he is to intepret his literal confinement in the past:

> Only teaching on Tuesdays, book-worming
> in pajamas fresh from the washer each morning,
> I hog a whole house on Boston's
> 'hardly passionate Marlborough Street . . .'

> These are the tranquillised *Fifties*
> and I am forty.

Lowell's detention in the respectable conformity of Boston is suffocating him. Familiarly in confessional poetry, we find the persona at odds with his environment.

As we move from this unsettling present to the past, imagining that in his memories Lowell finds consolation for his present distress, we discover, however, that he is a man for no season. For during the war he was again at a remove from the status quo – 'telling off the state and president'.

Lowell's social analysis and his private anxiety, however, are consumed in an essentially comic vision. It is a black comedy, to be sure, where sharp and shocking contrast is the principal method of humour. The fate of the 'jaundice-yellow' Abramowitz, a pacifist-vegetarian-philosopher, at the hands of the Hollywood pimps Bioff and Brown, is given stylised exaggeration through a kaleidoscope of clashing colours, set against a backdrop of 'bleaching khaki tenements': 'they blew their tops and beat him black and blue'.

The final portrait of Lepke, the doyen of murderers, is arguably the most brilliant moment in Lowell's poetry. We expect, at first, that Lepke will be lined up with the 'negro boy' and the Hollywood pimps, against Lowell, Abramowitz and the Jehovah's Witness. But as Lowell contemplates Lepke – notice the alliteration of their names – from the disadvantaged point of the 'tranquillised *Fifties*', the poet realises his spiritual community with the villain. For Lepke, like Lowell, flourished in a rebellious past before society rendered him incapable of passionate activity:

> Flabby, bald, lobotomized,
> He drifted in a sheepish calm.

Similarly, Lowell has been lobotomised by the society of the present decade.

He consummates his identification today with Lepke yesterday in a ringing phrase which inverts the catchcry of the Fifties – 'an agonizing reappraisal' –

■ designed to stir America out of the moral torpor to which she succumbed in that era. By applying this formerly era-bound term to Lepke's condition in the Forties –

> no agonizing reappraisal
> jarred his concentration on the electric chair

– Lowell links their fates across the decades. Lobotomised, too, Lowell like Lepke can live only for release from the bondage of existence:

> hanging like an oasis in his air
> of lost connections.

Question

How does Lowell link his situation to Lepke's, and what is the effect of the linkage?

SKUNK HOUR

The final poem in *Life Studies*, appropriately, is about the hour of death. In 'Skunk Hour', Lowell communicates his personal apprehension of purpose-lessness in the midst of universal despair. Each human figure in its doom-laden tableau is fatuous and self-deluding, diverting himself from his desperate condition by perverting the true nature of the world.

The second half of the poem concentrates on a fourth unnatural being – the poet himself:

> One dark night,
> my Tudor Ford climbed the hill's skull,
> I watched for love-cars.

At the end of his extensive *Life Studies*, Lowell presents himself as a voyeur.

The damning vision of the lovers amongst the gravestones, the object of the persona's perverse attention, displays the lustful lovelessness of modern passion. The cars' headlights are 'turned down' in this nightmare world, and the clandestine coupling of their occupants is set to music feebly serenading a 'love' that couldn't care less:

> 'Love, O careless love . . .'.

Writing of 'Skunk Hour', Lowell remarked that 'sterility howls through the scenery'.

The poet, however, is the dominant personality in these lines, and he is not exempt from daunting self-criticism – 'my mind's not right':

I hear
my ill-spirit sob in each blood cell,
as if my hand were at its throat.

The only escape from the trauma of perverted existence is the ultimate perversion of self-destruction. Pondering this, Lowell confronts himself as the incarnation of evil: 'I myself am hell'. Thus, with his faith in himself destroyed and his community with others disappointed – 'nobody's here' – Lowell remains without God or hope in the world. With the human order annihilated, skunks are free to consume its detritus.

This is 'skunk hour' indeed, as these creatures – combining a reputation for their notorious smell (when on the offensive) with a prettiness that makes them attractive – march in triumph 'up Main Street'. Their dominion, secured in the manner of an occupation force, supersedes the futility of man's aspirations (and occupation and spoiling of the planet), as their 'moonstruck eyes', burning with a diabolical 'red fire', ignore the chalk-dry spire of the Trinitarian Church.

The determined character of the skunks' business is established in a number of threateningly active verbs – 'march', 'swills', 'jabs' – perfectly evoking the sense of the unassailable victory of the animalic world and the superannuation of the human order. They are not anarchic, however. The mother skunk is attentive to her kittens' welfare, and the poet, as a surviving visionary, records their benign and secure domain from which all human threat has been removed:

a mother skunk with her column of kittens swills the garbage pail.
She jabs her wedge-head in a cup
of sour cream, drops her ostrich tail,
and will not scare.

Question
How do you read the arrival of the skunks and their appropriation of the human environment?

Assignment
Read all the *Life Studies* poems. Give your account of the sequence at large, in terms of the characteristics of Lowell's style and his essential concerns. With regard to these matters, is consistency or variety more evident?

V

One of the marks of later twentieth-century poetry is its concentration on the experiences of 'ordinary' people living ordinary lives. The age of democracy has emphasised the condition of the people, the *demos*. This has led increasingly to a preference for the small details of daily life and experience. A striking example of this shift of attention from the remarkable to the unremarkable – or, rather, to discovering the remarkable amongst the unremarkable – occurred in writing for the stage in the mid-1950s. In Britain, for example, prior to this theatrical revolution, dramatists were generally inclined to present images of individuals leading lives which were more sophisticated and intelligent (and better dressed and spoken) than that of their average audience members. The immense popularity of Terence Rattigan's plays, known as the 'French windows' genre (as that stage-setting was often employed in his plays of upper-middle-class conflict and passion – such as *Separate Tables* – as the windowed doors opened onto the suggestion of an elegant garden) was challenged by the 'kitchen sink' school, led by John Osborne, whose *Look Back in Anger* was first produced in 1956. Here were people getting about in singlets, talking in slang and exposing the grubby realities of their daily lives and relationships. The bright young things gave place to the angry young men. Rattigan attended the premiere of Osborne's play,

> and watched one of the seminal moments in the history of modern English drama unfolding on the stage…. Osborne's hero, Jimmy Porter, launched into a brilliant, eloquent attack on almost everything that a man [such as Rattigan] educated at Harrow and Oxford, who lived in Eaton Square, played golf and enjoyed weekend house parties stood for. It was a full frontal attack on the class privileges that Rattigan had taken for granted throughout his life, and a punch on the nose for the comfortable worlds of South Kensington, Albany, Little Court and Cannes.[2]

Osborne was not only initiating a theatrical revolution, but reflecting the momentous changes in society and culture, across the Western world, which were occurring in the 1950s. The advent of rock 'n' roll, in the same years, was another reflection of these radical movements. Remembering them alerts us tellingly to the ignorance of the now all but universally accepted caricature of the 1950s as a decade of mindless conservatism during which the arts were inert and change of any kind was ruthlessly suppressed.

Naturally, poetry similarly reflected and advanced these changes. In 1956, the same year as *Look Back in Anger*, Alan Ginsberg (1926–97) published *Howl*, his long poem of social protest, sexual promiscuity, drug-taking, psychiatric disorder and the literary life:

---

2. Geoffrey Wansell, *Terence Rattigan* (London: Fourth Estate, 1995), p. 270.

I saw the best minds of my generation destroyed by madness, starving
    hysterical naked,
dragging themselves through the negro streets at dawn looking for an
    angry fix,
angelheaded hispters burning for the ancient heavenly connection to
    the starry
dynamo in the machinery of night . . .
a lost battalion of platonic conversationalists jumping down the stoops
    off fire
escapes off windowsills off Empire State out of the moon,
yacketayakking screaming vomiting whispering facts and memories
    and anecdotes
and eyeball kicks and shocks of hospitals and jails and wars . . .

Of course, Ginsberg was writing at the extreme edge of social protest and was
determined to shock.

Yet poets at large, in these years, turned to the dull grimness of the banal lives
of unremarkable people, discovering in their stories the quiet desperation and
minor-key tragedies which would once have been considered too insignificant
for poetic treatment. This poem, by the Australian Gwen Harwood (1920–95),
shows how extraordinariness of insight and utterance can be wrought from
apparently unpromising material by a skilful wordsmith:

IN THE PARK
She sits in the park. Her clothes are out of date.
Two children whine and bicker, tug her skirt.
A third draws aimless patterns in the dirt.
Someone she loved once passes by – too late

to feign indifference to that casual nod.
'How nice', et cetera. 'Time holds great surprises'.
From his neat head unquestionably rises
a small balloon… 'but for the grace of God…'

They stand a while in flickering light, rehearsing
the children's names and birthdays. 'It's so sweet
to hear their chatter, watch them grow and thrive',
she says to his departing smile. Then, nursing
the youngest child, sits staring at her feet.
To the wind she says, 'They have eaten me alive'.

In this sonnet, with its conventional divisions into two quatrains and a sestet,
Harwood moves from the details of a simple scene to contemplate issues of love,
fate and despair in the human condition. As a sonnet-writer, she must encom-

pass this material in fourteen lines and adhere to the sonnet's convention of completeness. The reader should sense, at the end, that all that needs to be said about the subject has indeed been said.

The monosyllabic opening sets the scene, straightforwardly:

> She sits in the park.

But the second part of the first line introduces a tone of pathos as the apparel of the unnamed 'she' is noted:

> Her clothes are out of date.

This does not only indicate poverty, but also carelessness and indifference. She has no reason to keep up to date, no one for whom it is important to appear at her best. Tugging at her old-fashioned skirt are two children who, in onomatopoeia, 'whine and bicker'. A third (as if two ill-behaved, whingeing children were not enough to bear)

> draws aimless patterns in the dirt.

Family life, as she knows it, has no rewards, only burdens.

A man 'she loved once', representative of the romance and affection that have utterly passed from her life, is seen walking by. She would pretend to be indifferent to his presence, but she cannot help detaining him, so starved is she of emotional fulfilment. And they exchange some meaningless courtesies, 'rehearsing / the children's names and birthdays'. If the man is not the children's father, her absent husband, he is emblematic of that figure who was once loved, but who treated her casually (like this man's 'casual nod'). Now he is permanently associated in her life and consciousness, with the act of 'departing' – like this man, in the sestet – leaving her in lonely despair.

Looking at the scene, the man surmises 'but for the grace of God': if he had reciprocated her love, he could be saddled with her and the three children. Just possibly, there may be the implication, again, of the man as her departed husband. Had he not deserted her, he would be trapped in this deplorable domesticity.

The setting at the beginning of the sestet is evocative, in the reference to 'flickering light', of fitful, failing hope. The day is declining into night's even darker domain, when she must return home alone (although in the company, which is no company, of her children). In the hypocrisies of social intercourse, she pretends that she has found fulfilment in motherhood:

> It's so sweet
> to hear their chatter, watch them grow and thrive.

In the honesty of her address to the unsettling wind, however, she declares the truth: 'They have eaten me alive'.

'In the Park' may be read from a feminist perspective, as an indictment of the situation of an abandoned mother. Certainly, the detachment of the man from the woman's plight adds substance to this reading. It may also be construed as Harwood's realistic analysis and evaluation of states of life, marriage and motherhood, that were usually romanticised when Harwood wrote the poem. Again, 'In the Park' may be seen as a philosophical reflection on the way our lives may deviate from the hope and joy we plan and anticipate, as in the pursuit of love and family life. It exposes the disjunction between the ideal and reality.

Harwood's accomplishment in this poem is that she has included these (and, indeed, other) possibilities of interpretation in the small, disciplined space of the sonnet.

Question

What is the effect, in this poem, of Harwood's use of the traditional form of the sonnet in the representation of the banal modern reality of the woman's situation? Is the form of the poem well chosen?

SPECIAL STUDY 15

Philip Larkin (1922–85)

ABOUT THE AUTHOR

Larkin was born in the English Midlands, at Coventry. He excelled in English at King Henry VIII Grammar School but found the other subjects tiresome interruptions to his principal interest. In the poem 'I Remember, I Remember', Larkin dismisses his Coventry childhood as a nothingness.

Going up to St John's College, Oxford, early in the Second World War, Larkin read English, graduated with a first-class degree in 1943 and was appointed Librarian at Wellington in Shropshire. Two novels, *Jill* (1946) and *A Girl in Winter* (1947), were written at this time, as well as his first collection of poems – *The North Ship* (1945) – which showed few signs of the qualities of style and the thematic preoccupations which readers came to appreciate in his later verse.

Larkin's next post as Librarian was at the then University College, Leicester, followed by the Sub-Librarianship at Queen's University, Belfast. By this time, he was concentrating almost entirely on poetry, having given up an attempt at a third novel.

While at Belfast, Larkin wrote most of the poems for his first mature collection, *The Less Deceived* (1955). This established his reputation and advanced that of the group of writers to which he belonged, known as 'the

Movement'. This was a reaction against the dominant influence of Modernism in poetry which, Larkin argued, had taken poetry away from the general reader, being too learned and complex, and made it the preserve of literary scholars and intellectuals. This was, he contended, an aspect of a widespread tendency in twentieth-century art:

> Up to this [twentieth] century literature used language in the way we all use it, painting represented what anyone with normal vision sees, and music was an affair of nice noises rather than nasty ones.

In 1955, Larkin was appointed to the position which he was to hold for the rest of his professional life – Librarian at the University of Hull in northern England. Two more collections of poems followed: *The Whitsun Weddings* (1964) and *High Windows* (1974). In these years, Larkin developed the reputation – supported by many of his poems with their apparently autobiographical sources – of the lonely, bookish, bachelor, librarian-poet, with a detached and cynical view of life.

Larkin died on 2 December 1985.

Question

What is your response to Larkin's observation, quoted above ('Up to this century . . .'), with regard to poetry?

SELECTED POEMS FROM *THE WHITSUN WEDDINGS*

THE LARGE COOL STORE
The large cool store selling cheap clothes
Set out in simple sizes plainly
(Knitwear, Summer Casuals, Hose,
In browns and greys, maroon and navy)
Conjures the weekday world of those

Who leave at dawn low terraced houses
Timed for factory, yard and site.
But past the heaps of shirts and trousers
Spread the stands of Modes For Night:
Machine-embroidered, thin as blouses,

Lemon, sapphire, moss-green, rose
Bri-Nylon Baby-Dolls and Shorties
Flounce in clusters. To suppose
They share that world, to think their sort is

■ Matched by something in it, shows
How separate and unearthly love is,
Or women are, or what they do,
Or in our young unreal wishes
Seem to be: synthetic, new,
And natureless in ecstasies.

Essential to the themes of detachment and alienation in Larkin's poetry is his
concentration on his dissociation from women and love. This persists through
his four collections of poems. In *The Less Deceived*, for example, in 'Reasons
for Attendance', he portrays himself observing a dance from outside through
a window, and evaluating his separation from its sociability and sexuality.

By *High Windows*, his last collection, Larkin has completely divorced
himself from any possibility of this kind of relationship. He whimsically
assesses his position in 'Annus Mirabilis':

Sexual intercourse began
In nineteen sixty-three
(Which was rather late for me)

He more seriously evokes his transcendence of what he ironically calls 'happiness' in the title poem of that book.

In 'The Large Cool Store' — as in several other poems in *The Whitsun
Weddings* — Larkin seems still to be coming to terms with his lot as a single
man. He is especially determined to explain to himself the unattainable
'otherness' of women.

The store, symbolic of the world, is spacious and cool. This immediately
conveys (in the title and its repetition in the opening line) a sense of a
passionless, even frigid condition. It is the contradiction of the small spaces
and warmth of intimacy. Moreover, it is ordinary in its merchandise, conjur-
ing thoughts of the 'weekday world'. This is an unromantic setting. Yet within
it are objects gesturing towards the possibility of love and passion — at a
distance (we note) from the familiar and accessible untidiness of masculinity
which is metaphorically represented by 'heaps of shirts and trousers'. These
are women's night-dresses:

Bri-Nylon Baby-Dolls and Shorties . . .

They are delicate, decorated and colourful, like femininity itself, as Larkin
perceives it. But for all their prettiness, these commodities do not evoke a
living, breathing sensuality. They are synthetic and unnatural in their studied
passionateness. They do not disturb the coolness of the store. They only
serve, through their strangeness, to indicate to the speaker the gulf that is
between himself and love — that is to say, himself and women. It is at once an

■ idealisation of their domain and a despairing recognition that it is closed to him: 'how separate and unearthly love is'.

As in so many of his poems, Larkin uses the occasion for this unusual reflection on love to record, with his keenly visual cataloguing talent, aspects of contemporary Englishness. The store is a working-class emporium, frequented by those who live in 'low terraced houses', who rise for work at dawn at the 'factory, yard and site'. In a sense, this exaggerates the speaker's isolation – for this is not his store, he is even further removed from the 'Modes For Night'.

'The Large Cool Store' is as chilling as the store itself. This is a world of ersatz passion, in contradiction of nature. Such was Larkin's view of the dehumanising forces of modern life. His personal sense of alienation from love is consumed by a more general vision.

Question

To what extent, and through the use of which linguistic techniques, does Larkin depersonalise his ideas here?

MR BLEANEY

In spite of Larkin's determination to dissociate his poetic writing from Eliot's Modernist school, this poem is immediately reminiscent of the world of Eliot's early poems, such as the 'Preludes', both in the characterisation of Mr Bleaney (whose mean-sounding name recalls the sterility of Eliot's 'Prufrock') and the sordid setting:

> Flowered curtains, thin and frayed,
> Fall to within five inches of the sill.

The language of the poem is a significant ingredient of its tone and, so, of its meaning. The sound of 'Bleaney' is more pointedly mean than 'Gridley', which was Larkin's original choice. The alliteration, in the first stanza, of 'flowered', 'frayed', 'Fall' and 'five' brings together the potentially attractive with its decay and emphasises (particularly with the positioning of 'Fall' at the beginning of a line) the fallibility of life – one of Larkin's preoccupations.

In the tradition of the English lodger, Bleaney – like Prufrock – is remembered as an isolated figure, detached from family and affection, and housed uncomfortably in these sparsely furnished lodgings:

> Bed, upright chair, sixty-watt bulb, no hook
> Behind the door, no room for books or bags.

In this visual critique, we notice, however, a certain delight on Larkin's part

■ in the careful description of a familiar mode of English life. 'The Bodies' is probably the name of Mr Bleaney's employers who (according to the landlady) have 'moved him' on to another location. (It also conveys the sense of a morgue and a corpse.)

The distinction, in the second stanza, between the objective description of the land around the house – 'tussocky, littered' – and the landlady's romanticising of her 'bit of garden' indicates the gulf that is fixed between reality and social and personal ideals.

The persona of Mr Bleaney provides, for the speaker, an objective focus for his own condition, for he succeeds Bleaney in the room – and so, in a sense, is to be identified with him. Larkin is suggesting, wittily, that there is a community amongst isolates. One's sense of aloneness is not peculiar to oneself. But this does not diminish any person's loneliness. If anything, it adds to its enormity: 'So it happens that I lie / Where Mr Bleaney lay'. This imagery (like 'The Bodies') is evocative of the dead. The room (later described as a 'hired box') makes us think of a coffin. The condition is that of death-in-life.

Larkin's negative evaluation is emphasised by a sequence of onomatopoeic verbs – 'stub', 'stuffing', 'jabbering' – describing unattractive actions and sounds. Yet, again, his details about the annual rituals of Mr Bleaney's life have a certain Betjemanesque charm:

> the Frinton folk
> Who put him up for summer holidays,
> And Christmas at his sister's house in Stoke.

Alliteration, again, in the third stanza, adds force to the onomatopoeia of 'stub' – 'the same saucer-souvenir' with that emphasis mocking the object, a once special saucer, that is receiving the stubbing with 'fags'. That innocuous colloquialism conveys, in English culture, a culture and a whole way of life. The focus and emphasis is demotic.

The two closing stanzas amplify the unconsoling setting introduced at the beginning, with a 'frigid wind' and the 'fusty bed', as Larkin, wondering about Mr Bleaney's speculations and his assessment of his life ('at his age having no more to show / Than one hired box'), finds an objective method for asking the same questions about himself.

As so often in Larkin (as in the poets he admired, such as Thomas Hardy), the essence of this poem is a general moral observation: 'how we live measures our own nature'. Mr Bleaney may not have been moved by such considerations, Larkin notes dismissively – 'I don't know'. There is no doubt, however, that Larkin was, and his idea that others, in the same situation, might not be only increases the sense, which his poetry conveys, of his persona as an outsider.

Question

How and why does Larkin both identify with Mr Bleaney and differentiate himself from him?

THE WHITSUN WEDDINGS

This poem should be read in conjunction with 'Here' (in the same collection), where the poet introduces the idea of travel through England as a metaphor of his disengagement from life. In 'The Whitsun Weddings', the process of 'Here' is reversed. Larkin's speaker is now discovered, at the Christian season of Whitsun, journeying southward to London. At first, he is his characteristically autonomous self. From the interior of the speeding train, 'three-quarters-empty', he records the appearances of the separate external world:

> Wide farms went by, short-shadowed cattle, and
> Canals with floatings of industrial froth;
> A hothouse flashed uniquely: hedges dipped
> And rose: and now and then a smell of grass
> Displaced the reek of buttoned carriage-cloth
> Until the next town, new and nondescript,
> Approached with acres of dismantled cars.

These scenes are devoid of humankind. But Larkin's separateness is to be circumscribed. Noticing only distant vistas, then preoccupied with his reading, he is unaware that he is being drawn into the rites of life, until the celebratory sounds from the platforms at each station begin to demand his attention:

> At first, I didn't notice what a noise
>   The weddings made
> Each station that we stopped at.

His disengagement arrested, he now attends more closely, evaluating the scene critically but indulgently:

>   Struck, I leant
> More promptly out next time, more curiously,
> And saw it all again in different terms:
> The fathers with broad belts under their suits
> And seamy foreheads; mothers loud and fat;
> An uncle shouting smut.

His particularity of observation and his evaluative analysis secure his proximity to the event and his involvement in it. And at the heart of the poem, in the next stanza – as 'fresh couples' climb aboard and fill his carriage –

■ Larkin's key word, the affirming ejaculation 'Yes', consummates his marriage to the occasion he describes and assesses. This is *his* Whitsun wedding. The 'I' of the opening stanza has become the 'we' of a shared experience:

> We hurried towards London, shuffling gouts of steam.

Yet the exhilaration of the occasion is short-lived. The afternoon of the journey's climax declines into the evening of its end. Larkin ponders his fortuitous meeting with the couples and the accident of their unions in marriage. Both represent a 'frail / Travelling coincidence'. Ominously, he wonders about the future:

> What it held
> Stood ready to be loosed with all the power
> That being changed can give.

The indefiniteness of this speculation is itself negative. For marriages at least begin with the prospect of happiness. And it remains unresolved in the last lines, with their appropriately sexual reference, as Larkin closes in a puzzlingly paradoxical simile:

> We slowed again,
> And as the tightened brakes took hold, there swelled
> A sense of falling, like an arrow-shower
> Sent out of sight, somewhere becoming rain.

Arrows may wound and kill, and rainfall is the natural accompaniment of melancholy. But a summer shower is benign and rainwater is also productive of fertility. From Larkin's perspective, the effect of the 'dozen marriages' is uncertain. But his Whitsun wedding has produced the progeny of a poem. 'Struck' by the event, he too has been 'changed' by it. Its power in his life becomes the poetry in which he preserves it. In this way, we see that the remote Christian origins of Whitsun are immediately relevant to his work. For the celebration of Pentecost (another name for the Christian feast) is the affirmation of verbal inspiration.

'The Whitsun Weddings' is a poem about poetry, where Larkin affirms the importance for his creativity of the settings and the events of ordinary human experience, the subjectivity of his moral vision of them and his happiness in bringing his ideas and emotions to artistic birth.

Question

Why is the setting of a train journey especially useful and apt for the unfolding narrative and argumentative structure of this poem?

> ### Assignment
> Read widely in Larkin's poetry. It belongs to a world that is precisely limited, in time and place – in later twentieth-century England – and, some would say further, even to a masculine and middle-class view of life. In consideration of all the poems that you have read, would you argue that Larkin's concerns are nonetheless universal and timeless, in spite of such 'limitations' of setting, subject matter and response?

VI

One of the most remarkable social phenomena of twentieth-century life was the feminist movement and its achievements in the ongoing process of achieving women's equality with men. Particularly in the feminism of the 1960s and 1970s, the pioneering advocacy for women's rights of such as the Suffragettes at the beginning of the century began to make an impact not only in the public and legislative matters of rights to vote, access to higher education, the representation of women in various domains formerly exclusive to or dominated by men but also in marriage and the family and in women's individual lives. This has brought about changes in those areas – such as later marriage ages, fewer children (and borne later in life), the removal of the stigma associated with the unmarried woman – that are now having momentous social consequences (not, however, universally regarded as beneficial, even by women themselves).

Women's poetry, inevitably, reflected these momentous changes, as well as the larger social contexts of radical thought in the 1960s.

We should conclude our study of poetry of the second half of the twentieth century with a special study of the work of Sylvia Plath, one of the most important women poets of the twentieth century and, then, of her husband Ted Hughes. Their turbulent marriage is as famous as their poetry and provided a rich source of material for it.

SPECIAL STUDY 16

Sylvia Plath (1932–63)

ABOUT THE AUTHOR

Sylvia Plath's father, Otto, emigrated to the United States from a Prussian town in northern Germany in 1901. He had a distinguished academic career in zoology and received his doctorate from Harvard University in 1928. In childhood, Sylvia was the centre of her father's attention, while her sickly brother, Warren, occupied most of his mother's time. Otto Plath's health

■ deteriorated due to diabetes and he died in November 1940, devastating his young daughter.

Successful in high school, Plath went on to prestigious Smith College in 1950. By 1952, she was taking honours in English but was increasingly worrying about her abilities. In her journal in November 1952 she wrote: 'God, if ever I have come close to wanting to commit suicide, it is now.' She was also apprehensive, at this time, about her future as a writer and gloomy about the state of the world at large. She attempted suicide by cutting her legs and by taking an overdose. She was given psychiatric treatment at the Massachusetts General Hospital. This experience is recounted in detail in Plath's novel *The Bell Jar.*

Working on her undergraduate thesis on Dostoevsky at Smith, Plath applied for entrance to Oxford and Cambridge universities in England. She was accepted for both, chose Cambridge and was awarded a Fulbright Scholarship in 1955. She was writing both poetry and short stories in these years and winning literary awards.

Plath was a striking figure at Cambridge and greatly in demand socially. But the male company she encountered was not as sophisticated as she had expected. The resolution of this situation seemed to appear in 1956, when she went to a Cambridge literary party and met 'that big, dark, hunky boy, the only one there huge enough for me . . . it was Ted Hughes'. A Yorkshireman and Cambridge graduate, Hughes had by this stage decided to dedicate his life to poetry. They were married in London in June 1956. A honeymoon in Europe followed, which had its highs and lows.

Plath and Hughes returned to Cambridge so that she could finish her degree. In June 1957 they were relieved to be able to leave England for America as Plath had been offered an instructorship at Smith. In spite of this bright future, Plath's negative side continued to haunt her: 'I cannot ignore this murderous self', she wrote in her journal in October 1957. Hughes gave a reading of his poems at Harvard and was establishing his reputation. In 1958 they moved to Boston and became associated with the rich literary life of the city, meeting such poets as Robert Lowell and Elizabeth Hardwick and attending Lowell's writing seminar at Boston University. During this period, Plath was having weekly psychiatric therapy sessions.

Plath and Hughes drove across America in 1959 and returned to the east for two months of uninterrupted writing at the Yaddo community in upstate New York. Although she accomplished much during this period, Plath found the atmosphere at Yaddo stifling and they left America for England in November 1959. Their first child, Frieda, was born in April 1960. Hughes's reputation was expanding with broadcasts for the BBC and the publication of *Lupercal*, but Plath was struggling to find a new style of writing.

She suffered a miscarriage in 1961 and 'jolting jealousies' about Hughes's supposed unfaithfulness. At one point she tore up all his work in progress. More happily, they found an old thatched rectory in Devon to which they moved in 1961. At the beginning of the following year, their second child, Nicholas, was born. Plath was still anxious about her marriage, however, and she confronted Hughes with his unfaithfulness.

Between September and December 1962, Plath wrote the forty poems by which she has become famous and which were published after her death in the *Ariel* collection. She made arrangements to rent a flat in London, moving there in December with her two children. The following January was the worst winter in England in living memory. Plath's children became sick and, being house-bound, she began to lose her grip on reality. She committed suicide on 11 February by gassing herself in the flat's oven. She left bread and milk for the children.

LITERARY IMPORTANCE

The attention which is paid to the poems of Plath's last, troubled months obscures the fact that she had been writing poetry (and short stories) from childhood. Her quest was to find her own voice in poetry and, to achieve this, she experimented with many styles. To appreciate the characteristics of her last poems and the freedom of expression that she discovered in writing them, it is important to recognise that their qualities arose out of a long apprenticeship. They are 'confessional' poems, speaking directly and often with rawness and bitterness about her personal suffering, but they are also superbly crafted. From her years of experimentation with poetic form, Plath had learned the necessity of ordering her material.

The more closely we look at Plath's poetry, even when it seems to be expressing outbursts of uncontrolled emotion, as in 'Daddy', the more we realise how carefully arranged are the images, rhythm and vocabulary of the writing. The first point to make about Plath's literary importance is the recognition of her ability to express her highly individual experience of life in forms that are lively and structured.

A second aspect of her achievement is her expression of the pain of mental illness. The various ways in which she reveals the suffering of her speakers, their vulnerability and fragility, has an honesty that both instructs and elicits sympathy, even when their emotions are at their darkest and most punitive. In exploring her own world in this way, Plath makes it available to her readers. The problem which she identifies (in 'Lady Lazarus' for example) of the readers becoming voyeurs of her distress nonetheless remains. But she would argue, as she does in 'Kindness', that there is no stopping the 'blood jet' of poetry.

■ SELECTED POEMS FROM *ARIEL*

ARIEL

The title poem of Plath's last collection of poems, published after her suicide, recalls her experience of learning to ride a horse called Ariel on Dartmoor in Devonshire. This is probably combined with another experience of horse-riding in Cambridge, remembered in Ted Hughes's poem 'Sam'. Plath was carried away by Sam who galloped out of control. She remembered the experience as both terrifying and exhilarating. The poem's title also recalls the spirit in Shakespeare's play *The Tempest*. Ariel, there, represents poetry and artistry.

The poem begins in stillness and darkness, at daybreak. By its second line, it is set in motion:

> Then the substanceless blue
> Pour of tor and distances.

As the landscape of Dartmoor unfolds before the rider, her own actions begin to unfold on horseback and her unity with the horse starts to be established:

> God's lioness,
> How one we grow.

While the setting and elements are primarily physical, the vocabulary suggests a spiritual or transcendental element: 'substanceless', 'God'. Like the name 'Ariel' itself, representing both a horse and a spirit, the poem operates on at least these two levels of meaning.

The rider's unity with the horse is stressed in the description of poise: 'pivot of heels and knees'. This is accomplished riding, not that of somebody learning to ride. The poem is about the freedom which comes from mastery and Plath may be referring not only to horseriding but to artistic creativity and to life itself. Ariel in Shakespeare's *Tempest* is an accomplished singer. It was Plath's quest to write poetry that was free from restrictions and artificiality. It was also her hope to live in this way.

She gladly follows where the horse leads, in verbs of speedy activity: 'splits and passes'. Attempts are made to hold her back: 'Nigger-eye / berries cast dark / Hooks'. These belong to the dark world of 'shadows' and blackness. She would thrust forward into light. In contrasting imagery, she sees herself like 'White / Godiva'. The reference is to a horsewoman who rode naked. The nakedness expresses the freedom Plath's speaker yearns for:

> I unpeel
> Dead hands, dead stringencies.

Again, we see how these lines can be read, realistically, as referring to the moment when horseriding becomes freedom and not a lesson and, metaphorically, as referring to the freedom poets experience when they find their own voice and freedom in life itself. Plath does not underestimate the difficulty of the procedure. She needs to be 'hauled' through the air, like a heavy object. But she becomes lighter and brighter as she goes:

> I
> Foam to wheat, a glitter of seas.

The ride has accomplished the abandonment of her childish self. She leaves that behind and it fades into the distance: 'The child's cry / melts in the wall'. The 'cry' suggests all her suffering, particularly her grief, in childhood, over her father's death, which Plath saw as the source of her unhappiness.

Changing the metaphor from a rider on horseback, she now sees herself as 'the arrow' and 'the dew'. These are ambiguous metaphors. The arrow, shot with skill, is admirable as it flies fast and sure to its target. But it is also used to kill. Dew is attractive in the early morning, but it is fleeting as the sun quickly dries it up. Plath plays with the verb 'flies'. An arrow flies to its destination and dew flees on encountering the sun's rays. The irony of the poem is that it seems to be a celebration of the ecstasy of horseriding and creativity and freedom but it is finally the expression of a desire to escape completely from life, to be

> at one with the drive
> Into the red
>
> Eye, the cauldron of morning.

Psychologically, that 'drive' is the death-wish (described by Sigmund Freud in *Beyond the Pleasure Principle*, 1920). Plath expressed that wish in her series of suicide attempts. The final colour in the poem, red, emphasises the difference and surprise at the end by being different from those which have appeared before. Earlier, Plath sought whiteness to escape from darkness. But it is the redness of the fiery sun to which she is finally drawn. The imagery of the cauldron suggests that the sun will consume her. More positively, it may also indicate that she will be refined there, completely purified of this world's restrictions. A further irony is that in such a death she imagines she will escape from the deadness of life in this world.

Questions
1. What is the significance of the poem's title?
2. How does the poem 'work', on several levels of meaning?

■ LADY LAZARUS

In the title of the poem, Plath indicates that she is a female version of the biblical figure Lazarus, whom Jesus raised from the dead. The story is told in St John's Gospel (11: 1–44). This immediately confers significance upon her story and situation. Lazarus is a famous biblical character and the subject of numerous paintings. If the person in this poem is a female version of him, then she not only undergoes what he experienced – returning to life from death – but she is a figure as notable and as worthy of artistic commemoration.

The title sets the tone for the poem. It is a proud statement, drawing attention to the speaker's extraordinary life-story, which ordinary human beings will admire. But it is also an ironic statement. Lazarus was raised from the dead by his friend Jesus. It was not only a miracle, but an entirely happy event. In Plath's poems, the series of deaths she is referring to are her suicide attempts, coming from extreme unhappiness. In Christian teaching, suicide is a forbidden act. Unlike Lazarus, she does not have Jesus' friendship to revive her from her self-inflicted deaths. So the poem is also scornful of the story of Lazarus. Plath's speaker is saying that even after attempted suicides she rises from death and does so under her own powers:

> Dying
> Is an art, like everything else.
> I do it exceptionally well.

The series of neat stanzas in which 'Lady Lazarus' is written contrasts with the emotional wreckage which leads a person to suicide, but may also reflect the often-documented sense of purpose which people who have decided to commit suicide have, after the chaos which has led them to this definite act.

Plath introduces the idea of herself as a victim of Nazi persecution in the simile in the second stanza. Like the reference to Lazarus in the title, this links her personal situation to a famous phenomenon. She compares her suicide attempts to the deaths of Jews in the concentration camps run by the Nazis during the Second World War. Plath makes this comparison in a number of poems and she has been much criticised for it. First, because it gives an unjustified significance to her personal suffering: one woman's psychological pain, however intense, cannot be compared to the sufferings of the Holocaust and, in any case, Plath was not a Jew. Second, she portrays her father, Dr Otto Plath, in the role of a Nazi persecutor. In fact, the mild-mannered Dr Plath was a critic of Nazism.

The speaker imagines her body being displayed after another of its miraculous risings from death: 'Peel off the napkin / O my enemy'. The 'enemy' is the person, perhaps a doctor or Dr Plath himself, who brings her back to life and insists that she continues the cycle of living and dying: 'like the cat I have nine times to die'. Plath maintained that her father had ruined her life by dying when she was a child. This cruel act had deprived her of a father's love and, seeking it, she regularly attempted to get back to him by dying. But it is also a process of getting back at him, for hurting her in this way. This explains the violence of her portrayal of him.

She realises the wastage of her suicidal processes – 'What a trash / To annihilate each decade' – but, at the same time, thrills to the extraordinary display of herself and her emotions which these acts achieve. Scornful of ordinary people, she imagines them pressing forward to look at her body, like the audience at a freak show, as it is revived once again:

> The peanut-crunching crowd
> Shoves in to see
>
> Them unwrap me hand and foot –
> The big strip tease.

The several references to skin and flesh are typical of Plath's poetry in concentrating on the sense of her bodily fragility which is a metaphor for the fragility of her mental state. As her body is exposed to various assaults – they 'had to pick the worms off me like sticky pearls' – so her mind and emotions are vulnerable and responsive to the world's assaults: 'I turn and burn'.

At the centre of the poem, the rhythm is intensified to the point of hysteria:

> I do it so it feels like hell.
> I do it so it feels real.

The intensity of her emotion is like the single-minded devotion of a martyr-saint, prepared to die for faith. She has a similar vocation: 'I guess you could say I've a call'. And like the saints, relics are made available for human beings less devoted to their vocations to view: 'a bit of blood / Or a piece of my hair or my clothes'. It is, finally, the dissimilarity between her situation and that of the saints, however, which strikes us. They die for a cause beyond themselves. The suicide is utterly self-obsessed.

The poem closes with Plath focusing on the person she blamed for her psychological illness, her father. She presents him as a cruel and oppressive Nazi (using the German 'Herr' for 'Mr') and also as Satan, the devil himself: 'Herr Lucifer'. Sarcastically, she remarks: 'Do not think I underestimate your great concern'. In fact, if he had been concerned about her, she is arguing, he would not have died and left her. Having been so mistreated by a man, she will take out her revenge on all men:

> Out of the ash
> I rise with my red hair
> And I eat men like air.

Questions

1. Why does Plath compare her situation to that of the Jews in the Holocaust? Is the comparison justifiable – morally, poetically?
2. What is the thematic effect of the technique of short stanzas and of the rhythm of the poem?

DADDY

The poem opens in an insistent repetition as the speaker sets the tone of rejection: 'You do not do, you do not do'. This negativity, immediately after the apparent warmth of the title of the poem, makes that title ironic. It is hatred rather than affection which is conveyed. The autobiographical source of this emotion was Dr Otto Plath's death in 1940. He did not wilfully allow himself to die, as Plath has suggested in her poetry, but neither does he appear to have made a special effort to live. When she was told about the death, Plath angrily declared to her mother: 'I'll never speak to God again'. The ambiguous psychology of Plath's situation with regard to her father needs to be understood if her poems about him are to be appreciated. It was because of her love for him that his death, so early in her life, was such a shock. So her love turned to hatred, because he had inflicted this pain upon her: he had abandoned her and betrayed her love.

The opening stanza portrays the speaker as trapped in a 'black shoe'. This will be linked with the later imagery of Nazi jackboots. Here, the shoe resembles a coffin in which she is encased. In order to live herself, she must escape and kill her captor. From her childhood, she remembers her father as a vast being, like a seal stretching from the west coast of the United States ('Frisco', San Francisco in California) to the east coast, 'the freakish Atlantic'. It is a grotesque image, both in terms of the size of the creature and its association with ghastliness.

The thirty years she has spent under daddy's influence have brought her to the point where she is determined to be free. She will no longer 'pray to recover' him. Instead, she will kill him, finally. 'Ach, du' – 'oh, you' – she says accusingly and, by using German, begins to create the picture of Otto Plath as an oppressive Nazi and of herself as his Jewish victim. As we have already mentioned, in discussing 'Lady Lazarus', these are fictions which Plath developed. Her father was opposed to the Nazis and Plath herself was certainly not Jewish.

Tracing her father back to his origins, she presents him as a foreign being from an evil place with a history of 'wars, wars, wars'. The mystery of his precise birthplace adds to her sense of alienation from him: 'I could never tell where you / Put your foot, your root'. There is the sense that he is ashamed of his past and deliberately hid it from her. Communication between them is impossible: 'the tongue stuck in my jaw'. She associates her German-speaking father with the German people of the 1940s and, particularly, the Nazis and their concentration camps. As the Jews were victimised and slaughtered in the Holocaust, so her distant father inflicted cruelty on her, to the point where she identified with the Jews' suffering:

> I began to talk like a Jew.
> I think I may well be a Jew.

This is the voice of madness, of absurd fantasy. In the next stanza, Plath draws back a little from her absurd claim: 'I may be a bit of a Jew', but persists with the nonsense of enlisting her father (who had died when the war had scarcely begun and was an American citizen) in the German forces:

> I have always been scared of you,
> With your Luftwaffe, your gobbledygoo.
> And your neat mustache
> And your Aryan eye, bright blue.
> Panzer-man, panzer-man, O You.

Poetry does not have to be biographically or historically accurate. What matters here is that Plath is being true to her emotions. This is how she saw her father and how she chooses to describe her reaction to him. As biography or history it is a shocking libel on an innocent, dead man. But it undoubtedly reveals the truth of Plath's psychosis. The double repetition of 'brute', with its rhythmical insistence and the rude sound of the word, is a focus of the brutality Plath claims to have experienced as a result of her father's life and death.

She not only compares her father to the Nazis and, in the later reference to *Mein Kampf (My Struggle)*, Hitler's political autobiography, to their leader (another father-figure) but also compares him to the 'devil' and 'the black man', one of the terms for the devil. She had tried, through suicide, to get back to daddy, but each attempt failed. This was because of her love for him. But then she thought she had figured out a solution to her problem: 'I knew what to do'. She transferred her love to a living man, similar in appearance: 'a man in black with a Meinkampf look' and married herself to that 'model' or copy of the original: 'And I said I do, I do'. This is a reference to Ted Hughes, Plath's husband, with his dark looks and black jacket. But he turned out to be another cruel individual who treated her badly, abandoning her. 'Daddy' was written after Hughes had left Plath for another woman. So now she realises that the only solution is to kill off the men in her life: 'so daddy, I'm finally through'. And the only way to accomplish that is to kill herself (which she did, a few months after writing this poem):

> The black telephone's off at the root,
> The voices just can't worm through.

■ The final stanza tells of the killing off of this two-in-one Daddy. The 'villagers' refers primarily to Otto Plath's Prussian origins, with the sinister suggestion that the people realised his crimes (totally imaginary) against them: 'they always *knew* it was you'. It may also include a reference to Hughes's rural background. The last line is a bitter message to both men and a forecast of Plath's suicide:

> Daddy, daddy, you bastard, I'm through.

It sounds triumphant, but it is also desperate. The only way she can kill off the demons of her daddies is, finally, not only to kill them psychologically but to kill herself, bodily.

> **Question**
>
> How does Plath both express and discipline her emotions in this poem?

■ **SPECIAL STUDY 17**

Ted Hughes (1930–98)

ABOUT THE AUTHOR

Ted Hughes was born in Yorkshire in 1930 and educated at Mexborough Grammar School and Pembroke College, Cambridge. In 1956 he married Sylvia Plath, the American poet (see Special Study 16). They had two children, Frieda and Nicholas. Plath committed suicide in 1963.

In more than forty books of poetry, Hughes explored all aspects of the natural and animal world, from early collections such as *The Hawk in the Rain* (1957), through *Crow* (1970) to *River* (1983). He also wrote prose and produced translations, such as his *Tales from Ovid* (1997). From 1984 until his death in 1998, Hughes was Poet Laureate.

Just before his death, Hughes published *Birthday Letters*, a collection of poems dealing with his troubled relationship with Plath. Written over twenty-five years, after her death, all but two are addressed to her.

LITERARY IMPORTANCE

In Hughes's poetry we discover the marriage of two separate traditions of twentieth-century verse. The first of these has its roots in the Romantic movement of the nineteenth century. It engages with the idea of recovering and celebrating the processes and the beings of the natural world as a means

■ of coming to an understanding and appreciation of ourselves as human animals.

This is a profoundly reactionary influence in Hughes's poetry, for it contrasts starkly with the priorities of a civilisation that is the product of the scientific and industrial revolutions. For Hughes, the materialist spirit of our times has been fatally dehumanising. The only antidote to this poisoning of thought and emotion is to look beyond or behind our flawed human culture and observe and learn to identify with the sensuality and spirituality of the natural world, and especially the animals.

Hughes explores in detail every conceivable facet of animal behaviour. He analyses its violence and cruelty (as we perceive it) as well as its spontaneous sensuality and beauty. Probably as a result of Hughes's study of anthropology and archaeology, he brings a kind of scientific rigour and detachment to his careful and detailed portrayals of natural phenomena and the creatures. His poetic conspectus of the natural world ironically possesses something of the method and system of science.

The other tradition that Hughes draws upon in his poetry is the very opposite of the Romantic identification with nature we find in his subjects. It is an un-Romantic objectification and restraint in his style. Hughes is passionate in his ideology, but his expression is usually detached, and this strengthens the poetry, avoiding any decline into sentimentality.

Hughes's output was extraordinary by any standards. In addition to his hundreds of poems, there are his plays and prose. And his career reveals some remarkable changes of emphasis within the broad framework of his concerns. In his first period, in the 1950s, he began in a formal, rhetorical style. In the second period, in the 1960s after the suicide of Sylvia Plath, his style became more direct in manner, but despairing and sometimes surreal in its themes. Then, in the 1970s, a more hopeful frame of mind produced poems tending towards a spiritual solution to the tragedies of modern life. His last collection, *Birthday Letters*, reveals a more confessional mode.

His development, stylistically, was from lyricism and rhetoric to a plainer style. But as his poetry drew upon immense learning in both Western and Eastern thought, and an interest in the occult, he remained often difficult and obscure.

Some readers have objected to Hughes's preference for the dark aspects of nature, particularly its violence, and to his unremittingly scathing denunciation of modern life. Certainly, his poetry is more often disturbing than consoling. In many ways, Hughes is the most unlovable and unaccommodating of poets. Yet perhaps it is precisely this characteristic which makes his work so evocative of our age of confrontation and violence. He speaks to a world in which the processes of dehumanisation can seem irreversible.

■ FROM *BIRTHDAY LETTERS*

Hughes had remained largely silent about his relationship with Sylvia Plath and his separation from her prior to her suicide in 1963. In contrast, Plath's version of the disintegration of her marriage and her mind had been revealed both in her poems (especially the *Ariel* collection, which appeared after she died) and in her published letters. She had come under the influence of the 'confessional' poets of the 1950s, such as Robert Lowell, and believed in the importance of poetry for telling the truth about its writer's life and, especially, his or her relations with others.

In contrast, Hughes's poetry was notably impersonal. He focused on the external world of nature and its creatures. In some cases, it seemed as though the animals, in particular, represented aspects of the poet's personality. But the allusions, if they did exist, were at best indirect. This is why *Birthday Letters* is so striking in the context of Hughes's poetry at large. This is biographical and autobiographical writing, addressed to Hughes's dead wife, and describing their relationship.

Hughes probably intended to convey the truth of his relationship with Plath and the individual truths of their separate selves. But he sees that truth from his angle, in situations, furthermore, that were often highly emotional. Plath did not live to read the poems and to respond to them, perhaps to correct the impressions of the truth which they convey. Further, Hughes is writing in the compressed form of poetry. It is a selective and artificial representation of the truth. This does not mean that the poems are not true, but they invite interpretation and paraphrase of their meaning, which is the same as saying that they will produce different versions of the truth they represent as readers respond to them differently.

Because the poems are obviously confessional, we need to be careful about automatically assuming that they 'tell the truth'. A more cautious approach would be to describe the poems of *Birthday Letters* as striving to convey something of the truth of the relationship of Plath and Hughes. The ultimate truth of that private matter can never be certainly known by anyone.

Assignment
What are some of the problems of telling the truth in poetry? Think about this issue with reference to two or three poets' works which you have studied.

FULBRIGHT SCHOLARS

Fulbright scholars, such as Sylvia Plath, were clever young men and women who travelled on their scholarships, usually for postgraduate study, and often overseas. Plath, who had done well at prestigious Smith College in the United States, won a Fulbright Scholarship for further study at the similarly prestigious University of Cambridge in England. It was there that she met a fellow student, Ted Hughes, whom she married.

In this, the first poem in *Birthday Letters*, Hughes characterises the collection as a chronological, historical, biographical and autobiographical account of their relationship. He begins by thinking about the first encounter he may have had with Plath, possibly looking at a photograph of a particular year's 'intake / Of Fulbright Scholars':

> Were you among them?

This first poem is an important introduction to the collection. We notice, on the one hand, the poet's desire to get to the truth, but we also notice, on the other, his uncertainties about it. The first sentence of the poem (and so of *Birthday Letters*) is a query about the truth:

> Where was it?

The second, as we have seen, is a query about Plath. Was she included in the photograph that he remembers seeing? These uncertainties are reinforced by the repetition of 'maybe'.

He is more certain that he would have taken particular notice of the girls and, had he done so, he would have been struck by Plath's distinctive appearance:

> Noted your long hair, loose waves –
> Your Veronica Lake bang.

These features are known because of numerous photographs of Plath at that time, so this truth is indisputable. But the query remains as to whether Hughes had the experience he half remembers.

He is also uncertain about himself:

> Was it then I bought a peach?

And he notes his general ignorance at that stage of his life:

> At twenty-five I was dumbfounded afresh
> By my ignorance of the simplest things.

'Fulbright Scholars' is a poem about the difficulty of telling the truth, especially in the context of remembering the receding past. It is a text for *Birthday Letters* as a whole in which all the poems are recollections of what happened years before and are touched by the uncertainties of such recollections. It also makes clear that we are seeing the truth of past events through one person's eyes – someone who confesses not to his unique access to the truth but to his 'ignorance'.

■
Question
How does 'Fulbright Scholars' bring the truth into question?

THE MINOTAUR

In classical legend, the Minotaur was a monster, half bull, half man, which was fed with human flesh and lived in the labyrinth (or complicated passage-way) in Crete. It was killed by Theseus. In this poem, Hughes sees Plath as a death-bringing force, attempting to slay her Minotaur-father but destroying everything else in the process, the mahogany table-top, the high stool, their marriage, their children, her mother and finally herself. Her father, already dead, is risen, so her quest is futile, from Hughes's perspective.

The destructive power of her personality is vividly conveyed through verbs such as 'smashed', with its onomatopoeia, and 'swung', with its sense of overstated activity. We see the truth from Hughes's perspective when he explains that the cause of Plath's hysterical behaviour was his unpunctuality. She was

> Demented by my being
> Twenty minutes late for baby-minding.

That she was 'demented' may have been due simply to his trivial error (and we would then concur that her behaviour was an over-reaction) or that care-lessness on Hughes' part may have been the last straw in a sequence of events which had driven her mad.

He imagines that there is an evil spirit, a goblin, in her mind which took the criticism that Hughes made of Plath during these domestic confronta-tions and gave her the excuse to behave as she did, unravelling their marriage and neglecting their children.

The quoting of speech has the ring of truth about it, or at least that Hughes is certain that this is what was spoken at the time: '"Marvellous!" I shouted'. But here, as elsewhere in the poem, we sense that Hughes is blaming Plath for their troubles and portraying himself as attempting to retrieve the situa-tion. He tells her, for example, to put her anger into her poems and all will be well: 'we'll be away'. Again, this may be true, but we are justifiably scep-tical about its absolute truth when we are hearing one version of the events from someone deeply involved in them. Hughes had been customarily portrayed (probably equally unfairly and usually by feminist writers) as the villain of the piece.

It is possible that Hughes's anecdotes in a poem such as this are, in fact, attempts to redress the balance of Plath's poems, journals and published letters to her mother which laid the blame at his feet for the disintegration of their marriage.

■ The poem is savage in its criticism. Plath is seen as destroying the lives of all those closest to her in a quest to punish the one family member beyond her reach, her dead and 'risen father'. Finally, she punishes herself in her suicide, in a bloody sequence concluding in 'your own corpse'.

Question

How does the language of the poem suggest that we are hearing Hughes's version of the situation?

SAM

In her first year at Cambridge, Plath hired a horse called Sam that was supposed to be old and gentle but which bolted with the inexperienced rider on his back. While it was a frightening and dangerous experience, Plath recalled it as a time when she felt immensely alive. It formed the basis of the thrilling horse-ride described in the title poem of her last collection, *Ariel*.

Telling the truth of the experience, in 'Sam', Hughes focuses on the physical details of the event. We are given a description of Sam, reminiscent of Hughes's numerous poems about animals, with their carefully observed details: 'the white calm stallion'. The location of the event is noted – 'down the white line of the Barton Road' – and the series of actions which Plath experienced as she lost control: 'you slewed under his neck'. Such detail plainly indicates the truth of the poem's report. Added to it is the sense of the danger and horror of the situation for the rider:

An upside-down jockey with nothing
Between you and the cataract of macadam.

Poetic techniques of imagery and onomatopoeia give the scene an extra dramatic dimension:

But the propeller terrors of his front legs
And the clangour of the iron shoes, so far beneath you.

In the poem's second section, Hughes is less assured of the truth, as a series of questions indicates: 'How did you cling on?' 'What saved you?' Her poems were saved by the hammock in which she carried them.

He repeats his questioning in the third section: 'How did you hang on?' We realise that the query is not only about the incident with Sam but relates to Plath's life at large. In spite of the terrors of her existence, she managed to cling to life, but not through any ability that she could recognise: 'something in you not you did it for itself'.

Hughes also sees the experience with the horse as related to his marriage to Plath. In 'one giddy moment', like her 'upside-down jockey experience', she fell off Hughes, after attacking him, wilfully flinging herself off him to trip him and 'lay dead'. The event, like that with Sam, was 'over in a flash'. It is also a description of the end of her life.

Arguably, the poem attempts to suggest too much, moving from one incident clearly described to a portrayal of the marriage and an encapsulation of Plath's life, which is in the mode of speculation rather than clear revelation. But such speculation is one of the characteristics of poetry, an art of suggestion as much as an art of statement.

Question

Compare this poem with Plath's 'Ariel'. What similarities and differences would you note?

RED

Hughes begins decisively: 'Red was your colour'. This appears to be a factual statement, a simple declaration. But immediately, he undermines it: 'if not red, then white'. And when he tries to understand why red might have been so important to Plath, he puts his suggestion in the hesitation of a question: 'Was it blood?'

To support the originally firm statement that red was Plath's colour, Hughes presents evidence which clearly supports it: 'Our room was red'. Curtains, cushions and window-seat all matched. But there was an exception: 'the bookshelves escaped into whiteness'. The verb is important. That the bookshelves 'escaped' suggests that they were exceptional and liberatingly so. So, again, the idea of red as Plath's colour is reinforced. Flowers in the garden, her dress and her lipstick are also various shades of red.

Redness is present physically, but for Hughes it is metaphorical. It suggests a bleeding wound which is itself representative of Plath's psychological condition.

A third colour concludes the poem – blue. This was not Plath's colour, Hughes is arguing, but it was 'better for you'. It has healing powers. Whiteness, with its 'bone-clinic' quality, and the extremity of redness represent the polarities of her life, her quest for purity and the pain and passion of her existence. What destroyed her, Hughes concludes, was her inability to be nurtured by the kindly spirit of blue:

But the jewel you lost was blue.

Assignment

'Hughes confesses the truth about himself, in *Birthday Letters*, by appearing to tell the truth about Plath.' Do you agree? Refer to two or three poems in the collection and, perhaps, to some of Plath's in *Ariel*.

Contemporary
poetry

13

In reading and evaluating poetry by living writers, we come to the position of being unconfident about which poets and poetry will satisfy one of the accepted tests of artistry – that of time. History shows that poets who have been very popular in their lifetimes can be quickly forgotten, while others, insufficiently appreciated when they were alive, grow in stature with readers in the centuries after their deaths. Robert Bridges believed – no doubt correctly – that the audience for the poetry of his friend Gerard Manley Hopkins, did not exist during Hopkins' lifetime (1844–89) and delayed its appearance until a generation later, publishing it in 1918. Walter Savage Landor (1775–1864), popular in his day and an important influence on many poets, such as Robert Browning and Ezra Pound, would have few readers now. The same can be said of Coventry Patmore (1823–96), the most popular of poets in his lifetime, now the least read of his period. When T. S. Eliot burst controversially upon the literary scene in 1917, with *Prufrock and Other Observations*, no one could have predicted (indeed, many of the most astute critics would have regarded the idea as ludicrous) that, at century's end, eighty years hence, he would be universally esteemed as the most influential poet of the twentieth century, probably its most important and, many would say, its greatest. Other poets can gain a certain reputation during their lives, be neglected for centuries and then be rediscovered. John Donne is an example of this variety of the uncertainties of poetic reputation.

The bewildering scope of human experience today (in the English-speaking world alone, immediately accessed at our fingertips on the Internet) and the unprecedented number of poets vying for readers' attention may have brought us to a position where the idea of a single poet's voice (and assessment of human life and experience) speaking generally of the conditions of his or her times and of mankind en masse in that contemporary milieu – as Eliot did to the post-war generation in *The Waste Land* in 1922, or as Tennyson did for the Victorians in *In Memoriam* in 1850 – may no longer apply as a measurement of poetic importance, let alone greatness.

Nonetheless, many poets writing today have at least established secure contemporary reputations and have taken their places in anthologies, as editors select from their published works to date, while their bodies of work (like their lives) have yet to be completed. This, too, of course, is another of the uncertainties of time and literary reputation. Works of poets appreciated by readers during the writers' lifetimes may give place to others, later. And poems which the poets themselves believe to be their most important work may be regarded, by posterity, with less esteem than other poems they have written.

To close, we should look at some of the poetry of several contemporary writers, all of them from the 'new world', as evidence of the ongoing fertility of inventiveness, imagination and thought which continues to animate poetry in the English language, for writers and readers alike and, in the process of our study, discern qualities and characteristics of contemporary poetry which may be indicative of its future direction(s) in the twenty-first century.

Derek Walcott (1930–)

Walcott is the best known of contemporary West Indian poets. His writing focuses on the tensions, experienced in his own life, between the West Indian and European cultures. Bilingual (speaking English and Creole), he writes in both standard English and in West Indian dialect, calling himself, accordingly, 'a mulatto of style'. Walcott has spent most of his life in Trinidad, but has travelled and worked regularly in Europe and North America, having been, for example, Professor of Poetry at the University of Boston.

Recognition of his poetry came with the publication of *In a Green Night* (1964), with its West Indian themes, while in *The Fortunate Traveller* (1981) and *Midsummer* (1984) Walcott concentrated on the position of a black writer in America, distanced from his origins in the Caribbean. Cultural estrangement is also the theme of *Castaway* (1965) and *The Gulf* (1969).

His long work of sixty-four chapters, *Omeros*, inspired (as its title indicates) by Homer, applies the Greek epic drama to the Caribbean world. This was published in 1990. Two years later, Walcott received the Nobel Prize for literature. In his lecture on receiving the prize, he declared that

> there is the buried language and there is the individual vocabulary, and the process of poetry is one of excavation and self-discovery.

Walcott's engrossingly atmospheric poem 'Nights in the Gardens of Port of Spain' is initiated with the personification of 'Night' as a woman. Although the title refers to plural 'nights', it is the specific individuality of this night which Walcott records. However, there is the sense, too, that it could be any night in the West Indies, in the seaport capital of Trinidad, Port of Spain. All the elements of that title conjure up an exotic air. Night-time, gardens and the town reminiscent of Spain. Sensuousness dominates from the beginning. Walcott's dedication to portraying the spirit of West Indian life and culture – its otherness and uniqueness – animates the poetry.

The sense of the concentration of experience on this particular night is conveyed in the first, striking verb: 'simplifies'. The complexities of a 'black summer' Night are focused in the communal scene the poet will describe. Especially, we notice that it is her 'smells' which will be conveyed. It is a decidedly ambiguous term, as simplification becomes complex. Walcott does not, for example, use the more positive 'scents' or 'aromas'. Smells may be tantalising, can be revolting. This ambiguity is pursued in 'the impenetrable / musk of the negro'. Here is a smell that cannot be defined or fully known and 'musk', like 'sweat' which follows it, is more usually associated with negative smells. The reference to 'the negro' is more confronting now that the word is banned, as the poetry slides into an intensified olfactory negativity: 'her alleys odorous with shucked oyster shells'. We notice the poised precision of Walcott's word choice: how 'shucked' echoes 'musk', and the use of assonance and alliteration, uniting the presentation.

The air of developing sensuality, as Night becomes more intensely herself, as 'her heat' increases (both temperature-wise and sexually), calls forth a variegated colouring of the dark scene: 'coals of gold oranges, braziers of melon'. Certainly, we are encountering them as they are consumed by fiery Night, but the remembrance of their vivid colours adds to the sensuality, also increased by the sheer sounds of phrases such as 'gold oranges'. Every sense is being appealed to here in an evocation of a supremely sensual and feminine world.

Yet, at the heart of the poem, it might seem that that sensuality is cheapened by the presence of the 'whorehouse', the commercialising of sexuality, although the beauty of the metaphor describing its clients: 'a surf of sailors' faces crests' precariously retains that ambiguity present from the beginning. The nightclubs where their desire had been kindled 'tinkle like fireflies in her thick hair'. The onomatopoeia is pretty (but possibly tawdry, too); her 'thick hair' is lustrous, yet invaded. The antithesis of 'Hellfire or the whorehouse' at the poem's centre may indicate the essential, stark simplicity of human existence in such an environment, where the sensual is so palpable and available and, yet, where the European inheritance of sin and punishment – especially for sexual sins – remains potent.

Night transcends the domain to which she nonetheless belongs: 'she lifts her face from the cheap, pitch oil flare / towards white stars'. The juxtaposition (again) is extreme, of the world of 'Hellfire' and that of Heaven. But these 'white stars' may only be the neon lights of the seaport by which she is constrained, 'burning to be the bitch she must become'. The animalic reference, increased in intensity by the alliteration with 'burning' (gathering up the several references to fire in the poem) combines denigration with a certain fascination in the presence of such sensual determination.

The coda to the poem brings us rudely to daybreak. The peasant with his open cart has gathered the remains of the night's festivity – 'hacked, beheaded coconuts'. That Walcott uses the unusual word 'tumbril' for the cart, recalling the way victims were taken to their deaths by guillotine in the French Revolution, seems to pronounce a judgement on those who have submitted their lives to Night, the bewitching enchantress, but there is no denying the allure of her world, as he conveys it.

Question

How does Walcott present these nights in ambiguous ways? Why might he do so?

Les Murray (1938–)

This Australian poet was born at Nabiac, in the Manning River district of north ern New South Wales. He attended Taree High School, where he began reading poetry. In 1957, he entered the University of Sydney to study Arts. Murray moved to Canberra in 1963 where he worked at the Australian National University as a translator of foreign scholarly and technical materials. In 1964, he converted to Roman Catholicism and, in 1965, published his first collection of poems *The Ilex Tree*. After living in Europe, Murray returned to Australia in 1968 and settled in Sydney. He completed his BA in 1969. In 1975, he bought part of the family dairy farm at Bunyah and, in 1985, returned to live there permanently.

Murray has been writer-in-residence at several institutions, co-editor of *Poetry Australia* and literary editor of the conservative periodical *Quadrant*. He has won many literary awards, including the Grace Leven Prize (1980 and 1990), the Petrarch Prize (1995) and the T. S. Eliot Award (1996). In 1999 he was awarded the Queen's Gold Medal for Poetry on the recommendation of Ted Hughes.

Murray's poetry conveys his interpretation of life at large, profoundly influenced by his religious outlook; a particular kind of Australian response to human existence – dry, whimsical, yoked to the landscape and 'the Bush', to Aboriginal culture and the history of European settlement; and in a language that is, by turns, colloquial and talkative, meditative, universal and personal.

THE MITCHELLS
I am seeing this: two men are sitting on a pole
they have dug a hole for and will, after dinner, raise

I think for wires. Water boils in a prune tin.
Bees hum their shift in unthinning mists of white
bursaria blossom, under the noon of wattles.
The men eat big meat sandwiches out of a styrofoam
box with a handle. One is overheard saying
drought that year. Yes. Like trying to farm the road.

The first man, if asked, would say *I'm one of the Mitchells.*
The other would gaze for a while, dried leaves in his palm,
and looking up, with pain and subtle amusement,

say *I'm one of the Mitchells.* Of the pair, one has been rich
but never stopped wearing his oil-stained felt hat. Nearly everything
they say is ritual. Sometimes the scene is an avenue.

(1977)

In this sonnet, Murray reveals his commitment as a poet, exploring and presenting the ordinariness of Australian life and finding (in the process of that exploration and presentation) essential qualities of Australianness, and even of
humanity at large.

The opening declaration – 'I am seeing this' – affirms the role of the poet as
a seer: one who registers what is before him but also has the vision to penetrate
the surface appearance of situations. Yet 'I think', also in the opening verse-
sentence, indicates a certain detachment from (and, therefore, uncertainty
about) what he is seeing. The scene is paradoxically striking in its everyday characteristics: 'two men are sitting on a pole', and so on. The Mitchells are seen in
the midst of their activity, resting for a meal. The details of their actions and the
objects around them give the poem the quality of a realistic painting – an
Australian country scene. But the setting is described aurally as well as visually.
In 'boils' we hear the bubbling water and in 'hum' the sound of the bees. The
environment has the characteristics of an Australian pastoral:

in unthinning mists of white
busaria blossom, under the noon of wattles.

Such lyrical presentation of nature is celebratory, even idealising. But Murray
quickly returns to the realistic banalities of the situation: 'the men eat big meat
sandwiches'.

Even such almost photographic detail as this, however, might be read as not
merely realistic but celebratory of the big men, larger than life, of the Australian
bush with its trials and challenges. For the octave of the sonnet closes with one
of the Mitchells reflecting on the arduousness of taming the outback: 'drought
that year. Yes. Like trying to farm the road'. The simple observation expands into
a poetic simile. The laconic speech of an Australian farmer may include some

arresting observations. We see that Murray is not only 'seeing this' but over-hearing it too and delighting in the qualities of speech he records.

In the sestet, the two Mitchells are particularised, but their reluctance to reveal very much of themselves means that we leave the poem uncertain even of their relationship: father and son? Brothers? Their lives are as mysterious and elusive as the outback: they are a 'pair', but 'one has been rich'. In what circumstances? Their speech reveals little of their true selves: 'Nearly everything / they say is ritual'.

Murray's evaluation of what he is seeing is ambiguous. He is drawn to the men and their condition. But as a seer he would penetrate their beings, which are impenetrable. Yet he defers to their laconic ceremony and would set the men, in a staged tableau, in an idealised location with a theatrical dimension:

> Sometimes the scene is an avenue.

An avenue is a ceremonial road, with trees (or perhaps poles) in order. As the men's talk and behaviour is ritualised, so they should be seen in such a place, as Murray has captured them here, in the literary ceremoniousness and order of the sonnet form.

Question

How does the language of Murray's poem (his choice of vocabulary and quoted speech, in particular) encourage us to probe the larger meaning of the situation which, on the surface, seems so plain and realistic?

Margaret Atwood (1939–)

A Canadian writer best known for her novels, Atwood is also a poet, short-story writer and literary critic. Born in Ottawa, she went to university in Toronto and later in the United States and has taught in several Canadian universities. She won the Booker Prize in 2000 for *The Blind Assassin*, her tenth novel, having been shortlisted for it on previous occasions. The recipient of numerous international honours and awards, Atwood has published several collections of poetry, includ-ing *Power Politics* (1973), *Two-headed Poems* (1978) and *Interlunar* (1984). She writes in free verse and her themes include the position of women in society and relations between the sexes and between nations, in the context of a vision of life that is usually ironic and often pessimistic.

> UP
> You wake up filled with dread.
> There seems no reason for it.

Morning light sifts through the window,
there is birdsong,
you can't get out of bed.

It's something about the crumpled sheets
hanging over the edge like jungle
foliage, the terry slippers gaping
their dark pink mouths for your feet,
the unseen breakfast – some of it
in the refrigerator you do not dare
to open – you will not dare to eat.

What prevents you? The future. The future tense,
immense as outer space.
You could get lost there.
No. Nothing so simple. The past, its density
and drowned events pressing you down,
like sea water, like gelatin
filling your lungs instead of air.

Forget all that and let's get up.
Try moving your arm.
Try moving your head.
Pretend the house is on fire
and you must run or burn.
No, that one's useless.
It's never worked before.

Where is it coming from, this echo,
this huge No that surrounds you,
silent as the folds of the yellow
curtains, mute as the cheerful

Mexican bowl with its cargo
of mummified flowers?
(You choose the colours of the sun,
not the dried neutrals of shadow.
God knows you've tried.)

Now here's a good one:
You're lying on your deathbed.
You have one hour to live.
Who is it, exactly, you have needed
all these years to forgive?

(1995)

The preposition of the title introduces several ideas and expectations which are to be frustrated, sounding the familiar ironic tone of Atwood's poetry. As well as getting up (and 'up', there, could also – ironically – be an imperative verb), there is the idea of looking up, and that of elevation being associated with idealism and 'the good'. 'Down', and 'being down', in contrast, have as many negative connotations. So we see that, in this contemporary poem, one of the ancient arts of poets continues to be practised – the stirring-up of expectation in the title of a poem.

Atwood uses the second-person address throughout – 'you'. This, to a degree, depersonalises a personal experience. There is the sense that the reader will understand what is being described here and has indeed experienced it (along with the speaker). On the other hand, such a usage – again, very familiar in poetry (Eliot uses it in 'Preludes', in a very similar situation: 'You tossed a blanket from the bed') – may suggest to a reader unfamiliar with the experience what it is like for those who know it well.

The opening line has the key word 'dread'. The poem evokes the dreadful experience of daily life, especially at the beginning of the day when every person has to stir themselves to begin its routine. Atwood asks why it should be so dreadful when the surrounding physical circumstances are benign, even beautiful. 'There seems no reason for it':

> Morning light sifts through the window,
> there is birdsong.

She begins to engage with the reason for this inability to 'get out of bed', in the second stanza, by referring to the disorder of the sheets in a striking simile – 'hanging over the edge like jungle / foliage' (as we note the line, in imitation, hanging over the edge, into the next line). The terry-towelling slippers have been transformed, by this psychological dread, into sinister life: 'gaping / their dark pink mouths for your feet'. And beyond the bedroom is breakfast waiting in the refrigerator 'you do not dare / to open' and a meal 'you will not dare to eat'. By this stage in the poem, it is clear that an extreme mental condition of debility and despair, the physical dysfunction produced by psychological depression, is being described.

How does this come about? Atwood suggests that the refusal to get 'up' is due to a reluctance to engage the future – 'immense as outer space' – deriving from the experience of the past, with its 'density / and drowned events'. It is not a matter merely of getting lost in the future tense ('Nothing so simple'), but having to endure more of what the past has already delivered. Such a reflection indicates an individual who has experienced a deal of life, so the poem conveys the idea of a middle-aged anxiety and world-weariness. It was published when Atwood was 56.

Physical motions to dispel these metaphysical miseries are then invoked – 'try moving your head' – but to no avail. Atwood continues to worry the question:

> Where is it coming from, this echo,
> this huge No that surrounds you . . .

Her negativity encloses here as if she were a mummy in a tomb. She has tried various strategies to lighten this oppressive dread, as she notes wryly:

> (You chose the colours of the sun,
> not the dried neutrals of shadow.
> God knows you've tried.)

The poem closes with one last, desperate plea to get up. If the pretence that the house is on fire will not work, then perhaps this strategy could be tried:

> You're lying on your deathbed.
> You have one hour to live.
> Who is it, exactly, you have needed
> All these years to forgive?

The poem does not indicate whether that proves efficacious, and the phrase: 'Now here's a good one' seems to suggest that it is going to be another failed attempt. But it also indicates a reason for the inability to affirm one's life by dispelling the surrounding disabling negativity. The speaker has not forgiven herself. Burdened with the guilt of her existence, she has made it worse by despairing of its worth.

Question

The poem, in a meditative, occasionally conversational free-verse style, is yet richly poetic in its language. To what aspects of Atwood's technique would you refer in demonstrating this?

Michael Ondaatje (1943–)

A Canadian poet of Sinhalese, Tamil and Dutch origin, Ondaatje was born in Colombo, Ceylon (now Sri Lanka). When his parents separated, he moved with his mother to England and attended Dulwich College. His university education was undertaken in Canada, where he has remained, and he has been a member of the staff of the English Department at Glendon College, York University in Toronto since 1971. Ondaatje has received numerous honours and awards and in 1992 was presented with the Booker McConnell Prize for his novel, *The English Patient* (adapted for the screen in 1996).

Among Ondaatje's best-known collections of poetry are *The Collected Works of*

Billy the Kid: Left Handed Poems (1970) and *There's a Trick with a Knife I'm Learning to Do: Poems 1973–1978* (1979).

Ondaatje focuses on personal situations which reveal individuals in conflict with society, drawing on autobiographical material, but locating this in histori- cal and mythological contexts.

In 'Letters & Other Worlds' (1979), we locate Ondaatje in the confessional mode of poets such as Robert Lowell (see Special Study 14). Particularly, we identify the theme of fraught familial relationships (between husbands and wives and across the generations) which recurs in confessional poetry – such as that of Sylvia Plath (see Special Study 16). The problem with this material, in poetry, is its personal character; the challenge is to make the autobiographical subject available to the reader. That 'availability' (or accessibility) can be achieved, as Lowell often achieves it, through making the study of individual lives a study of life in general. Another procedure – which is Ondaatje's here – is to reveal a personal history sufficiently bizarre as to stir our interest in and engagement with this essentially private world of his alcoholic father and of his mother, estranged from her husband.

As if hyper-alert to the necessity to poeticise the intimately personal elements of this poem, Ondaatje's begins with an epigraph that compares his father with 'Adam before the fall' – the everyman of human history – and it opens with richly metaphorical language:

> My father's body was a globe of fear
> His body was a town we never knew.

This is personal, certainly – 'my father' – but the metaphors enlarge the refer- ence (globally) for the reader's engagement. The negativity of fear and the unknown town are balanced with 'the logic of his love'. The alliterated phrase (combining thought and emotion) establishes a complexity of response to the subject which also engages the reader. This is not going to be simply a demoli- tion of his father's character.

The literariness of his father's letters also assists the process of transforming the autobiographical exercise into a poetic presentation. Yet Ondaatje is true to the confessional mode in providing documentary details of his father's life and death:

> He came to death with his mind drowning.
> On the last day he enclosed hmself
> in a room with two bottles of gin . . .

Again, 'the last day' is both personal and universal. This type of Adam, at the beginning of time – before the fall – is now envisaged at the Day of Judgement. And the image of his drowning mind has a surreal quality that is not merely documentary. Further, that the father achieves 'a new equilibrium' in death preserves the ambiguity of judgement of the son.

The need to touch the ordinary with extraordinariness to justify the confessional approach is clear in the fourth stanza. Ondaatje observes that 'his early life was a terrifying comedy'. In that oxymoron (for comedies are usually amusing), the life is transformed into a literary mode and the memory that 'my mother divorced him again and again' is a fictional way of registering her recurring despair of the marriage. But then, the poetry takes a distinctly crazy turn as we see the father rushing 'into tunnels magnetized / by the white eye of trains'. And the anecdote which follows is sufficiently bizarre to compel the reader's attention:

> Once, gaining instant fame,
> Managed to stop a Perahara in Ceylon   [Perahara = annual religious festival]
> – the whole procession of elephants dancers
> local dignitaries – by falling
> dead drunk onto the street.

That this is a sad comedy alleviates the personal, factual component, while simultaneously intensifying the humanly tragic aspects of father's 'other world'.

The much-complained-of tendency of some modern poetry to appear to be little more than prose cut up into uneven lines can be substantiated by Ondaatje's next stanza (if it might be so called):

> As a semi-official, and semi-white at that,
> the act was seen as a crucial
> turning point in the Home Rule Movement
> and led to Ceylon's indepenedence in 1948.

There is nothing here, vocabulary-wise or in terms of the cadence of the phrases, that is 'poetic', by any ordinary understanding of the term. Even as prose, it is flat, with the cliché of a 'turning point'. Yet, surrounded by more consciously 'poetic' language, it has its own effect at the heart of the poem, being indicative of the ordinary factuality of the father's life, but whether the language in which that is conveyed needs to be as journalistic as this is for each reader to decide.

Further anecdotes follow, until the two final sections of the poem where the recovery of the initial poetic discourse begins to be achieved. The image of the man as 'the silent drinker' presents both Ondaatje's father and an image of the isolated individual of twentieth-century literature and life. And in the closing lines, metaphor ('the clarity of architects'), a catalogue of epistolary subjects (beginning with 'the row of blue flowers'), a mimesis of language and sense ('widening and widening and widening' in the clipped one-line phrases detailing the stages of the father's decline), the poem wittily finishes with a recognition of the exhaustion of poetic speech – 'the blood searching in his head without metaphor'. The means of the father's communication with the outside world (through his letters) dies as the poet's means of expressing his father's world (principally, through metaphor) also ends.

Question

Do you find this poem too personal? If so, why? If not, why not? Does it matter that it may be?

Joanne Burns (1945–)

Born in Sydney, Burns graduated from the University of Sydney in 1966 and subsequently taught in both schools and tertiary institutions. She lived in England in the early 1970s and travelled in Europe and, later, in Asia. She was one of the Four Australian Poets group which toured North America in 1985 and in 1990 was writer-in-residence at the University of Wollongong. Burns' seventh book of poems, *penelope's knees*, appeared in 1996.

Her work has been widely published in magazines, journals and anthologies and been produced for theatre and radio. The title piece from *blowing bubbles in the 7th lane* has been produced as a radio drama by the Australian Broadcasting Commission.

HOW

how these pieces of paper: lined unlined small large crinkled smooth smudged spotless, become pieces of first draft scribble, of typescript, of 'writing', become texts for performance, works in progress, submissions to magazines and journals, become copyright, enter folders in filing cabinets, become manuscripts, literature, the numbered pages of published books, isbn-d.

how these books are launched admired read reviewed squeezed alongside within between a crowd of others on the shelves in private and public places. how these books will be remaindered, garage saled, dumped in glad bags along with old newspapers, junk mail and ageing christmas cards, turn up as brief mentions in fifty years time in someone else's biography, or within the meticulous index in the work of a fastidious literary historian securing a career.

how these books will return to pulp, through diligent efforts to beat the world's timber crisis, how these books will turn into serviettes paper towels and parking tickets, into pieces of paper, become torn food wrappings lifting in the wind

This is a prose poem about manuscripts and texts and their evolution from 'pieces of paper' to 'pieces of paper' again:

torn food wrappings lifting in the wind.

As such, it is a poem about the literary life and about life itself: its beginnings and endings, its cyclic quality.

The work is integrated by an incantatory repetition on the simple monosyllable 'how', which turns out not to be as simple as it seems. For it introduces both a question – 'How is it that . . . ?' – and a statement: 'I have noticed how . . . '. What the speaker has observed prompts her to wonder why this process takes place. It is particularly pertinent for a writer to raise the question. Will this be the fate of her poems?

The process is a fated one. The various forms of paper that a writer uses are described:

> lined unlined small large crinkled smooth smudged spotless

and the creation of a text, its performance, applications to place it somewhere, the records that are kept about it, the accretion of its details and its cataloguing: 'isbn-d' (a reference to the international classification of each published text).

The success of a published book is briefly noted – and that brevity is a judgement in itself on the futility of the writer's life – before it is 'remaindered' (as booksellers attempt to dispose of it cheaply), then (worse) garage-saled (like 'isbn-d', another inventive verb) and, most ignominiously:

> dumped in glad bags along with old newspapers.

Note the onomatopoeic bathos of 'dumped' and the irony of 'glad bags' on this sad occasion.

Finally, the author's book or text vanishes from existence, pulped in the recycling process. Although Burns notes the worthy motives of such 'efforts to beat the world's timber crisis', there is the judgement that the recycled paper that is produced will be used for less worthy purposes in the future:

> serviettes paper towels and parking tickets . . . torn food
> wrappings lifting in the wind.

The use, again, of the phrase 'pieces of paper' at the end emphasises the cyclic process of the poem. But it is not only a work about the literary life and its productions. It is a comment on the vanity of all human endeavour.

Questions

1. How do Burns' concerns about writing and its fate expand into a larger comment about life itself?

2. What is your assessment of the style and technique of prose-poetry used here? Do you enjoy this kind of experimental approach to poetic form, or would you prefer a more traditional style? Argue your case. (You are not required to affirm experiment.)

Judith Beveridge (1956–)

Judith Beveridge was born in London in 1956 and migrated to Sydney, Australia in 1960. At school, she 'hated poetry for the first few years . . . until we came to some modern contemporary writers, like Robert Lowell'.[1] After university, where she graduated in communications in 1977, Beveridge determined to become a poet, working as a research officer at a publications firm to support herself.

Beveridge's first collection of poems, *The Domesticity of Giraffes* (1987), won the Dame Mary Gilmore Award, the NSW Premier's Award and the Victorian Premier's Award in 1988. Her poetry has been set for study on the New South Wales Higher School Certificate curriculum (1993–5) and she has conducted classes in poetic writing at the University of Technology, Sydney, as well as at adult colleges. In 2000, she worked as poetry advisor for the journal *Kalimat*, which promotes Australian and Arabic literature and she co-edited the poetry anthology *A Parachute of Blue* (1995). Beveridge published *Accidental Grace*, her second collection of poetry, in 1996.

Hers is a structured, subtle poetry in which she is deftly critical of much of contemporary Australian life. Asked what her assessment of Australia would be, as reflected in her poetry, she replied:

> I'm happy to live here. But what worries me is the Americanisation of Australia – our uncritical adoption of the worst aspects of that culture, and the resulting watering-down of our own. The increase in violence is also very alarming, and I worry about the isolation of people in our society: the old, migrants and individuals. The disparity between rich and poor is growing, I think, and that is wrong. The materialism of Australian society is depressing.[2]

ORB SPIDER
I saw her, pegging out her web
thin as a pressed flower in the bleaching light.
From the bushes a few small insects
clicked like opening seed-pods. I knew some
would be trussed up by her and gone next morning.
She was so beautiful spinning her web
above the marigolds the sun had made
more apricot, more amber; any bee
lost from its solar flight could be gathered

---

1. Interview with Judith Beveridge, in Barry Spurr, *The Poetry of Judith Beveridge* (Glebe: Pascal Press, 1993), pp. 31–2.
2. Ibid., p. 34.

back to the anther, and threaded onto the flower like a jewel.
                    She hung in the shadows
as the sun burnt low on the horizon
mirrored by the round garden bed. Small petals
moved as one flame, as one perfectly-lit hoop.
I watched her work, produce her known world,
a pattern, her way to traverse
a little portion of the sky;
a simple cosmography, a web drawn
by the smallest nib. And out of my own world
mapped from smallness, the source
of sorrow pricked, I could see
immovable stars.
                    Each night
I saw the same dance in the sky,
the pattern like a match-box puzzle,
tiny balls stuck in a grid until shaken
so much, all the orbits were in place.
Above the bright marigolds
of that quick year, the hour-long day,
she taught me to love the smallest transit,
that the coldest star has a planetesimal beauty.
I watched her above the low flowers
tracing her world, making it one perfect drawing.
                                    (1987)

In this poem of delicate observation, Beveridge concentrates on and celebrates
the minute creatures of nature, objectively noting nature's processes, including
its cycle of life and death, particularised in the spider's entrapment of its prey.

'Orb Spider' opens in an anecdotal way – 'I saw her' – as the speaker records
the web-spinning in sunlight that she has observed, in a perfect summer, in the
past. The speaker immediately establishes, in a simile, the delicate beauty of this
creation:

> thin as a pressed flower in the bleaching light.

The visual is embellished by the aural in the onomatopoeia of the accompanying
sounds from the bush:

> a few small insects
> clicked like opening seed-pods.

And the speaker matter-of-factly recognises that the spider is spinning there
because of the proximity of her prey:

> I knew some
> would be trussed up by her and gone next morning.

This observation, however, is neutral. Beveridge chooses not to take this opportunity to reflect on the cruelty (from the human perspective) of nature. Her argument here is of a different kind and immediately she resumes, without irony, her praise of the spider's beauty:

> She was so beautiful spinning her web
> above the marigolds the sun had made
> more apricot, more amber.

The web, indeed, could be benign for insects: a bee unable to find the marigold's anther could be led to the pollen by the web and threaded onto it (in an exquisite simile) 'like a jewel'. This first verse-paragraph is a celebration of the design of the natural world, its creatures and plants.

The larger processes of nature – the rising and setting of the sun on which it ultimately depends – give unity to the poem's structure as we move to the second verse-paragraph. Again, the orb spider is the centre of attention:

> she hung in the shadows
> as the sun burnt low on the horizon.

Beveridge catches these familiar sights of the hanging spider in her web and the shadows cast by the setting summer sun, and of that web on the 'round garden bed'. The design of the first verse-paragraph is now celebrated with symbolic resonance, as everything conforms to perfect circularity – the roundness of the garden bed, the 'perfectly-lit hoop' of petals and the microcosm of the orb of the spider's world:

> I watched her work, produce her known world,
> a pattern, her way to traverse
> a little portion of the sky.

We discern that this descriptiveness is growing into a statement of moral importance. In her domain, the orb spider has the fulfilment of perfect satisfaction:

> a simple cosmography, a web drawn
> by the smallest nib.

For all its smallness, it has that large validity. Consequently, the spider and its web – that is, its world – can teach the human observer, less sufficient in her environment, a universal truth:

> And out of my own world
> mapped from smallness, the source
> of sorrow pricked, I could see
> immovable stars.

What the speaker has seen and grows to love, in other words, has taken her out of her own cosmos with its pettiness and unhappiness, and revealed the order of nature and the universe, represented by 'immovable stars'. The poem has moved, appropriately, to evening, the time of vision and revelation.

Her preoccupation with the orb spider becomes a nightly appreciation of the natural world and its rituals:

> Each night
> I saw the same dance in the sky.

Beveridge affirms the ultimate rightness of the design, in spite of all the inexplicable appearances of nature:

> the patterns like a match-box puzzle,
> tiny balls stuck in a grid until shaken
> so much, all the orbits were in place.

This imagery is true to the central argument of the poem, whereby the microcosm (as in the spider's being and behaviour) discloses the macrocosm of creation. The speaker celebrates the vitality of the living cosmos, which is heightened in the poetic description of a fast-passing year, 'that quick year, the hour-long day'. She reflects how her observation of the orb spider concentrated and intensified her appreciation of nature's works, both minute and momentous:

> she taught me to love the smallest transit,
> that the coldest star has a planetesimal beauty.

And the poem closes, after tracing that large orbit of creation, by returning to the microcosmic orbit which was its inspiration:

> I watched her above the low flowers
> tracing her world, making it one perfect drawing.

The haunting quality of this poem abides in its implicit religious significance. Nowhere does Beveridge explicitly speculate on the fundamental theological issue which the recognition of design, in nature, has always aroused: that design implies a designer. She is satisfied to be reverent before the insect as before the coldest star; to affirm that they both reflect the order of creation, and to argue that such recognition of harmony and beauty transfigures the pain and inadequacies of human existence into a profound experience of love derived from a sense of the ultimate purposefulness of the world.

By analogy, the spider is representative of the poet and her web represents poetry.

Questions

1. How do the technical characteristics of this poem reflect and enhance its theme(s)?

2. While recognisably a 'contemporary' poem, 'Orb Spider' is more technically and formally constructed than much contemporary verse. Do you agree? Do you enjoy this kind of writing or would you prefer a different style?

Having studied these six poems, by six different poets, all contemporary, we can see certain thematic preoccupations and technical characteristics which are familiar in present-day poetry at large and which we could imagine, therefore, will continue to be familiar in poetry in the foreseeable future. Who can tell, however, whether some revolution in verse, like that of the Romantics (at the beginning of the nineteenth century) or the Modernists (in the early years of the twentieth), will make momentous changes in the subject matter and style of poetry later in this new century? It is possible that the writers we have selected are representative of the end of a tradition. On the other hand, they may be indicative of its robust qualities of endurance, for nothing that we read in their works, even as we acknowledge the differences between these poets and their unique talents – and dozens of others who could have been cited – is revolutionary in terms of what we have been encountering in poetry for at least fifty years.

A prominent theme in contemporary poetry is the preoccupation with personal experience (often focused on its negative aspects) and the ways in which this can be mediated in verse. We have seen this in Michael Ondaatje's poem about his father and, less directly, in Margaret Atwood's 'Up'. Yet Les Murray's account of the Mitchells and, even more strikingly, Judith Beveridge's celebration of the orb spider show that the pursuit of a certain detachment – 'impersonality' – has also persisted in contemporary poetry.

Technical variety and experimentation is undoubtedly a quality of modern verse, often to the point – and beyond the point – where many readers would no longer recognise the writing as 'poetic' in any sense. There were sections, as we saw, in Ondaatje's poem where the writing could only be described as prosaic (but used for a deliberate, contrasting effect in the larger context of the poem), while Joanne Burns' 'How' is in a long modern tradition (one thinks of e. e. cummings, for example) of striking inventiveness in language use, pushing the boundaries of how language can be used poetically. Yet her incantatory use of the word 'how' takes us back to the very source of poetic language in rhythmical, repetitive speech.

That most humane of activities and pleasures, the study of poetry, continues to be animated and stimulated by the practitioners of this ancient artistry of words and language, to inspire and challenge all those who (in William Blake's phrase) will hear the voice of the Bard.

Historical tables

Writers' lives	II Literary events (with dates of publication of significant texts)
Dante Alighieri 1265–1321 Francesco Petrarch 1304–74 John Wyclif 1320?–84 John Gower 1325–1408 William Langland 1330(?)–1400(?)	1362 English becomes the official language in Parliament and the Law Courts
Geoffrey Chaucer 1343(?)–1400	1387–1400 Writing of Chaucer's *Canterbury Tales*
	1454 First dated printing from movable types in Europe

EDWARD IV 1442–83
r. 1461–83

EDWARD V 1470–83
r. 1483

RICHARD III 1452–85
r. 1483–5

HENRY VII 1457–1509 r. 1485–1509	1485	Battle of Bosworth Field: beginning of the Tudor period in England
	1488	Bartholomew Diaz rounds the Cape of Good Hope
	1494	With the support of the Pope, Spain and Portugal agree to divide the unexplored part of the world
HENRY VIII 1491–1547 r. 1509–47	1513	Accession of Pope Leo X, the zenith of the Renaissance papacy
	1515	Cardinal Thomas Wolsey, Lord Chancellor of England
	1517	Reformation begins: Martin Luther's theses
	1519	Magellan begins circumnavigation of the world
	1534	Henry asserts control over English Church
	1545	Counter-Reformation begins: Council of Trent

EDWARD VI 1537–53
r. 1547–53

MARY I 1516–58 r. 1553–8	1555	Latimer and Ridley burned by Mary
	1556	Cranmer burned
ELIZABETH I 1533–1603 r. 1558–1603	1563	Elizabethan Church Settlement
	1570	Elizabeth anathematised by the Pope

| | | 1476 | Caxton sets up his press at Westminster |

Sir Thomas More 1476–1535	1516	Thomas More's *Utopia*
Sir Thomas Wyatt 1503–42	1535	Coverdale's English Bible
Henry Howard, Earl of Surrey 1517–47		

| | 1549 | First Book of Common Prayer |

| Edmund Spenser 1552–99 | 1557 | *Tottel's Miscellany* |
| Sir Philip Sidney 1554–86 | 1579 | Edmund Spenser's *Shepheardes Calendar* |

Francis Bacon, 1561–1626	1590	Spenser's *Faerie Queene*
Christopher Marlowe 1564–93	1591	Philip Sidney's *Astrophil and Stella*
William Shakespeare 1564–1616		

	1577	Drake begins voyage around the world
	1578	Execution of Mary, Queen of Scots
	1588	Defeat of the Spanish Armada

JAMES I 1566–1625 r. 1603–25	1603	Union of English and Scottish crowns
	1605	Gunpowder Plot
	1607	Colonisation of Virginia
	1608	Quebec founded
	1616	Inquisition issues edict against Galileo's astronomy
	1620	Pilgrim Fathers settle in New England

CHARLES I 1600–49 r. 1625–49	1628	William Harvey's theory of the circulation of the blood
	1629	Charles rules without Parliament
	1633	William Laud appointed Archbishop of Canterbury
	1640	Charles defeated by the Scots; Long Parliament begins
	1642	Beginning of the Civil War
	1644	The North lost to Charles
	1645	Battle of Naseby: Royalist army crushed
	1648	Second Civil War; New Model Army defeats Scots and Royalists
	1649	Charles executed

OLIVER CROMWELL 1599–1658
r. 1653–8

RICHARD CROMWELL 1626–1712
r. 1658–9

CHARLES II 1630–85 r. 1660–85	1660	Restoration of the monarchy and the episcopate; Royal Society founded
	1665	Great Plague of London

John Donne 1572–1631 Ben Jonson 1573–1637 George Herbert 1593–1633	1592 Christopher Marlowe's *Hero and Leander* 1595 Sidney's *Defence of Poesy* 1601–9 period of Shakespeare's great tragedies and romantic comedies
Sir Thomas Browne 1605–82 John Milton 1608–74 Samuel Butler 1612–80 Richard Crashaw 1613–49	1605 Francis Bacon's *Advancement of Learning* 1611 Authorised (King James) version of the Bible 1616 Ben Jonson Poet Laureate; his *Works* published
Andrew Marvell 1620–78 Henry Vaughan 1621–95 John Bunyan 1628–88 John Dryden 1631–1700	1623 First Folio of Shakespeare's plays 1633 Publication of John Donne's *Poems* and George Herbert's *The Temple* 1637 John Milton's *Lycidas* 1642 Theatres closed
	1651 Thomas Hobbes's *Leviathan*
Jonathan Swift 1667–1745	1667 Milton's *Paradise Lost* 1668 John Dryden Poet Laureate 1675 John Bunyan's *Pilgrim's Progress* composed

	1666	Great Fire of London; Newton discovers law of gravity
	1673	Test Act deprives English Catholics and Nonconformists of public offices
	1675	Greenwich Observatory founded
	1678	'Popish Plot'
	1681	Charles rules without Parliament
JAMES II 1633–1701 r. 1685–8	1688	'Glorious Revolution'
WILLIAM III 1650–1702 r. 1689–1702	1689	Bill of Rights
	1690	Battle of the Boyne James II defeated by William III
	1695	Freedom of the press in England
	1701	Act of Settlement establishes Hanoverian succession
ANNE 1665–1714 r. 1702–14	1707	Act of Union unites English and Scottish Parliaments
	1710	Tory government
GEORGE I 1660–1727 r. 1714–27	1714	Beginning of Hanoverian succession; Whig oligarchy
	1721	Robert Walpole, first Prime Minister
GEORGE II 1685–1760 r. 1727–60	1729	Methodists begin at Oxford
	1733	John Kay invents flying shuttle, first great textile invention; Jethro Tull advocates new agricultural methods
	1742	Fall of Walpole
	1743	George defeats the French (last English monarch to command troops in the field)
	1745	Jacobite rebellion
	1746	Jacobites destroyed

	1681 Andrew Marvell's *Poems*; Dryden's *Absalom and Achitophel*
John Gay 1685–1732	

Alexander Pope 1688–1744

James Thompson 1700–48

| Samuel Johnson 1709–84 | 1712   first version of Alexander
Pope's *The Rape of the Lock* |

| Thomas Gray 1716–41 | 1726   Jonathan Swift's *Gulliver's Travels* |

Oliver Goldsmith 1730–74	1728 Pope's *Dunciad* 1730 James Thomson's *The Seasons* 1733–4 Pope's *Essay on Man*
James Boswell 1740–95	1751 Thomas Gray's *Elegy*
George Crabbe 1754–1832 William Blake 1757–1827	

| | 1757 | Pitt, Secretary of State |
| | 1759 | 'Year of Victories'; canal transport begins |

GEORGE III 1738–1820	1761	Fall of Pitt
r. 1760–1820	1764	James Hargreaves invents spinning jenny
	1768	Royal Academy of Arts founded
	1769	Richard Arkwright erects spinning mill
	1770	James Cook discovers Australia
	1773	'Boston Tea Party'
	1774	Joseph Priestley discovers oxygen
	1775	American War of Independence
	1776	American Declaration of Independence
	1779	Samuel Crompton invents spinning mule
	1783	American Independence recognised; Pitt the Younger, Prime Minister; first hot-air and hydrogen balloon flights
	1789	Washington, first President of USA; French Revolution
	1792	France becomes a republic
	1800	Union of Great Britain and Ireland
	1804	Napoleon Bonaparte, Emperor of France
	1805	Battle of Trafalgar, Nelson's victory and death
	1807	Abolition of the slave trade in the British Empire
	1811	Luddite riots
	1815	Battle of Waterloo
	1819	'Peterloo' demonstration

| GEORGE IV 1762–1830 | 1825 | First railway opened |
| r. 1820–30 | 1829 | Catholic Emancipation; Metropolitan Police established |

William Wordsworth 1770–1850 Samuel Taylor Coleridge 1772–1834	1770 Oliver Goldsmith's *The Deserted* *Village*
Jane Austen 1775–1817	
	1779–81 Samuel Johnson's *Lives of the* *Poets* 1783 George Crabbe's *The Village*
George Gordon, Lord Byron 1788–1824	1791 James Boswell's *Life of Samuel* *Johnson*
Percy Bysshe Shelley 1792-1822	1792 Mary Wollstonecraft's *A* *Vindication of the Rights of Woman* 1794 William Blake's *Songs of* *Innocence and of Experience*
John Keats 1795–1821	1798 *Lyrical Ballads* published by Wordsworth and Coleridge
Elizabeth Barrett Browning 1806–61 Alfred, Lord Tennyson 1809–92 Robert Browning 1812–89 Charlotte Brontë 1816–55	1818 Byron begins *Don Juan*; Mary Wollstonecraft Shelley publishes *Frankenstein* 1819 Shelley's and Keats's 'great year': many of their famous poems written

Matthew Arnold 1822–88

WILLIAM IV 1765–1837 r. 1830–7	1832	First Reform Bill; Morse invents electric telegraph
	1833	Oxford Movement begins in Anglicanism; first Factory Act
	1834	'Tolpuddle Martyrs'
	1836	Chartists begin
VICTORIA 1819–1901 r. 1837–1901	1838	National Gallery opened
	1846	Repeal of the Corn Laws; Peel resigns
	1847	British Museum opened
	1848	General revolutionary movement throughout Europe; *Communist Manifesto* produced by Marx and Engels; gold discovered in California
	1851	Great Exhibition; gold discovered in Australia
	1854	Crimean War
	1856	Livingstone crosses Africa
	1857	Indian Mutiny
	1861	American Civil War begins
	1865	President Lincoln assassinated; slavery abolished in USA; antiseptic surgery introduced by Lister; Salvation Army founded
	1867	Second Reform Bill
	1868	Disraeli, then Gladstone, Prime Ministers
	1874	Disraeli succeeds Gladstone
	1877	Victoria, Empress of India
	1878	Edison and Swan produce electric light
	1880	Gladstone, Prime Minister
	1884	Fabian (socialist) Society founded
	1895	Marconi sends wireless message; Roentgen discovers X-rays; Freud publishes theory of psycho-analysis
	1899	Boer War begins

1833 Thomas Carlyle's *Sartor Resartus*

Gerard Manley Hopkins 1844–89

1850 Tennyson succeeds Wordsworth
as Poet Laureate, publishes *In Memoriam*
1853 Matthew Arnold's *Poems*
1855 Robert Browning's *Men and Women*
1857 Elizabeth Barrett Browning's *Aurora Leigh*
1859 Charles Darwin's *Origin of Species*; John Stuart Mill's *On Liberty*
1862 Christina Rossetti's *Goblin Market*
1864 John Henry Newman's *Apologia Pro Vita Sua*

William Butler Yeats 1865–1939

1873 Walter Pater's *Renaissance*

T. S. Eliot 1888–1965

1895 Oscar Wilde's *The Importance of Being Earnest*
1896 A. E. Housman's *A Shropshire Lad*
1898 Thomas Hardy's *Wessex Poems*

	1900	Australian Commonwealth proclaimed
EDWARD VII 1841–1910 r. 1901–10	1902	Boer War ends
	1903	First flight of heavier-than-air machine (Wright brothers) in USA
	1906	San Francisco earthquake; suffragette movement begins; vitamins discovered by Hopkins
	1908	Asquith, Prime Minister
	1909	Henry Ford produces Model T chassis
GEORGE V 1865–1936 r. 1910–36	1911	Parliament Act reduces power of House of Lords; pay for members of Parliament introduced
	1914–18	First World War
	1916	Easter Uprising in Ireland
	1917	Revolution in Russia
	1919	Peace treaty with Germany at Versailles
	1926	General Strike
	1928	Women given the vote
	1934	Hitler becomes Dictator
	1936	Accession and abdication of Edward VIII; civil war in Spain
GEORGE VI 1895–1952 r. 1936–52	1939–45	Second World War
	1946	United Nations assembly opens in New York
	1947	India and Pakistan become Dominions
	1948	Republic of Ireland Bill
	1950	Korean War begins
	1951	Festival of Britain

Ted Hughes 1930–98

1914	W. B. Yeats's *Responsibilities*
1915	D. H. Lawrence's *The Rainbow*
1917	T. S. Eliot's *Prufrock and Other Observations*
1922	Eliot's *The Waste Land* and James Joyce's *Ulysses*
1925	Virginia Woolf's *Mrs Dalloway*
1930	W. H. Auden's *Poems*
1934	Dylan Thomas's *Eighteen Poems*

Seamus Heaney 1939–

1944	Eliot's *Four Quartets*
1949	George Orwell's *Nineteen Eighty-Four*

ELIZABETH II 1926–
r. 1952–

1952	Samuel Beckett's *Waiting for Godot*
1957	Stevie Smith's *Not Waving but Drowning*
1964	Philip Larkin's *The Whitsun Weddings*
1969	Samuel Beckett awarded Nobel Prize for Literature
1970	Ted Hughes's *Crow*
1984	Seamus Heaney's *Station Island*
1998	Ted Hughes's *Birthday Letters*

Glossary of literary terms

Note: This glossary is not exhaustive. It lists and briefly defines the most common technical terms used in this book. Students of poetry should possess a detailed dictionary of literary terminology, such as M. H. Abrams's *A Glossary of Literary Terms* (3rd edition; New York: Holt, Rinehart and Winston, 1971).

allegory   An extended and often complex metaphorical presentation, usually in narrative form, of philosophical, spiritual or moral matters, to give them physical (and often personal) expression, as in Edmund Spenser's *The Faerie Queene*, John Bunyan's *The Pilgrim's Progress* and John Dryden's *Absalom and Achitophel*.

alliteration   A method of emphasis where words with the same initial consonant are found in close proximity, for connective and cumulative effect:

> O **w**ild **W**est **W**ind, thou breath of Autumn's being . . .
> (Percy Shelley, 'Ode to the West Wind')

assonance   The repetition of identical or similar vowel sounds in stressed syllables, where the surrounding consonants are different:

> Such weight and thick pink bulk . . .
> (Ted Hughes, 'View of a Pig')

ballad   A narrative poem, telling a simple dramatic story of love, war or adventure, with a brisk rhythm and a regular rhyme, e.g. John Keats's 'La Belle Dame sans Merci'.

blank verse   Unrhymed iambic pentameter (see under **metre** below), which has been a favourite form in English for dramatic writing as it represents the rhythms of ordinary speech, e.g. in Shakespeare's plays.

blazon   The description, usually idealised and of a woman, of physical beauty, often beginning with the hair and forehead and eyes and moving downwards. (Sometimes known as the device of *descriptio*.)

caesura   A break in a poetic line, occurring where a phrase, clause or sentence ends, causing a pause in the rhythm, marked in the following example (as often) by a comma:

> I sit in the top of the tree, my eyes closed
> (Ted Hughes: 'Hawk Roosting')

374

canto   One of the divisions of a long (usually epic) poem (from the Italian for 'song').

carpe diem   Meaning (from Latin) 'seize the day' ('enjoy the moment'), a common form of lyric poetry where the speaker emphasises that life is short and that he and the auditor (usually a reluctant beloved) should make love now, e.g. Andrew Marvell's 'To His Coy Mistress'.

confessional poetry   Frank description of personal experiences, including family problems and the poet's mental and emotional life, as found in much modern poetry, e.g. Robert Lowell's *Life Studies*.

couplet   A sequence of two rhymed lines, usually rhythmically identical too and often forming a complete unit of thought:

> Then flashed the living lightning from her eyes,
> And screams of horror rend the affrighted skies.
>
> (Alexander Pope, *The Rape of the Lock*, III)

dramatic monologue   A lyric poem in which a single speaker reveals his or her ideas and emotions, to the reader, usually in the account of interactions with other individuals or events, e.g. T. S. Eliot's 'The Love Song of J. Alfred Prufrock'.

elegy   A formal poem of mourning for the dead, e.g. John Milton's *Lycidas* (remembering one dead person) or Thomas Gray's elegy commemorating a community. Often, the elegy is used as an occasion for meditation on other serious matters (see, for example, W. H. Auden's elegy on W. B. Yeats at the time of the outbreak of the Second World War).

emblem poetry   Poems (particularly in the seventeenth century) which imitate the shapes of their subjects, such as George Herbert's 'The Altar' and 'Easter Wings'.

enjambement   This occurs when the sense and rhythm of a poetic line is carried on into the next line:

> The tide is full, the moon lies fair
> Upon the straits.
>
> (Matthew Arnold, 'Dover Beach')

epic   A long narrative poem, recounting a great story of heroic deeds in an elevated language, e.g. John Milton's *Paradise Lost*.

hyperbole   Meaning (from Greek) overshooting, where fact is extravagantly exaggerated for serious or comic effect, as in Iago's address to Othello in Shakespeare's play:

> Not poppy nor mandragora,
> Nor all the drowsy syrups of the world,
> Shall ever medicine thee to that sweet sleep
> Which thou ow'dst yesterday.

image   A figure of speech or of descriptive writing which, through comparing the subject to something else, usually visualised, increases understanding of it. In 'The Lake Isle of Innsifree', W. B. Yeats presents the island as an image of peace and contemplation.

lyric   A general term for the shortest poems, usually with a regular rhyming and rhythmical pattern and deriving from the idea of poetry being written to be set to music and sung. It includes several forms of poetry, e.g. the sonnet, ode, elegy, dramatic monologue and hymn.

metaphor   Used to refer to one thing in terms of another unlike thing, for the purpose of vivid presentation and deepening of meaning. In 'The Road Not Taken', Robert Frost uses two roads metaphorically: one standing for the populous way of ordinary existence, the other 'less travelled by' – a metaphor for the lonelier life of the artist.

metre   The repetitive pattern of rhythm or stresses in poetry. This sign / is used above a syllable or word that is stressed; this ˇ indicates an unstressed syllable. Very common in English poetry is the unstressed followed by the stressed syllable: ˇ / which is an **iambic** foot (from the Greek *iambus* for this arrangement of emphasis). **Iambic pentameter,** five iambic feet in a line, is the most common metre in English poetry (and is easily identified if we read the line with exaggerated emphasis):

> ˇ /   ˇ   / ˇ / ˇ / ˇ /
> A small house agent's clerk, with one bold stare . . .
>
>   (T. S. Eliot, *The Waste Land*, III)

Iambic tetrameter, with four feet in a line, sounds like this:

> ˇ   /   ˇ   /   ˇ / ˇ /
> The bride hath paced into the hall . . .
>
>   (S. T. Coleridge, *The Rime of the Ancient Mariner*)

The reverse of the iambic rhythm is the **trochaic**, where the stress falls on the first syllable of the foot:

> / ˇ   / ˇ   /   ˇ   ˇ   / ˇ
> Father, father, where are you going?
>
>   (William Blake: 'The Little Boy Lost')

Less urgent, but more poignant is the **dactylic**:

> /   ˇ   ˇ /   ˇ   / ˇ ˇ   /
> Death stands above me, whispering low.
>
>   (W. S. Landor, 'Death Stands Above Me')

The **hexameter** has six feet in a line. An iambic hexameter is known as

the **Alexandrine**, as in the last lines of Edmund Spenser's stanzas in
The Faerie Queene:

$$\breve{\ } \ / \ \breve{\ } \ / \ \breve{\ } \ / \ \breve{\ } \ / \ \breve{\ } \ / \ \breve{\ } \ /$$
And diverse plots did frame, to maske in strange disguise.

Rarely encountered are the monometer (one foot), dimeter (two feet)
and heptameter (seven feet).

Other patterns of rhythmical feet are the **anapestic** – two
unstressed syllables, followed by a stressed syllable – and the
spondaic, which consists of two successive stressed syllables.

Free verse, common in twentieth-century poetry, does not have
fixed rhythmical or rhyming patterns, but its freedom is often limited
by other constraints of rhythm, such as incantation and repetition.

ode A formal poem of commemoration, derived from classical Greek and
Roman poetry on serious themes. See, for example, Wordsworth's
'Ode: Intimations of Immortality'.

onomatopoeia The sounds of words imitate or mime the sound being
described:

The redbreast **whistles** from a garden-croft;
And gathering swallows **twitter** in the skies.

(John Keats, 'To Autumn')

oxymoron A contradiction in terms, often used by the Petrarchan poets of
the English Renaissance who would describe their 'pleasing pains' of
love. Milton describes what one sees in Hell as 'darkness visible'.

pastoral An elaborately conventional poem, idealising the natural setting and
life of shepherds and rural people, e.g. Christopher Marlowe's pastoral
lyric 'The Passionate Shepherd to His Love'.

personification To give human qualities to inanimate or non-human things.
In the following example it is combined with onomatopoeia:

The hour-glass whispers to the lion's roar.

(W. H. Auden, 'Our Bias')

quatrain A four-line unit of usually rhyming poetry, the most common
length for a stanza.

refrain A word or line usually repeated at the end of each stanza of a poem,
such as 'Nevermore' in Edgar Allan Poe's 'The Raven'.

rhyme The quality by which the same sounds in different words link those
words, usually at the end of successive poetic lines, giving unity to the
poem's structure. Rhyme distinguishes poetry from ordinary speech,
though it is not necessarily present (as in blank verse and much contemporary poetry).

rhythm   (see **metre**)

satire   Poetry that is usually comic or witty, but which has the serious purpose of reforming some aspect of society or human behaviour, e.g. Alexander Pope's *The Dunciad*.

simile   Similar to the metaphor, but always introduced by 'like' or 'as', for the purpose of making a comparison in order to intensify and expand meaning:

> Come with soft rounded cheeks and eyes **as bright**
> **As sunlight** on a stream.

(Christina Rossetti, 'Echo')

sonnet   A poem of fourteen lines, divided (in the 'Italian/Petrarchan' style) into eight lines (octave) and six lines (sestet), usually concluding with a rhyming couplet. Shakespeare (developing the 'English' variation of this, with three quatrains and a couplet) is the author of a famous sequence of sonnets.

stanza   The recurring unit of a poem, often a quatrain. Where the unit becomes long (as in the sections of poetry in the books of *Paradise Lost*), the term 'verse-paragraph' is more appropriate.

symbol   It is not merely a comparison (like a simile) or extended identification (like a metaphor) or even a more sustained analogy (like an image). A symbol represents a larger, more profound and complex idea than itself. The rose, for example, is a symbol which calls forth various associations, sensual and spiritual.

tone   The result of the treatment and development of the subject of a poem by the poet. A frivolous tone suggests that the poet regarded the theme light-heartedly, as in 'The White Knight's Song' by Lewis Carroll. Then the tone might be melancholy, as in Christina Rossetti's 'Amor Mundi', or satirical (in T. S. Eliot's 'Whispers of Immortality') or anguished (in G. M. Hopkins's 'Thou Art Indeed Just, Lord') or exultant (in John Milton's 'On the Morning of Christ's Nativity'). The tone of a poem, the combination of subject and style, is the best guide to its meaning.

Further reading

The New Princeton Encyclopedia of Poetry and Poetics, ed. Alex Preminger and T. V. F. Brogan (Princeton, NJ: Princeton University Press, 1996).

The New Princeton Handbook of Poetic Terms, ed. T. V. F. Brogan (Princeton, NJ: Princeton University Press, 1994).

Abrams, M. H., *The Mirror and the Lamp: Romantic Theory and the Critical Tradition* (Oxford: Oxford University Press, 1971).

Brooks, Cleanth and Warren, Robert Penn, *Understanding Poetry* (New York: Holt, Rinehart & Winston, 1960).

Buchbinder, David, *Contemporary Literary Theory and the Reading of Poetry* (South Melbourne: Macmillan, 1991).

Burton, S. H., *The Criticism of Poetry* (London: Longmans, 1950).

Dyson, A. E. (ed.), *Poetry Criticism and Practice* (London: Macmillan, 1968).

Eliot, T. S., *On Poetry and Poets* (London: Faber and Faber, 1957).

Furness, Tom and Bath, Michael, *Reading Poetry* (New York: Prentice Hall, 1996).

Goodman, Lizbeth (ed.), *Literature and Gender* (London: Routledge, 1996).

Gunn, Thom, *The Occasions of Poetry* (London: Faber & Faber, 1982).

Gurrey, P., *The Appreciation of Poetry* (London: Oxford University Press, 1938).

Levi, Peter, *The Art of Poetry* (New Haven, CT: Yale University Press, 1991).

Moon, Brian, *Studying Poetry* (Cottesloe: Chalkface, 1998).

Raffel, Burton, *How to Read a Poem* (New York: New American Library, 1984).

Raine, Kathleen, *The Inner Journey of the Poet* (London: Allen & Unwin, 1982).

Robinson, Peter, *In the Circumstances: About Poems and Poets* (Oxford: Clarendon Press, 1992).

Reed, Jeremy, *Madness: The Price of Poetry* (London: Peter Owen, 1989).

Scully, James, *Modern Poetics* (New York: McGraw-Hill, 1965).

Wain, John, *Professing Poetry* (London: Macmillan, 1977).

Wimsatt, W. K., *Day of the Leopards: Essays in Defense of Poems* (New Haven, CT: Yale University Press, 1976).

Index